Bibliography of
Japanese
New Religions

T0346690

Bibliography of Japanese New Religions

WITH ANNOTATIONS AND AN INTRODUCTION TO JAPANESE NEW RELIGIONS AT HOME AND ABROAD

● PLUS AN APPENDIX ON AUM SHINRIKYŌ ●

Edited by Peter B. Clarke

Routledge
Taylor & Francis Group

LONDON AND NEW YORK

First published 1999 by
JAPAN LIBRARY

2 Park Square, Milton Park, Abingdon, Oxon OX14 4RN
711 Third Avenue, New York, NY 10017, USA

Routledge is an imprint of the Taylor & Francis Group, an informa business

BIBLIOGRAPHY OF JAPANESE NEW RELIGIONS
WITH ANNOTATIONS
AND AN INTRODUCTION TO JAPANESE
NEW RELIGIONS AT HOME AND ABROAD

First issued in paperback 2016

British Library Cataloguing in Publication Data
A CIP catalogue entry for this book is
available from the British Library

ISBN 978-1-873410-80-6 (hbk)
ISBN 978-1-138-96465-5 (pbk)

Typeset in Stone 9½ on 11½pt by LaserScript, Mitcham, Surrey

Contents

Contributors

The editor, Peter Clarke is the Professor of History and Sociology of Religion and Director of the Japanese New Religions Project, Department of Theology and Religious Studies, King's College, University of London.

The introduction and appendix were written by Peter Clarke and the annotated bibliography was compiled by Sonia Crivello, Research Assistant, Japanese New Religions Project, Department of Theology and Religious Studies, King's College, University of London. The summaries of individual movements were compiled by Helen MacNaughtan, Doctoral Student, London School of Economics and Political Science. The summary of Kōfuku-no-Kagaku was written by Masaki Fukui, Doctoral Student, Department of Theology and Religious Studies, King's College, University of London. Special thanks must be extended to Keishin Inaba, Doctorial student, Department of Theology and Religious Studies, King's College, University of London, who kindly read the whole manuscript at proof stage and provided invaluable assistance regarding errors and omissions.

Other contributors were Louella Matsunaga, Lecturer in Anthropology, University of Oxford; Sanda Ducaru, Doctoral Student, Japanese New Religions Project, Department of Theology and Religious Studies, King's College, University of London. Professor Susumu Shimazono, Faculty of Letters, University of Tokyo; Professor Michael Pye, Department of Religious Studies, University of Marburg; Professor Emiko-Tierney, Department of Anthropology, University of Wisconsin; Professor Gary Bouma, Department of Anthropology and Sociology, Monash University of Melbourne; Catherine Cornille, Professor of Comparative Religion, Catholic University of Louvain; Professor Ari Pedro oro, Department of

Anthropology, Federal University of Rio Grande do Sul; Professor Klaus Peter Koepping, Institute of Ethnology, University of Heidelberg, Dr Tina Hamrin, Department of Comparative Religion, University of Stockholm and Elizabeth Arweck, Doctoral Student, Department of Theology and Religious Studies, King's College, University of London.

Using the Bibliography

To assist readers to find the information they require as quickly as possible the bibliography has been constructed in the following way:

MAIN BIBLIOGRAPHY

This section consists of an alphabetical list by author of references, the majority of which refer to Japanese new and new, new religions outside Japan. Apart from a small number in French, German, Japanese, and Portuguese, these references are in English. Some of the titles have been translated from the Japanese.

The references include material published by the new and new, new religions themselves and research-based material published by academics and serious students of new religions.

We have included some material on new and new, new religions in Japan itself where we felt this was relevant to the study of these religions abroad.

Few of our references predate 1960 since little literature exists on Japanese new religions abroad prior to that time.

SUMMARIES OF JAPANESE NEW RELIGIONS

This section provides summaries of some of the main Japanese new and new, new religions that are active outside Japan. They are: Agonshū, Aum Shinrikyō (see appendix) Byakkō Shinkō Kai, Honmichi, Kōdō Kyōdan, Kōfuku-no-Kagaku, Konkōkyō, Kurozu-mikyō, Mahikari, Ōmotokyō, Perfect Liberty Kyōdan', Reiha no Hikari, Reiyūkai, Risshō Kōsei Kai, Seichō-no-Ie, Sekai Kyūseikyō, Shinnyoen, Sōka Gakkai and Tenrikyō.

The summaries are based on information provided by the movements themselves with the exception of Aum Shinrikyō. On account of its impact and notoriety we decided to include a special appendix containing a brief history and select bibliography on Aum Shinrikyō. The historical account of Aum is an interpretative essay by Peter Clarke based on scholarly research and analysis of this phenomenon (pp 265ff).

In addition to each summary there is a list of references in alphabetical order by author which refer specifically to that movement and includes both primary and secondary source material. These references also appear in the main bibliography but are listed here for quick reference.

SUGGESTIONS FOR FURTHER READING

For a detailed earlier bibliography see: H. Byron Earhart's *The New Religions of Japan: A Bibliography of Western Language Materials*, Ann Arbor: Michigan Papers in Japanese Studies, No. 9, 1983.

The *Japanese Journal of Religious Studies* published by the Nanzan Institute for Religion and Culture is also extremely useful, as is the *Journal of Japanese Religions* published by the NCC Centre for the Study of Japanese Religions in Kyoto.

Japanese New Religions Abroad – The Way of the *Kami* in Foreign Lands

By Peter B. Clarke

T he main focus of this annotated bibliography is the academic and serious literature, mainly but not exclusively in English, as well as the internal literature produced by the movements themselves that is relevant to the process of the internationalization of Japanese new religions. The bibliography builds upon the reference work of Earhart (1983) and was motivated by my own research on Japanese new religions in Brazil, Europe and parts of Africa which began in the early 1980s.

A previous volume (Clarke and Somers, 1994) referenced some of the scholarly writings on Japanese new religions in the West, but it was only in editing that volume that I came to realize the need for a more comprehensive work that would bring together under one cover the growing literature on the international dimension of Japanese new religions on a much wider scale. A short appendix has been added containing a select bibliography on Aum Shinrikyō, the movement on trial in Japan for the sarin gas attack on the Tokyo underground in March 1995 and many other heinous crimes. This movement has subsequently come to be regarded as one of the principal defining moments in the history of Japanese new religions, generating there and globally many of the same fears and suspicions about new religions and prompting many of the same questions about the nature of contemporary society as did the holocaust in Jonestown Guyana in 1979 when over 900 members of the People's Temple were either murdered or committed suicide under orders from their leader the Reverend Jim Jones (Hall,1987).

Other great tragedies involving new religions in recent times that have displayed the enormous tension that can be generated between new forms of religious belief and practice and their interpretation, implementation and goals, real or imaginary, and the wider society, include: the Branch Davidian community in Waco, Texas in February 1993, where there was tragic loss of lives on both sides in what some experts believe was a totally unnecessary conflagration that occurred in a stand-off between the leadership of the movement and the Federal Bureau of Investigation (FBI), (Lewis, 1993), and the 53 violent deaths in the Solar Temple movement in October 1994 (Palmer, 1996).

It would be difficult to exaggerate the effects on popular perceptions of religion nationally and internationally of these tragedies. Focusing on the fall-out from the Aum Shinrikyō attack on the Tokyo underground one Japanese observer wrote of the 'Death of Religion in Japan' (Yamaori, 1995). If it is too early to speak of the death of religion it is certainly not too soon to detect a radical rethink in Japan on the value of religion offered by new and new, new religions and a questioning of the methods used to achieve the goals of this-worldly and other-worldy benefits that are promised to practitioners.

During research in Japan, Europe and Brazil after the Aum Shinrikyō incident I personally found that in many cases interviewees would begin to respond to questions by distancing themselves from Aum Shinrikyō and from violence and fanaticism, afraid that I might imply that these were characteristics of all Japanese new and new, new religions.

What are commonly referred to as new religions are a feature of the religious, and very often political and social, life of almost every country in the world. Wherever these new religions have emerged they have been the subject of controversy, in some cases dividing communities and families that are usually in agreement on essentials, and in others uniting groups that are in principle antagonistic and hostile to each other, for example supporters of the Communist party and conservative politicians in Japan in the 1970s.

Although Aum Shinrikyō provides, with hindsight, an unambiguous illustration of the two-edged character of charismatic authority based on claims to mystical power in which good and evil are not simply opposite sides of the same coin but can change places so easily, it is, nevertheless, important not to generalize by interpreting the beliefs and activities of all Japanese new religions in the same way in the light of the Aum incident.

Japanese new religions are now to be found in most countries of the world. There are over thirty such religions in Brazil which, with an estimated 1.3 million inhabitants of Japanese descent, has the largest population of people of Japanese origin in the world outside Japan. Elsewhere in South America the numbers are smaller, for example, in Peru, Paraguay, Colombia, Chile and Argentina. Mexico has a number of Japanese new religions, the largest of them being Sōka Gakkai or Value Creation Society. The new religions of Japan have also spread to the Caribbean. Mahikari, for example, has a following on the islands of Guadeloupe and Martinique where it is undergoing a process of assimilation that will possibly eventually have the effect of obscuring its Japanese character (Hurbon, 1991). Japanese new religions elsewhere are on the whole more cautious about adaptation.

Since the new immigration law of 1965 which placed Asian immigrants on a par with Europeans for the first time since 1924 the United States has come to be home to almost as many Japanese new religions as Brazil. The international dimension to Japanese new religions is also evident in much of the Far East and South East Asia. There are new movements in Mongolia, China – including Hong Kong – Taiwan, Korea, Indonesia, Thailand, Malaysia and Singapore. A number of African countries, among them the Democratic Republic of the Congo, Ghana, Kenya, Angola, Nigeria and South Africa are home to Japanese new religions, as are India and Nepal.

All the main Japanese new religions are to be found in Europe. This development is relatively recent, apart from a Tenrikyō presence in Britain since c.1910. For most of the others the mission to Europe began in the 1970s as Japanese business and commerce increased there (Clarke and Somers, 1994). The largest Japanese new religion in Europe is Sōka Gakkai followed by Mahikari.

There are many aspects of this expansion abroad that are as yet little understood and little researched. For example, movements that have made considerable headway in one or two countries have been unsuccessful in others. Sekai Kyūseikyō (The Church of World Messainity) has acquired a large membership in Brazil of about 330,000 since its beginnings there in 1955, and over 250,000 in Thailand over a similar period of time, but has failed to reach more than 5,000 in the United States in over forty years of mission activity. The realization of the need to adapt and the will to adapt in Brazil from the 1960s, and in Thailand, partly explain the movement's success in those countries. In the United States adaptation was not as

3

easily undertaken for historical, political and cultural reasons, and as a consequence Messianity has remained an 'ethnic religion'.

The progress of Tenrikyō (Religion of Heavenly Origin) abroad has also been extremely variable. It is the second oldest new religion in Brazil arriving there in 1931, two years after Ōmotokyō, and yet one of the smaller ones, with far fewer members than Sekaikyusei Kyo, Perfect Liberty Kyōdan, Seichō-no-Ie (House of Growth) and Sōka Gakkai. On the other hand, it has a long history in Korea also but there it has been highly successful for a Japanese new religion with over 100,000 members. In Hawaii where Tenrikyō dates back to 1908 it has never been numerically strong and is in a state of decline and the same holds for the mainland of the United States where, since 1938, it has failed to make any noticeable inroads into the wider American community or to attract more than a handful of non-Japanese Americans. One point worth noting is that in Korea the leadership of Tenrikyō is local and the liturgy is in Korean, broadly demonstrating that the most effective carriers of a religion are the local people and the most effective means of communicating its message is through the vernacular language.

While more will be said on the factors making for success and failure later, a short introduction such as this is not the place to offer a full treatment of this extremely complex question which I hope to consider as an in-depth study, with special reference to Japanese new religions, at a future date.

UNPACKING THE TERMS 'NEW' AND 'NEW, NEW' RELIGIONS

While, as previously noted, the content of this annotated bibliography concerns Japanese new religions abroad the Japanese context in which they emerged cannot be ignored if their presence overseas is to be fully understood. This means the provision here of a brief account of their rise in Japan and an explanation of the sense in which they can usefully be described as new.

Modern Japanese religions come in two basic forms: that of new religions (shin shūkyō) and that of new, new religions (shin shin shūkyō). Shimazono (1991) has identified a third category: the new spirituality movements (Shin Reisei Undō).

Scholarly opinion in Japan, as elsewhere, is divided on the question of the value of using the term 'new', and also 'new, new'. I have already discussed the question of new in the context of Japan (1994) and the West (1997) and do not wish to enter into a detailed account of the debate here, or of the reasons why I prefer to continue to use this term despite its obvious limitations I will simply make a few comments in support of my position that are sometimes overlooked by participants in the debate. Two general and basic points need to be made to begin with: firstly, because a belief or idea can be shown to have antecedents this does not strip it of the quality of newness or originality; new does not have to imply a fundamental or radical innovation or change in doctrine and ritual in an objective sense, although this may well be the perception of believers. And secondly, a religious movement does not have to be defined unequivocally as either new or old, but may be one or the other depending on the angle from which it is being observed. Looked at diachronically many new religions, Japanese and other, are most likely to appear to be highly derivative, drawing many of their beliefs and practices from long established religious traditions, while if studied synchronically, their new features appear much more obvious.

As one would expect, most historians treat them diachronically, while most social scientists take a synchronic approach. The most fruitful approach is to examine them from both angles while avoiding the pitfalls of an exaggerated evolutionist and essentialist interpretation. This is by no means easy. Earhart (1989), who has made one of the most thoroughgoing attempts at such an approach, sees the new religions of Japan as 'developing out of the general background of Japanese religion' which he views as: the unified religious world view of the Japanese people' (Ibid:11).

He stresses that there is no substantial break or discontinuity between new and old religion in Japan (Ibid:11). New religions such as Gedatsu-kai, Earhart believes, are but a 'miniature contemporary version of this heritage' (Ibid: 10). He comments:

Gedatsu-Kai is a reformulation of the unified world view of Japanese religion that enables members to go back to the heart of their tradition while at the same time going forward into the future (Ibid: XIV).

While Earhart's analysis seeks to do justice to the contribution of both past and the present, the old and the new, to the content and ritual of Japanese new religions, his overall interpretation is possibly overly metaphysical and essentialist. He loudly echoes Durkheim's essentialism and evolutionism in his contention that Japanese religion has an essence or core that persists amid all cultural, economic, historical, political and social change, and the idea that it is transmitted from generation to generation in the same form risks over-emphasizing the element of continuity. Every belief has a material, intellectual, emotional and cultural aspect, and while the form in which it is expressed may persist seemingly unchanged, these 'internal' elements will be shaped and moulded by different kinds of experience.

Earhart is also in danger of giving the appearance of homo-geneity, unity and uniformity were they never existed, and of obscuring the significant changes in content, structure, function and meaning that have occurred, and the differences in the way of being religious that have been developed at different periods of history. As is well known, the Japanese religious outlook has been characterized by diversity for a very long time with Confucianism influencing Shinto and the converse, and Buddhism being affected by and affecting both. Moreover, there have been and continue to be local and regional variants of the traditional models of Shinto, and a variety of forms of Buddhism have existed in Japan for a very long time, making for variation in the interpretation of the content and the form of the rituals associated with these traditions.

These qualifications of Earhart's position are not meant to deny its obvious merits or the existence of a paradigmic worldview or set of interpenetrating worldviews, and of characteristic features in the religious life of the Japanese that have persisted over centuries down to the present. However, in the script of most paradigms there are a number of blank spaces, so to speak, that leave open possibilities for innovation. What appears to be complete allows for interpretation and even originality. New experiences make demands on the existing belief systems which they cannot always satisfactorily respond to, either because their ideology of change is inappropriate or they have become too closely associated with the mainstream, orthodox view of things and have been commandeered by the establishment and its supporters and used to legitimate their power and authority. It is in this context that seemingly peripheral movements emerge, some of which mount a challenge to the status quo, become the mainstream themselves in time and go on to experience the same opposition.

Acknowledgement, therefore, of the existence of paradigmatic aspects of Japanese religious belief, practice and orientation, and that new religions come under a broadly inclusive cover called Japanese religion, should not be taken to imply that these religions are not in any doctrinal, ritual or ideological sense original or new. As previously pointed out, the new is often wrapped in the clothes of the old and needs to be unpacked to be observed. While, as Reader and Tanabe (1998) point out, there are, and have been, constants in the religious practice of the Japanese – praying for practical benefits, *genze riyakū*, has been among the most common and persistent religious activities in Japan – the purposes that cosmologies, beliefs and rituals are designed to serve can change and indeed have changed to give them a new meaning in both an objective and subjective sense.

Generally, new religions see themselves as belonging to an old tradition and at the same time revealing for the first time eternal truths that are part of that tradition but have never previously been known or correctly understood. Thus, the tradition is presented as faulty at its foundations and this provides an opening for an extremely radical view of the past. Agonshū claims to be new or original as a result of its founder, Seiyū Kiriyama, having discovered the *Agama* sutras which it claims are the earliest of the Buddhist sutras and previously unknown, while Shinnyo'en simultaneously emphasizes the Shugendo and Shingon roots of its founder Shinjō Itō and points to the latters 'discovery' of the *Mahaparinivana* sutra, said to contain the last teachings of the Buddha, and the essence of all he had previously been searching for and all he had so far learned. Out of the old comes something completely new; by basing their teachings on the ancient texts of the *Agama* sutras in the first case and on the *Mahaparinirvana* sutra in the second these two movements claim uniqueness.

There are variations on this approach to originality found, for example, in the claim made by movements that they are providing a deeper understanding of a long-established belief or practice, a method adopted by Shōkō Asahara who, shortly after establishing Aum Shinrikyō, explained his teaching and practices relating to the attaining of *satori* or enlightenment as a deepening of the long-established Buddhist practice of, in Japanese, *shinensho* or the fourfold meditation to eliminate false views (Shimazono, 1995: 389).

New religions need not, therefore, be considered new in the sense of providing entirely new beliefs and rituals but in the way they have restructured aspects of Japanese cosmology with a long history and interpreted long-standing ritual practices to serve different ends than was once the case. Yamashita (1998) makes the point that Tenrikyō (Religion of Heavenly Truth), Tenri Honmichi (Original Way of Heavenly Truth), a splinter group from Tenrikyō founded by the former Tenrikyō minister Aijirō Ōnishi (1881–1958) – he was one of a number of founders of Japanese new religions who either denied the emperor's divinity or strongly denounced his rule and was subsequently arrested and imprisoned for lese-majeste – and Ōmotokyō (Religion of Great Origin), while they have all derived much in the way of ritual and belief from Shinto have, nonetheless, an eschatological element not found in that belief system. Yamashita also credits the foundress of Tenrikyō, Miki Nakayama (1798–1887), with providing in the Ofudesaki – revelations made to her by God the Parent – a new version of the myth of human creation:

> The Koki (myth of human creation) in the Ofudesaki is highly original because the idea of equality (therein) stood in sharp contrast to the reality of contemporary society in which the concept of karma was used to justify unequal treatment of people. (Ibid: 132).

Examples of how traditional religious ideas and practices have been made new by leaders of new religions abound. Ooms (1993) interprets the use made of possession, *kamigakari*, by the founders of several Japanese new religions including Nao Deguchi (1836–1918) the foundress of Ōmotokyō (Religion of the Great Origin) which dates from 1895, in this way. Seeing these founders as essentially mediums and faith-healers Ooms observes that they extended the related functions of possession and faith-healing to cover wider issues than was traditional:

> Unlike traditional mediums who articulated and structured the experience of their patients in terms of *prevailing models of reality* the founders of new religions made their patients' experiences meaningful in terms of the *new vision of reality* which they were constructing. A successful cure could result, therefore, in the dissociation of the individual from the *established socio-cultural system*. The patient was instead converted to the founders *new world view* and integrated into a *new community* of fellow believers. The founders thus *expanded the function of faith-healing far beyond the provision of immediate benefits*. They used it as a highly effective means of proselytization, for it enabled them to communicate a *new view* of the world by making it meaningful with regard to an individual's unique experience (my italics) (Ibid: 17).

Referring specifically to Nao Deguchi, Ooms explains how the foundress of Ōmotokyō radically transformed the character and purpose of possession or *kamigakari* as traditionally understood. She did this principally by declaring herself to be the final and ultimate source of revelation, and by preaching to others that their salvation was not dependent on this traditional means of access to supernatural help but on obedience to the will of the deity who possessed and revealed his truth to her, Ushitora no Konjin. Ooms comments:

> Kamigakari now represented not only a source of miscellaneous insights and immediate benefits, but also a source of a total and radically *new view* of the world and the individual's relation to the sacred (Ibid: 16).

Hardacre (1990) also recognizes the ingenuity of Nao Deguchi and highlights this in her discussion of the foundress of Ōmotokyō's interpretation and application of the Buddhist notion of Transformed Male (henjonanshi) and Transformed Female (henjonyoshi). Nao claimed to have been changed by the command of the deity Ushitora no konjin into a transformed male, or a female in a male body. Her co-founder Onisaburō Deguchi (1871–1948) underwent a parallel change to become a transformed female in a male body. Hardacre, commenting on the 'originality' of the foundress's interpretation of *henjōnanshi* and *henjōnyoshi* which, she points out, has no antecedents in traditional Buddhist terminology, writes:

> Nao invented a neologism having the same pronunciation but written with different characters than the Buddhist term, and she interpreted the basic idea to mean a symbolic change of gender rather than a change of sex (Ibid: 51).

This idea of a Transformed Male and a Transformed Female collaborating in a divine mission to transform the world was new, as was Nao's decision to separate out sex from gender when previously they were seen as matching each other. This did not mean a change in her thinking concerning the characteristics of femaleness and maleness. On these questions Nao remained traditional associating the former with perseverance, self-effacement and modesty and the latter with initiative, authority, and force (Ibid: 53). Indeed, as Hardacre explains, she used this dyad of transformed male and transformed female as a device for controlling her co-founder, Onisaburō who was often in conflict with her (Ibid).

Without overlooking the conventional and traditional in either Nao or Onisaburō Deguchi's attitude, outlook, behaviour, and beliefs, both displayed considerable creativity and originality which extended beyond the sphere of religion, as commonly understood, in western society into the world of art, calligraphy, agriculture, botany and ceramics. At times these spheres overlapped as in the case of Onisaburō's raku-ware productions. For example, using this medium he developed new symbols relating to the notion of world transformation or reconstruction, *tatekae-tatenaoshi*, the central idea in Ōmotokyō's teaching, and the main motivation for their activities, including the construction of a model of a terrestrial paradise at Ayabe. The differences that Onisaburō Deguchi created are best described by the widely respected Japanese art critic, the art historian Giichirō Katō (d.1974) whose fascination for and depiction of tea bowl 'Paradise 28' reveals unmistakably why it should have constituted so expressive and persuasive a symbol of an earthly paradise in a Japanese context.

Kato (1975) wrote of the originality, beauty and purity of the colours of Onisaburō Deguchi's tea bowls in general which 'surpassed in value those which we knew', and was stunned by 'Paradise 28' which he struggled to name. Onisaburō Deguchi's design, and his choice and use of colours in creating this tea bowl provided, Katō was convinced, a most potent symbol of paradise in that it broke with tradition and resulted in the creation of an object that was to deepen understanding and feelings – for many not only the very stuff of paradise on earth but also of originality – in ways previously unimagined. He wrote:

> This wonderful tea bowl ('Paradise 28') could not have escaped my notice ... The day on which I discovered it I consulted the dictionary far into the night to find a suitable word to christen it. I finally made up 'scintillating bowl, Yowan: the character Yo signifies star light, shining of stars. Such compound words as 'brilliance', 'shiny bowl', 'beautiful bowl', 'excellent bowl', 'elegant bowl' could not satisfy me. I wished to find a genuine brilliance even in the name to be applicable (sic) to such a bowl.
>
> ... On a white ground bright ultra-marine and crimson were daubed in mixture with the dominant colour of bluishgreen, but also yellow was there. They mixed with each other to turn into orange and purple in some places. To my surprise these colours were past the colour feeling we normally have: they were far brighter and more cheerful and genuine. The roundness, full of an inner force in perfect harmony, and the quietness of the inside bottom, are characteristics. The shaping of the kodai, the bottom, has a charm innocent and spontaneous, a perfection. Again, a peculiar expression are the three lines engraved around the rim of the bottom, and the fine lines that radiate upwards. Titled pores, like venesection, lie innumerably about

the body of the bowl, resembling a starry sky. Such venesection-like tilts are symbols of prayer, each thrust was made by one prayer. These all show the viewers the mystery of pottery and the extraordinary enthusiasm of the creator. (Ibid).

It could, of course, be argued, as the above quotation implies, that such creativity in such a central area of traditional culture was, in intention, revivalist, a device meant to shock people into returning to the 'core' and 'substance' of their culture, and a way of asserting the priority of content over form which often succeeds in dominating it.

While, therefore, there was much that was conventional in the life and activities of Onisaburō Deguchi and Nao Deguchi they, nonetheless, developed new concepts, offered new interpretations of some long standing beliefs, widened the scope of traditional rituals and developed new symbolic expressions of the new transformed world to be brought into being by the deity Ushitora no Konjin.

Their movement, Ōmotokyō, gave rise to a number of new religions, among them the previously mentioned Sekai Kyūseikyō or The Church of World Messianity, or simply Messianity, founded in its original form in 1928 as Dainihon Kanonkai (Great Japan Association for the worship of the Boddhisattva Kannon) by Mokichi Okada (1882–1955). Once again a comparison between these movements shows change amid continuity, and perhaps more of the latter than the former. One of the more obvious areas in which this change is apparent is in the content, spirit and goals of their millenarianism, a dimension in which both display originality in the Japanese context. Ōmotokyō's millenarianism is concerned primarily with the complete transformation of the present world by returning it to its pristine condition under the benevolent rule of Ushitora no Konjin (Berthon, 1985 and Ooms, 1993) while Messianity's vision looks forward to the creation of a New Age that has never before existed (Clarke, 1999 b).

More generally, the new and new, new religions of Japan have made a difference to the religious life of Japan by their new emphasis in their teaching on pacifism, the energy they put into recruitment and expansion overseas among non-Japanese, about which more will be said below, in the stress they place on lay spirituality, in the provision of techniques to enable devotees to reach the summit of the spiritual mountain, and in the significance they give to the laity as primary evangelists. Also, as was suggested elsewhere (Clarke, 1994: 5), from the nineteenth century the

Japanese new religions can be understood as vehicles for the development of non-establishment, essentially lay spirituality in Japan, and in this respect provide a parallel with the rise of Protestantism in sixteenth-century Europe.

Establishing a chronological framework of Japanese new religions is also problematic and decisions taken on this front have an obvious bearing on the question of terminology just discussed (Inoue, 1991). The first quarter of the nineteenth century is one possible starting point when movements such as Kurozumikyō was founded (1814) by the Shinto priest Kurozumi Monetada (1780–1850). Another, more historically convincing, starting point would be the middle years of the nineteenth century which saw the emergence of two movements – Tenrikyō (1838), and Konkōkyō (1859) – which were to exert a considerable influence on many future new religions.

The period 1890–1910 in which Ōmotokyō (1895) was founded – a movement which derived much from Konkōkyō and in turn gave rise to several new religions – is preferred by others as a starting point for similar reasons. A fourth possible starting date would be the late 1920s which saw the emergence of a number of splinter groups from Ōmotokyō including not only Sekai Kyūseikyō (Church of World Messianity) but also Seichō-no-Ie (House of Growth) in 1930 and the beginnings of Sōka Gakkai (Value Creation Society), founded in 1930 by Makiguchi Tsunesaburō (1871–1944). The preference here is for the middle years of the nineteenth century largely on account of the influence exerted by the movements that emerged in this period on the later 'new' and 'new, new' religions.

The term 'new, new' which has been used frequently here does not encapsulate all the features of those movements to which it is applied nor does it identify the differences there can be in the emphasis they place on material as opposed to spiritual goals or the variation in their response to the world. As we have seen, Aum is one kind of a new, new religion, Agonshū is another. Nor does it imply a radical discontinuity between the movements so labelled and the new religions themselves, nor is it chronologically mean-ingful. Examples of new, new religions include Agonshū, Mahikari, an offshoot of Sekai Kyūseikyō, Shinnyoen, Kōfuku-no-Kagaku (Institute for Research in Human Happiness) and Byakkō Shinkōkai (The White Light Association).

It is chiefly the fact that these and other movements labelled 'new, new' began to flourish in the 1980s when the new religions had deemed to have peaked, and their greater emphasis on traditional values, on ancestor veneration, on spiritual notions of causality, and the dynamism with which they spread their teachings that distinguish them from the latter. The growth rate of these 'new, new' religions in the 1980s paralleled that achieved by new religions such as Sōka Gakkai in the 1960s, a growth-rate that was itself phenomenal by any standards. At its peak this movement was estimated to have had around sixteen million members (Reader, 1991:196).

It is not uncommon for a Japanese new religion to claim to have a following of several hundred thousand members or several million and more members. Aside from Sōka Gakkai, those with a million or more members include the new, new religions Shinnyoen and Kōfoku-no-Kagaku and, given the chronological starting point suggested here, the oldest of the Japanese new religions, Tenrikyō, included in the periodization favoured here, established as it was back in 1838. The term membership is, as is well known, highly problematic in the Japanese context, meaning different things and requiring varying and different kinds of commitment at different times, and this applies even within the same movement. In Kōfoku-no-Kagaku the requirements of membership have changed on at least three occasions in the past five years, and new kinds of membership have also been introduced. Again, as in Seichō-no-Ie (House of Growth), conditions and terms of membership are often different for members in Japan compared with those for overseas members. Generally, there are full-time ministers of varying grades, active 'lay' members, occasional members and sympathizers who subscribe to the movement's literature, but do little else.

In line with the aims of sociology many scholars have sought to provide causal explanations for the rise of new religions in the Japanese context and elsewhere, and it is not the intention to rehearse these here but rather to limit the discussion to a number of comments, beginning with a question about the value of attempting to explain the causes of such a phenomenon. Given the complexity and diversity of the phenomenon I suggest that it might be more fruitful to search for reasons for new religions rather than for their causes. This is sometimes a question of emphasis and some scholars do both. However, the stress in much of the literature has been on causes producing general theories of rapid social change and the like as explanations. While the identification of causes in this way has its merits it also limits discussion of their scope and vision in ways that the pursuit of reasons, being less scientific and empirical and more wide-ranging, does not.

It is commonly claimed that Japanese new religions have arisen in response to rapid, even unprecedented levels of social change (McFarland, 1967) and this view throws much light on the growth of these movements after World War II. The basis of McFarland's thesis is that Japan, a largely agricultural country characterized by high levels of interdependence and cooperation, both of which are necessitated by the demands of irrigation for rice production among other activities, and by social conformity, was transformed into an industrial society over a relatively short period of time. Beginning in the middle years of the nineteenth century, the pace of change accelerated rapidly after World War II, at a time when the country experienced its first defeat at the hands of a foreign power and was deeply demoralized and traumatized by this and the atomic bombing of Hiroshima and Nagasaki.

I would like to add here that this catapulting of the country from a largely rural, agricultural society to one of the world's most urbanized and industrialized countries was accomplished in its later stages not only in the midst of traumatic setbacks but also, and most importantly, without any compelling ideology of change either of a political and/or religious kind, and under the authority and will of a foreign power. It is worth noting in this context, and this is the essence of my refinement to McFarland's position, that almost all of the Japanese new and new, new religions of the period discussed here either were or continue to be strongly millenarian, providing this indispensable ideology of change.

This millenarian focus may work against the fortunes of some of these movements in the present, especially those which, in taking their members back to the past, to tradition, have simply encouraged them to remain there as if the past itself were a utopia. Others have taken members back to the past to move forward into a future new world which they intend to build, while others have simply paid lip service to Japan's past and looked for other foundations – mainly American – on which to construct a new world.

DECLINE OR DEATH?

Most of those interested in the phenomenon of Japanese new religions are of the opinion that these movements are no longer as numerically strong today as they once were. Tenrikyō's membership was around four-and-a-half million in the late 1930s compared with

14

about one-and-a-half million today, but it is worth noting that this extraordinary early expansion was favoured by the political circumstances of the time that the movement decided to benefit from (Yamashita, 1998).

Though in decline Tenrikyō is by no means a spent force. On 19 April 1998, the day following the celebrations of the 200 birthday of the foundress, Miki Nakayama, I personally estimated, and had this estimate confirmed independently by two other participants and by official sources, that at least one hundred thousand members – the vast majority were Japanese, with small delegations from Korea, Taiwan, Brazil, Hawaii, India and Europe – attended the Women's Association annual meeting in the square in front of her sanctuary. During the period of the birthday celebrations which lasted from 18–26 April 1998 several times that number visited Tenrikyō's main sanctuary.

Thus, while concentrating on their relatively poor performance in recent times it needs to be pointed out, Japanese new religions are still large compared with similar movements elsewhere. If the new religions known as the Independent African Churches, particularly in West and South Africa, are excluded and the Hare Krishna and Sathya Sai Baba movements are seen as distinct from traditional Hinduism, there are very few, if any examples, of new religions anywhere else in the world attracting such large numbers as the Japanese new religions.

In addition to the Aum Shinrikyō factor, lack of growth in contemporary Japan can also be attributed to the lack of fit between the models of society the new religions are providing and the changing outlook of the Japanese population, particularly those under thirty years of age. While providing an egalitarian, lay form of religious life the new and new, new religions also place a great deal of stress on active participation in, loyalty to and working competitively and exclusively for the religious organization, much in the same way as employees of a company. Such a relationship was always reciprocal and depended on the guarantee of a life-long job and financial security.

The present difficult economic situation has forced even companies themselves to rethink their strategy of offering life-time employment and total involvement and this is leading to considerable change in the way people think about such wholehearted belonging. With overtime cut employees have much more free time to devote to spiritual causes but with less inclination to do so and less resources to spare.

15

An even greater impediment to growth than those mentioned so far is that of motivation, particularly the motivation of the second and third generations. This was singled out as a major difficulty in interviews on a number of occasions with evangelists and officials of new and new, new religions including Perfect Liberty Kyōdan (April, 1996), Risshō Kōsei Kai (April, 1997) and Sekai Kyūseikyō (April, 1998). To give but one example to illustrate the point. A young Japanese-Brazilian minister of Sekai Kyūseikyō who recently arrived in Japan to care for the Japanese-Brazilian members of the movement that have returned there for work spoke of the surprise and even shock at the lack of enthusiasm and inactivity among Japanese second and third generation members that he had encountered compared to Brazil (Interview, Atami, April, 1998). In Japan itself, and Hawaii, many of the Japanese new religions have lost their evangelical, sectarian fire and have taken on the settled character of denominations.

There are things that affect their growth that religions can do little about, changes the outcome of which they can neither prepare for or predict. In the present morally and socially uncertain situation few people, including the religious specialists and visionaries, have a clear idea of what the future will be like, nor has any religious organization been able to provide a convincing and compelling preview of it. New and new, new religions, as we have seen, have tried millenarianism as a strategy to carry people over into the next stage in their social and moral history, and to great effect.

They have preached and continue to preach the imminent end of the present order, usually through a titanic struggle between the forces of good and evil, with good triumphing and all the just surviving to enjoy perfect bliss in a totally transformed life on earth. This ideology of change, grounded on the twin pillars of fear and hope, is still effective psychologically, but on a lesser scale than in the period c1940–80. The Aum incident has greatly reduced its potential, for the time being at least, leaving an ideological vacuum at a time when the future appears to be increasingly uncertain and unattractive.

The new and new, new religions of Japan will no doubt survive for a long time to come – albeit with more intense competition from new religions from outside the country – for many of them have a strong institutional base with a hard core of dedicated members and are major players in the cultural, commercial, and educational life of the country. There is not, however, the same consumer demand for the spiritual message they have to offer in the form it is being offered.

Japanese people of all generations – particularly since the Aum Affair, although the beginnings of this change were observable before then – are not only more sceptical of new forms of religious organizations, but are generally less content to have their spiritual life organized and packaged in a specific, undifferentiated form. They want more room to select those spiritual techniques which they themselves see as directly relevant to their needs, without the obligations and duties of attendance, voluntary activity and giving, that come with membership and guarantee spiritual development. Increasingly, beliefs and rituals are being detached from a particular institutional base as individualism becomes more apparent in the sphere of religion as elsewhere, processes in line with what Shimazono terms the growth of the new spirituality movements (Shin Reisei Undō) (1991).

SUCCESS AND FAILURE ABROAD

There are many similarities between the pattern of the spread of Japanese religions, both old and new, outside Japan and that of the religions of other peoples. Immigration, commerce, trade and colonialism, singly or in combination, have often been the catalysts for a religion to undertake missionary activity in 'foreign lands'. The converse also holds in that these processes have followed on the heels of missionary expansion. Both courses were followed in the spread of Christianity and Islam to various parts of the world.

In the Japanese case in modern times, that is from the Meiji restoration (1868) onwards, Japanese religions, rather than serving as flag bearers of colonialism, commerce, trade and immigration, have expanded overseas – Manchuria, Korea and Taiwan in the pre-World War II era were partial exceptions – in the wake of these processes. Modern Japanese immigration began in the late nineteenth century, effectively from 1885, as people left their homeland in search of a livelihood (Suzuki, 1969). 1885–1923 is known as the Hawaiian period on account of the fact that 46.6 per cent of the 487,000 Japanese who emigrated during that period settled on those islands while some 21 per cent went to the United States mainland. Severe restrictions were placed on Japanese immigration to Hawaii and the United States mainland by the Gentlemen's Agreement between the United States and Japan, concluded in 1908. Primary Japanese and other Asian immigration were banned completely to the United States by the Asian Immigrant Exclusion Act of 1924 which was only finally repealed in 1965. Immigration to Peru was also severely restricted from 1924.

1924–1934 is known as the Brazilian period for during that decade 63 per cent of the 214, 000 Japanese emigrants who took up residence abroad went to that country. Between 1935–45 the wave of Japanese emigration turned in the direction of Manchuria which absorbed 85 per cent of the total, taking in over 50,000 immigrants in 1940 and 270,000 overall (Suzuki:16). Repatriation followed the ending of the World War II, immigration beginning again in the early 1950s, but not on anything like the previous scale. Between 1952–62 Brazil once again became the main destination.

Japanese religions, whether old or new, had had little contact with Europe and the mainland of the United States outside California until the 1960s, and the same holds for Australia, New Zealand, Africa, large parts of Asia, including India, Indonesia, Thailand, Singapore and Malaysia. The repeal in the United States in 1965 of the law excluding Asia immigrants, along with Japan's growing economic and commercial influence, provided Japanese religions, among others from Asia, with greater and easier access to that country. Cultural contacts facilitated by improved communications and travel have also been important, as has the military presence of the United States in Japan in the expansion of Japanese new religions overseas. The widening and deepening of Japanese commercial and trading interests in Latin America, particularly Brazil, Argentina, Chile and Peru, Western Europe, and in a number of the countries mentioned above, have also contributed to the arrival and establishment of Japanese religions there.

Prior to the 1960s most Japanese religions, both new and old, directed their attention almost exclusively to the Japanese living abroad. They were largely non-proselytizing, ethnic religions, and when members from outside the Japanese community joined, little or no effort was made to accommodate them by, for example, providing translations of the chants and prayers into their language.

While there are certain obvious measures that can be taken in certain contexts to facilitate the diffusion of a non-indigenous religion in an alien culture the process of religious adaptation is not only an extremely complex one but also highly variable. Considerations not only of a religious and cultural kind but also of economics, geography, history, and politics can have a decisive influence on the progress made by a religion, as is evidenced in the development of Buddhism, Christianity and Islam outside the regions in which they began.

The endeavours of Stark (1987; 1996) notwithstanding, there is no entirely satisfactory general theory of religious success and/or failure, nor is there any sociological or anthropological tool kit available to ensure that a process of adaptation undertaken by a new movement will be successful. Yet to fail to adapt is to fossilize, while to over-adapt can also be highly dangerous in that a religion risks obscuring the distinctive character of its message and with it much of its appeal.

As previously mentioned, adaptation was not a main priority for Japanese religions abroad prior to World War II and for some time after it had ended. The intention of immigrants was to return home and in their absence they knew others were venerating the ancestors on their behalf. It was only when they settled permanently and realized they themselves would be the ancestors in their new land that immigrants, now residents, began to create a religious infrastructure to cater for this eventuality. The same pattern has been followed by immigrants elsewhere including Muslims in Britain and in the rest of Europe (Clarke, 1998 a).

In Brazil it was not until the late 1960s that new religions began in earnest to devise strategies that would enable them to attract members from among the non Japanese population. Even as late as this a number of new movements, including Tenrikyō, did little to open themselves up to the wider society, retaining their distinctively Japanese character. This introversionism is easier to understand in the context of the state of Sao Paulo which has the highest concentration of Japanese and descendants of Japanese in Brazil than in Recife, situated in the northeast of the country, where there are probably less than two hundred Japanese in this city of five million inhabitants. Nonetheless, the ethnic composition of the Tenrikyō church in Recife, now in its twenty first year there, is around fifty percent Japanese. A similar situation exists in San Francisco where the same church has been present for over one hundred years. The majority of the members, who total less than one hundred, is still Japanese or of Japanese descent. This is not a deliberate policy on the part of the local church. The Tenri pastor in San Francisco would welcome a more multi-ethnic congregation and strives hard to built one, but the liturgy of Tenrikyō constitutes a major obstacle to the realization of this goal.

The way the headquarters in Japan understands the role of the church overseas and the decisions it takes, based on this understanding, can also be determinative of the way in which a Japanese new religion develops abroad. Mission can mean different things to pastors and church members on the spot than to policy-makers who man the international departments of the new religions in Japan. By way of contrast with the evangelist on the spot who seeks to adapt and acculturate, the international departments in Japan appear to be more preoccupied with the question of the preservation of Japanese culture and religion overseas, however limited these become in terms of their force and scope, and with questions of control.

It is these matters, and a concern with potential centrifugal tendencies abroad that most influence mission thinking and strategy. After a presence in Honolulu of almost ninety years, one Japanese new religion with a shrinking membership, and in need of winning the support of the younger generation of Japanese Americans, recently appointed (1996), to the disappointment of local, committed church members, a non English-speaking bishop. While the rationale behind the appointment was clearly based on the idea of mission as caring for the Japanese abroad, even this cannot be accomplished through Japanese members since most of these, as well as potential members of Japanese origin, are barely literate in the Japanese language. Examples of this kind of decision could be multiplied many times over, and it is worth noting again in this context that the most successful overseas Tenrikyō church is in Korea where the leadership is almost entirely indigenous, and where the prayers that accompany the rituals are performed in the vernacular.

Generally, the Japanese new and new, new religions abroad have been better at adapting than the older ones, and, as a consequence, have had a much greater impact. The more established Japanese religions abroad include the Pure Land schools of Jōdo Shū (Pure Land) and Jōdo Shinshū (True Pure Land), Sōtō Zen and Rinzai Zen, and Shingon Buddhism. With the exception of Zen, these traditions have remained, for the most part, ethnic Japanese religions and in the opinion of some observers are on a path to extinction.[1]

Those on the spot believe that success is heavily dependent on their movement's ability to develop a measure of cultural continuity in certain essentials of ritual and belief with the local culture and religious tradition. They point to the need to adapt and inculturate if their church or movement is to survive, let alone grow, even among nisei, sansei, yonsei – the second, third and fourth generation descendants of Japanese – many of whom have no more than a smattering of the Japanese language and culture.

Local pastors of Japanese religions in Brazil, including some who are Japanese or of Japanese descent, have pointed out in interviews the absolute necessity of adopting Catholic belief and ritual, at least in a juxtaposed or parallel form. In the words of a Perfect Liberty

Kyōdan minister in Sao Paulo: 'There can be no religion in Brazil without Jesus and Mary, and if we are to survive we must have both.'[2] Another interviewee explained the importance of his Catholicism – he still declares himself to be a Catholic – to his mission on behalf of Kōfuku-no-Kagaku in Brazil.[3]

The success of, if not the largest, then one of the largest, Japanese new religion and/or religious philosophy in Brazil, Seichō-no-Ie can be attributed, at least in part, to the significance it gives in its teachings to Jesus. Many members, life-time Catholics, claim to have come to understand for the first time, through the writings of Masaharu Taniguchi, the movement's founder, the meaning of the life and message of Jesus. Members of Sekai Kyūseikyō – The Church of World Messianity – in Brazil have spoken in a similar vein. There is, nevertheless, a possible danger in becoming too Catholic in Brazil for, as research indicates (Clarke,1998 b), there is a substantial number of members of Seichō-no-Ie, Sekai Kyūseikyō, Perfect Liberty Kyōdan and Mahikari under the age of thirty who no longer identify with Catholicism and for whom membership of a Japanese new religion is in part a path from Rome.

Overall, in the world of Japanese new and new, new religions abroad, there is a general tendency for them to expand faster in the so-called developing countries and in countries where there is a greater empathy for spiritual explanations of life, especially in the existential sphere, and in the areas of health and personal relationships. Their relational character is also often greatly appealing, linking, as it does, the living and the dead, and people with their natural environment. Though in many cases it is felt that growth has been slow – some missionaries really believed the word of their leader was so powerful and persuasive that they would have hundreds of thousands of followers in Europe within a matter of a decade – there are signs, Sōka Gakkai's activities in China being one, and those of Messianity, Seichō-no-Ie and Kōfuku-no-Kagaku's in Brazil being others – that the mission abroad continues to grow in importance as the home base shrinks.

NOTES

1 Interview with Professor George Tanabe, Hawaii, 9 January 1997.

2 Interview with the Reverened Yumi Fuji Kura, Perfect Liberty Kyōdan, Sao Paulo, 8 September 1997.

3 Interview with a member of Kōfuku-no-Kagaku, Sao Paulo, 5 September 1997.

REFERENCES

Berthon, Jean-Pierre (1985) *Espèrance millenariste d'une nouvelle religion japonaise*, Paris: Cahiers d'etudes et de documents sur les religions du Japon, No.6, Atelier Alpha Bleu.

Clarke, Peter B and Somers, Jeffrey (eds) (1994) *Japanese New Religions in the West*, Folkestone Japan Library/Curzon Press

Clarke, Peter B (1997) 'Change and Variety in New Religious Movements in Western Europe, c.1960 to the Present' in E. Arweck and Peter Clarke, New Religious Movements in Western Europe. An Annotated Bibliogrpahy, Westport,CT: Greenwood Press, 1997.

Clarke, Peter B (ed) (1999a), *New Trends and Developments in the World of Islam*, London: Luzac Oriental.

Clarke, Peter B (1998 b) 'The Brazilian Response to Japanese Millenarianism' in *Japanese New Religions in Global Perspective*, (ed) Clarke, Peter B, London: Curzon Press (forthcoming).

Byron Earhart, Harry (1983) *The New Religions of Japan. A Bibliography of Western Language Materials*, Ann Arbor, Michigan: Centre for Japanese Studies.

—— (1989) *Gedatsu-Kai And Religion in Contemporary Japan. Returning to the Centre*, Bloomington and Indianapolis: Indiana University Press.

Hall, John H (1987) *Gone From the Promised Land: Jonestown in American Cultural History*, New Brunswick, NJ: Transaction.

Hardacre, Helen (1990) 'Gender and the Millennium in Ōmotokyō, a Japanese New Religion', in *Senri Ethnological Studies*, No 29, pp. 42–60.

Hurbon, Laennec (1991) 'Mahikari in the Caribbean' in *Japanese Journal of Religious Studies*, 18, 2–3, pp. 242–264.

Inoue, Nabutaka (1991) *New Religions. Contemporary Papers in Japanese Religions* 2, Tokyo: Institute for Japanese Culture and Classics (IJCC), Kokugakuin University.

Kato, Giichiro (1975) 'Yowan and Me' in *Cahiers De La Ceramique Du Verre Et Des Arts Du Feu, Revue Trimestrielle*, No 11, 1975 pp. 1.

Lewis, James ed., (1993) *From the Ashes: Making Sense of Waco*, Lanham, Maryland: Rowman and Littlefield

McFarland, H. Neill (1967) *The Rush Hour of the Gods: A Study of New Religious Movements in Japan,*, New York: Macmillan.

Groszos Ooms, Emily (1993) *Women and Millenarian Protest in Meiji Japan, Deguchi Nao and Ōmotokyō*, Ithaca, New York: East Asia Program, Cornell University.

Palmer, Susan (1996) 'Purity and Danger in the Solar Temple' in *Journal of Contemporary Religion*, Vol.11, No 3, October pp. 303–319.

Reader, Ian and Tanabe, George (1998) *Practically Religious. Worldly Benefits and the Common Religion of Japan*, Honolulu: Hawaii University Press.

Reader, Ian (1991), *Religion in Contemporary Japan*, Basingstoke and London: Macmillan.

Shimazono, Susumu (1991) 'New Religions and New Spirituality Movements: Two Types of Religious Movements in Advanced Industrial Societies'. (Paper presented at the Fifth Annual International Conference on Religion, May 16–17, 1991, at Buellton, California.

Stark, Rodney (1987) 'How New Religions Succeed: A Theoretical Model' in D. Bromley and P.Hammond (eds), *The Future of New Religious Movements*, Macon: Mercier University Press, pp. 11–29
—— (1996) 'Why New Religious Movements Succeed or Fail. A Revised General Model', in *Journal of Contemporary Religion*, Vol. 11, No. 2, May, pp. 133–146.
Suzuki, Tetsuo (1969) *The Japanese Immigrant in Brazil*, Vol. 2, Tokyo: Tokyo University Press.
Yamaori, Tetsuo (1995) 'The Aum Affair and the Death of Religion in Japan' in *Shokun* 27: 6, 34–47.
Yamashita, Akiko (1998) 'The "Eschatology" of Japanese New and New, New Religions: From Tenrikyō to Kōfuku-no-Kagaku', in *Japanese Religions*, Vol 23 (1 & 2), pp 125–142.

Main Bibliography

1 ABE, Y. (1968). 'Religious freedom under the Meiji Constitution.' *Contemporary Religions of Japan* 9(4): 268–338.

2 ABE, Y. (1969). 'Religious freedom under the Meiji Constitution.' *Contemporary Religions of Japan* 10(1–2): 57–98.

3 ABE, Y. (1969). 'Religious freedom under the Meiji Constitution.' *Contemporary Religions of Japan* 10(3–4): 181–203.

4 ABE, Y. (1970). 'Religious freedom under the Meiji Constitution.' *Contemporary Religions of Japan* 11(1–2): 27–79.

5 ABE, Y. (1970). 'Religious freedom under the Meiji Constitution.' *Contemporary Religions of Japan* 11(3–4): 223–296.

6 ABE, N. (1992). 'Sōka Gakkai kai'in ni tsugu.' Bungei Shunjū 70(2): 167–75.
A proclamation to the members of Sōka Gakkai.

7 *Agonshū Homa.* Tokyo, Agon Shu.
Sent to holders of Agonshū monthly good luck charm.

8 *Agonshū Dharma Cakra.* Tokyo, Agonshū.
Monthly Magazine.

9 *Agonshū Kaigai Kaiho.* Kyoto, Agonshū.
Monthly magazine aimed at people overseas.

10 *Agonshū Meitoku Kuyo Experience.* Tokyo, Agonshū.
A newsletter for those who have experienced Meitoku Ko.

11 Agonshū (1982). *Agonshū no shiori.* Tokyo, Agonshū Sōhonzan Shuppan-kyoku.
A guidebook to Agonshū.

12 Agonshū (1984). Imakoso Agonshū! Tokyo, Agonshū.

13 Agonshū (1986). Senzo kuyō (Memorial Services for the Ancestors). Tokyo, Shūkyōhōjin Agonshū Kyōgebu.

14 Agonshū (1989). The Agonshū (The Original Teachings of Lord Buddha). Tokyo, Agon Shu.
A pamphlet giving a brief outline of Agonshū teachings in English and Japanese.

15 Agonshū (1992). The Official Foundation Ceremony of the Sohonzan Sōhonden-Shakazan Daibodaiji. The Main Temple of Agonshū Buddhism, Agonshū.

16 Agonshū (1994). Agonshū. Tokyo, Agon Shu International Department.
A booklet introducing the teachings and activities of Agonshū.

17 AKAMATSU, P. (1972). *Meiji 1868: Revolution and Counter-revolution in Japan.* London, George Allen & Unwin Ltd.
The book describes the forces at work in the conversion of a feudal state into a modern power within a few decades.

18 AKATA, M. (1986). Sorei Shinkō to Takai Kan. Tokyo, Jinbun Shoin.
This text is about beliefs in Ancestral Spirits and the Concept of the other World.

19 AKIBA, Y. (1991). 'Shinnyoen ni okeru "reinō".' Bukkyō 16: 56–66.

20 AKIZUKI, R. (1990). New Mahāyāna: Buddhism for a Post-Modern World. Berkeley, California, Asian Humanities Press.

21 ALLAM, C. (1990). 'The Nichiren and Catholic confrontation with Japanese nationalism.' Buddhist-Christian Studies 10: 35–84.

22 ALMOND, P. C. (1988). The British Discovery of Buddhism. Cambridge, Cambridge University Press.
Examines the British discovery of Buddhism during the Victorian period.

23 ANDERSON, R. (1988). *Taiken: Personal Narratives and Japanese New Religions,* PhD. Indiana University: 380.

24 ANDERSON, R. W. (1994). Taiken – Nippon Shinshūkyō no taiken no fōkuroa. Tokyo, Gendai Shokan.
The folklore of experiences in Japanese New Religions.

25 ANDERSON, R. W. (1994). 'Risshō Kōseikai and the Bodhisattva Way.' *Japanese Journal of Religious Studies* 21(2–3): 311–337.
This article concerns conflicts that arise in families associated with Risshō Kōsei Kai as a result of the sect's emphasis on 'following the bodhisattva way.'

26 ANDERSON, R. and MARTIN, E. (1997). 'Rethinking the Practice of **Mizuko Kuyō** in Contemporary Japan: Interviews with Practitioners at a Buddhist Temple in Tokyo.' *Japanese Journal of Religious Studies* 24(1–2): 121–144.

27 ANDREASEN, E. (1997). Popular Buddhism in Japan. Sandgate, Folkestone, Japan Library.

28 ANESAKI, M. (1916). *Nichiren: The Buddhist Prophet.* Cambridge, Harvard University.

29 ANESAKI, M. (1930). *History of Japanese Religion: With special reference to the social and moral life of the nation.* London, Routledge and Kegan Paul.

30 ANESAKI, M. (1938). *Religious Life of the Japanese People: its present status and historical background.* Tokyo, Kokusai Bunka Shinkōkai (Society for International Cultural Relations).

31 ANESAKI, M. (1949). *Nichiren, The Buddhist Prophet.* London, Oxford University Press.

32 ANESAKI, M. (1963). *History of Japanese Religion.* Vermont and Tokyo, Tuttle Co.

33 AOKI, T. (1972). Some Remarks on the New Religious Movements in Contemporary Japan. The Symposium on Family and Religion in East Asian countries. C. Nakane and A. Goto. Tokyo, The Centre for East Asian Cultural Studies: 106–12.

34 AOKI, M. Y. and DARDESS, M. B., Eds. (1981). As the Japanese See It: Past and Present. Honolulu, University of Hawaii Press.

35 AONO, M., Ed. (1984). Nihonjin no shūkyō ishiki (The Religious Consciousness of the Japanese). Tokyo, NHK.

36 ARAI, K. (1972). *New Religious Movements. Japanese Religion, a Survey by the Agency of Cultural Affairs.* I. Hori, F. Ikado, T. Wakimoto and K. Yanagawa. Tokyo, Kōdansha: 89–104.

28

A useful, though now somewhat outdated overview of the development and main characteristics of Japanese New Religious Movements.

37 ARAI, K. (1982). Minshūteki shōsasshi ni okeru meshianizumu – Burajiru hokutōbu no shūkyōteki ideorogī (Religious Ideology in North-east Brazil). Kamigami no sōkoku. H. Nakamaki. Tokyo, Shinsensha.

38 ARAI, K. (1996). *New Religions. Religion in Japanese Culture.* N. Tamaru and D. Reid. Tokyo, Kōdansha: 97–114.

39 ARAKI, M. (1982). *Kōnkō Daijin and Konkō-Kyō: A Case Study of Religious Meditation.* PhD. Chicago, University of Chicago.

40 ARIGA, T. (1954). 'The So-called "Newly-arisen Sects" in Japan.' Occasional Bulletin, Missionary Research Library, New York 5(4).

41 ARMSTRONG, R. C. (1950). *An Introduction to Japanese Buddhist Sects.* Oxford, Oxford University Press.

42 ARWECK, E. and CLARKE, P. B. (1997). *New Religious Movements in Western Europe. An Annotated Bibliography.* Westport, C.T, Greenwood Press.

43 ASAHARA, S. (1986). Chōnōyoku: Himitsu no kaihatsu hō (A Secret Method to the Development of Psychic Power). Tokyo, Aum Shuppan.

44 ASAHARA, S. (1991). Nosutoradamusu himitsu no daiyogen (The Secret Prophecy of Nostradamus). Tokyo, Aum Shuppan.

45 ASAHARA, S. (1992). *Declaring Myself the Christ: Disclosing the True Meanings of Jesus Christ's Gospel.* Fujinomiya, Aum Publishing Co.

46 ASAHARA, S. (1992). *The Teachings of the Truth.* Fujinomiya, Aum Publishing Co.

47 Asahi Shimbunsha Tōshobu, Ed. (1953). Shinkō, Shūkyōshin to Konnichi no Kyōdan (Faith, Religious Belief and Present-Day Religious Organizations). Tokyo, Asahi Shimbunsha.

48 ASTLEY, T. (1992). 'A Matter of Principles: A note on the recent conflict between Nichiren Shōshū and Sōka Gakkai.' *Japanese Religions* 17: 167–75.

49 ASTLEY, T. (1995). 'The Transformation of a Recent Japanese New Religion.' *Japanese Journal of Religious Studies* 22(3–4).
Examines the rise to prominence of Kōfuku-no-Kagaku, the way in which its organization, teachings and public profile have changed in the course of the movement's development.

50 AZUMI, K. (1967). Functions of Sōka Gakkai Membership (Unpublished Paper), Columbia University.

51 AZUMI, K. (1967). Social basis of a New Religious Party: The Kōmeitō of Japan, Unpublished Paper delivered at meeting of American Sociological Association.

52 BABBIE, E. T. (1966). 'The Third Civilization: An Examination of Sōka Gakkai.' Review of Religious Research 7: 101–121.
Babbie presents a case study of Sōka Gakkai as an international religious movement, reflecting on the factors determining its success as a world-proselytizing religion. Briefly tracing the origins and growth of the movement, Babbie then reviews the literature on the study of religious organizations using this as a basis to present the main theme of his

paper: a developmental model of a successful world-proselytizing religion. Babbie's model contains four elements: field, message, initial group, and expansion phase which he applies to the case of Sōka Gakkai.

53 BACH, M. (1971). The Power of Perfect Liberty. Out of Japan: A Creative Breakthrough in Humanity's Quest for a New Man in a New Age, Englewood Cliffs, USA.
Details the author's personal contact with Perfect Liberty, discussing its teachings and values, its leader and members, and its vision of world peace.

54 BAIRY, M. A. (1959). *Japans neue Religionen in der Nachkriegszeit.* Bonn, Ludwig Röhrscheid Verlag.

55 BALET, L. (1909). 'Le Tenrikyō, religion de la raison celeste.' Melanges Japonais 6: 23–24.

56 BANCROFT, A. (1979). *Zen: Direct Pointing to Reality.* London, Thames & Hudson.

57 BASABE, F. M., ANZAI, S. and LANZACO, F. (1967). *Religious Attitudes of Japanese Men: A Sociological Survey.* Tokyo, Sophia University Press.
A survey of the religious concerns of Japanese young men (aged 20–45), mainly college students and so-called salaried men, including an attempt to classify them as believers, atheists and indifferent.

58 BASABE, F. M., ANZAI, S. and ALPHONSO M. NEBREDA (1967). *Japanese Youth Confronts Religion: A Sociological Survey.* Tokyo, Sophia University Press.

59 BASABE, F. M. (1978). Japanese Religious Attitudes. Maryknoll, New York, Orbis.
Analysis of 1966 questionnaire data from Japanese university students, showing little religious belief. A tradition and denomination breakdown is included. Pilot studies of law and science students and adult urban males.

60 BATCHELOR, S. (1994). *The Awakening of the West – the Encounter of Buddhism with Western Culture.* Berkeley, California, Parallax Press.

61 BEARDSLEY, R. K. (1959). *Village Japan.* Chicago, University of Chicago Press.
This book is a complete study of a social microcosm in every aspect of its activity and organization. An excellent starting point for understanding the people of rural Japan.

62 BEASLEY, W., Ed. (1975). *Modern Japan: Aspects of History, Literature and Society.* London, Allen and Unwin.

63 Becker, C. B. (1995). 'Mechanisms and Features of Religious Healing.' Tenri Journal of Religion 23(March): 105–116.
A description and assessment of experiments performed to measure the efficacy of different types of religious healing.

64 BECKFORD, J. (1978). 'Cults and Cures.' *Japanese Journal of Religious Studies* 5(4): 225–.
An examination of the pseudonym 'unity Cult' focusing on ex-members of the movement in the U.K. Beckford seeks to test the hypothesis that New Religious Movements play an integrative social role. He finds there is no evidence that the unity Cult acts as a mechanism for social integration, and suggests that withdrawal from such movements is too complex a process to lend itself to a single explanation.

65 BECKFORD, J. (1984). 'Holistic Imagery and Ethics in New Religious and Healing Movements.' *Social Compass* **31**(2–3).

66 BELLAH, R. N. (1957). *Tokugawa Religion: The Values of Pre-industrial Japan.* Glencoe, Illinois, Free Press.
A seminal work which examines the extent to which religious-based values favoured the industrialization of Japan.

67 BELLAH, R. N. (1958). 'Religious Aspects of Modernization in Turkey and Japan.' *American Journal of Sociology* **64**(1).

68 BELLAH, R. N. (1962). 'Traditional Values and the Modernization of Japan.' *Contemporary Religions of Japan* **3**(3): 207–219.

69 BELLAH, R. N. (1962). *Nihon kindaika to shūkyō rinri.* Tokyo, Miraisha.
Concerning Japanese modernization and religious ethics.

70 BELLAH, R. N. (1965). *Epilogue: Religion and Progress in Modern Asia.* Religion and Progress in Modern Asia. R. Bellah. New York, Free Press.
A discussion of the problem of religion and modernity in terms of 'progress'.

71 BELLAH, R. N. (1968). Shinto and Modernization in Continuity and Change. 2nd International Conference for Shinto Studies, Institute for Japanese Culture and Classics, Kōkagakuin University, Tokyo.

72 BELLAH, R. N. (1985). *Tokugawa Religion: The Cultural Roots of Modern Japan.* New York, New York Free Press.

73 BENZ, E. (1971). *Neue Religionen.* Stuttgart, Ernst Klett Verlag.
General reference work on Japanese New Religions.

74 BERTHON, J.-P. (1985). *Ōmoto – Espérance millénariste d'une nouvelle religion japonaise.* Paris, Atelier Aipha Bleu.

75 BERTHON, J.-P. (1987). 'Les Nouvelles Religions.' Echanges France-Asle 5(87).

76 BERTHON, J.-P. (1989). 'La Voix des Dieux: Possession et Communication avec les Esprits dans les Nouvelles Religions Japonaises.' Cahiers de Littérature Orale **26**: 153–81.

77 BERTHON, J.-P. (1991). 'Kofuku-no-Kagaku ou la Science du Bonheur: La Naissance d'une Nouvelle Religion Japonaise.' France-Japan Eco.

78 BERTHON, J.-P. (1992). 'Japon: Une Religion Sans Croyance ou la Prégnance de L'activité Rituelle.' Psychanalystes **41** (Special Issue: Destins des rituels): 123–33.

79 BERTHON, J.-P. (1993). *Les nouvelles religions et les jeunes. Pratiques et représentations sociales des Japonais.* J. Cobbi. Paris, L'Harmattan: 177–195.

80 BERTHON, J.-P. (1995). Religions Historiques et Nouvelles Religions Japonaises: Les Figures Différenciées du Renouveau Religieux. Y a-t-il un Renouveau Religieux dans les Sociétés Asiatiques Contemporaines? C. Clémentin-Ojha, Ecole français d'Extrême-Orient.

81 BEST, E. (1977). 'The Definition of Religion and the Interpretation of Evidence: The Role of Religion in contemporary Japanese Society.' *Studies in Religion*/Sciences religieuses 6(1): 5–16.

82 BETHEL, D. M. (1973). *Makiguchi-The Value Creator*. New York, John Weatherhill Inc.
The book traces the development of Tsunesaburo Makiguchi's philosophy and its influence on his educational theories. The author draws on new research, personal interviews, and Makiguchi's own writings to give a clear picture of the magnitude and revolutionary quality of his theories and the role these theories played in the development and growth of Sōka Gakkai. (from flaptext)

83 BLACKER, C. (1962). 'New Religious Cults in Japan.' *Hibbert Journal* **60**: 305-13.

84 BLACKER, C. (1964). 'Le Sōka Gakkai Japonais; L'activisme Politique d'une Secte Bouddhiste.' Archives de sociologie des religions **17**.

85 BLACKER, C. (1971).'*Millenarian Aspects of the New Religions of Japan. Tradition and Modernization in Japanese Culture.*' D. H. Shiveley. Princeton, Princeton University Press: 563-600.
This article gives an overview of millenarian movements worldwide and considers the extent to which new religions in Japan can be classified as millenarian.

86 BLACKER, C. (1986). *The Catalpa Bow: A Study of Shamanistic Practices in Japan*. London, Unwin Hyman Ltd.
This was the first full-length book to make a study of shamanism in Japan. Dr. Blacker describes the various shamanic figures surviving in Japan today, and describes many rituals in which she either witnessed or participated.

87 BLACKER, C. (1991). 'Magic and Mystery-and Modern Japan.' *Japan Digest*. 1: 22-25.
Interview with Carmen Blacker talking about her background and the religious tradition of Japan.

88 BLACKER, C. (1994). 'The Goddess Emerges from her Cave: Fujita Himiko and her Dragon Palace Family.' *Japanese New Religions in the West*. P. B. Clarke and J. Somers. Folkestone, Kent, Japan Library: 25-32.
This article discusses the emergence of a 'new, new' religions, Ryūgū Kazoku or the Dragon Palace Family which was founded in 1973 after a dramatic initiatory vision revealed to the founder the task she was to perform in this life.

89 BLOOM, A. (1965). 'Observations in the Study of Contemporary Nichiren Buddhism.' *Contemporary Religions of Japan* **VI**(1): 58-74.
This article reflects on the myriad of organizations deriving their doctrines and activities from Nichiren Buddhism. Following interviews, the author depicts the nature of thought in these Nichiren organizations, in particular Sōka Gakkai.

90 BLOOM, A. (1965). *Shinran's Gospel of Pure Grace*. Tuscon, University of Arizona Press.

91 BLOOM, A. (1998). Shin Buddhism in the West: An Overview. *Japanese New Religions in Global Perspective*. P. R. Clarke. Richmond, Curzon Press.

92 BOBILIN, R. T. (1968). *Japanese Peace Movements. The Religious Situation: 1968*. D. R. Cutler. Boston, Beacon Press. Annot Earhart

93 BOCKING, B. (1981). 'Reflections on Sōka Gakkai.' *The Scottish Journal of Religious Studies* **2**(1): 38-52.

94 BOCKING, B. (1987). 'The Japanese Religious Traditions in Today's World: The Religious Situation of the World from 1945 to the Present Day.' *Religion in Today's World*. F. Whaling. Edinburgh, T & T Clarke.

95 BOCKING, B. (1994). 'Of Priests, Protests and Protestant Buddhists: the Case of Sōka Gakkai International.' *Japanese New Religions in the West*. P. B. Clarke and J. Somers. Folkestone, Kent, Japan Library: 117–131.
This article discusses Sōka Gakkai, the most well known and most successful of the post-war Japanese lay religious movements. It considers the direction of development of Sōka Gakkai International following the split between the Sōka Gakkai organizations and the Nichiren Shōshū sect of which it was a lay movement.

96 BOCKING, B. (1995). 'Fundamental Rites? Religion, State, Education and the Invention of Sacred Heritage in post-Christian Britain and pre-War Japan.' *Religion* 25: 227–247.
This article focuses on the evolution of prewar 'state Shinto' in Japan as an analogy to contemporary developments in Britain. It considers the relations between state, education and religion and examines the 1988 Education Reform Act and 1994 government 'guidance' to schools, particularly Religious Education (RE) and its concern with 'morality'.

97 BOUMA, G., SMITH, W. et al. (1998). Japanese Religion in Australia: Mahikari and Zen in a Multicultural Society. *Japanese New Religions in Global Perspective*. P. B. Clarke. Richmond, Surrey, Curzon Press.

98 BRAND, J. A., S.J (1961). 'Shinkōshūkyō – As religiões novas do Japāo (Shinkōshūkyō – The New Religions of Japan).' *Estudos* 21: 23–35.

99 BRANNEN, N. (1961). 'A Visit to Taisekiji, Head Temple of Sōka Gakkai.' *Contemporary Religions in Japan* II(2/June): 13–30.

100 BRANNEN, N. (1961). 'A Visit to Sōka Gakkai Headquarters.' *Contemporary Religions in Japan* 2(1 March): 55–62.

101 BRANNEN, N. (1962). 'The Teaching of Sōka Gakkai.' *Contemporary Religions in Japan* 3(3): 247.

102 BRANNEN, N. (1964). 'False Religions, Forced Conversions, Iconoclasm.' *Contemporary Religions in Japan* V: 232.

103 BRANNEN, N. (1964). 'Sōka Gakkai: New Religious Sect or Third World Power?' *Japan Studies* 1(2).

104 BRANNEN, N. (1964). 'Sōka Gakkai's Theory of Value.' *Contemporary Religions of Japan* 5(2): 143–54.
This article discusses Tsunesaburo Makiguchi's 'theory of life' from which Sōka Gakkai derived its name, depicting how this philosophy of utilitarianism was utilized as a fundamental basis for the teachings of the Nichirenshū sect, and the inconsistencies it has exposed.

105 BRANNEN, N. S. (1966). 'Religion and Politics: Sidelights on Sōka Gakkai.' *Japanese Religions* 4(4).

106 BRANNEN, N. S. (1967). 'Happiness and Life's Objective (Chapter 4 of Shakubuku Kyōten).' *Contemporary Religions of Japan* 8(2).

107 BRANNEN, N. (1968). *Sōka Gakkai: Japan's Militant Buddhists*. Richmond, Virginia, John Knox Press.

108 BREMEN, J. V. and MARTINEZ, D. P., Eds. (1995). *Ceremony and Ritual in Japan.* Nissan Institute/Routledge Japanese Studies Series. London, Routledge.
The book focuses on the traditional and religious aspects of Japanese society from an anthropological perspective, presenting new material and making cross-cultural comparisons. It also considers how far ritual and religion are incorporated into everyday life in Japan, both in the domestic sphere and in industry.

109 BRETT, C. C. (1979). 'The Kōmeitō and Local Japanese Politics.' *Asian Survey* **19**: 366–78.

110 BROOKS, A. P. (1981). '**Mizuko Kuyō** and Japanese Buddhism.' *Japanese Journal of Religious Studies* **8**(3–4): 119–47.

111 BROWN, D. M. (1968). 'Japan's Century of Change: The Religious Factor.' *Japan Christian Quarterly* **35**(1): 24–33.

112 BUCKNELL, R. S. (1992). The Buddhist Experience in Australia. Religion and Multiculturalism in Australia – Essays in honour of Victor C. Hayes. N. C. Hable. Adelaide, Australian Association for the Study of Religion: 214–225.

113 BURGESS, J. and M. ISIKOFF (1984). 'Moon's Japanese Profits Bolster Efforts in US.' *Washington Post.*

114 BURKERT, R. (1929). 'Ōmoto oder von der Hütte Gottes auf Erden.' Die Glocke **9**.

115 BYŌDO, F. (1987). Shūkyō 'kaiki' genshō o yomu -shakai ishiki chōsa no bunseki (Interpreting Mysterious Phenomena of a Religious Kind: Analysis of a Social Opinion Poll). Gendai nihon no shūkyō. H. Yamamoto. Tokyo, Shinsensha: 11–30.

116 CALDAROLA, C., Ed. (1982). *Religions and Societies: Asia and the Middle East.* Berlin, Mouton Publishers.
The book studies the patterns of interaction between religion and society and a scholarly introduction to the sociology of religion in non-western countries. It includes a section by Caldarola on Japan: Religious Syncretism in a Secular Society.

117 CALDAROLA, C. (1982). *Japan: Religious Syncretism in a Secular Society. Religions and Societies: Asia and the Middle East.* C. Caldarola. Berlin, Mouton Publishers.

118 CARPENTER, R. T. and ROOF, W. C. (1995). 'The Transplanting of Seichō-no-Ie from Japan to Brazil: Moving Beyond the Ethnic Enclave.' *Journal of Contemporary Religion* **10**(1): 41–54.
Analyses the growth of Seichō-no-Ie in Brazil and how it has been successfully transplanted from Japan, focusing on a framework centred on ideology, practice, environment and organization.

119 CAUSTON, R. (1988). *Nichiren Shōshū Buddhism.* London, Rider & Co. Ltd.
The author who was chairman of Nichiren Shōshū Buddhism UK (Sōka Gakkai) explains the teachings and practice of the movement and gives examples of how individuals and families have overcome problems through practising the teaching.

120 CERMENO, A. (1955). 'Las religiones novismas del Japon.' Siglo Mision **42**: 423–26.

121 CHANDRA, L. (1996). 'The Lotus Sutra and the Present Age: The Philosophy of SGI President Daisaku Ikeda.' Tokyo, Institute of Oriental Philosophy.

122 CHANG, C. K. (1988). Some Correlations between the Early Religions of Japan and Korea. Shamanism:The Spirit World of Korea. R. Guisso and Chai-shin Yu. Berkeley, Asian Humanities Press: 52–59.
Examines the close relationship between Japan and Korea in the realm of religion by comparing sacred regalia, sacred implements, shaman rituals, the form of shrines and the form of ritual worship of both countries.

123 CHAPEL, G. W. (1989). 'Synthesizing Eastern and Western Religious Traditions: The Rhetoric of Japan's Seichō-no-Ie Movement.' *The Journal of Communication and Religion* 12 -**March.**

124 CHINNERY, T. E. (1971). *Religious Conflict and Compromise in a Japanese Village: A First-Hand Observation of the Tenrikyō Church.* Vancouver, The University of British Columbia.

125 CHURCH OF WORLD MESSIANITY World Messianity Newsletter. Long Beach, California, The Church of World Messianity.

126 CHURCH OF WORLD MESSIANITY MOA Newsletter. Long beach, California, Mokichi Okada Association (MOA).

127 CHURCH OF WORLD MESSIANITY (1965). Fragments from the Teachings of Meishu-sama. Atami, Japan, Church of World Messianity.

128 CHURCH OF WORLD MESSIANITY (1974). Excerpts from the Teachings of Meishu-sama. Atami, Japan, Church of World Messianity.

129 CHURCH OF WORLD MESSIANITY (1976). Ohikari. Los Angeles, California, Church of World Messianity. 1.

130 CHURCH OF WORLD MESSIANITY (1976). Introductory Course of World Messianity and Joining the Church. Los Angeles, California, Church of World Messianity.

131 CHURCH OF WORLD MESSIANITY (1977). Sampai. Los Angeles, California, Church of World Messianity.

132 CHURCH OF WORLD MESSIANITY (1978). Foundation of Paradise on Earth. Los Angeles, California, Church of World Messianity.

133 CHURCH OF WORLD MESSIANITY (1979). Hōshi ('Giving of Service'). Los Angeles, California, Church of World Messianity. 4.

134 CHURCH OF WORLD MESSIANITY (1983). The Light from the East. Atami, Japan, MOA Productions.

135 CHURCH OF WORLD MESSIANITY (1984). Foundation of Paradise: From the teachings of Meishu-sama, Church of World Messianity.

136 CHURCH OF WORLD MESSIANITY (n.d). Member's Handbook. Atami, Japan, Church of World Messianity.

137 CLARK, E. T. (1949). The Small Sects in America. New York.

138 CLARKE, P. B., and SOMERS, J., Ed. (1994). *Japanese New Religions in the West.* Sandgate, Folkestone, Kent, Japan Library.

139 CLARKE, P. B. (1994). 'Japanese "Old", "New" and "New, New" Religious Movements in Brazil.' *Japanese New Religions in the West*. P. B. Clarke and J. Somers. Folkestone, Kent, Japan Library: 149–160.
This article considers the nature of appeal and the impact of two Japanese new religions in Brazil: Seichō-no-Ie and Sekai Kyūsei Kyō.

140 CLARKE, P. B. (1995). 'The Cultural Impact of New Religions in Latin and Central America and the Caribbean with Special Reference to Japanese New Religions.' Journal of Latin American Cultural Studies 4(1 (June 1995)).

141 CLARKE, P. B. (1998). 'Modern Japanese Millenarian Movements: Their Changing Perception of Japan's Global Mission with Special Reference to the Church of World Messianity in Brazil.' *Japanese New Religions in Global Perspective*. P. B. Clarke. Richmond, Curzon Press.

142 CLARKE, P. B. 'Japanese New Religions in Global Perspective.' *Japanese New Religions in Global Perspective*. P. B. Clarke. Richmond, Surrey, Curzon Press.

143 CLARKE, P. B. (1998). The Success and Failure of Japanese New Religions Abroad. Japanese New Religions in Global Perspective. P. B. Clarke. Folkestone, Kent, Curzon Press.

144 CONNER, J. W. (1977). *Tradition and Change in Three Generations of Japanese Americans*. Chicago, Nelson Hall.

145 CONNOLLY, P. (1985). 'Buddhism in Britain: History, Variety and Prospects.' *The Presence and Practice of Buddhism*. P. Connolly and C. Erricker, West Sussex Institute of Higher Education.

146 COOK, F. H. (1975). 'Japanese Innovations in Buddhism.' *Buddhism: A Modern Perspective*. C. S. Prebish. University Park and London, Penn State University Press.

147 COOKE, G. (1974). 'Traditional Buddhist Sects and Modernization in Japan.' *Japanese Journal of Religious Studies* (4): 267–330.

148 CORNILLE, D. C. (1991). The Phoenix Flies West. The Dynamics of Mahikari in Northern Europe. 5th International Conference on 'New Religions in a Global Perspective', Santa Barbara, California.
This paper is valuable in helping to understand how Mahikari functions in Europe and how it is being received in Europe. It describes the new dynamics of interaction between Mahikari and the new culture in which it is becoming established. The new religion no longer spontaneously emerges in answer to existing needs, but is superimposed upon a tradition in which it must either cater for different needs or bring about a redefinition of needs within its own context.

149 CORNILLE, D. C. (1992). Sekte of Kunst? Mahikari, een nieuwe Japanse godsdienst in de Nederlanden. Religieuze Bewegingen in Nederland 24. R. Kranenborg. Amsterdam, VU Uitgeverji.

150 CORNILLE, D. C. (1994). Different Forms of Spirit Meditation in Mahikari and Shinnyo-en: Shamanism East and West. Le Défi Magique. J.-B. Martin, Presses Universitaires de Lyon. 2.

This contribution was a paper given at the CESNUR Conference of 1992 in Lyon concerning 'Magic and Occultism in Contemporary Societies'. It focuses on Mahikari and Shinnyo-en, new religions having similar worldviews and consideration of different forms of shamanism as a factor for their expansion.

151 CORNILLE, C. (1994). 'Jesus in Japan: Christian Syncetism in Mahikari.' *Japanese New Religions in the West*. P. B. Clarke and J. Somers. Folkestone, Kent, Japan Library: 88–102.
A discussion of the syncretism of Christian elements in one of the 'new, new' religions, Mahikari.

152 CORNILLE, C. (1998). New Japanese Religions in the West: between Nationalism and Universalism. *Japanese New Religions in Global Perspective*. P. B. Clarke. Richmond, Surrey, Curzon Press.

153 COWAN, J. (1982). 'The Buddhism of the Sun.' Richmond, Surrey, Nichiren Shōshū of the United Kingdom.
Essays by various members of the movement discussing teaching and practices.

154 DALE, K. J. (1969). 'Authority in Risshō Kōsei Kai.' *Japan Missionary Bulletin* 23(8).

155 DALE, K. J. (1970). An Investigation of the Factors Responsible for the Impact of Hōza of Risshō Kōsei Kai as a Means of Religious Propagation and Education in Contemporary Japan. City of New York, Union Theological Seminary.

156 DALE, K. J. (1975). *Circle of Harmony: A Case Study in Popular Japanese Buddhism*. Tokyo, Seibunsha.

157 DALE, P. N. (1986). *The Myth of Japanese Uniqueness*. New York, St. Martin's Press.
An analysis and critique of the Nihonjinron phenomenon and an attempt to dispel the notion of Japanese inscrutability.

158 DAN, I. (1986). Shinkō Shūkyō no Ura ga wakaru Hon. Tokyo, Seikai Ōraisha.
Concerns the hidden aspects of the New Religions.

159 DATOR, J. (1965). 'The Sōka Gakkai: A Socio-Political Interpretation.' *Contemporary Religions in Japan* 6(3): 205–242.
Examines why Sōka Gakkai has been successful as a social and political force. There is discussion about its establishment as 'organizational group' within Japan's social environment, the appeal of its teachings in contemporary society and the organization's political strategy. The last section examines the dangers facing the Sōka Gakkai and offers suggestions for its future.

160 DATOR, J. (1967). 'The Sōka Gakkai in Japanese Politics.' A Journal of Church and State IX: 211.

161 DATOR, J. (1968). 'Demographic and Attitudinal Data on Sōka Gakkai Members' (Unpublished paper prepared for presentation at the annual convention of Association for Asian Studies), Association for Asian Studies. (also published by Stanford University, California).

162 DATOR, J. A. (1969). *Sōka Gakkai-Builders of the Third Civilization*. Seattle and Washington, University of Washington Press.
An examination of Sōka Gakkai from a sociological and political perspective, detailing the movement's organization and expansion, the composition of both its American and Japanese members and its appeal as a religious and ideological group.

163 DAVIES, A. (1990). 'Kidnappings in Japan and America.' Barrytown, New York, Unification Theological Seminary.

164 DAVIS, R. E. (1970). *Miracle Man of Japan: The Life and Work of Masaharu Taniguchi*. Lakemont, GA, CSA Press.

165 DAVIS, W. B. (1977). 'Toward Modernity: A Development Typology of Popular Religious Affiliations in Japan.' Ithaca, New York, Cornell China-Japan Program.

166 DAVIS, W. (1980). *Dojo: Magic and Exorcism in Modern Japan*. Stanford, California, Stanford University Press.
An ethnographic description and theoretical analysis of the history, teachings and practices of Sūkyō Mahikari with particular focus on possession and healing through exorcism.

167 DAVIS, W. (1980). 'The Secularization of Japanese Religion: Measuring the Myth and the Reality.' *Transitions and Transformations in the History of Religions*. F. E. Reynolds and T. M. Ludwig. Leiden, E. J. Brill.

168 DAVIS, W. (1983). 'Japanese Religious Affiliations: Motives and Obligations.' Sociological Analysis **44**(2).

169 DAVIS, W. (1989). 'Buddhism and the Modernization of Japan.' *History of Religions* **28**(4).

170 DAVIS, W. (1991). 'Fundamentalism in Japan: Religious and Political.' *Fundamentalisms Observed*. M. E. Marty and R. S. Appleby. Chicago and London, University of Chicago Press: 782–813.
Davis analyses Japan's society, politics and religion under the concept of fundamentalism. He discusses prewar political fundamentalism in terms of 'civil religion' and gives an historical outline of the state's use of both Buddhism and Shinto in national development and the way in which religion and government were unified to enforce a structure of national identity. Davis then looks at political fundamentalism in the postwar concentrating on Japan's new religions, especially Risshō Kōsei Kai, Mahikari and Sōka Gakkai. He outlines their theology and activities including political activity. Finally he discusses whether the New Religions can be termed fundamentalist, how they relate to Japan's socio-political and cultural realities and the contemporary influence of historical fundamentalism.

171 DAVIS, W. (1992). *Japanese Religion and Society: Paradigms of Structure and Change*. Albany, New York, State University of New York Press.
The relationship between Japanese religions, culture and values on the one hand and society, social change and economic development on the other. This is a carefully analysed interpretation and critical assessment of both Japanese religion and the Japanese and Western scholarship on the subject.

172 DEED, M. L. (1966–7). 'Itto En: Compound of One Light.' *Journal of Religious Thought* **23**(1).

173 DEGUCHI, O. (1957). 'A Guide to God's Way.' Kameoka, Ōmoto Central Office.

174 DEGUCHI, N. (1957). 'Scripture of Ōmoto' by Deguchi Nao, Ōmoto Central Office.

175 DEGUCHI, I. (1963). 'Ōmoto (Great Foundation).' *Contemporary Religions in Japan* 4(3): 230–247.

176 DEGUCHI, K. (1973). *The Great Onisaburō Deguchi.* Kyoto, Japan, Ōmoto Foundation: 266.
This book is the English translation of a biographical portrait of Onisaburō Deguchi, the driving force behind the Ōmoto sect written by his grandson.

177 DEGUCHI, E. (1978). Ōmoto. Shinshūkyō no Sekai. Tokyo, Daizo Shuppan. IV: 7–48.

178 DEGUCHI, H. (1994). In Search of Meaning. Kyoto, The Ōmoto Foundation.

179 DELIKHAN, G. A. (1964). 'Sōka Gakkai's Starting Success.' *The Asia Magazine* 4(42 (October 18th)): 4–5.

180 DERRETT, E. M. A. (1983). 'The International Face of a Japanese New Religion: Sekai Kyūseikyō in Brazil and Thailand.' *Religion* 13: 205–17.

181 DERRETT, E. M. A. (1984). 'The International Face of a Japanese "New Religion" – the Beliefs and Expansion of Sekai Kyūsei Kyō.' PhD. Theology and Religious Studies. London, King's College.
In this thesis, while initially placing the teachings of Sekai Kyūsei Kyō's founder, Okada, in the cultural context of late nineteenth century Japan, the author then examines and contrasts the expansion of this religion in Brazil and Thailand and the degree of receptiveness of the foreign members to its most distinctive teachings and practices.

182 DERRETT, E. M. A. (1984). 'A Japanese "New" Religion in Britain: Sekai Kyūseikyō.' *Religion Today* One(2/3): 12–13.
An introduction to the movement Sekai Kyūseikyō describing its founding and teachings and how it is establishing itself in Britain.

183 DERRETT, E. M. A. (1987). 'Signs Along a Better Way: The Methods of Evangelization of a Japanese "New Religion" in Brazil and Thailand in *The New Evangelists. Recruitment Methods and Aims of New Religious Movements.* (Ed.) P. B. Clarke. London, Ethnographica.
Derrett examines evangelistic methods used by Sekai Kyūsei Kyō (SKK) in Brazil and Thailand. Four methods are examined: miracles, heightening of pleasurable emotion, teachings and guidance and the example of the faithful, and their appeal to and interpretation by members in both countries is compared and contrasted. Derrett's theme is that these methods are interpreted by members as 'signs' of a religious success and determine a religion's authority and thus expansion.

184 DEVOS, G. (1960). 'The Relation of Guilt Toward Parents to Achievement and Arranged Marriage among Japanese.' *Psychiatry* 23: 287–301.

185 DEVOS, G. (1982). 'Afterward.' *The Quiet Therapies: Japanese Pathways to Personal Growth.* D. Reynolds. Honolulu, University of Hawaii Press.

186 DOBBELAERE, K. (1986). 'Civil Religion and the Integration of Society: A Theoretical Reflection and an Application.' *Japanese Journal of Religious Studies* **13**(No. 3): 127–146.

187 DORE, R. (1958). *City Life in Japan: A Study of A Tokyo Ward*. Berkeley, California, University of California Press.
   A detailed ethnography of an area of Tokyo in the 1950s, before Japan's economic boom. Reprinted with new Introduction, 1999. Japan Library.

188 DŌYŪSHA (ed) (1953). Kyōgikōshūkairoku (Record of Teaching Lectures). Tenri, Dōyūsha.

189 DRUMMOND, R. H. (1964). 'Japan's "New Religions" and the Christian Community.' Christian Century **81**(50): 1521–23. Annot Earhart

190 DUCARU, S. (1993). *The Role of Charismatic Leaders in the New Religious Movements in Japan: Sources of Authority and Popularity*. Cambridge, University of Cambridge.
   The primary focus of this thesis is to look at the strong female orientation of the Japanese new religions as contrasted with Western new religious movements. Women in Japan are not only active members of these movements but also function as teachers, missionaries and leaders. Ducaru suggests a new hypothesis and looks at the ways in which women are manipulating religion as an avenue to power.

191 DUMOULIN, H. (1963). Sōka Gakkai, eine moderne Volksreligion: ein Besuch im Haupttempel Taisekiji. Das Moderne Japan: Einführende Aufsätze. J. Roggendorf.

192 DUMOULIN, H. (1964). 'Sōka Gakkai.' Die Katholischen Missionen **83**.

193 DUMOULIN, H. (1969). 'Buddhismus im modernen Japan.' Saeculum **20**: 291–351.

194 EARHART, H. B. (1965). Shugendō, the Traditions of En no Gyōja and Mikkyō Influence. Studies of Esoteric Buddhism and tantrism. Koyasan, Koyasan University: 297–317.

195 EARHART, H. B. (1969). 'The Interpretation of the 'New Religions' of Japan as Historical Phenomena.' *Journal of the American Academy of Religion* **37**(3): 237–48.

196 EARHART, H. B. (1970). A Religious Study of the Mount Haguro Sect of Shugendō. Tokyo, Sophia University.

197 EARHART, H. B. (1970). 'The Ideal of Nature in Japanese Religion and its possible significance for environmental concerns.' *Contemporary Religions of Japan* **11**(1–2): 1–26.

198 EARHART, H. B. (1970). 'The Significance of the 'New Religions' for Understanding Japanese Religion.' KBS Bulletin on Japanese Culture **101**: 1–9.

199 EARHART, H. B. (1971). 'Recent Publications on the Japanese New Religions.' History of Religions **10**(4): 375–85.

200 EARHART, H. B. (1974). *Religion in the Japanese Experience; Sources and Interpretations*. Belmont, California, Wadsworth.
   This book contains essays by eminent scholars on various aspects of Japanese religion including Japanese New Religion.

201 EARHART, H. B. (1974). 'The Interpretation of the "New Religions" of Japan as New Religious Movements.' *Religious Ferment in Asia*. R. J. Miller. Lawrence, University Press of Kansas: 170–88.

202 EARHART, H. B. (1974). 'The New Religions of Korea: A Preliminary Interpretation.' Transactions of the Korean Branch of the Royal Asiatic Society **49**: 7–25.

203 EARHART, H. B. (1975). 'The Japanese Dictionary of Religious Studies.' *Japanese Journal of Religious Studies* **2**(1): 5–44.

204 EARHART, H. B. (1975). 'Statistics on Religious Organizations in Japan 1947–72.' *Japanese Journal of Religious Studies* **2**(1): 5–44.

205 EARHART, H. B. (1976). 'Recent Publications on Sōka Gakkai.' *History of Religions* **15**(3): 264–88.

206 EARHART, H. B. (1980). 'Gedatsukai: One Life History and Its Significance for interpreting Japanese New Rreligions.' *Japanese Journal of Religious Studies* **7**(2–3): 227–57. Annot Earhart

207 EARHART, H. B. (1980). 'Toward a Theory of the Formation of the Japanese New Religions: A Case Study of Gedatsu-kai.' *History of Religions* **20**(1–2): 175–97.
In this article Earhart presents a theory of the formation of Japanese new religions, arguing against the prevailing explanation that Japanese NRMs have a causal relationship with social disruption and anxiety. His theory emphasises the importance of the historical details surrounding the formation of a new religion, including social conditions, religious history and personal innovation of founders. Earhart's model derives from his study of the formation of Gedatsu-kai which he uses as an analytical case study.

208 EARHART, H. B. (1981). 'New Religions for Old.' *Monumenta Nipponica* **36**: 328–34.

209 EARHART, H. B. (1982). *Japanese Religion: Unity and Diversity*. Belmont, California, Wadsworth.
This book gives a general introduction to the history and dynamics of Japanese religion. It includes a chapter on religion in contemporary Japan and an extensive annotated bibliography.

210 EARHART, H. B. (1983). *The New Religions of Japan: A Bibliography of Western-Language Materials*. Ann Arbor, Centre for Japanese Studies at the University of Michigan.
A comphrehensive bibliography of Japanese New Religions in the West including a bibliography of individual religions.

211 EARHART, H. B. and MIYAKE, H., Eds. (1983). Dentōteki shūkyō no saisei: Gedatsukai no shisō to kodō. (Concerning the Regeneration of a Traditional Religion, Gedatsukai.). Tokyo, Meichō.

212 EARHART, H. B. (1983). 'New Religions.' *Kōdansha Encyclopedia of Japan*. Tokyo, Kōdansha International. 5: 366–368.

213 EARHART, H. B. (1984). *Religions of Japan: Many traditions within one sacred way*. San Francisco, Harper and Row.

214 EARHART, H. B. (1987). 'Japanese Buddhism and New Religions: Buddhism as Power.' *Japanese Buddhism: Its tradition, New Religions, and Interaction with Christianity.* A. Miruara. Tokyo and Los Angeles, Buddhist Books International: 64–68.

215 EARHART, H. B. (1989). *Gedatsu-kai and Religion in Contemporary Japan.* Bloomington, Indianapolis, Indiana University Press.
   The book traces the origins of Gedatsu-kai in its founder's experiences and documents the movement's growth using a variety of methods-life histories of members, a nationwide member survey, and participant observation of meetings and major rituals. In his study, Earhart enables us to examine the views of Japanese members balancing his outsider view with the insider outlook of members.

216 EDER, M. (1978). Japan mit und unter dem Buddhismus: Geschichte der Japanischen Religion. Nagoya, Asian Folklore Studies.

217 ELLWOOD, R. S. J. (1969). 'Models, Metaphors and Religious Movements.' *Tenri Journal of Religion* **15**.

218 ELLWOOD, R. S. J. (1972). *Religious and Spiritual Groups in Modern America,* Englewood Cliffs.

219 ELLWOOD, R. S. (1974). *The Eagle and the Rising Sun: Americans and the New Religions of Japan.* Philadelphia, Westminster Press.
   Ellwood examines the impact of five 'new religions' in America: Tenrikyō, Sōka Gakkai, Sekai Kyūseikyō, Seichō-no-Ie and Perfect Liberty. The cultural exchange between East and West as presented by the development of these movements in America is discussed.

220 ELLWOOD, R. S. (1979). *Alternative Altars: Unconventional and Eastern Spirituality in America.* Chicago, University of Chicago Press.

221 ELLWOOD, R. S. (1982). *Tenrikyō: A Pilgrimage Faith, The Structure and Meanings of a Modern Japanese Religion.* Nara, Tenri University.
   In the foreword, Ellwood states that this study is intended to be a description and an interpretation along the lines of empathetic phenomenology of Tenrikyō.

222 ELLWOOD, R. S. (1985). *Japanese Religion: A Cultural Perspective.* Englewood Cliffs, Prentice-Hall.

223 ENDŌ, Y. (1964). 'Sōka Gakkai, the Study of a Society for the Creation of Value.' Anglican Theological Review 46: 131–141.

224 ENDŌ, T. (1996). The Lotus Sutra and the Philosophy of Sōka Gakkai. Tokyo, Institute of Oriental Philosophy.

225 EPP, R. (1971). 'Review of Nihon no shinkō shūkyō (Japan's New Religions) by Hiroo Takagi.' *Japan Christian Quarterly* 37: 53–55.

226 EPP, R. (1980). 'Some Aspects of Daisaku Ikeda's Thought.' Japan Christian Quarterly 46.

227 Ethnic Studies Oral History Project, Ed. (1982). *Uchinanchu: A History of Okinawans in Hawaii.* Honolulu, Hawaii, University of Hawaii Press.
   Also in conjunction with University of Hawaii and United Okinawan Association of Hawaii.

228 FALK, N. A. and GROSS, R. M. Eds. (1980). *Unspoken Worlds. Women's religious lives in non-Western Cultures.* San Francisco, Harper and Row.

Contains an article by Nakamura on Kitayama Sayō, founder of the new religion Tensho-kōtai-jingū-kyō, contesting previous claims of feminist tendencies in this movement.

229 FANTOLI, A. (1967). 'L'attuale situazione religiosa del Giappone.' Civiltà cattolica **115**: 527–41.

230 FARR, K. (1935). *Tenrikyō: Teaching of the Heavenly Reason*, University of Washington.

231 FAURE, B. (1987). 'The Daruma-shū, Dōgen, and Sōtō-Zen.' *Monumenta Nipponica* **42**(1): 25–55.

232 FERNANDES, G. (1941). Uma seita nipo-brasileira: a Associação Universal Humanitaria. O Sincretismo Religioso no Brasil. G. Fernandes. Curitiba, Guaria: 77–94.

233 FIELDS, R. (1992). *How the Swans came to the Lake – a Narrative History of Buddhism in America*. Boston and London, Shambhala.

234 FINNEY, H. C. (1991). 'American Zen's "Japan Connection": A Critical Case Study of Zen Buddhism's Diffusion to the West.' Sociological Analysis (52): 379–396.

235 FITZPATRICK, C. (1989). 'Letter from Aomori.' *Far Eastern Economic Review* **143**(11): 42–3.

236 FOARD, J. (1982). 'The Boundaries of Compassion: Buddhism and National Tradition in Japanese Pilgrimage.' *Journal of Asian Studies* **41**(2): 231–51.

237 FRAGER, R. and T. P. ROHLEN (1976). 'The Future of a Tradition: Japanese Spirit in the 1980s.' *Japan: The Paradox of Progress*. L. Austin. New Haven, Connecticut, Yale University: 255–78.

238 FRANCK, F. (1975). An Encounter with Ōmoto. 'The Great Origin', A Faith Rooted in the Ancient Mysticism and the Traditional Arts of Japan. New York.

239 FUJIEDA, M. (1960). 'The Church of World Messianity.' *Contemporary Religions in Japan* **1**(4): 24.

240 FUJI, T. (1983). The Process of Making Teachings: Founder, Okano of Gedatsu-kai. Revival Of Traditional Religions. H. Miyake and H. B. Earhart, Meichō Shuppan.

241 FUJI, T. (1987). The Founder of the Buddhism Salvation Army as seen from followers' viewpoints. Kyōsō to sono shuhen (Founders and their Periphery). S. t. S. Kenkyū-kai, Uzankaku.

242 FUJI, T. (1990). Seikatsu kiritsu to rinrikan (Discipline in Living and Moral Values). Shinshūkyō Jitten (Dictionary of New Religions). N. Inoue, Kobundo.

243 FUJI, T. (1990). Tenshō Kōtai Jingū Kyō (The Dancing Religion). Shinshūkyō Jitten (Dictionary of New Religions). N. Inoue. Kobundo.

244 FUJII, M. (1972). Gense riyaku (This-Worldly Benefits). Girei no Kōzō (The system of ritual). N. Tamaru. Tokyo, Kōsei Shuppan: 179–238.

245 FUJII, M. (1974). 'Gendaijin no shinkō kōzō (The Faith System of Contemporary People).' Nihonjin no kōdō to shisō (The Behaviour and Thought of the Japanese)(32).

246 FUJII, M. (1977). Shinshūkyō no tanjō to hatten (Development of NRMs in Japan). Nihon Shūkyō Shi. K. Kasahara. Tokyo, Yamakawa Shuppan-sha: 362–396.

247 FUJII, M. (1981). Shinshūkyō no Shugyō. Religious Training. K. Sasaki, N.Miyata and T.Yamaori. Tokyo, Shunjusha. 4: 97–114.

248 FUJII, T. (1983). Kyōso-Okano Seiken no shishō keisei(Political Views of the Founder, Okano). Dentōteki shūkyō no saisei: Gedatsukai no shishō to kodō. H. B. Earhart and H. Miyake. Tokyo, Meichō: 1–78.

249 FUJII, M. (1986). Nihonjin to Goriyaku Shinkō (Concerning the Japanese and their beliefs in the material world). Tokyo, Kōdansha.

250 FUJIKURA, Y. (1992). Alguns Aspectos de Inculturação no Trabalho Missionário da Perfect Liberty Kyōdan no Brasil (Some Aspects of Inculturation in the Missionary Work of PL in Brazil). São Paulo, Pontiícia Universidade Católica.

251 FUJIMOTO, K. (1977). Gasshō no seikatsu. Tokyo, Sōtōshūshūmuchō.

252 FUJIWARA, H. (1970). 'I Denounce Sōka Gakkai.' Tokyo, Nisshin Hōdō.

253 FUKAYA, T. (1955). 'The Fundamental Doctrines of Tenrikyō.' *Tenri Journal of Religion* 1.

254 FUKAYA, T. (1956). Tenrikyō Nyūmon. Tenri, Dōyūsha.
The introductory text of Tenrikyō

255 FUKAYA, T. (1956). Yōkigurashi e no Michi (The Road to the Yōkigurashi – a way of life). Tenri, Dōyōsha.

256 FUKUDA, Y. (1955). Outline of Sacred Teaching of Kōnkō Religion. San Francisco, Kōnkō Missions of North America.

257 FUKUDA and UYENO (1984). 'The Gulag in Japan: Religious Persecution by the Communist Party.' Tokyo, Research Institute on Communism and Religious Issues.

258 FUKUDA, Y. (n.d). *Hand Book of the Kōnkō Mission*. San Francisco, Kōnkō Mission.

259 FUKUI, M. (1997). 'A Study of Kōfuku-no-Kagaku as a Millenarian Movement.' Unpublished M. A. dissertation Department of Theology and Religious Studies. London, King's College London.

260 GAMOU, M. (1957). Amazonia ni okeru nikkei colonia no dōkadatei-Tomé-Açu Shokuminchi. Imin. I. Seiichi, Kokin.
Concerns the process of assimilation of peoples of Japanese descent in the Amazon.

261 GARRIGUES, S. L. (1975). 'The Sōka Gakkai Enshrining Ceremony: Ritual Change in a Japanese Buddhist Sect in America.' *Eastern Anthropologist* 28(2).

262 GAY, J. L. (1965). 'Las nuevas religiones en Japán.' Misiones Extranjeras 45: 41–63.

263 GEDATSUKAI (1976). Shibuchō-kanji no kokoroe. Tokyo, Gedatsukai.
The instructions for leaders and secretaries of branches.

264 GEDATSUKAI (1979). Gedatsu Kongō den. Tokyo, Gedatsu Shuppanbu.
The Biography of Gedatsu Kongō.

265 GERLITZ, P. (1975). 'Kathartische und therapeutische Elemente in der Seelsorge der Risshō Kōsei Kai.' Zeitschrift für Religions-und Geistes-geschichte **27**(4).

266 GERLITZ, P. (1977). Gott erwacht in Japan: Neue fernöstliche Religionen und ihre Botschaft vom Glück, Verlag Herder.

267 GINOZA, S. (1988). Zen'yaku: Ryūkyū Shintō-ki. Tokyo, Tōyō Tosho Shuppan.

268 GITTINGS, J. A. (1967). 'Politics of Mercy in Sōka Gakkai.' Japan Christian Quarterly **33**: 197–99.

269 GLOCK, C. Y. and BELLAH, R. N. Eds. (1976). The New Religious Consciousness. Berkeley, University of California Press.

270 GOA, D. J. and COWERD, H. G. (1983). 'Sacred Ritual, Sacred Language: Jodo Shinshu religious forms intransition.' Studies in Religion **12**(4).

271 GOMBRICH, R. and BECHERT, H. Eds. (1984). The World of Buddhism. London, Thames and Hudson.
A substantial volume looking at Buddhism's influence on Asiatic civilizations and includes a chapter on its revival in the West.

272 GOMBRICH, R. and OBEYESEKERE, G. (1988). *Buddhism Transformed: Religious Change in Sri Lanka*. Princeton, New Jersey, Pronceton University Press.
This book examines the recent changes in popular religion of Sri Lanka.

273 GOMBRICH, R. (1994). 'A Buddhologist's Impression of Japanese Buddhism.' *Japanese New Religions in the West*. P. B. Clarke and J. Somers. Folkestone, Kent, Japan Library: 15–24.
The article offers brief remarks on three salient features of Japanese Buddhism: its relation to other religions in the same culture; Japanese ritualism; and the role of performance of the Buddhist clergy.

274 GONÇALVES, R. M. (1971). A religião no Japão na época da emigração para o Brasil e suas repercussões em nosso pais (Religion in Japan in the Period of Emigration to Brazil and its Repercussions in Our Country). O Japonês em São Paulo e no Brasil. São Paulo, Centrode Estudos Nipo-Brasileiros: 58–73.

275 GORAI, S., Ed. (1980). Minzoku shūkyō to shakai (Folk Religion and Society). Kōza Nihon no minzoku shūkyō (Series on Japanese Folk Religions). Tokyo, Kōbundō.

276 GOWEN, H. H. (1935). 'Tenrikyō, the Religion of Heavenly Reason.' *Journal of the Society for the Study of Religions* **12**.

277 GöSSMANN, E., Ed. (1991). Japan-ein Land der Frauen? München, Iudicium Verlag.

Reconsiders the position of women in Japan giving views from the inside rather than standard Western feminist interpretations. Articles on women in general by Okano and Immoos.

278 GRAPARD, A. (1991). 'Visions of Excess and Excesses of Vision: Women and Transgression in Japanese Myth.' *Japanese Journal of Religious Studies* 18(1): 3.

279 GRAPARD, A. G. (1992). *The Protocol of the Gods: A Study of the Kasuga Cult in Japanese History.* Berkeley and Los Angeles, University of California Press.
The book presents the cult of Kasuga as a structural model of Japanese culture.

280 GRAY, W. (1974). 'Ōmoto and Teihard de Chardin: Two Case Studies in Revitalization.' *Japanese Religions* 8.

281 GREENE, D. C. (1901). 'Renmon Kyō Kai.' *Transactions of the Asiatic Society of Japan* 29.

282 GRESSER, J. (1966). *Kōmeitō: An Assessment of Its Political Orientation and Future Course*, Unpublished paper, Harvard University.

283 GROSS, C. H. (1970). 'Sōka Gakkai and Education', Michigan State University, College of Education, Institute for International Studies.

284 GUARIGLIA, G. (1959). Prophetismus und Heilserwartungs-Bewegungen als völkerkundliches und religionsgeschichtliches Problem. Horn and Vienna, Verlag Ferdinand Berger.

285 GUTHRIE, S. E. (1976). *A Japanese 'New Religion': Risshō Kōsei Kai in a Japanese Farming Village*, Yale University.

286 GUTHRIE, S. (1988). *A Japanese New Religion: Risshō Kōsei-Kai in a Mountain Hamlet.* Ann Arbor, Centre for Japanese Studies, University of Michigan.

287 HAAS, H. (1900). Tenrikyō order ein neues synkretistische Religionsge-bilde in Japan unserer Tage.

288 HAAS, H. (1903). 'Renmon Kyō, die Lotustorsekte.' Zeitschrift für Missionskunde und Religionswissenschaft 18.

289 HAAS, H. (1910). 'Tenrikyō: Ein neues synkretistisches Religionsgebilde in Japan unserer Tage.' Zeitschrift für Missionskunde und Religionswis-senschaft 25.

290 HAAS, H. (1910). 'Die Tanzpsalmen der Tenrikyō-kwai.' Zeitschrift für Missionskunde und Religionswissenschaft 25.

291 HAAS, H. (1914). '3 Religionen der Japaner.' Archiv für Religionswis-senschaft 17.

292 HAGA, M. (1995). 'Self Development Seminars in Japan.' *Japanese Journal of Religious Studies* 22(3–4).
Looks at the growth of self-development seminars in Japan and assess the reason for their appeal.

293 HAKUCHO, M. (1957). 'Thoughts on the New Religions.' *Japan Quarterly* 4: 65–.

294 HALL, J. W. (1956). *Changing Conceptions of Modernization in Japan.* Princeton, Princeton University Press.

295 HAMADA, T. (1990). Tenrikyō: Zonmei no kyōso Nakayama Miki (The Living Founder of Tenrikyō-Nakayama Miki). Tokyo, Kōdansha.

296 HAMBRICK, C. H. (1974). 'Tradition and Modernity in the New Religious Movements.' *Japanese Journal of Religious Studies* 1(2–3): 217–252.
Hambrick questions in what specific ways the new religious movements are new and to what extent traditional elements are to be found in them. In doing so he analyses both Japanese 'traditional' religion and the concept of 'modernity' under an overall theme of change in Japan during the last century. Finally he relates these traditional and 'modern' characteristics to new religious movements in Japan.

297 HAMMER, R. (1961). The Idea of God in Japan's New Religions – with Special Reference to Tenrikyō, Konkōkyō, Sekai Kyūseikyō, Ōmotokyō, Reiyūkai, Risshō Kōsei Kai, PL Kyōdan, Seichō-no-Ie and Annaikyo. PhD. University of London, London.

298 HAMMER, R. (1962). *Japan's Religious Ferment.* New York, Oxford University Press.

299 HAMMER, R. J. (1963). 'The Scriptures of Perfect Liberty Kyōdan: A Translation with a Brief Commentary.' *Japanese Religions* 3(1).

300 HAMMER, R. J. (1963). 'Popular Religion and the New Religions of Japan.' *Japanese Religions* 3(2): 1–9.

301 HAMMER, R. J. (1971). 'Japan.' *Religions of the World: From Primitive Beliefs to Modern Faiths.* G. Parrinder. New York, Grosset & Dunlap.

302 HAMMITZSCH, H. (1968). 'Die Religionen als gesellschafts und staatsbildende Faktoren in neuen Japan.' Saeculum: 74–82.

303 HAMRIN, T. (1996). The Dancing Religion in a Japanese-Hawaiian Immigrant Environment via Healers and Shin Buddhist Clergy to Nationalistic Millenarianism. Stockholm, Almqvist & Wiskell International.

304 HAMRIN, T. (1999). Illness and Salvation in Tenshō-Kōtai-Jingū-Kyo: The Dancing Religion. *Japanese New Religions in Global Perspective.* P. B. Clarke. Richmond, Surrey, Curzon Press.

305 HARA, K. (1960). Kurozumi Munetada (The founder of Kurozumikyō). Tokyo, Yoshikawa Kōbunkan.

306 HARA, K. (1970). 'Kōmei tennō to Kurozumikyō.' Kokoro 23(9 (September)): 65–71.

307 HARDACRE, H. (1979). 'Sex-role Norms and Values in Reiyūkai.' *Japanese Journal of Religious Studies* 6: 445–60.
Based on concrete examples, Hardacre presents a full picture of the roles women are expected to fulfil in one of the Japanese New Religious Movements.

308 HARDACRE, H. (1982). 'The Transformation of Healing in the Japanese New Religions.' *Journal of the History of Religions* 20(3): 305–320.

309 HARDACRE, H. (1983). 'The Cave and the Womb World.' *Japanese Journal of Religious Studies* 10(2–3): 149–176.

310 HARDACRE, H. (1984). *Lay Buddhism in Contemporary Japan: Reiyūkai Kyōdan*. Princeton, Princeton University Press.

311 HARDACRE, H. (1986). *Kurozumikyō and the New Religions of Japan*. Princeton, Princeton University Press.
A detailed analysis of a particular new religion, this book goes beyond that to present the shared assumptions and world view of the majority of Japanese NRMs.

312 HARDACRE, H. (1986). 'Creating State Shinto: The Great Promulgation Campaign and the New Religions.' *Japanese Journal of Religious Studies* 12(4): 29–64.
The first part of this paper examines the way in which the Japanese state attempted to create a state religion through the Great Promulgation Campaign of 1870–1884. The latter part of the paper analyses the effect of this campaign on two of the New Religions, Kurozumikyō and Konkōkyō.

313 HARDACRE, H. (1987). 'Hōza: The Dharma Seat.' *Japanese Buddhism: Its Tradition, New Religions, and Interaction with Christianity*. M. K. et. al. Tokyo, Los Angeles, Buddhist Books International: 96–105.

314 HARDACRE, H. (1988). 'Maitreya in Modern Japan.' *Maitreya, the Future Buudha*. A. Sponberg and H. Hardacre. Cambridge, Cambridge University Press: 270–284.
The author makes a study of the significance of Maitreya in Reiyūkai Kyōdan.

315 HARDACRE, H. (1988). 'Gender and the Millenium in Ōmoto Kyōdan: the Limits of Religious Innovation.' *Innovation in Religious Traditions: Essays in the Interpretation of Religious Change*. M. Williams, C. Cox and M. S. Jaffe. Berlin and New York, Mouton de Grutyer.
The founders of Ōmotokyō, Deguchi Nao and her son-in-law, Deguchi Onisaburō, practised a gender-role reversal in which she was a male spirit in a female body and he was a female spirit in a male body. The author examines the Buddhist antecedents for this reversal and its relation to millenarian thought, but argues that the challenge the founders represented to the traditional gender system was never extended to their followers.

316 HARDACRE, H. (1989). *Shinto and the State (1868–1989)*. Princeton, Princeton University Press.

317 HARDACRE, H. et al., eds. (1990). *Japanese Civilization in the Modern World*. Osaka, Senri Ethnological Studies.

318 HARDACRE, H. (1994). 'Conflict between Shugendō and the New Religions of Bakumatsu Japan.' *Japanese Journal of Religious Studies* 21(2–3): 137–166.
The subject of this article is the conflict that arose during the Bakumatsu period (mid-nineteenth century) between Shugendō and three newly emerging religious associations: Kurozumikyō, Tenrikyō and Konkōkyō. The points of conflict were the healing rituals and constructions of gender.

319 HARDACRE, H. (1994). Japanese New Religions: Profiles in Gender. *Fundamentalism and Gender*. J.S.Hawley. New York and Oxford, Oxford University Press.

320 HARDACRE, H. (1995). *Aum Shinrikyō and the Japanese media: The Pied Piper meets the Lamb of God.*, Columbia University.

321 HARDACRE, H. (1996). Shinmeiaishinkai and the Study of Shamanism in Contemporary Religious Life. *Religion in Japan: Arrows to Heaven and Earth.* P. F. Kornicki and I. J. Mullen. Cambridge, Cambridge University Press.
Discusses differentiating features of 'new, new religions' as compared to 'new religions' with particular reference to Shinmeiaishinkai.

322 HASHIMOTO, H. and MCPHERSON, W. (1976). 'Rise and Decline of Sōka Gakkai: Japan and the United States.' *Review of Religious Research* **17**: 82–92.

323 HASHIMOTO, H. and MCPHERSON, W. (1976). 'Rise and Decline of Sōka Gakkai: Japan and the US.' *Review of Religious Research* **17**(2).

324 HATANAKA, S. (1987). Gendai no Kokoro: Sūkyō Mahikari. Tokyo, Ōbunsha.

325 HAWLEY, J. S., Ed. (1994). *Fundamentalism and Gender.* New York and Oxford, Oxford University Press.
Contains an essay by Helen Hardacre on women in the Japanese New Religions providing general background information on the New Religions and their common world view, a discussion of the ideologies of gender and the family since the Meiji Civil Code and a methodology for identifying fundamentalism within the new movements.

326 HAYASAKA, M. (1972). 'Issues Surrounding the Official Recognition of Tenrikyō and Konkōkyō.' *Tenri Journal of Religion* **18**.

327 HAYASHI, M. (1988). Learning from the Japanese New Religions, PhD. Fuller Theological Seminary, School of World Mission: 477.
Analyses the growth of 'new religions' from a missological perspective, describing their expansion through social and communicational factors detailing their world view and addressing the missological implications. There are chapters on Ōmoto, Reiyūkai, and Agonshū.

328 HAYASHI, M. and YAMANAKA, H. (1993). 'The Adaptation of Max Weber's Theories of Religion in Japan.' *Japanese Journal of Religious Studies* **20**(2–3).

329 HAYASHI, B. M. (1995). *'For the Sake of Our Japanese Brethren': Assimilation, Nationalism, and Protestantism among the Japanese of Los Angeles, 1895–1942.* Stanford, California, Stanford University Press.

330 HEISIG, J. (1990). 'Magic and Morality in Modern Japanese Exorcistic technologies – A Study of Mahikari.' *Japanese Journal of Religious Studies* **17**(1): 29.

331 HELTON, W. R. (1965). 'Political Prospects of the Sōka Gakkai.' *Pacific Affairs* **38**(314): 231–244.

332 HENDRY, J. (1993). *Wrapping Culture.* Oxford, Clarendon Press.
The first part of the book is a detailed study of Japanese presents and their wrappings and then the notion of wrapping is extended to include many aspects of Japanese culture such as language (the wrapping of thoughts and emotions), the body, and in the social and

political domain. For those interested in cross-cultural communication in the Far East this book puts the previous knowledge of Japan in a new and stimulating perspective.

333 HEPNER, C. W. (1935). *The Kurozumi Sect of Shinto*. Tokyo, Meiji Japan Society.
The author states that the object of his dissertation is to show the relationship of the Kurozumi-Sect to the historical antecedents of Shinto development, to present a complete study of the Sect and to place a valuation on its teachings and practical work.

334 HERBERT, J. (1967). *Shinto: The Fountainhead of Japan*. London, George Allen & Unwin Ltd.
Classical study of the history, organization, belief system ('metaphysics'), and worship of Shinto. Particularly useful for its detailed mythology and level-headed approach.

335 HERRIGEL, E. (1985). *Zen in the Art of Archery*. London, Penguin.
The author describes how he was initiated into the 'Great Doctrine' of archery. It is a lucid introduction to one of the most subtle spiritual traditions in the world.

336 HESSELGRAVE, D. J. (1965). A Propagation Profile of the Sōka Gakkai, PhD. University of Minnesota.

337 HESSELGRAVE, D. J. (1965). 'Resurgent Buddhism of the Sōka Gakkai.' *Christianity Today* 9((7 May 1965)): 45–46.

338 HESSELGRAVE, D. J. (1978). Nichiren Shōshū Sōka Gakkai: The Lotus Blossom in Modern Japan. *Dynamic Religious Movements*. D. J. Hesselgrave. Grand Rapids, Michigan, Baker Book House.

339 HIBBARD, E. L. (1962). 'Interview with Leaders of Ōmoto-kyo.' *Japan Christian Quarterly* 28.

340 HINO, I. P. (1964). 'Comments by a Disciple of the Master Onisaburō Deguchi on "Modern Japanese Religions" by Offner and Van Straelen and "The New Religions of Japan" by H. Thomsen.' Contemporary Religions of Japan 5(1): 75f.

341 HINO, I. P. (1970). The Outline of Ōmoto. Kameoka, Japan, Ōmoto Foundation.

342 HINO, I. P. (1974). Ofudesaki: The Holy Scriptures of Ōmoto. Kameoka, Ōmoto.
This is a translation of the holy scriptures by Hino.

343 HIRASAWA, H. (1963). 'Tenrikyō Followers' Views of Disease Seen From Patients with Malignant Tumours.' *Tenri Journal of Religion* 9.
Contrasts views of disease from a medical and religious perspective, and discusses the varying ways in which followers of Tenrikyō being treated at Tenri hospital for malignant tumours, accommodated these two perspectives.

344 HIROTA, M. (1974). 'Bakumatsu, isshin-ki no Kurozumikyō (Kurozumi-kyō at the Last Days of the Tokugawa government and the Meiji Restoration).' Okayama daigaku hōbungakubujutsu kiyō (Okayama University Hobungakubujutsu bulletin)(34 (October)): 13–25.

345 HIROTA, M. (1990). Shinnyōen: sono gendaisei to kakushinsei. Tokyo.

346 HOLMES, F. L. and TANIGUCHI, M. (1962). *The Science of Faith: How To Make Yourself Believe*. Tokyo, Nippon Kyobun-sha.

50

347 HOLTOM, D. C. (1939). *The National Faith of Japan*. London, Kegan Paul.

348 HOLTOM, D. C. (1943). *Modern Japan and Shinto Nationalism*. Chicago, University of Chicago Press.

349 HOLTZAPPLE, V. R. (1977). Sōka Gakkai in Midwestern America: A Case Study of a Transpositional Movement. PhD. St. Louis, University of Washington.
Participant observation and study in a midwestern American city in which movement elite and local members were in conflict over recruitment practices.

350 HOLZMAN, D. and MOTOYAMA Y. et al., Eds. (1959). Japanese Religion and Philosophy: A Guide. Ann Arbor, Centre for Japanese Studies, University of Michigan.

351 HONBU, T. K. (1956). Tenrikyō kyōsoden. Tenri City, Tenrikyō Dōyūsha.
Biography of the founder of Tenrikyō

352 HORI, I. (1958). 'Mountains and their Importance for the Idea of the Other World in Japanese Folk Religion.' History of Religions 1(1).

353 HORI, I. (1958). 'On the concept of the Hijiri (holy man).' Numen 5(April).

354 HORI, I. (1962). Nihon shūkyō no shakaiteki yakuwari. Tokyo.
Discussion of the social role of Japanese Religions.

355 HORI, I. (1968). *Folk Religion of Japan*. Chicago and London, Chicago University Press.
This book contains a final chapter on the Japanese New Religions viewing them as a continuation of the shamanic and folk tradition.

356 HORI, I. (1970). Three Types of Redemption in Japanese Folk Religion. *Types of Redemption*. R. J. Z. Weblowsky and C. J. Blacker, Leiden.

357 HORI, I., IKADO, F. et al., Eds. (1972). *Japanese Religion: A Survey by the Agency for Cultural Affairs*. Tokyo, Kōdansha International Ltd.
A survey on religion in Japan presented in a handbook form. The first half of the book describes the main religions in Japan: Shinto, Buddhism, Christianity, NRMs, Confucianism and Folk Religion, while the second half presents a selection of the main organizations within the above religions, listing briefly their history, address and vital statistics.

358 HORI, I. (1975). 'Shamanism in Japan.' *Japanese Journal of Religious Studies* 2(4): 231–287.
In this article, Hori presents the main characteristics of shamanism and the history of its influence on spirituality in Japan. He considers the origins, magical charisma and role of shamanism in Japan by placing it within the general histiography of religion.

359 HORINOUCHI, I. (1973). Americanized Buddhism: A Sociological Analysis of a Protestantized Japanese Religion, PhD. University of California.

360 HOSHINO, E. (1982). 'Amerika Shakai ni okeru Zen Bukkyō no Shintō (The Penetration of Zen Buddhism into American Society).' Shūkyō Kenkyū 55(3): 268–269.

51

361 HOSHINO, E. and TAKEDA, D. (1987). 'Indebtedness and Comfort – the Undercurrent of Mizuko Kuyō in contemporary Japan.' *Japanese Journal of Religious Studies* 14(4): 305–20.

362 HOURMANT, L. (1989). 'Ascèse, rationalité, modernité en contexte oriental: le bouddhisme de la Sōka Gakkai.' Social Compass 36(1): 83–94.

363 HOURMANT, L. (1990). 'Transformer le Poison en élixir.' L'alchimie du désir dans un culte néo-bouddhique, la Sōka Gakkai Française. De L'Emotion en Religion. F. Champion and D. Hervieu-Léger. Paris, Centurion: 71–119.

364 HOURMANT, L. (1993). La relation à l'objet sacré dans un culte néo-bouddhique: la Sōka Gakkai française. Systèmes de pensée en Afrique noire (Fétiches II. Puissance des objets, charme des mots 12.): 145–171.

365 HOURMANT, L. (1995). 'Les nouveaux mouvements religieux japonais en France entre laïcisation et euphémisation du sacré.' Social Compass 42(2): 207–220.

366 HSU, F. L. K. (1971). 'Variations in Ancestor Worship Beliefs and Their Relation to Kinship.' *Southwest Journal of Anthropology* 25: 153–72.

367 HUANG, C.-H. (1989). 'Tenrikyō no Taiwan ni okeru dendō to juyō.' Minzokugaku kenkyū 54(3): 292–306.
A discussion of evangelism and acceptance of Tenrikyō in Taiwan.

368 HUBBARD, J. (1992). 'Premodern, Modern and Postmodern: Doctrine and the Study of Japanese Religion.' *Japanese Journal of Religious Studies* 19(1): 3–28.

369 HUMPHREYS, C. (1937). The Development of Buddhism in England. London, Buddhist Lodge.

370 HURBON, L. (1980). 'La Double Fonctionnement des sectes aux Antilles Le Cas du Mahikari en Guadeloupe.' Archives de sciences sociales des religions 25: 50–1.

371 HURBON, L. (1986). New Religious Movements in the Caribbean. *New Religious Movements and Rapid Social Change.* J. A. Beckford. Newbury Park, California, Sage: 145–176.
This article looks at a range of new religious movements in the Caribbean including Mahikari. It draws a contrast between Mahikari and some Christian sects, especially Jehovah's Witnesses and Seventh Day Adventists, in that Mahikari validates and strengthens African ideas of spirit possession. Mahikari is seen here as offering an alternative to Western based models of modernity and that is more supportive of Caribbean Africans' sense of ethnic identity.

372 HURBON, L. (1991). 'Mahikari in the Caribbean.' *Japanese Journal of Religious Studies* 18(2–3): 243–264.
An examination of the way in which Mahikari has found widespread acceptance in the Caribbean cultural context because of the way in which Mahikari teachings are perceived by the movement's members to echo Caribbean folk beliefs regarding the ancestors and spirit possession.

373 HURST, J. D. (1980). *The Nichiren Shōshū Sōka Gakkai in America: The Ethos of a New Religious Movement*, PhD. Temple University: 401.
This dissertation examines Nichiren Shōshū of America (NSA) and its history as an international movement and its development in America. The implications of its ethos and world view for American culture are analysed.

374 HURST, J. (1992). *Nichiren Shōshū Buddhism and the Sōka Gakkai in America: The Ethos of a New Religious Movement*. New York, Garland Publishing Inc.
One of the most recent and complete accounts of the development and spread of the movement within the US with particular reference to the ethos (as opposed to 'world view') of the group.

375 IENAGA, S. (1960). 'The Japanese and Religion.' Contemporary Religions in Japan (December): 1.

376 IGETA, M. (1983). 'The Image of Woman in Sermons – Anju in "Sanshō Dayū".' Japanese Journal of Religious Studies 10(3).
Examines the sister/brother archetypes in Japanese myths and religions, contrasting them with the Great Mother type of deity.

377 IIDA, T. (1958). 'Tenrikyō and Humanism.' *Tenri Journal of Religion* 4.

378 IIDA, T. (1986). 'Shūkyō to kezai-Tenrikyō no baai(Religion and economics: The case of Tenrikyō).' Tenri Daigaku gakuhō 151: 15–38.

379 IKADO, F. (1968). Trends and Problems of New Religions: Religion in Urban Society. *The Sociology of Japanese Religion*. K. Morioka and W. N. Newell. Leiden, E.J. Brill: 101–117.
Examines organisational aspects of new religions, comparing them with political organisations and with businesses. It also explores social factors in post-war Japan encouraging proliferation of new religious movements.

380 IKADO, F. (1972). 'Genze riyaku-sono ronri to shinri (This-worldly benefits: the logic and ethic).' Nihon Bukkyō (Japanese Buddhism)(34 (February 1972)): 1–23.

381 IKEDA, D. (1961). Sōka Gakkai. Tokyo, Seikyō Shimbunsha.

382 IKEDA, D. (1965). Science and Religion. Tokyo, Sōka Gakkai.

383 IKEDA, D. (1966). Guidance Memo. Tokyo, Seikyō Press.

384 IKEDA, D. (1972). The Human Revolution. New York and Tokyo, John Weatherhill Inc. 1.
A thinly disguised 'fictional' account of the appearance, spread and persecution of Sōka Gakkai.

385 IKEDA, D. (1973). *Yesterday, Today, Tomorrow*. Santa Monica, California, World Tribune Press.

386 IKEDA, D. (1975). *Guidance Memo*. Santa Monica, California, World Tribune Press.

387 IKEDA, D. (1976). *Dialogue on Life*. Tokyo, Nichiren Shōshū International Center. 2.

Explores the nature and expression of life from Buddhist perspectives and with reference to scientific and philosophical analyses. Ikeda hopes to illustrate a clear path to human happiness and prosperity, a revolutionary change in individual spiritual values.

388 IKEDA, D. (1976). *Buddhism: The Living Philosophy*. Tokyo, The East Publications Inc.

The book is a clear and general account of the way the Buddhist life philosophy can help man understand his true place in the universe and live in harmony and happiness with the universal laws governing all life. Ikeda discusses the nature and goals of the Sōka Gakkai.

389 IKEDA, D. (1976). *The Living Buddha: An Interpretive Biography*. Tokyo, Japan, John Weatherhill Inc.

390 IKEDA, D. (1976). *Advice to Young People*. Los Angeles, World Tribune Press.

391 IKEDA, D. (1976). *Daily Guidance*. Los Angeles, World Tribune Press.

392 IKEDA, D. (1977). *Buddhism, The First Millennium*. Tokyo, Kōdansha International.

393 IKEDA, D. (1977). *Heritage of the Ultimate Law of Life*. Santa Monica, California, World Tribune Press.

394 IKEDA, D. (1977). *On Requital for the Buddha's Favor*. Santa Monica, California, World Tribune Press.

395 IKEDA, D. (1978). *Songs from My Heart*. New York and Tokyo, John Weatherhill Inc.

Poems and photographs of Daisaku Ikeda.

396 IKEDA, D. (1978). *The True Object of Worship*. Santa Monica, California, World Tribune Press.

397 IKEDA, D. (1979). *On the Japanese Classics*. New York and Tokyo, John Weatherhill Inc.

A series of conversations between Daisaku Ikeda and Makoto Nemoto in which they discuss the great works of Japanese literature.

398 IKEDA, D. (1979). *Glass Children and Other Essays*. Tokyo, Kōdansha International.

Essays on a wide variety of subjects concerning the application of Buddhism in everyday life: socialisation of children, family life, world peace etc.

399 IKEDA, D. and INOUE, Y. (1980). *Letters of Four Seasons*. Tokyo, Kōdansha International.

400 IKEDA, D. and HUYGHE, R. (1980). La Nuit Appelle L'Aurore. Dialogue Orient-Occident sur la crise contemporaine. France, Flammarion.

401 IKEDA, D. (1980). *Shinpan Ikeda kaichō zenshū 10, Kōgihen* (Collected works of President Ikeda, New Edition). Tokyo, Seikyō Shinbunsha. **10.**

402 IKEDA, D. (1981). *A Lasting Peace*. New York and Tokyo, John Weatherhill Inc. **1.**

In his second collection of addresses the honorary president of Sōka Gakkai confronts the most pressing issues of today: nuclear disarmament and environmental destruction, the

54

polarization of the globe into east and west, north and south, education, cultural pluralism, and the need for human spiritual renewal. His remarks on all these themes are well considered and well reasoned, but what makes them remarkable is his deep commitment to the resolution of these problems from the standpoint of religious conviction and the transformation of the self. (from flaptext)

403 IKEDA, D. (1982). *The Human Revolution.* New York and Tokyo, John Weatherhill Inc.
Five volumes

404 IKEDA, D. (1982). *Life: An Enigma, a Precious Jewel.* 1982, Kōdansha International.

405 IKEDA, A. (1982). Ōmoto shiryō shūsei (Collected Historical works on Ōmoto). Tokyo, San'ichi Shobō.

406 IKEDA, D. and B. WILSON (1984). *Human Values in a Changing World: A Dialogue on the Social Role of Religion.* London & Sydney, Macdonald.
This is series of conversations-recorded and edited between Daisaku Ikeda-Japanese leader of Sōka Gakkai and Professor Bryan Wilson of All Souls College, Oxford, Britain's foremost sociologist of religion. A wide range of issues are discussed including the social role of religion, ethics of the modern age, the character of nationalism etc.

407 IKEDA, D. (1985). *Buddhism and the Cosmos: Daisaku Ikeda in conversation with Masayoshi Kiguchi and Eiichi Shimura.* London, Macdonald.
A series of conversations between the leader of Sōka Gakkai, Daisaku Ikeda and a respected astronomer (Kiguchi) and journalist (Shimura). In this wide-ranging and controversial series of conversations Ikeda presses both science and mysticism into the service of the Human Revolution and the delineation of the way forward. He explores the implication of recent astronomical and cosmological findings, clarifying their meaning for the world in the light of Buddhist wisdom.

408 IKEDA, D. (1986). *The Flower of Chinese Buddhism.* New York and Tokyo, John Weatherhill Inc.
The fascination of the story of introduction of Buddhism to China lies in the meeting of two great civilizations in Asia: India, the cradle of Buddhism, and China where Buddhism was transformed and transported to Korea and Japan. Ikeda traces the history of Buddhism in China, including discussion of the translations of Buddhist scriptures and the scholarly activity in China.

409 IKEDA, D. (n.d). Sōka Gakkai-Its Ideals and Traditions.

410 IKEDA, D. (n.d). A Historical View of Buddhism.

411 IKOMA, F. (1950). Tenrikyō Yōgi (The Tenrikyō Textbook). Tenri, Dogensha.

412 IKOMA, F. (1955). Kyōsama Goshōden (A Small Biography of the Founder). Tenri, Dōyūsha.

413 IMAMURA, E. (1955). Tenrikyō Nyūmon (The Introductory Textbook of Tenrikyō). Tenri, Dōyūsha.

414 IMMOOS, T. (1991). Land der maechtigen frauen. Japan: ein Land der Frauen? E. Gössmann. Muenchen, Ooa, iudicum verlag.

A fresh perspective on the shamanic and cult functions of women in ancient Japan and survivals of those rituals in the present day.

415 INABA, K. (1998). 'Altruism in the Contemporary Religions and the network of altruistic practice: A case study of Risshō Kōsei-Kai.' Journal of the Japanese Association for the Study of Religion and Society **4**: 151–177.

This article deals with altruism in Japanese contemporary religions including an examination of two concepts namely 'Harmony Ethics' described by Shimazono (1992) and 'Vitalism' suggested by Tsushima et al. (1979) as the common structure and the world view of the beliefs and teachings of Japanese NRMs. There is an overview of altruism in Risshō Kōsei-Kai.

416 INAGAKI, S. (1953). Shinkō Shūkyō no Hihan (Criticism of New Religions). Kyoto, Nagata Bunshōdō.

417 INGRAM, P. (1969). 'Sōka Gakkai and the Kōmeitō: Buddhism and Political Power in Japan.' Contemporary Religions in Japan **10**(3–4): 155–.

418 INOUE, N. et al., (1981). Shinshūkyō Kenkyū Chōsa Handobukku (Handbook for Study and Field Research of the New Religions). Tokyo, Yūzankaku.

419 INOUE, N. (1981). 'Ibunka no naka no shinshūkyō undō (New Religion Activities Within Foreign Cultures).' Shūkyō kenkyū **249**: 1–36.

420 INOUE, N. (1981). Hamamatsu ni okeru Kurozumikyō no juyō to tenkai (The Acceptance and Development of Kurozumikyō in Hamamatsu). Toshi shakai no shūkyō (Religions in Urban Society). N.Tamaru. Tokyo, Tokyo daigaku shūkyōgaku kenkyūshitsu.

421 INOUE, N. (1982). 'California ni okeru Nikkeijin Community Nihon Shūkyō (Japanese-American Communities and Japanese Religions in California).' Shūkyō Kenkyū **55**(3): 266–267.

422 INOUE, N. (1982). 'Hokubei ni okeru Konkōkyō no Tenkai (Jyō) (The History of Kōnkō Church in North America).' Shinto Shūkyo **107**: 26–53.
Also additional articles in Shinto Shūkyō Nos. 109 and 110.

423 INOUE, N. (1983). NSA and Non-Japanese members in California. Japanese Religions in California: A Report of Research Within and Without the Japanese-American community. K. Yanagawa. Tokyo, Department of Religious Studies, University of Tokyo: 99–161.

424 INOUE, N. (1985). Umi o watatta Nihon shūkyō-Imin shakai no uchi to soto (Japanese Religions Overseas: Within and Without Immigrant Communities). Tokyo, Kōbundō.

425 INOUE, A. and EYNON M. (1987). A Study of Ofudesaki. Tenri, Tenrikyō Dōyūsha.

426 INOUE, N. (1988). Higashimawari no seiyōfukyō – Nihon Bukkyō no Amerika shinshutsu (Propagation of the West via the East: Japanese Buddhism's advance into America). Ronshū Nihon Bukkyōshi 9: Taishō-

Shōwa jidai (Collected Essays on the History of Japanese Buddhism: The Taishō and Shōwa Periods). K. Mitsugi. Tokyo, Yūzankaku.

427 INOUE, N. et al. (1990). Shinshūkyō jiten. (Dictionary of New Religions). Tokyo, Kōbundō.
This dictionary represents a collaborative effort on behalf of many researchers and their extensive study of specific New Religions. More than half the book is devoted to topics including organisation, teaching and practice, societal response, overseas expansion and biographies of founders. There is an alphabetical listing of the more well known NRMs in present day Japan and addresses and a chronological table of the appearance an development of these religions. The dictionary combines easy access to basic information as well as in-depth analysis of topics with numerous case studies.

428 INOUE, N., Ed. (1991). *New Religions: Contemporary Papers in Japanese Religion*. Tokyo, Institute for Japanese Culture and Classics, Kokugakuin University.
A collection of five essays which amount to a general survey in Japanese New Religions and include the following movements: Renmonkyō, Shinsei Ryūjinkai, Reiyūkai-derived groups, and Tenshō Kōtai Jingūkyō.

429 INOUE, N. (1991). 'The Dilemma of Japanese-American Society – A Case Study of Konkōkyō in North America.' *Japanese Journal of Religious Studies* 18(2–3): 133–150.

430 INOUE, N. (1991). Recent Trends in the Study of Japanese New Religions. Contemporary Papers in Japanese Religion(2). I. Nobutaka. Tokyo, Kokakaguin University: 4–24.
Examines the present state and predicts future developments in the field of religious studies in Japan. His comments on the feminist impact on the study of religions are especially interesting.

431 INOUE, N. (1993). Shinshūkyō no kaidoku (Interpreting New Religions). Tokyo, Chikuma.

432 INOUE, N., Ed. (1994). Gendai nihon no shūkyōshakaigaku (Sociology of Religion in Today's Japan). Tokyo, Sekaishishōsha.

433 INOUE, N. and TAKEDA, M. et al. (1995). Aum Shinrikyō towa nanika: gendai shakai ni toikakeru mono (What is Aum Shinrikyō? Some Problems in the Modern World), Asahi.

434 INOUE, N., Ed. (1996). Shinshūkyō: Kyōdan Jinbutsu Jiten (Dictionary of Groups and People in New religious Movements). Tokyo, Kōbundo.

435 Inoue, N. (1996). Religion and Education. Religion in Japanese Culture. T. Noriyoshi and D. Reid. Tokyo, Kōdansha: 137–155.

436 Inoue, N. (1996). Naze Wakamono wo Shinshūkyō ni Hikareru no ka (Why are Young People Attracted by New Religions?). Gakko no naka no Shūkyō (Religions in Schools). T. Shimomura. Tokyo, Jijitushinsha.

437 INOUE, N. (1996). Aum Shinrikyō Jiken no Teiki suru mono (After the Aum Shinrikyō Affair). Gakko no naka no Shūkyō (Religions in Schools). T. Shimomura. Tokyo, Jijitushinsha.

438 INOUE, N. (1997). The Information Age and the Globalization of Religion. *Globalization and Indigenous Culture*. N. Inoue. Tokyo, Institute for Japanese Culture and Classics, Kokugakuin University: 80–96.

439 INOUE, N. (1997). 'Shin shinshūkyō, Gainen no Gakujutsuteki Yūkōsei ni tsuite (The Efficiency of the Concept "Neo-new Religion".' *Shūkyo to Shakai* (Religion & Society) **3**: 3–36.

440 International Institute for the Study of Religions (1958). New Religions, Bahai, Islam and the Japan Free Religious Association. Tokyo, International Institute for the Study of Religions.

441 International Institute for the Study of Religions (1960). 'Sōka Gakkai and the Nichiren Shū Sect.' *Contemporary Religions in Japan* **1**(1).

442 INUI, T. and OGUCHI, I. et al. (1955). Kyōso-Shomin no Kamigami (Founders – the gods of the people). Tokyo, Aoki Shoten.

443 IONESCU, S. (1998). 'Women in Japanese New Religions in Germany: The Understanding and Construction of Self.' Unpublished PhD. dissertation. *Theology and Religious Studies*. London, University of London.

444 IONESCU, S. (1998). 'Adapt or Perish: The Story of Sōka Gakkai in Germany.' *Japanese New Religions in Global Perspective*. P. B. Clarke. Richmond, Surrey, Curzon Press.

445 ISHII, K. (1983). Beikoku gedatsu kyōkai – nikkei shinshūkyō no hen'yō (Gedatsukai in America-The Changing Face of a Japanese New Religion). Dentōteki shūkyō no saisei: Gedatsukai no shisō to kodō (The Regeneration of Traditional Religion: The Thought and Conduct of Gedatsukai). H. B. Earhart and H. Miyake. Tokyo, Meichō: 361–407.

446 ISHII, K. (1983). Transformation of a Japanese New Religion in American Society: A Case Study of Gedatsu Church of America. Japanese Religions in California. K. Yanagawa. Tokyo, Department of Religious Studies, University of Tokyo.

447 ISHII, K. (1996). Urbanization, Depopulation and Religion. *Religion in Japanese Culture*. N.Tamaru and D. Reid. Tokyo, Kōdansha: 156–171.

448 ISHII, K. (1996). Aum Shinrikyō. *Religion in Japanese Culture*. N. Tamaru and D. Reid. Tokyo, Kōdansha: 209–216.

449 ISHIMOTO, B. S. (1935). *Facing Two Ways: The Story of My Life*. London, Toronto, Melbourne and Sydney, Cassell & Company Ltd.
A brief and candid chapter on the author's own search for a meaningful religion, with references to Pure Land, Zen and Nichiren Buddhism.

450 ISHIZU, I. (1970). The Basis of the Idea of Redemption in Japanese Religions. *Types of Redemption*. R. J. Z. Werblowsky and J. Bleeker. Leiden, E.J.Brill.

451 ITALIAANDER, R. (1973). *Sōka Gakkai: Japans Neue Buddhisten*. Erlangen, Verlag Der Evangelisch-Lutheran Mission.

452 ITŌ SHINJŌ (n.d). Tomoshibi Nen Nen (Buddha's Light Everlasting), Shinnyoen.

453 ITO TOMOJI SHŌJUIN (1992). *A Wisteria Cluster.* Tokyo, Shinnyoen.
Two volume set of sermons by the wife of the founder of Shinnyoen.

454 ITŌ, M. (1987). 'On the track of "Divine Sales" People.' Japan Quarterly (34): 300–304.
A short journalistic article discussing the issue of door-to-door sales people, believed to be predominantly 'moonies' who prey upon middle-aged women selling articles such as seals, miniature pagodas and ginseng. These sales people claim to be able to 'cleanse' and 'remove curses'. Annual sales are estimated at £70-£80 billion and Itō speculates on how the money is spent.

455 IWAI, T. (1932). The Outline of Tenrikyō, Tenrikyō Dōyūsha.

456 IZUMI, S. (1957). Brasil imin no jittai chōsa (Research on Japanese Society in Brazil). Kokin.

457 JABBOUR, M. E. (1958). *The Sect of Tenshō-Kōtai-Jingū-kyō: The Emergence and Career of a Religious Movement,* University of Hawaii, USA.

458 JACOBS, J. L. (1991). 'Gender and Power in New Religious Movements.' Religion **21**: 345–356.

459 JAECKEL, T. (1960). 'Psychological and Sociological Approaches to Japan's New Religions.' Japanese Religion 2(1): 6–13.

460 JANSEN, M. B., Ed. (1965). *Changing Japanese Attitudes Toward Modernization.* Princeton, Princeton University Press.
This book contains essays by leading experts on Japan, including two studies by important Japanese scholars, covering numerous aspects of Japanese thought about the impact of modernization on the life of the country.

461 *Japan Times* (1979). Ikeda Quits Presidency of Sōka Gakkai Group. *Japan Times Weekly.* Tokyo.

462 JOHNSON, T. W. (1970). 'Japan's New Religions: A Search for Uniformities.' Kroeber Anthropological Society Papers **42**: 99–118.

463 KAGEYAMA, G. (1975). Nicherenshū fukyō no kenkyū (Research on the Propagation of Nichirenshū). Kyoto, Heirakuji shoten.

464 KAJIMURA, N. (1988). Nihonjin no Shūkyō (The Religion of the Japanese). Tokyo, Chūōkōronsha.

465 KAMATA, H. (1966). Daughters of Gods: Shaman priestesses in Japan and Okinawa. Folk Cultures of Japan and East Asia. J. Pittau. Tokyo.

466 KAMATA, H. (1972). 'The Role of the Priestess in Ryukyu Ritual Performance.' Japanese Religions 17(4): 11–17.
Discusses Okinawan folk religion and the important role played by women as priestesses. Focuses on how they are chosen and their interaction with deities.

467 KAMOMIYA, J. (1952). Shinkō Taikenshū (Faith Experiences). Tokyo, Risshō Kōseikai Shūgaku Kenjō.

468 KAMOMIYA, J. (1961). 'Risshō Kōsei Kai.' *Contemporary Religions in Japan* 2(1): 30.

469 KAMSTRA, J. H. (1960). 'Japans grosste-Gefahr-die Sōka Gakkai(1).' Zeitschrift fur Missionwissenschaft und Religionswissenschaft **44**(1): 41–51.

470 KAMSTRA, J. H. (1960). 'Japans grosste-Gefahr-die Sōka Gakkai(2).' Zeitschrift fur Missionwissenschaft und Religionswissenschaft **44**(2): 98–106.

471 KAMSTRA, J. H. (1994). Japanese Monotheism and New Religions. *Japanese New Religions in the West*. P. B. Clarke and J. Somers. Folkestone, Kent, Japan Library: 103–116.
Polytheism, the belief in myriads of deities has been one of the pillars of Shinto in particular and of Japanese religion in general. This article highlights the contrast with the new religions such as Tenrikyō, Konkōkyō and Ōmotokyō which believe in deities with monotheistic qualities. Kamstra analyses the impact of Christian theistic qualities on Japanese new religions.

472 KANDA, H. (1993). Kinsei kōki ni okeru shūkyō ishiki no hen'yō to tōgō (The Change and Unification of Religious Belief in Recent Times). Nihonshi Kenkyū (*Research on Japanese History*).

473 KANGAKURYŌ, Ed. (1953). Shinkō Shūkyō Kaisetsu (Explaining New Religions). Kyoto, Hayakkaen.

474 KAPLEAU, P. (1980). *The Three Pillars of Zen. Teaching, Practice and Enlightenment*. New York, Anchor/Doubleday.
Alongside lectures on Zen training and teachings, the book also contains dialogues with ten western devotees and eight contemporary enlightenment experiences.

475 KASAHARA, K. (1976). Gendai Shakai to Sōka Gakkai (Modern Society and Sōka Gakkai). Gendai Bukkyo (Contemporary Buddhism). N. Hajime. Tokyo, Kōsei Shuppansha. 20: 123–207.

476 KASAHARA, K. (1977). Nihon shūkyōshi (The History of Religions in Japan). Tokyo, Yamakawa shuppansha.

477 KASAHARA, M. (1985). 'The Moonies Make a Comeback.' *Japan Quarterly* (32): 46–50.

478 KASAI, M. (1983). 'Mekishiko genchijin ni okeru Nihon bunka juyō no ichi keitai-Nichiren Shōshū dendō ni kansuru jirei kenkyū (One Form of Acceptance of Japanese Culture Among Native Mexicans: A Case Study of Nichiren Shōshū Proselytization).' Nanbu Mekishiko sonraku ni okeru Katorikku-kei bunka no kenkyū 2.

479 KASHIMA, T. (1977). *Buddhism in America: The Social Organization of an Ethnic Religious Institution*. Westport, Connecticut, Greenwood Press.

480 KASHIO, N. (1996). Gendai Furansu toshi to shinshukyo undo: Pari Mahikari no jirei (The Modern French City and New Religious Movements: The Case of Mahikari in Paris). Cities and Civilization. T. Makoto, Mineruva Shobo.

481 KAWAHASHI, N. (1995). 'Jizoku (Priest's Wives) in Sōtō Zen Buddhism.' *Japanese Journal of Religious Studies* 22(1–2).

Since Buddhism is still regarded as a world-renunciating religion, priests' wives are an ambiguous category, despite the fact that most of the priests are married and that their wives play an important part in the day-to-day running of the temple.

482 KERNER, K. (1970). 'Japan's New Religions.' *Japan Interpreter* 6(2): 135–50.

483 KERNER, K. (1974). The Malevolent Ancestor: Ancestral Influence in a Japanese Religious Sect. *Ancestors*. W. H. Newell. Hague, Mouton: 205–217.

484 KERNER, K. (1979). *Building God's Kingdom: Society and Order in a Japanese Utopian Community*. PhD. New York, Columbia.

485 KERR, A. (1982). 'Ōmoto and Other Religions.' Ōmoto International April–June: 30–34.

486 KERR, A. (1983). 'Ōmoto and Other Religions.' Ōmoto International January–June: 9–13.

487 KIMBALL, B. A. (1979). 'The Problem of Epistemology in Japanese New Religions.' *Tenri Journal of Religion* 13: 72–93.

488 KIMURA, Y. (1988). *Issei: Japanese Immigrants in Hawaii*. Honolulu, Hawaii, University of Hawaii Press.

489 KIRBY, R. J. (1910). 'Ancestral Worship in Japan.' *Transactions of the Asiatic Society of Japan* 38: 233–267.

490 KIRIMURA, Y. (1977). Fundamentals of Buddhism. Tokyo, Nichiren Shōshū Center.

491 KIRIMURA, Y., Ed. (1982). Outline of Buddhism. Tokyo, Nichiren Shōshū International Center.

492 KIRIMURA, Y. (1982). The Life of Nichiren Daishonin. Tokyo, Nichiren Shōshū International Center.

493 KIRIYAMA, S. (1971). Henshin no genri (The Principles of Transformation). Tokyo, Kadokawa Bunsho.

494 KIRIYAMA, S. (1978). Agon mikkyō ima (Agon Esotericism now!). Tokyo, Hirakawa.

495 KIRIYAMA, S. (1981). Ryūjin ga tobu-kaun o yokusuru shugojin shugorei no mochikata (The Dragon God Flies-The Way to Acquire Protective Deities and Spirits to Improve Family Fortunes). Tokyo, Hirakawa.

496 KIRIYAMA, S. (1987). Hito wa donna innen o motsu ka (What Types of Karma do People Have?). Tokyo, Agonshū.

497 KIRIYAMA, S. (1994). Hannya Shingyō Meisōhō (Hanya Shingyo Meditation Methods), Agonshū.

498 KIRIYAMA, S. (1995). *Aum Shinrikyō to Agonshū*. Tokyo, Agonshū Press.
The response of Kiriyama, founder of Agonshū, to the Aum Shinrikyō affair.

499 KISALA, R. (1992). Gendai shūkyō to shakai rinri. Tokyo, Seikyūsha.
Contemporary Religion and Social Ethics.

500 KISALA, R. (1994). 'Etica sociale e attività di welfare delle nouve relgioni. Il caso del Tenrikyō e del Risshō Kōsei Kai.' Religioni e Società 17.

501 KISALA, R. (1994). 'Sōka Gakkai, Kōmeitō and the Separation of Religion and State in Japan.' Nanzan Bulletin **18**.

502 KISALA, R. (1994). Social ethics and the Japanese New Religions: the Social Welfare Activities of Tenrikyō and Risshō Kōseikai. New Religious Movements in Asia and the Pacific Islands: Implication of Church and Society. R. C. Salazar. Manila, De La Salle University.

503 KISALA, R. (1994). 'Contemporary Karma-Interpretations of Karma in Tenrikyō amd Risshō Kōsei Kai.' *Japanese Journal of Religious Studies* **21**(1): 73–92.

504 KISALA, R. (1995). 'Aum Alone in Japan: Religious Responses to the Aum Affair.' *Bulletin of the Nanzan Institute for Religion and Culture* **19**(Spring): 6–34.

505 KISALA, R. (1996). Japanese New Religions and the Concept of Peace. Research in the Social Scientific Study of Religion. Joanne M. Greer et al. Greenwich, CT, JAI Press. **7**: 145–60.

506 KISALA, R. (1998). '1999 and Beyond: The Use of Nostradamus' Prophecies by Japanese Religions.' *Japanese Religions* **23**: 1–15.

507 KISALA, R. (1998). 'Coercion and Power Relationships Within the Leadership of the AUM Spiritual Truth Church in Japan.' *Wolves Among the Fold*. A. Shupe. New Brunswick, NJ, Rutgers University Press.

508 KISHIDA, E. (1969). The Character and Doctrine of Gedatsu Kongo, Gedatsu Church of America.

509 KISHIMOTO, H. (1958). The Role of Mountains in the Religious Life of the Japanese People. Proceedings of the Ninth International Congress for the History of Religions, Tokyo.

510 KISHIMOTO, H. (1960). 'The Problem of Religion and Modernization in Japan.' *Contemporary Religions in Japan* **1**(3): 1–19.

511 KITAGAWA, J. M. (1961). 'The Contemporary Religious Situation in Japan.' *Japanese Religions* **2**(2–3): 24–42.

512 KITAGAWA, J. M. (1965). 'The Buddhist Transformation of Japan.' *History of Religions* **4**(2): 310–36.

513 KITAGAWA, J. M. (1966). *Religion in Japanese History*. New York, Columbia University Press.
   The book is based on a series of lectures given in 1962–3 under the auspices of the Committee on the History of Religions of the American Council of Learned Societies. The purpose of the lectures was to delineate both for a general audience and scholars alike, the significance, inner logic, and patterns of religious phenomena in Japan both historically and structurally.

514 KITAGAWA, J. M. (1971). New Religions in Japan: A Historical Perspective. *Religion and Change in Contemporary Asia*. R. Spencer. Minneapolis, University of Minnesota Press: 27–43.

515 KITAGAWA, J. M. (1981). 'The Career of Maitreya, with Special Reference to Japan.' *History of Religions* **21**(2): 107–125.

516 KITAGAWA, J. M. (1987). *On Understanding Japanese Religion*. Princeton, Princeton University Press.
A collection of articles spanning three decades on various aspects of Japanese religion including history, pilgrimage, festivals, shintoism buddhism and present-day religious ethos.

517 KITAMURA, T. (1958). Oyashikiri Taikenshū (Experiences of Oyashikiri). Tondabayashi, PL Shuppansha.

518 KITAMURA, S. (1961). 'Tenshō Kōtai Jingū-kyō: The Dancing Religion.' Contemporary Religions in Japan 2(3): 26–.

519 KIYOTA, M. (1969). 'Buddhism in Postwar Japan: A Critical Survey.' *Monumenta Nipponica* 24(1–2): 113–136.

520 KIYOTA, M. (1982). Gedatsukai: Its Theory and Practice (A Study of a Shinto-Buddhist Syncretic School in Contemporary Japan). Los Angeles – Tokyo, Buddhist Books International.

521 KLEIN, N. H. (1968). 'On the Doctrine of Sōka Gakkai.' *Japanese Religions* 5(3).

522 KNECHT, P. and HATANAKA, S. (1993). 'Dentō o kumu shinshūkyō: Mahikari.' Academia (Jinbun-Shakaikagakuhen) 57(7–271).

523 KNECHT, P. (1995). 'The Crux of the Cross: Mahikari's Core Symbol.' *Japanese Journal of Religious Studies* 22(3–4).
Explores the symbolism of the cross in both sects of Mahikari (Sekai Mahikari Bunmei Kyōdan and Sūkyō Mahikari). It also discusses the importance of Japan in Mahikari's teachings, and identifies some of the sources drawn upon by the founder of Mahikari.

524 KNOTT, K. (1988). New Religious Movements. *The British: Their Religious Beliefs and Practices 1800–1986*. T. Thomas. London, Routledge.
An account of the growth of new religious movements in the U.K. A number of movements are discussed, including Baha'i, the Unification Church, ISKCON, Scientology and the Rajneesh Movement. Sōka Gakkai, Sōtō Zen, and Nichiren Shōshū are also mentioned, but are not discussed in detail.

525 KOBAYASHI, S. (1958). 'Sōka Gakkai, A Strange Buddhist Sect.' *Japan Christian Quarterly* 24(April): 104–111.

526 KOBAYASHI, S. (1959). 'The Peaceful Co-existence of intellectual and Magical Elements in Japan's New Religions.' *Japanese Religion* 1(4): 28–35.

527 KOBAYASHI, S. (1960). 'Ōmoto: A Religion of Salvation.' *Japanese Religions* 2(April): 38–50.

528 KOBAYASHI, T. (1991–3). 'Japanese Immigrants in Toronto: The Case of Emigrants from Wakayama Prefecture.': 95–110.

529 KOBAYASHI, A. (1994). A Study of a Japanese New Religion: The Institute for Research into Human Happiness. Unpublished M.A. thesis. Theology and Religious Studies. London, King's College.
A study of a Japanese New Religion which includes interviews with some members in the UK.

530 KOBAYASHI, H. (1994). Agonshū. Shinshūkyō jidai. M. Shimizu. Tokyo, Daizō Shuppan. 2: 63–118.

531 KODAIRA, Y. (1958). Sōka Gakkai. Tokyo, Nihon Hōsō Shuppansha.

532 KODERA, M. (1971). 'Kurozumikyō no rekishiteki seikaku (Kurozumikyō in History).' Okayama shigaku(24 (September)): 39–64.

533 KOEPPING, K. P. (1967). 'Sekai Mahikari Bunmei Kyōdan: A Preliminary Discussion of a Recent Religious Movement in Japan.' *Contemporary Religions in Japan* 8(2): 101–134.

534 KOEPPING, K.-P. (1968). Pattern and Function in Cultural Processes: The Study of Religious Dynamics in Post-war Japan. VIIIth International Congress of Anthropological and Ethnological Sciences, Tokyo.

535 KOEPPING, K.-P. (1969). 'Sōka Gakkai, eine kämpferische neue Religion Japans.' Indo-Asia 3: 247–258.

536 KOEPPING, K.-P. (1970). 'Motive und Taktiken der Japanischen Studenten-Rebellion.' Indo-Asia 4: 168–186.

537 KOEPPING, K.-P. (1971). Wogegen Japan's Studenten revellieren. Japan, Beharrung und Wagnis. G. Wirsing. München: 57–60.

538 KOEPPING, K. P. (1974). Religiöse Bewegungen im Modernen Japan ais Problem des Kulturwandels. Cologne, Wienand Verlag.

539 KOEPPING, K. P. (1976). 'On the Epistemology of Participant Observation.' Occasional Papers in Anthropology 6: 159–77.

540 KOEPPING, K. (1977). 'Ideologies and New Religious Movements. The case of Shinrikyo and its Doctrines in Comparative Perspective.' *Japanese Journal of Religious Studies* 4(2–3): 103–50.

541 KOEPPING, K. P. (1980). 'Japanese Religious Movements: The Semiology of Revolutionary Ideologies.' Anthropological Forum IV(3–4): 375–385.

542 KOEPPING, K. P. (1981). 'Women as Religious Founders: Japan's Living Goddesses.' *Journal of Religion and Culture* 16(3): 265–282.
A discussion of some of the numerous charismatic female founders of New Religions in the light of Shimazono's 'ikigami' theory with special emphasis on Kiriyama Sayo, the founder of Tenshō Kōtai Jingu Kyō.

543 KOEPPING, K. P. (1990). Die Neuen Regionen Japans. Tokyo, OAG.

544 KOEPPING, K.-P. (1994). Manipulated Identities: Syncretism and Uniqueness of Tradition in Modern Japanese Discourse. *Syncretism/Anti-syncretism: The politics of religious synthesis.* C. Stewart and R. Shaw. London and New York, Routledge: 161–177.
Koepping examines the modern concern with cultural and national identity in Japan, with reference to the notion of syncretism and from an anthropological perspective. He looks at cultural change in the Meiji period focusing on the reformer Nishimura Shigeki and then discusses syncretism in the new religions.

545 Kōfukū no Kagakū Kōhō-Kyōku (1995). Daishinsai sabaibaru manyuaru. Kore de anata wa sukuwareru (Survival Manual for the Great Earthquake: This is How You Will Be Saved). Tokyo, IRH.

546 Kōfuku-no-Kagaku (1989). The No Shi (*Brain Death is No Death*). Tokyo, IRH Press.

547 Kōfuku-no-Kagaku (1991–). Kōfuku-no-Kagaku. Tokyo, IRH Press. *Monthly Magazine.*

548 Kōfuku-no-Kagaku (1994). *Love is for Giving.* Tokyo, IRH Press.

549 Kōfuku-no-Kagaku (1995). Sōka Gakkai Ruining Japan. Tokyo, Kōfuku-no-Kagaku General Headquarters.

550 Kōfuku-no-Kagaku (1995). Genron no Jiyu tai Shikyo no Jiyu (Freedom of Speech vs. Freedom of Religion). Tokyo, Kōfuku-no-Kagaku General Headquarters.

551 KOHLER, W. (1962). Die Lotus-Lehre und die modernen Religionen in Japan. Zurich, Atlantis Verlag.

552 KOMOTO, M. (1988). 'The Place of Ancestors in the New Religions: The Case of Reiyūkai-derived Groups.' Transaction of the Institute for Japanese Culture and Classics 62.

553 KŌMOTO, K. (1976). Kyōsosama no oitsuwa (Tales of the Founder). Okayama, Kurozumikyō Nisshinsha.

554 KŌMOTO, M. (1991). The Place of Ancestors in the New Religions: The Case of Reiyūkai Derived Groups. *Contemporary Papers in Japanese Religion* (2). N. Inoue. Tokyo, Kokagakuin University: 93–124.

555 KONDŌ, D. K. (1982). *Work, Family and the Self: A Cultural Analysis of Japanese Family Enterprise*, PhD. Harvard University.
An examination of the ways in which mature gendered identities are constructed in Japan. This study, based on participant observation in a small factory in downtown Tokyo, focuses particularly on gender issues in the work place.

556 Konkōkyō *Konkō Review.* Los Angeles, California, Konkōkyō.

557 Konkōkyō (1933). The Sacred Scriptures of Konkōkyō. Konko-cho, Japan, Konkōkyō Hombu.

558 Konkōkyō (1954). Konkōkyō kyogi (Konkōkyō Doctrines), Kōnkō Honbu Kyocho.

559 Konkōkyō (1959). Konkōkyō Kyoten (Konkōkyō Scriptures), Kōnkō Hombu Kyocho.

560 Konkōkyō (1971). Daily Service Book. San Francisco, Ministerial Staff of Kōnkō Churches of America.

561 Konkōkyō (1976). Konkōkyō's 50 Years in America. San Francisco, Kōnkō Churches of America.

562 Konkōkyō (1981). Kōnkō Daijin, A Biography. San Francisco, Kōnkō Churches of America.

563 Konkōkyō (1996). Voice of the Universe: Selected Teachings of Konkōkyō. Tokyo, Konkōkyō.

564 KORNICKI, P. F. and I. J. MULLEN, Eds. (1996). *Religion in Japan: Arrows to Heaven and Earth.* Cambridge, Cambridge University Press.
A collection of essays on different aspects of religion in Japan, ranging from the eighth century to the present day. Includes an article by Helen Hardacre on a 'new, new religion',

Shinmeiaishinkai, as well as aspects of contemporary religious practice such as pilgrimage (Reader) and Mizuko Kuyō (Harrison) and the wrapping of sacred space (Hendry).

565 KOTANI, K. (1958). A Guide to Reiyūkai. Tokyo.

566 KOTANI, K. (1958). Watakushi no shugyō seikatsu sanjū nen (My Thirty Years Practice). Tokyo, Reiyūkai Kyōdan.

567 KOTANI, K. (1958). Watakushi no shugyō seikatsu, sanjūgo nen. (My Religious Life of 35 years). Tokyo, Reiyūkai.

568 KOUAME, N. (1995). 'Tenri: les trois visages d'une ville religieuse.' Etudes Japonaises 8: 57–75.

569 KUDŌ, T. (1961). 'The Faith of Sōka Gakkai.' *Contemporary Religions of Japan* 2(2): 1–12.

570 Kumamoto Nichinichi Shinbun, Ed. (1992). Aum Shinrikyō to mura no ronri. Fukuoka, Ashi Shobō.

571 KUMASAKA, Y. (1966). 'Sōka Gakkai: Group Psycholoic Study of a New Religio-Political Organization.' *American Journal of Psychotherapy* 20(July): 462–70.

572 KURITA, Y. (1982). 'California no Bon Odori: Amerika Shakai to Nikkeijin no Ikikata (Bon Festival in California: Japanese Americans in American Society).' Kikan Minzokugaku 21: 6–17.

573 KUROZUMI, M. (1974). Kurozumikyō kyōsho (The Founder of Kurozumikyō). Okayama, Kurozumikyō Nisshinsha.

574 KUROZUMI, T. (1976). Kurozumikyō kyōsoden (Tales of the Founder of Kurozumikyō). Okayama, Kurozumikyō Nisshinsha.

575 Kurozumikyō (1957). Kurozumikyō. Okayama, Ōmoto.

576 Kurozumikyō (1981). Taiyo Amaneku (The Sun Sheds Its Blessing Universally). Okayama, Kurozumikyō Nissinsha.

577 KYŌCHŌ, K. H. (1953). Kōnkō daijin (The Great God Konko). Okayama, Konkōkyō Honbu Kyōchō.

578 KYŌCHŌ, K. H. (1972). Gaisetsu: Konkōkyō (The Explanation: Konkōkyō). Okayama, Konkōkyō Honbu Kyōchō.

579 LAFLEUR, W. (1992). *Liquid Life: Abortion and Buddhism in Japan.* Princeton, Princeton University Press.
This book treats a topic of widespread concern and has been written in part to explain how Japan has avoided polarizing society over the issue of abortion. The author argues that Japanese Buddhists have devised a religious view that can accept the termination of foetal life even in the face of Buddhism's denunciation of killing.

580 LAM, A. (1992). 'Women and Equal Employment Opportunities in Japan.' Nissan Occasional Paper Series, Oxford No. 16.
A look at how and to what extent the 1987 Equal Employment Opportunities Law has been implemented in Japanese companies.

581 LANCZKOWSKI, G. (1974). Die neuen Religionen. Franfurt, Fischer Taschenbuch Verlag.

582 LANDE, A. and CLARKE, P. B. (1988). Japan (New Religious Movements). The World's Religions. S. Sutherland, L. Houlden, P. B. Clarke and F. Hardy. London, Routledge: 932–44.
A short summary of the features of several Japanese New Religious Movements including Sōka Gakkai, Nichiren Shōshū, Sekai Kyūseikyō, Ōmotokyō, PL Kyōdan, Risshō Kōsei Kai, Konkōkyō, Tenrikyō, Mahikari, Seichō-no-Ie and Reiyūkai.

583 LANTERNARI, V. (1963). *The Religions of the Oppressed: A Study of Modern Messianic Cults.* London, MacGibbon & Kee.

584 LAUER, H. (1975). 'A Study of the Nichiren Shōshū Academy of America.' *CCNY Journal of Anthropology* 1(1): 7–26.

585 LEBRA, W. P. (1966). *Okinawan Religion,* University of Hawai Press.
A systematic, descriptive account of the indigenous religion of Okinawa discussing concepts of the supernatural, religious practices and its relationship to the social structure.

586 LEBRA, T. S. (1967). *An Interpretation of Religious Conversion: A Millenial Movement among Japanese – Americans in Hawaii,* PhD. University of Pittsburgh.

587 LEBRA, T. S. (1969 –70). 'Logic of Salvation: The Case of a Japanese Sect in Hawaii.' *The International Journal of Social Psychiatry* 16(1): 45–53.

588 LEBRA, T. S. (1970). 'Religious Conversion as a Breakthrough for Transculturation: A Japanese Sect in Hawaii.' *Journal for the Scientific Study of Religion* 9(3): 181–96.
Examines the transformation of the sick role in Tenshō Kōtai Jingū Kyō in Hawaii. Lebra argues that in this NRM, the Japanese norm of sickness providing a socially acceptable means of seeking emotional support is reversed with sickness among Tenshō Kōtai Jingū Kyō members attracting condemnation so that the legitimacy of the sick role is denied.

589 LEBRA, T. S. (1974). Taking the Role of the Supernatural 'Other': Spirit Possession in a Japanese Healing Cult. *Culture-Bound Syndromes, Ethnopsychiatry and Alternative Therapies.* W. P. Lebra. Honolulu, University of Hawaii Press.

590 LEBRA, T. S. (1974). 'The Interactional Perspective of Suffering and Curing in a Japanese Cult.' *The International Journal of Social Psychiatry* 20: 281–86.

591 LEBRA, T. S. (1974). Ancestral Influence on the Suffering of Descendants in a Japanese Cult. *Ancestors.* W. H. Newell. Hague, Mouton: 219–30.
Reassess the general anthropological theory on ancestors in the light of her research in Japan. Suggests that Japanese material does not readily fit then-existing models and suggests that this may be in part due to the blurring of boundaries between ancestors and their descendants in the Japanese case.

592 LEBRA, T. S. (1976). *Japanese Patterns of Behaviour.* Honolulu, University of Hawaii Press.

593 LEBRA, T. S. (1977). Religious Conversion and Elimination of the Sick Role: A Japanese Sect in Hawaii. *Culture, Disease and Healing: Studies in Medical Anthropology.* D. Landy. New York, Macmillan: 408–15.

Examines the elimination of the sick role in Tenshō Kōtai Jingu Kyō in Hawaii through the re-evaluation of illness as a sign of dereliction of duty, so that illness becomes a source of shame to the afflicted individual. This is contrasted with the sick role in mainstream Japanese Society, where illness provides a socially sanctioned means for the afflicted person to be cared for and indulged by those around him.

594 LEBRA, T. S. (1984). *Japanese Women: Constraint and Fulfilment*. Honolulu, University of Hawaii Press.
One of the first and most thorough studies of the position of Japanese women in the context of social structure, based on a life-cycle description that combines statistics with personal accounts.

595 LEBRA, T. S. (1986). Self Reconstruction in Japanese Religious Psychotherapy. *Japanese Culture and Behaviour*. T. S. Lebra and W. P. Lebra. Honolulu, University of Hawaii Press.
Lebra examines the reconstruction of self implicit in the healing practices of Gedatsukai, and draws parallels with some of the Japanese psychotherapies such as Naikan and Morita therapy.

596 LEWIS, D. C. (1985). 'Japanese Religion: A Unity Behind Diversity?' *Japanese Religions* 14(4): 47–59.
Based on research and interviews concerned with Japanese 'religious behaviour', Lewis presents principal themes found to permeate 'religious' activities as well as society and culture in general. Lewis discusses how these concerns with community, identity, age and the lifecycle, memory and nostalgia, purity and pollution and safety suggest an interweaving of religious and secular life in Japan.

597 LEWIS, D. (1986). 'Religious Rites in a Japanese Factory.' *Japanese Journal of Religious Studies* 13(4): 261–75.
Outlines the main religious rites practised in one Japanese factory. These include general rites, with parallels in other company and non-company contexts, and rites specific to this factory. Lewis argues that the existence of numerous religious observances in a modern factory undermines the theory that industrialization is always accompanied by secularization. He notes the low degree of general involvement in many of these rites, coupled with a high degree of scepticism about their efficacy and argues that these features cast doubt on the validity of a Durkheimian analysis in the context of Japanese factories.

598 LLOYD, A. (1911). *The Creed of Half Japan*. London, Smith, Elder & Co.
Historical Sketches of Japanese Buddhism

599 LOCK, M. (1980). *East Asian Medicine in Urban Japan*. Berkeley, University of California Press.

600 LOFTIN, M. T. (1951). *Japanese in Brazil: A Study in Immigration and Acculturation*, PhD. Vanderbilt University.

601 Look (1963). A New Face Called Sōka Gakkai Raises Old Problems in Modern Japan. Look: 18.

602 LUERAS, L., Ed. (1987). *Kanyaku Imin: A Hundred Years of Japanese Life in Hawaii*. Honolulu, Hawaii, University of Hawaii Press.

603 MACIOTI, M. I. (1996). Il Buddha che è in noi (The Buddha Within Ourselves). Rome.
Dr Macioti's Study of Sōka Gakkai in Italy

604 MAEDA, T. (1976). Ancestor Worship in Japan: Facts and History. *Ancestors*. W. H. Newell. The Hague, Mouton Publishers: 139–61.

605 MAEYAMA, T. (1967). O Immigrante e Riugião: Estudo de uma Seita Religiosa Japonesa em São Paulo. São Paulo, Escola de Sociologia e Política de São Paulo.

606 MAEYAMA, T. (1967). Brasil no nikkei minority shakai ni okeru shukyō kōdō ni okeru ichikōsatsu (Observaçao sobre o comportamento religioso na cominidade minoritária nikkei do Brasil), Centro de estudos Nipo-Brasileiros.

607 MAEYAMA, T. (1972). 'Ancestor, Emperor and Immigrant: Religion and Group Identification of the Japanese in Rural Brazil (1908–1950).' *Journal of Inter-American Studies and World Affairs* 14(2): 151–182.

608 MAEYAMA, T. (1979). 'Ethnicity, Secret Societies and Associations: The Japanese in Brazil.' *Comparative Studies in Society and History* 21(4): 589–610.

609 MAEYAMA, T. (1982). 'Burajiru no Nikkeijin ni okeru Aidentitii no Hensen: Tokuni sutoratejii tono kanren ni oite.' *Latin American Studies* 4: 181–219.

610 MAEYAMA, T. (1983). 'Religion, Kinship and the Middle Classes of the Japanese in Urban Brazil.' *Latin American Studies* 5: 56–82.

611 MAEYAMA, T. (1983). Japanese Religions in Southern Brazil: Change and Syncretism, The University of Tsukuba.
This article discusses the religious life of the Japanese in southern Brazil by presenting ethnographical case studies of religious organizations. It begins with an outline of Japanese emigration and how this influenced the general absence of traditional Shinto religion in Brazil. This leads to the central discussion of New Religions, first focusing on the activities of six movements: Ōmoto, Tenrikyō, Sēicho-no-Ie, Sekai-Kyūsei-Kyō, P.L Kyōdan and Sōka Gakkai. The next section presents five Nippo-Brazilian new religions, groups originating in Brazil but rooted in Japanese cultural and religious tradition: Shirei-kyō, Fudō Myō, Inari Daimyōjin, Kaminoya Yaoyorozukyō and Nossa Senhora de Kannan.

612 MAEYAMA, T. and R. J. SMITH (1983). Ōmoto: A Japanese 'New Religion' in Brazil, University of Tsukuba.

613 MAEYAMA, T. (1984). 'Brasil nikkeijin ni okeru ethnicity to identity-ninshikiteki, seijiteki genshō toshite (Ethnicidade e identidade entre os nikkeis do Brasil – como fenômenos epistemológico e político).' Minzokugaku kenkyu (Estudos Etnológicos) 4(48): 444–58.

614 MAEYAMA, T. (1986). The division and integration among Brazilian Japanese – The Issue of Ethnicity and Identity. Gendai Asia Imin: Sono kyosei genri o motomete (Contemporary Asian Immigrants: Their Symbiotic Principle). S. Shigematsu. Nagoya, Nagoya University Press.
This book contains contributions on various aspects of immigrants in different countries including an article on Brazilian Japanese.

615 MAEYAMA, T. (1987). 'Contato entre diferentes culturas e mudanças culturas – a luz do caso dos nikkeis do Brasil.' Philosophical Society, University of Shizuoka: 1–27.

616 Mahikari Primary Training Reference Textbook. Takayama Gifu Prefecture: Sūkyō Mahikari H.Q, L.H Yōkōshi no Tomo.
There is also an Intermediate and Advanced Training Reference Textbook.

617 Mahikari (1977). Yokoshi Norogoto Shu. Los Angeles, California, Sekai Mahikari Bunmei Kyōdan of America.

618 Mahikari (1985). Gendai no kokoro: Sūkyō Mahikari (The Spirit of Today: Sūkyō Mahikari). Tokyo, Ohbunsha.

619 Mahikari (1985-). Mahikari. Tokyo, Yoko Shuppan.
Monthly Magazine.

620 Mahikari (1989). Mahikari Mondō. Tokyo, L.H. Yōkōshi Shuppan.

621 MAKIGUCHI, T. (1937). Sōka Kyōikuho no Kagakuteki Chōshūkyōteki Jikken Shōmei (Practical Experimentation in Value-Creating Educational Methods Through Science and Supreme Religion). Tokyo, Sōka Kyōiku Gakkai.

622 MAKIGUCHI, T. (1943). Kachi Sōzō (The Creation of Value). Tokyo, Soka Kyoiku Gakkai.

623 MAKIGUCHI, T. (1953). The Theory of Value. Tokyo, Sōka Gakkai.

624 MAKIGUCHI, T. (1953). Kachiron (A Discussion of Value). Tokyo.

625 MAKIGUCHI, T. (1964). The Philosophy of Value. Tokyo, Seikyō Press.

626 MARRA, M. (1988). 'The Development of Mappō Thought in Japan (I).' *Japanese Journal of Religious Studies* 15(1): 25–54.

627 MARRA, M. (1988). 'The Development of Mappō Thought in Japan (II).' *Japanese Journal of Religious Studies* 15(4): 287–305.

628 MARRACH, L. (1978). Seichō-no-Ie: Um Estudo de sua penetração entre os Brasileiros. Comissão Julgadora. São Paulo, Pontiícia Universidade Católica: 166.

629 MARTINEZ, D. P. (1994). Japanese Religions. *Women in Religion*. J. Holm and J. Bourker. London, Pinter.
Examines women's roles in religion in Japan from the pre-Buddhist era to the present.

630 MASAMUNE, H. (1957). 'Thoughts on the New Religions.' *Japan Quarterly* 4(1): 65–69.

631 MASON, J. W. T. (1939). The Spirit of Shinto Mythology. Tokyo, The Fuzambo Company.
The book is a sympathetic exploration into Shinto mythology including Shinto myths.

632 MASUNAGA, R. The Sōtō Appproach to Zen, Layman Buddhist Press.

633 MATSUDA, M. (1988). Burajiru dendō no hanseiki (An Incomplete Record of Evangelism in Brazil). Tokyo, Nihon Kyōbunsha.

634 MATSUDA, M. (1989). Hikari wa kokkyō o koete (The Light Crosses National Boundaries). Tokyo, Nihon Kyōbunsha.

635 MATSUI, Y. (1994). Violence Against Women in Development, Militarism and Culture. Feminist Theology from the Third World. U. King. London, SPCK/Orbis Press: 124–135.
A shortened version of an article originally published in the 'Asian Journal of Feminist Theology' entitled 'In God's Image', the author links violence and abuse of women to development strategy, military aggression and culture. Fully aware that Japanese women play an ambiguous role in Asia, being seen both as victims and oppressors, she urges for more listening to the voices of oppressed women everywhere.

636 MATSUMOTO, S. (1976). In Quest of the Fundamental. Tenri, Japan, Tenrikyō Overseas Mission Department.

637 MATSUMOTO, S. (1981). Modern Society and Spiritual Maturity. Tenri, Japan, Tenrikyō Overseas Mission Department.

638 MATSUMURA, A. (1975). 'Psychological Approaches of the New Religions.' *Japan Christian Quarterly* **41**(2): 111–3.

639 MATSUNAGA, A. (1969). The Buddhist Philosophy of Assimilation: The Historical Development of the Honji-Suijaku Theory. Tokyo, Sophia University.

640 MATSUNAGA, L. (1999). Spiritual Company, Corporate Religion? Yaohan, Seichō-no-Ie and the developing work ethic in Japanese companies. *Japanese New Religions in Global Perspective.* P. B. Clarke (ed). Richmond, Surrey, Curzon Press.

641 MATSUNAGA, L. (1998). Spirit First, Mind Follows, Body Belongs: Notions of Health, Illness and Disease in Sūkyō Mahikari U.K. *Japanese New Religions in Global Perspective.* P. B. Clarke (ed). Richmond, Surrey, Curzon Press.

642 MATSUNO, J. (1976). Gendai Shakkai to Risshō Kōsei Kai (Contemporary Society and Risshō Kōsei Kai). Gendai Bukkyō (Contemporary Buddhism). H. Nakamura, K. Kasahara and H. Kaneoka. Tokyo, Kōsei Shuppansha. **9**: 209–295.

643 MATSUOKA, H. (1988). 'Waga Kuni ni okeru Ketsu-Bon-Kyo Shinkō nitsuiteno ichi Kosatsu.' Annual Review of Religious Studies of the University of Tokyo **11**: 85–100.
A study of Ketsu-Bon-Kyo Sutra Belief in Japan

644 MATSUOKA, H. (1993). 'Nikkei Shūkyō no Kaishin (Conversion to Japanese New Religion: The Case of Church of World Messianity).' *Journal of Religious Studies* **17**(2): 122–144.

645 MAY, C. L. (1954). 'The Dancing Religion, a Japanese Messianic Sect.' *South-western Journal of Anthropology* **Spring**: 119–137.

646 McCLAIN, C. S. (1995). *Women as Healers.* New Brunswick, New Jersey, Rutgers University Press.

647 McCRIMMON, M. (1964). 'From Christianity to Sōka Gakkai.' *The Japan Missionary Bulletin* **18**(July): 397–402.

648 McFARLAND, N. H. (1958). 'The New Religions of Japan.' *Perkins School of Theology Journal* **12**(1): 3–21.

649 McFARLAND, H. N. (1958). 'The Present Status of the Religions of Japan.' *Journal of Bible and Religion* **26**(3): 222–31.

650 McFARLAND, H. N. (1960). 'Japan's New Religions (a).' *Contemporary Religions of Japan*(June): 35.

651 McFARLAND, H. N. (1960). 'Japan's New Religions (b).' *Contemporary Religions of Japan*(Sept): 30.

652 McFARLAND, H. N. (1960). 'Japan's New Religions (c).' *Contemporary Religions of Japan*(Dec): 24.

653 McFARLAND, H. N. (1967). *The Rush Hour of the Gods: A Study of new Religious Movements in Japan*. New York, Macmillan.
One of the first books to give a general review which encompasses relevant Japanese history as well as socio-religious background. The author, a Professor of the History of Religion examines five new religions, Konkōkyō, PL Kyōdan, Seichō-no-Ie, Risshō Kōsei Kai, and Sōka Gakkai.

654 McGUIRE, M. (1995). *Ritual Healing in Suburban America*. Brunswick, New Jersey, Rutgers University Press.

655 McINTOSH, J. (1990). 'The Religious Pulse of Koreans in Japan.' *Japanese Religions* **16**(1): 1–15.

656 McVEIGH, B. (1991). Gratitude, Obedience and Humility of Heart: The cultural construction of belief in a Japanese New Religion. PhD. Princeton, Princeton University.
The dissertation has three main purposes: to present the ideology of Sūkyō Mahikari as a coherent, though syncretistic whole; to delineate the group's theory of human nature and to discuss the social construction of mind and spirit.

657 McVEIGH, B. (1991). 'Gratitude, Obedience, and Humility of Heart: The Morality of Dependency in a New Religion.' *Journal of Social Science* (International Christian University, Tokyo) **30**(2): 107–125.

658 McVEIGH, B. (1992). 'The Vitalistic Conception of Salvation as expressed in Sūkyo Mahikari.' *Japanese Journal of Religious Studies* **19**(1): 41–68.
This article seeks to apply to Mahikari the argument of Tsushima et al. (1979) that Japanese NRMs do possess a distinctive concept of spiritual salvation. McVeigh proposes a four aspect paradigm for understanding Mahikari and possibly other Japanese NRMs. In this paradigm, the crucial aspects of the movement are subsumed under the headings: Divine Source;Divine Power;Divine Personage; and Divine Practice.

659 McVEIGH, B. (1992). 'The Master Metaphor of Purity: The Symbolism of Authority and Power in Sūkyō Mahikari.' *Japanese Religions* **17**(2): 98–125.
This article examines the notions of purity in Mahikari, and suggests that purity forms a master metaphor running through all Mahikari ideology. It pays particular attention to the rituals designed to maintain purity.

660 McVEIGH, B. (1992). 'The Authorization of Ritual and the Ritualization of Authority: The Practice of Values in a Japanese New Religion.' *Journal of Ritual Studies* **6**(2): 39–58.

661 McVEIGH, B. (1993). 'Building Belief through the Body: The Physical Embodiment of Morality and Doctrine in Sūkyō Mahikari.' *Japanese Religions* 18(2): 140–161.

McVeigh outlines the main ideas on the body held by Sūkyō Mahikari members, reflecting on notions of the body as a physical, moral and spiritual entity and how this manifests itself in the movement's activities and rituals.

662 McVEIGH, B. (1995). 'Learning Morality Through Sentiment and the Senses: The Role of Emotional Experience in Sūkyō Mahikari.' *Japanese Religions* 20(1): 56–76.

Discusses how the religious organization Sūkyō Mahikari strategically uses sentiment and emotion to reinforce belief among their followers. McVeigh outlines fundamental principles and ethnomorality of Mahikari centring on the notion of dependency and then examines how emotional experience is utilised through the ritual practice of exorcism, testimonials and ceremonies.

663 McVEIGH, B. (1996). 'Spirit Possession in Sūkyō Mahikari: A Variety of Sociopsychological Experience.' *Japanese Religions* 21(2): 283–297.

An attempt to describe and explain spirit possession in Sūkyō Mahikari in socio-psychological terms.

664 MELTON, J. G. (1987). The Encyclopedia of American Religions. Detroit, Michigan, Gale Research Company.

665 MELTON, J. G. (1993). *Encyclopedia of American Religions*. Detroit, Gale Research Company.

666 MELTON, J. G. and JONES, C. A. (1994). New Japanese Religions in the United States. *Japanese New Religions in the West*. P. B. Clarke and J. Somers. Folkestone, Kent, Japan Library: 33–53.

A discussion about the appearance of Japanese New Religions in the USA.

667 MÉTRAUX, D. A. (1978). The Religious and Social Philosophy of Sōka Gakkai, PhD. Columbia University.

668 MÉTRAUX, D. (1979). 'The Sōka Gakkai's Philosophy of Life.' Proceedings of First International Symposium on Asian Studies.

669 MÉTRAUX, D. (1980). 'Why Did Ikeda Quit?' *Japanese Journal of Religious Studies* 7(1).

An attempt to explain the reason for Ikeda's abrupt resignation from his post as the president of Sōka Gakkai in 1970 and subsequent move to Sōka Gakkai International, the overseas development branch of the movement. This explanation reveals tensions between the priesthood and the lay organisation. The 1991 split between the two may show that Métraux's interpretation is correct.

670 MÉTRAUX, D. (1986). 'The Sōka Gakkai's Search for the Realization of the World of Rissho Ankokuron.' *Japanese Journal of Religious Studies* 13(1): 31–61.

Métraux discusses Sōka Gakkai's claim to be Nichirens' successor and focuses on the movements' emphasis of its peace movement which is based on Nichiren's treatise Risshō Ankokuron. ('Establishment of Righteousness and Security in the Country')

671 MÉTRAUX, D. (1988). *The History and Theology of Sōka Gakkai*. New York, Edwin Mellen Press.

A more up-to-date account of Sōka Gakkai both at home and abroad. Critical but by no means hostile. Includes a chapter on the success of Nichiren Shōshū in America.

672 MÉTRAUX, D. (1992). 'The Dispute Between the Sōka Gakkai and the Nichiren Shōshū Priesthood: A Lay Revolution Against a Conservative Clergy.' *Japanese Journal of Religious Studies* 19(4): 325–36.
Outlines the confrontation between Sōka Gakkai and the Nichiren Shōshū sect, describing the claims on both sides and the steps taken during the dispute. Métraux reflects on the ability of a new religious movement to prosper without an organised clergy.

673 MÉTRAUX, D. A. (1994). *The Sōka Gakkai Revolution.* Lanham, New York, London, University Press of America.
Métraux examines the activities of the Sōka Gakkai movement, including its history, relationship with politics, its concern with education, its conflict with the Nichiren Shōshū sect and its internationalisation. His theme is 'revolution' based on the movement's own use of the word to describe the human experience that members of Sōka Gakkai attain.

674 MICKLER, M. L. (1991). The Anti-Cult Movement in Japan. New Religious Movements in Global Perspective, Buelton, California.

675 MILLER, R. J. (1974). Ancestors and Nobility in Ancient Japan. *Ancestors.* W. H. Newell. The Hague, Paris, Mouton Publishers: 163–176.

676 MILLER, R. A. (1982). *Japan's Modern Myth.* New York and Tokyo, Weatherhill.

677 MILLER, A. (1992). 'Predicting Nonconventional Religious Affiliation in Tokyo: A Control Theory Application.' *Social Forces* 71: 397–410.

678 MILLER, A. S. (1995). 'A Rational Choice Model for Religious Behaviour in Japan.' *Journal for the Scientific Study of Religion* 34(2): 234–244.
This article adopts a modified rational choice model to explain religious behaviour in Japan, arguing that the Japanese participate in religious rituals and acts with the expectation of them serving specific practical purposes. Illness, death, 'superstition', old age and stages in the course of life precipitate involvement in religious ritual and membership in a new religion relates to a desire for social support. The article utilises data on religious belief from the Institute of Statistical Mathematics in Tokyo.

679 Ministry of Education. Shūkyō Nenkan (The Year Book of Religion).
This volume is published every year by the Ministry of Education.

680 MIURA, Y. (1963). Neue Religionen in Japan. Bad Salzuflen, MBK-Verlag.

681 MIYAKE, H. and e. al (1972). 'Genze riyaku kankei bunken mokuroku (Bibliography of this-worldly benefits).' Nihon Bukkyō (Japanese Buddhism) (34 (February)): 46–47.

682 MIYAKE, H. (1987). The Influence of Shugendō on the 'New Religions'. *Japanese Buddhism: Its Tradition, New Religions and Interaction with Christianity.* M. K. e. al. Tokyo-Los Angeles, Buddhist Books International: 71–82.

683 MIYANAGA, K. (1983). Social Reproduction and Transcendence: An Analysis of the Sekai Mahikari Bunmei Kyōdan, a Heterodox Religious Movement in Contemporary Japan. PhD. University of British Columbia.

684 MIYATA, N. (1963). '"Ikigami" shinkō no hatsugen (The Origins of Belief in "Living Gods").' Nihon minzokugaku kaihō **28**: 1–11.

685 MIYATA, N. (1968). '"Yonaoshi" to miroku shinkō:nihon ni okeru "yonaoshi" no minzokuteki imi' (World Renewal and Faith in Maitreya: The Folkloric Meaning of World Renewal in Japan).' Minzokugaku kenkyū 33(1): 32–44.

686 MIYATA, N. (1975). Miroku Shinkō no Kenkyū (A Study on Miroku (Maitreya) Belief). Tokyo, Miraisha.

687 MIYATA, N. (1979). 'Nihonjin no shūkyō seikatsu to gense riyaku (Religious Life of the Japanese and This-Worldly Benefits).' Nihon Bukkyō (Japanese Buddhism)(34): 43–57.

688 MIYATA, N. (1983). Various Types of Maitreya Belief in Japan – Unpublished manuscript.

689 MIYAZAKI, F. (1990). 'The Formation of Emperor Worship in the New Religions: The Case of Fujidō.' Japanese Journal of Religious Studies 17(2–3): 281.

690 MIZOGUCHI, A. (1978). Sōka Gakkai. Shinshūkyō no Sekai (The World of the New Religions). Nawata Sanae et al. Tokyo, Daizō Shuppan. II: 164–240.

691 MOGAMI, T. (1963). The Double Grave-System. *Studies in Japanese Folklore.* R. M. Dorson. Bloomington, Indiana, Indiana University Press.

692 MONTERO, D. (1980). *Japanese Americans: Changing Patterns of Ethnic Affiliation over Three Generations,* Westview Press.

693 MONTGOMERY, D. (1991). *Fire in the Lotus: The Dynamic Buddhism of Nichiren.* London, Mandala.
Contains a brief general history of Buddhism and its introduction to Japan, followed by a description of the development of Nichiren Buddhism in Japan. The founding of Sōka Gakkai is then described, and its subsequent expansion in Japan and later in the United States is outlined. A brief account of Reiyūkai, Risshō Kōsei Kai, and other smaller Nichiren groups abroad is also given. Appendix One contains Nichiren Buddhist prayers and sutras.

694 MOOS, F. (1963). 'Religion and Politics in Japan: The Case of Sōka Gakkai.' Asian Survey 3(3).

695 MORGAN, R. D. (1994). Sōtō Zen Buddhism in Britain. *Japanese New Religions in the West.* P. B. Clarke and J. Somers. Folkestone, Kent, Japan Library: 132–148.
This paper discusses how Sōtō Zen has become established in Britain and how it has acclimatized to a different culture during the past twenty years.

696 MORI, K. (1977). Study of Makiguchi Tsunesaburō: The Founder of Sōka Gakkai. Theology Department, Graduate Theological Union: 242.

697 MORI, Y. (1979). Perfect Liberty Kyōdan. Shinshūkyō no Sekai (The World of the New Religions). M. Shimizu. Tokyo, Daizo Shuppan. V: 83–124.

698 MORI, K. (1985). Brasil ni okeru Tenry-kyō no tenkai to soshikika no tokushitsu (Desenvolvimento da Tenry-kyō no Brasil e a peculiaridade

do seu processo de organizaçao). São Paulo, Centro de Estudos Nipo-Brasileiros.

699 MORI, S. (1995). 'Historical Trends in Religious Studies: Methodological Change in the Studies of Tenrikyō Religion by Christian Missionaries and Western Scholars of Religion.' Tenri Journal of Religion 23(March): 67–104.

700 MORIKAWA, M. (1982). Honkyō josei fukyōsha ni tsuite no ichishiron, toku ni shodai josei kyōkaicho ni tsuite. (A Comment on Missionaries of Our Religion Particularly about the First Female Founder.). Konkōkyō-gaku, Konkōkyō. 22: 76–95.

701 MORIOKA, K. and M. SHIMPO (1957). The Impact of the Physical Movement of Population on Japanese Religions after World War II. *Religion in Changing Japanese Society.* K. Morioka. Tokyo, University of Tokyo Press.

702 MORIOKA, K. (1967). 'Les Religions Contemporaines du Japon: Coexistence et Conflit.' *Revue françcaise de sociologie* 8 (July–September): 348–54.

703 MORIOKA, K. and W. H. NEWELL, Eds. (1968). *The Sociology of Japanese Religion.* International Studies in Sociology and Social Anthropology. Leiden, E. J. Brill.
A translation into English of a collection of articles by Japanese scholars on the sociology of religion. This includes two articles on Japanese New Religious Movements.

704 MORIOKA, K. (1968). Religious Behaviour and the Actor's Position in the Household. *The Sociology of Japanese Religion.* K. Morioka and W. H. Newell. Leiden, E. J. Brill: 143.

705 MORIOKA, K. (1969). Contemporary Changes in Japanese Religion. *Sociology and Religion.* N. Birnbaum and G. Lenzer. Englewood Cliffs, NJ., Prentice-Hall: 382–86.

706 MORIOKA, K. (1973). Gendai shakai no minshū to shūkyō (The People and Religion in a Modern Society). Nihonjin no kōdō to shisō (The Behaviour and Thought of the Japanese). Tokyo, Hyōronsha. 49.

707 MORIOKA, K. (1975). The Changing Family and Buddhism in Postwar Japan. *Religion in Changing Japanese Society.* Tokyo, Tokyo University Press: 99–113.

708 MORIOKA, K. (1975). Gendai Shakai no Minshū to Shūkyō (The Masses and Religion in Contemporary Society). Tokyo, Hyoronsha.

709 MORIOKA, K. (1975). Religion in Changing Japanese Society. Tokyo, University of Tokyo Press.

710 MORIOKA, K. (1976). Nihon no kindaishakai to kirisutokyō (Contemporary Japan and Christianity). Tokyo, Hyōronsha.

711 MORIOKA, K. (1977). 'The Appearance of 'Ancestor Religion' in Modern Japan: The Years of Transition from the Meiji to the Taisho Periods.' *Japanese Journal of Religious Studies* 4(2–3): 183–212.

712 MORIOKA, K. (1978). Hendōki no Ningen to Shūkyō (Man and Religion in Times of Social Change). Hendōki no Ningen to Shūkyō (Man and Religion in Times of Social Change). K. Morioka. Tokyo, Miraisha.
Features a general chapter on social change and religion by the editor followed by four specific studies of New Religions and several other studies on change and religion.

713 MORIOKA, K. (1979). 'The Institutionalization of a New Religious Movement.' Japanese Journal of Religious Studies 6(1–2): 239–280.

714 MORIOKA, K. and NISHIYAMA, S. (1980). 'Acceptance of a New Religion and Subsequent Changes in Religious Consciousness.' *Japanese Journal of Religious Studies* 7(4): 292–317.

715 MORIOKA, K. (1984). Ancestor Worship in contemporary Japan: Continuity and Change. *Religion and Family in East Asia.* G. A. DeVos and T. Sofue. Los Angeles, California, University of California Press.

716 MORIOKA, K. (1989). Shinshūkyō no kōgeki, ōsen to kiketsu – Risshō Kōseikai no 'Yomiuri jiken' (The Offence, Accepting Challenge and Conclusion Towards New Religions – Risshō Kōseikai's 'Yomiuri' Newspaper Case). Shinshūkyō undō no tenkai katei. K. Morioka. Tokyo, Sōbunsha.

717 MORIOKA, K. (1994). 'Attacks on New Religions: Risshō Kōseikai and the "Yomiuri Affair".' *Japanese Journal of Religious Studies* 21(2–3): 281–310.
Risshō Kōseikai, one of Japan's most successful New Religions faced a crisis in the mid–1950s when the 'Yomiuri Shinbun' published a series of articles criticising its activities. This essay examines the circumstances of the affair, analyses the response by Risshō Kōseikai and investigates how the incident affected the society's development.

718 MOROI, M. (1954). Moroi Masaichi Shū (A Collection of Moroi Masaichi's Writings). Tenri, Dōyūsha.

719 MOROI, M. (1954). Shinjitsu no Michi (The True Road). Tenri, Dōyūsha.

720 MOROI, Y. (1964). 'Tenri-kyō: Some Misconceptions Corrected.' *Contemporary Religions of Japan* 4(4): 304–324.

721 MOROI, Y. (1972). Contemporary Thought and Tenrikyō, Tenri: Tenrikyō Overseas Mission Department.

722 MORRIS, I. (1960). Nationalism and the Right Wing in Japan. New York.

723 MOUER, R. (1986). *Images of Japanese Society.* London and New York, Routledge and Kegan Paul International.
A clear, level-headed study of the stereotypical 'holistic' image of Japanese society, popular with both foreign observers and the Japanese themselves. The authors propose a new multidimensional stratification model which could lead to an entirely different approach in the social scientific research on Japan, while avoiding the extremism of Nihonjinron-bashing.

724 MULHOLLAND, J. F. (1970). Hawaii's Religions. Rutland Vermont, and Tokyo, Charles E. Tuttle Company.

725 MULLINS, G. A. (1969). 'Conversion: Risshō Kōsei-Kai and Christian.' *Japan Christian Quarterly* 35(2).

726 MULLINS, M. (1988). 'The Organizational Dilemmas of Ethnic Churches: A Case Study of Japanese Buddhism in Canada.' *Sociological Analysis* 49(3).

727 MULLINS, M. (1989). 'The Situation of Christianity in Contemporary Japanese Society.' *The Japan Christian Quarterly* 55(2).

728 MULLINS, M. R. (1989). 'Religious Minorities in Canada: A Sociological Study of the Japanese Experience.' *Canadian Studies* 4.

729 MULLINS, M. (1990). 'The Transplantation of Religion in Comparative Sociological Perspective.' *Japanese Religions* 16(2): 43–62.

730 MULLINS, M. R. (1990). 'Japanese Pentecostalism and the world of the dead: A study of cultural adaptation in Iesu no Mitama Kyōkai.' *Japanese Journal of Religious Studies* 17(4): 353–74.
This article discusses the process of transplantation of religion from one culture to another from a sociological perspective and examines social factors such as ideology, environment and organization. Mullins presents two case studies, Japanese Buddhism in Canada and Christianity in Japan and traces the historical process of transplantation in both.

731 MULLINS, M. R. and YOUNG, R. F., Eds. (1991). Japanese New Religions Abroad. Special Issue of Japanese Journal of Religious Studies. Tokyo, Nanzan Institute of Religion and Culture.

732 MULLINS, M. R. (1992). Japan's New Age and Neo-New Religions: Sociological Interpretations. *Perspectives on the New Age*. J. R. Lewis and J. G. Melton. Albany, New York, State University of New York Press: 232–46.
Gives a brief historical account of the emergence of NRMs in Japan from the Meiji restoration onwards, divided into four periods of growth. The main focus is on the last of these periods, beginning in the late 1970s when the influence of the New Age Movement began to appear in Japan. The neo-New religion Kōfuku-no-Kagaku is cited in this context as an example of a Japanese New Age Movement. In addition to tracing New Age influences on the Japanese neo-New Religions, this article strongly emphasises the importance of indigenous folk beliefs in these movements, in particular shamanism and magical practices.

733 MULLINS, M. R., SHIMAZONO S., SWANSON, PAUL. L, Ed. (1993). Religion and Society in Modern Japan. *Nanzan Studies in Asian Religions*. Berkeley, California, Asian Humanities Press.
This book is an anthology which seeks to provide readers with a selection of interpretations and perspectives on the significance of religion in modern Japan. The emphasis is on the sociocultural expressions of Japanese religions rather than on religious texts and traditions. Most of the studies are based on extensive field research and participant observation.

734 MUN, S. (1971). 'Fundamental doctrines of the New Religions in Korea.' Korea Journal 11(12): 1–21.

735 MURAKAMI, S. (1958). Kindai minshū shūkyō-shi no kenkyū (A Study of the History of Modern Folk Religions). Tokyo, Hōzōkan.

736 MURAKAMI, S. (1967). Kindai Nihon no Shūkyōsha (Religious Leaders of Recent Japan). Tokyo, Asoka Shuppansha.
A general study of twenty-seven religious leaders most of them founders of New Religions.

737 MURAKAMI, S. (1970). 'Les religions nouvelles au Japon.' Social Compass 17(1): 137–51.

738 MURAKAMI, S. (1972). New Religions of Japan. The Symposium on Family and Religion in East Asian Countries. C. Nakane and A. Goto. Tokyo, Centre for East Asian Cultural Studies: 17–27.

739 MURAKAMI, S. (1972). Kōnkō daijin no shōgai (The Life of Kōnkō Daijin). Tokyo, Iwanami shoten.

740 MURAKAMI, S. (1973). 'Minshū shūkyō no shisō (The Thoughts of Folk Religions).' Nihon shisō taikei 67.

741 MURAKAMI, S. (1978). Nihon shūkyō jiten (Encyclopedia of Religions in Japan). Tokyo, Kōdansha.

742 MURAKAMI, S. (1979). Ōmoto Shinyu: Ten no Maki (Ōmoto Divine Oracles: The Book of Heaven). Tokyo, Heibonsha.

743 MURAKAMI, S. (1979). Ōmoto Shinyu: Hi no Maki (Ōmoto Divine Oracles: The Book of Fire). Tokyo, Heibonsha.

744 MURAKAMI, S. (1980). *Japanese Religion in the Modern Period*. Tokyo, University of Tokyo Press.

745 MURAKAMI, S. (1980). Shinshūkyō: Sono Kōdōo to Shisō (The New Religions: Their Thought and Actions). Tokyo, Hyōronsha.

746 MURATA, K. (1959). Sōka Gakkai, Communist Envy. *Japan Times*. Tokyo.

747 MURATA, K. (1969). *Japan's New Buddhism – An Objective Account of Sōka Gakkai*. New York and Tokyo, Walker/Weatherhill.
An introductory book presenting basic teachings, history and organizational framework of the movement as well as an outline of its educational and social welfare activities. Deliberate contrast to the generally negative view of Sōka Gakkai at the time.

748 MURATA, K. (1971). *Japan's New Buddhism*. New York, John Weatherhill Inc.
An account of Sōka Gakkai by a Japanese journalist.

749 MURŌ, T. (1987). Agonshū Sekai heiwa e no michi (Agonshū: The Road to World Peace). Tokyo, Seiunsha.

750 MURŌ, T. (1987). Wakamono wa naze shin shinshūkyō ni hashiru no ka (Why are young people attracted to 'New, New Religions'?). Tokyo, Tokino Keizaisha.

751 NADOLSKI, T. (1973). Ōmoto and the Japanese Imperial Government. Nihon bunka kenkyū (Studies in Japanese Culture). 2: 26–32.

752 NADOLSKI, T. P. (1975). The Socio-Political Background of the 1921 and 1935 Ōmoto Suppressions in Japan, PhD. University of Pennsylvania.

753 NAGAI, M. (1992). 'Shinnyoen ni okeru reinō sōshō.' *Tokyo Daigaku shūkyōgaku nenpō* 9: 101–15.

754 NAGAI, M. (1993). 'Shin-shūkyō ni okeru shūyōsei to jujutsusei: Shinnyoen o jirei to shite.' Nenpō shakaigaku ronshū 6(167–78).

755 NAGAI, M. (1995). 'Magic and Self-Cultivation in a New Religion: The Case of Shinnyoen.' *Japanese Journal of Religious Studies* 22(3–4).
Analyses the role of magical practices and their relationship to self-cultivation in the teachings of Shinnyoen through an examination of reports of the transmission of spiritual power and through narratives of followers.

756 NAGATANI, C. (1995). Shinnyoen no sesshin shugyō to shinja no sekaikan henyō ni tsuite. Kyūshū Daigaku Bungakubu Hikaku Shūkyō-gaku Kenkyūshitsu. N. Sakai and S. Takezawa, Fukuoka.

757 NAKABA, T. (1968). Nihon no chōryū: Sōka Gakkai hatten no ayumi (A Japanese Trend: The History of Sōka Gakkai's Development).

758 NAKABA, T. (1972). Amerika no Nichiren Shōshū (Nichiren Shōshū in America). Tokyo, Senzeki Press.

759 NAKAHARA, Z. (1950). 'Ōmoto no kenkyū (A Study of Ōmoto).' Minzokugaku Kenkyū 15.

760 NAKAJIMA, H. (1956). 'The Conception of Death in Tenrikyō.' *Tenri Journal of Religion* 2.

761 NAKAJIMA, H. (1957). 'The Fundamentality of Tenrikyō's View of the Salvation.' *Tenri Journal of Religion* 3.

762 NAKAJIMA, H. (1961). 'The Basic Structure of the Idea of Salvation in Tenrikyō.' *Tenri Journal of Religion* 7.

763 NAKAJIMA, H. (1962). 'A Basic Structure of Revelation in Tenrikyō Doctrine.' *Tenri Journal of Religion* 8.

764 NAKAJIMA, H. (1964). 'The Divine model of the Foundress of Tenrikyō.' *Tenri Journal of Religion* 10.

765 NAKAJIMA, M. (1993). Economic Development in East Asia and Confucian Ethics. SISR XXII International Conference on Religion, Culture and Identity, Budapest.

766 NAKAMAKI, H. (1977). 'Hawai Nikkei shūkyō ni okeru Nihon shikō to Amerika shikō (Japan-orientated and American-orientated religions of the Japanese Americans in Hawaii).' Shūkyō Kenkyū 234: 20–22.

767 NAKAMAKI, H. (1980). 'Hawaii ni okeru Nikkei Reinōsha to Minkan-shinkō: Oahu Tō no Josei Reinōsha no Jirei (Japanese Religious Mediums and Folk Belief among Japanese Americans in Hawaii: Female mediums on Oahu Island).' Kokuritsu Minzokugaku Hakubutsukan Kenkyū Hōkoku 5(2): 317–375.

768 NAKAMAKI, H. (1982). 'Ajia no Shūkyō to Amerika Shakai (3) (Asian Religion and American Society (3)): Appeasing the Dead.' Loop 91: 10–14.

769 NAKAMAKI, H. (1982). 'Nikkei Kirisuto Kyōto no Shūkyō ishiki to Minzoku Ishiki (Religious Consciousness and Racial Consciousness among Christians of Japanese Ancestry).' Shūkyō Kenkyū 55(3): 265–266.

770 NAKAMAKI, H. (1983). 'Nikkei Kirisuto Kyōkai no Tenkai to Nikkei Kirisuto Kyōto no Ishiki: California Shū Sacramento no Jirei (The History

of Japanese Christian Churches and the Consciousness of Japanese Christians in Sacramento, California, USA).' Kokuritsu Minzokugaku Hakubutsukan Kenkyū Hōkoku 8(1).

771 NAKAMAKI, H. (1984). 'The Structure and Transformation of Religion in Modern Japan: In Search of a Civilization Studies Perspective.' *Senri Ethnological Studies* 16: 87–97.

772 NAKAMAKI, H. (1986). Shin-sekai no Nihon shūkyō – Nihon no kamigami to ibunmei (Japanese religions in the new world – The gods of Japan and different civilizations). Tokyo, Heibonsha.

773 NAKAMAKI, H. (1989). Nihon Shūkyō to Nikkei Shūkyō no Kenkyū – Nihon, America, Brasil (Studies on Japanese Religion and Religions of Japanese origin in Japan, America and Brazil). Tokyo, Tōsui Shobō Co. Ltd.

774 NAKAMAKI, H. (1991). 'The Indigenization and Multinationalization of Japanese Religion-Perfect Liberty Kyōdan in Brazil.' *Japanese Journal of Religious Studies* 18(2–3): 213–242.
Describes the history of PL Kyōdan in Brazil and analyses the way in which it has transformed itself into a multinational organization. Nakamaki seeks to show parallels between multinational religions and multinational enterprises and also argues for a link between the overseas expansion of Japanese enterprises and that of Japanese religions.

775 NAKAMAKI, H. (1992). Mukashi daimyō, ima kaisha – Kigyō to shūkyō (In the Olden Days Feudal Lords-Nowadays Companies: Business Enterprises and Religion). Kyoto, Tankōsha.

776 NAKAMAKI, H. (1992). Tōsuisuru bunka (The Culture that Intoxicates Central and South American Religion and Society). Tokyo, Heibonsha.

777 NAKAMAKI, H. (1994). 'The Japanese and Religion – a Consumer's Perspective.' *Kansai Forum*: 26–29.

778 NAKAMURA, T. (1920). Ōmotokyō no Kaibō. Tokyo, Nihon Seishin Igakkai.

779 NAKAMURA, T. (1932). 'Kokusai-shūkyō ōmoto-kyō (Ōmoto, the International Religion).' Kami no kuni(December): 44–49.

780 NAKAMURA, K., Ed. (1950). Shinkō Shūkyō (New Religions). Tokyo, Jeep Sha.

781 NAKAMURA, K. (1951). A Talk on the Tenrikyō Scriptures. Tenri, Dōyūsha.

782 NAKAMURA, K. (1953). Kyososama no Hinagata (A Model of the Founder). Tenri, Dōyūsha.

783 NAKAMURA, H. (1958). Present Situation and Future of Japanese Buddhism. Religions in Japan, at Present. Institute for Research in Religious Problems. Tokyo, Soshun: 11–15.
Brief note on the declining influence of Buddhism as seen in the late 1950s and predictions of the future as seen then.

784 NAKAMURA, K. (1980). No Women's Liberation: The Heritage of a Woman Prophet. Unspoken Worlds. *Women's religious lives in non-Western cultures.* N. A. Falk and R. M. Gross. San Francisco, Harper and Row.

785 NAKAMURA, K. (1981). 'Revelatory Experience in the Female Life Cycle: A Biographical Study of Women Religionists in Modern Japan.' *Japanese Journal of Religious Studies* 8(3–4): 187–205.

786 NAKAMURA, K. (1983). 'Women and Religion in Japan: Introductory Remarks.' *Japanese Journal of Religious Studies* 10(2–3): 115–121.
Introductory remarks to a volume of Japanese Journal of Religious Studies discussing women and religion in Japan. Nakamura outlines the status of women's studies in Japan and then comments on the essays in the volume.

787 NAKAMURA, I. and TADA, T., Eds. (1984). Jōrei: Divine light of Salvation: Okada Mokichi. Kyoto, Japan, Society of Jōrei.

788 NAKAMURA, K. (1997). 'The Religious Consciousness and Activites of Contemporary Japanese Women.' *Japanese Journal of Religious Studies* 24(1–2): 87–120.

789 NAKANE, C. (1970). *Japanese Society*. Berkeley, University of California Press.
A classic study of Japanese society which sets out to demonstrate that vertical relationships between senior and junior provide the basic organizational principle of Japanese society. The most basic social unit in Japanese society according to Nakane, is the household, or **ie,** *and it is the hierarchical relationships between members of the* **ie** *which provide the model for relationships within all other forms of organization in Japan.*

790 NAKANE, C. (1972). An Interpretation of the Size and Structure of the Household in Japan over Three Centuries. *Household and Family in Past Time*. P. Laslett. Cambridge, Cambridge University Press.

791 NAKANO, T. (1981). 'Amerika shakai to NSA – Hawai no baai (NSA in American Society – The Case of Hawaii).' Kōza Kyōgaku kenkyū 2.

792 NAKANO, T. (1990). 'New Religions and Politics on Post-War Japan.' *Sociologica* 14(12).

793 NAKANO, T. (1992). 'Ecumenism and Peace in Post-War Japan.' *Religion Today* 7(1): 7–9.

794 NAKANO, T. (1992). 'Sōka Gakkai and its Peace Movements: The Making of the Counter Communism?' *Religion Today* 7(2): 5–8.

795 NAKANO, T., F. IKADO, et al. (1992). 'Discussion: The traditional and the contemporary in religion.' *The Journal of Oriental Studies* 4: 1–22.

796 NAKANO, T. (1996). Religion and State. *Religion in Japanese Culture*. Tamaru, N. and D. Reid. Tokyo, Kōdansha: 115–136.

797 NAKAO, N., Ed. (1954). Shinkō Shūkyō no Kaibo (The Anatomy of New Religions). Tokyo, Tōsei Shuppansha.

798 NAKAYAMA, K. (1932). Kyōha Shintō no hassei katei (The Processes of Development of Sect Shinto). Tokyo, Moriyama shoten.

799 NAKAYAMA, S. (1954). The Doctrine of Tenrikyō. Tokyo, Tenrikyō.
The standard guide to the Tenrikyō faith

800 NAKAYAMA, S. (1954). On the idea of God in the Tenrikyō Doctrine, Tenri.

801 NAKAYAMA, S. (1957). On the Doctrine of Tenrikyō, Tenri.

802 NAKAYAMA, S. (1957). 'The Various Forms of Verbal Evolution in Tenrikyō Doctrine.' *Tenri Journal of Religion* **3**.

803 NAKAYAMA, S. (1957). 'Women's Position Viewed by Tenrikyō.' *Tenri Journal of Religion* **3**.

804 NAKAYAMA, S. (1958). The Missionary Spirit of the Foundress of Tenrikyō, Tenri.

805 NAKAYAMA, S. (1958). 'The Doctrine and Practice of Tenrikyō (Part 1).' *Tenri Journal of Religion* **4**.

806 NAKAYAMA, S. (1959). 'The Doctrine and Practice of Tenrikyō (Part 2).' *Tenri Journal of Religion* **5**.

807 NAKAYAMA, S. (1960). 'The Doctrine and Practice of Tenrikyō (Part 3).' *Tenri Journal of Religion* **6**.

808 NAKAYAMA, S. (1961). 'The Anniversary of the Tenrikyō Foundress.' *Tenri Journal of Religion* **7**.

809 NAKAYAMA, S. (1962). 'The Doctrine and Practice of Tenrikyō (Part 4).' *Tenri Journal of Religion* **8**.

810 NAKAYAMA, R. Y. (1979). Mind and Body. Tenri, Japan, Tenrikyō Overseas Mission Department.

811 NAKAZANO, M. (1976). Kotodama. Santa Fe, New Mexico, Third Civilization.

812 NAKAZANO, M. (1979). My Past Way of Budo. Santa Fe, New Mexico, Third Civilization.

813 NAKAZONO, M. (1972). Messiah's Return: The Hidden Kototama Principle. Santa Fe, New Mexico, Third Civilization.

814 NAWATA, S. (1978). Reiyūkai. Shinshūkyō no Sekai (The World of the New Religions). Tokyo, Daizo Shuppan. II: 5–81.

815 NAWATA, S. (1979). Reiyūkai. Shinshūkyō no sekai (The World of New Religions). Tokyo, Daizōkan. 2: 6–81.
This volume contains information concerning Reiyūkai, Risshō Kōsei Kai and Sōka Gakkai.

816 NAYLOR, C. (1991). 'Nichiren, Imperialism and the Peace Movement.' *Japanese Journal of Religious Studies* **18**(1): 51–78.

817 NEBREDA, A. M. (1960). 'L'étudiant japonais en face du problème religieux: Ombres et lumières.' Études **307**(December): 361–70.

818 NEBREDA, A. M. (1963). 'New Religions of Japan.' Hibbert Journal 62(244): 10–15.

819 NEFSKY, M. F. (1984). Women and the Religious Character of Contemporary Japan, PhD. University of Toronto.

820 NEFSKY, M. F. (1991). *Stone Houses and Iron Bridges: Tradition and the place of women in contemporary Japan.* New York, Peter Lang.

83

An objective look at the role of Japanese women in religion within the economic and social context of the so-called Fifteen Year War (1930–1945) and after the defeat.

821 NEFSKY, M. F. (1995). Liberator or Pacifier: Religion and Women in Japan. *Religion and Gender.* U. King. Oxford, Blackwell.
This is a critique of Western feminist approaches to the role of women in Japanese religions.

822 NEHRING, A. (1992). Risshō Kōsei Kai. Eine neubuddhistische religion in Japan. Erlangen, Verlag der Ev.-Luth Mission.

823 NEWELL, W. H. and DOBASHI, F. (1968). Some Problems of Classification in Religious Sociology as shown in the History of Tenri Kyōkai. *The Sociology of Japanese Religion.* Morioka, K. and W. N. Newell. Leiden, E.J. Brill: 94–100.
This article gives a history of Tenrikyō and analyses its organization and the way in which it has changed, especially in the post-war era.

824 NEWELL, W. H., Ed. (1974). *Ancestors.* The Hague, Mouton.

825 NEWNAN, E. S. (1956). Female Leadership Roles in Japan's New Religions: Their relation to Shamanism and Max Weber's Charisma Theory, University of Michigan.

826 NGOKWEY, N. (1989). 'On the Specificity of Healing Functions: A study of Diagnosis in Three Faith Healing Institutions in Feira (Bahia, Brazil).' Social Science and Medicine 29(4): 515–526.

827 NHK Seron Chōsabu (1984). Nihonjin no shūkyō ishiki (The Religious Consciousness of the Japanese). Tokyo, Nihon Hōsō Shuppan Kyōkai.

828 Nichiren Shōshū International Center, Ed. (1979). The Major Writings of Nichiren Daishonin. Tokyo, Nichiren Shōshū International Center.
Three volume set of books containing English translations of the doctrinal writings and letters of Nichiren Daishonin (1222–1282).

829 Nichiren Shōshū International Center (1987). Buddhism and the Nichiren Shōshū Tradition. Tokyo, Nichiren Shōshū International Center.

830 NICHOLSON, S. O. (1956). New Religious Movements in Japan, University of Michigan.

831 NIELSEN, N. C. J. (1957). 'Japan's New Religions.' Christian Century 74: 1196–98.

832 Nihon Bukkyō Kenkyūkai, Ed. (1970). Nihon shūkyō no gense riyaku (This-worldly Benefits of Religion in Japan). Tokyo, Daizō Shuppan.

833 Nihon Shisō Taikei (Japanese Thoughts) (1971). 'Minshū shūkyō no shisō (The Thought of Mass Religions).' Nihon Shisō Taikei 67.

834 Nipponzan Myōhōji (Nichirenshu Sect) (1995). (Monthly Magazine).
Monthly Magazine of Nipponzan Myōhōji. A monastic order of the Nichirenshu Sect.

835 NISHIJIMA, T. (1988). Shinshūkyō no kamigami (Gods of New Religions). Tokyo, Kōdansha.

836 NISHIMURA, S. (1956). Manual of Konkōkyō, Kōnkō Hombu Kyocho.

837 NISHIO, H. K. (1967). 'Comparative Analysis of the Risshō Kōseikai and the Sōka Gakkai.' Asian Survey 7(11): 776–790.
This article traces the historical development of the Risshō Kōsei Kai and the Sōka Gakkai religious movements, comparing and contrasting their membership, composition, their doctrinal orientations, recruitment methods, organizational structure, political activity and their general historical rivalry.

838 NISHITANI, K. (1960). 'The Religious Situation in Present-Day Japan.' Contemporary Religions in Japan 1(1 (March)): 7–24.

839 NISHIYAMA, S. (1978). Shinshūkyō no Juyō ni yoru Dentō teki Shūkyō Jissen no Henka (Change in the practice of Traditional Religions caused by the Acceptance of New Religions). Hendoki no Ningen to Shūkyō (Man and Religion in Transition). K. Morioka. Tokyo, Miraisha: 132–165.

840 NISHIYAMA, S. (1979). 'Shinshūkyō no Genkyo (The Present Condition of the New Religions).' Rekishi Koron 5(7 (July)): 33–37.

841 NISHIYAMA, S. and SHIMAZONO, S. et al. (1979). 'The Vitalistic Conception of Salvation in Japanese New Religions: An aspect of modern religious consciousness.' *Japanese Journal of Religious Studies* 6(1–2): 139–61.

842 NISHIYAMA, T. (1981). Introduction to the Teachings of Tenrikyō. Tenri, Japan, Tenrikyō Overseas Mission Department.

843 NISHIYAMA, S. and T. FUJII (1991). The Propagation and Spread of Tenshō Kōtai Jingūkyō within Japanese-American Society on Hawaii Island. Contemporary papers in Japanese Religion (2). N. Inoue. Tokyo, Kokagakuin University: 125–161.

844 NISHIYAMA, S. (1991). 'Youth, Deprivation, and New Religions: A Sociological Perspective.' *The Japan Christian Quarterly* 57(1): 4–11.

845 NIWANO, N. (1959). Hokkekyō no atarashii kaishaku (The new interpretation of Hokkekyō). Tokyo.

846 NIWANO, N. (1976). Niwano Nikkyō jiden (The biography of Niwano Nikkyō). Tokyo, Kōsei Shuppansha.
Niwano Nikkyō was a recent president of Risshō Kōseikai.

847 NIWANO, N. (1977). *A Buddhist Approach to Peace.* Tokyo, Kōsei Publishing Company.

848 NIWANO, N. (1978). *Lifetime Beginner: An Autobiography.* Tokyo, Kōsei Publishing Co.

849 Niwano, N. (1982). *My Father, My Teacher: A Spiritual Journey.* Tokyo, Kōsei Publishing Co.

850 NIWANO, N. (1989). Kokoro no naka no Sanpomichi (The Inward Path). Tokyo, Kōsei Publishing Company.

851 NIYEDA, R. (1958). New Religion in Japan-Japanese People's Religion. Religions in Japan at Present: 23–26.

852 NOBUHARA, T. (1980). *The Brilliant Life of Munetada Kurozumi: A Philosopher and Worshipper of the Sun.* Tokyo, PMC Publications.

853 NOBURO, M. (1970). Ikigami shinkō (The Belief in Living Gods). Tokyo, Kōshobō.

854 NORBECK, E. (1970). *Religion and Society in Modern Japan: Continuity and Change*. Houston, Tourmaline Press.

855 NORMAN, W. H. H. (1970). 'Sōka Gakkai, Kōmeitō and Freedom of Speech.' *Japan Christian Quarterly* 36: 258–265.

856 NUKARIYA, K. (1973). *The Religion of the Samurai*. London, Luzac and Company Ltd.
A study of Zen Philosophy and Discipline in China and Japan.

857 NUMA, G. (1954). 'Nichiren Kyōdan no Shakaigaku-teki Chōsa Kenkyū (A Sociological Study of the Nichiren Sect).' Bungaku-bu Ronsō 3: 3–26.

858 NUMATA, K. (1988). Gendai nihon no shinshūkyō (New religions in contemporary Japan). Tokyo, Sōgensha.

859 NUMATA, K. (1990). 'Shinnyoen no kenkyū.' Shakaigaku ronshū 24(1): 55–86.

860 OFFNER, C. B. and VAN STRAELEN, H. (1963). Modern Japanese Religions with special reference to their doctrines of healing. Tokyo, Enderle.
One of the first works on Japanese NRMs, now a classic.

861 OFFNER, C. B. (1969). 'Sōka Gakkai.' *Japan Christian Quarterly* 35(3).

862 OFFNER, C. B. (1973). 'Individual Values in the New Religious Movements of Japan.' *Japan Christian Quarterly* 39(1): 31–38.

863 OFFNER, C. B. (1982). 'Healing in the New Religions.' Japan Christian Quarterly XLV(1): 27–32.

864 OGASAWARA, K. (1985). Nihon-teki senzo saishi no Brasil – teki tenkai – Risshō Kōsei-kai to Reiyūkai no hikaku o tōshite (Desenvolvimento brasileiro do culto ao antepassado de estilo japonēs – pela comparação entre Risshō Kōsei-kai e Reiyūkai). Sān Paulo, Centro de Estudos Nipo-Brasileiros.

865 OGAWA, D. M. (1978). *Kodomo no tame ni-For the Sake of the Children*. Honolulu, Hawaii, Universiy of Hawaii Press.

866 OGUCHI, I. (1951). 'Shin Shūkyō Shūdan no Keisei to sono Kiban (The Formation of new Religious Groups and their Basis).' Shiso 327: 29–34.

867 OGUCHI, I. (1954). Nihon shūkyō no shakaiteki seikaku (Social character of Japanese Religions). Tokyo, University of Tokyo Press.

868 OGUCHI, I. and A. SAKI (1956). Kyōso (The Founder of a New Religion). Tokyo, Aoki-Shoten.

869 OGUCHI, I. (1956). 'Common People and Religion.' *Missionary Bulletin* 10(8,9,10).
Discussion of New Religions over several issues of the journal.

870 OGUCHI, I. and A. SAKI (1957). Sōka Gakkai. Tokyo, Aoki-shoten.

871 OGURI, J. (1972). Kindai shakai ni okeru kyōha Shintō no hatten (The development of Sect Shinto in a modern society).

872 OGURI, J. (1976). Nihon no kindai shakai to Tenrikyō (Modern Japanese Society and Tenrikyō). Tokyo, Hyōronsha.

873 OGURI, J. (1976). Nihon no kindai shakai to Tenrikyō. Nihonjin no kōdō to shisō (The behaviour and thought of the Japanese). Tokyo, Hyōronsha. 7.

874 OGURI, J. (1977). Tenrikyō no Tanjo to Hatten (The Birth and Development of Tenrikyō). Nihon Shūkyōshi (A History of Japanese Religion). K. Kasahara. Tokyo, Yamakawa Shuppansha. II: 227–247.

875 Oh, J. K.. (1972). 'Fusion of Politics and Religion in Japan: The Sōka Gakkai Kōmeitō.' *Journal of Church and State* **14**: 59–74.

876 Oh, J. K. (1973). 'The Nichiren Shōshū of America.' *Review of Religious Research* **14**: 169–177.

877 OHNUKI-TIERNEY, E. (1976). Shamanism and World View: The Case of the Ainu of the Northwest Coast of Southern Sakhalin. *In the Realm of the Extra-Human: Ideas and Actions*. A. Bharati. The Hague, Mouton Publishers: 175–200.
An attempt to situate the shamanistic practices of a specific Ainu group within the wider context of Ainu shamanism and culture.

878 OHNUKI-TIERNEY, E. (1976). The Shamanism of the Ainu of the Northwest Coast of Southern Sakahalin. *Culture Bound Syndrome*. R. C. Simons and C. C. Hughes. Dordrecht, Netherlands, Reidel.
A mainly descriptive paper of the shamanistic practices of a specific Ainu group (now resettled in Hokkaidō), with special reference to the spirits and deities involved, the shamanistic rites and the practitioners themselves.

879 OHNUKI-TIERNEY, E. (1980). 'Shamans and Imu: Among Two Ainu Groups: Toward a Cross-Cultural Model of Interpretation.' Ethos 8(3): 204–228.
The author shows the distinction between shamans perceived as genuine and accepted by the Ainu groups and those people, who, despite displaying similar symptoms are perceived as 'possessed'.

880 OHNUKI-TIERNEY, E. (1984). Illness and Culture in Contemporary Japan: An Anthropological View. Cambridge, Cambridge University Press.

881 OHNUKI-TIERNEY, E. (1985). Nihonjin no Byōkikan (Japanese concepts of Illness). Tokyo, Iwanami Shoten.

882 OHNUKI-TIERNEY, E. (1987). *The Monkey as a Mirror: Symbolic Transformations in Japanese History and Ritual*. Princeton, Princeton University Press.
This article offers a challenging anthropological work that examines Japanese ritual, history, and myth with regard to three intertwined relationships: the monkey metaphor, the special status people ('outcasts') and the monkey performance. The author's main focus is on 'intra-cultural variation and its effect upon the perception of ritual' by two groups of Japanese: the dominant Japanese and the special status people.

883 OHNUKI-TIERNEY, E. (1989). Health Care in Contemporary Japanese Religions. *Healing and Restoring: Health and Medicine in the World's Religious Traditions*. L. E. Sullivan. New York and London, Macmillan: 59–87.

Examines the role of Buddhist temples and Shinto shrines in healing practices in contemporary Japan.

884 OHNUKI-TIERNEY, E. (1990). 'The ambivalent self of the contemporary Japanese.' *Cultural Anthropology* **5**: 196–215.

885 OHNUKI-TIERNEY, E. (1991). 'The Emperor of Japan As Deity (*Kami*): An Anthropology of the imperial system in historical perspective.' Ethnology **30**(3): 1–17.
The author focuses on the cultural meanings assigned to the emperor and their changes over time and compares this with the notion of kami (deity) in Japanese religions. She argues for the initial shamanic function of the emperor.

886 OHNUKI-TIERNEY, E. (1993). *Rice as Self: Japanese identities through time.* Princeton, Princeton University Press.

887 OHNUKI-TIERNEY, E. (1994). 'Brain Death and Organ Transplantation: Cultural Bases of Medical Technology.' Current Anthropology **35**(3): 233–253.
The author argues, citing the case of Japan, that resistance to organ transplants is not a matter of economic or technological backwardness but of different cultural perceptions of life and death, nature and culture, self and other.

888 OHNUKI-TIERNEY, E. (1994). Rice as Metaphor of the Japanese Self. *Paths Toward the Past.* R. Harms, J. Miller, D. Newbury and M. Wagner. Atlanta, GA, African Studies Association Press: 455–472.

889 OHNUKI-TIERNEY, E. (1994). 'The Call for a New Asian Identity: An Examination of the Cultural Arguments and their Implications.' Japan Programs Occasional Papers **5**: 8–9.

890 OHNUKI-TIERNEY, E. (1996). The Self, Internal and External Others: Construction and Representation of Identities in Japanese Culture. *Narrative Agency: Self-Making in Chinese, Indian and Japanese Cultures.* W. Dissanayake. Minneapolis, University of Minnesota Press.

891 OHNUKI-TIERNEY, E. (1996). McDonald's in Japan: Changing Manners and Etiquette. *The Global in the Local: Transnational Fast Food Industries in East Asia.* J. Watson. Stanford, Stanford University Press.

892 OISHI, S. and e. al (1964). 'A Review Article: The New Religious Sects of Japan.' *Contemporary Religions of Japan* **5**(1): 47–78.

893 OKADA, M. (1947). Tengoku no fukuin (Gospels from Heaven). Atami, Sekai Kyūseikyō Shuppanbu.

894 OKADA, M. (1953). Amerika o Sukuu (Saving America). Atami, Sekai Kyūseikyō Shuppanbu.

895 OKADA, M. (1953). Sekai Kyūseikyō Kisekishu (The Miracles of Sekai Kyūseikyō). Atami, Sekai Kyūseikyō Shuppanbu.

896 OKADA, M. (1981). A Modern-Day Renaissance Man. New York, M. Okada Cultural Services Association.

897 OKADA, H. (1987). Gendai no kokoro: Sūkyō Mahikari (The Spirit of Today: Sūkyō Mahikari). Tokyo, Obunsha.

898 OKADA, Y. (n.d). Guse no Hikari (The Light of the Messiah). Atami, Sekai Kyūseikyō Hombu.

899 OKAMOTO, H. (1953). 'Nambei kaitaku ki: shinkō burajiru ni kagayaku made (A Journal of Pioneering in South America: to a Radiant Day in Advancing Brazil).' Kami no kuni (41): 50–55.

900 OKAMOTO, R. (1963). Japan: A New Faith Called Sōka Gakkai Raises Old Problems in Modern Japan. Look. **27**: 15–26.

901 OKANO, A. S. (1967). An Introduction to Kōdō Kyōdan Buddhism. Yokohama, Kōdō Kyōdan.
Written by the founder of Koko Kyōdan, this book sets out the teachings, faith and practice of the religion.

902 OKANO, K. L. (1970). The Heart of a Bodhisattva. Yokohama.
Written by Lady Okano, the wife of the founder of Kōdō Kyōdan, this book discusses the principles and teachings of Buddha and the application of these practices in the context of daily life as a Mahayana Bodhisattva.

903 OKANO, H. (1976). Die Stellung der Frau im Shinto. Wiesbaden, Otto Harrassowitz.
A well-documented, detailed presentation of women's symbolic and actual functions in Shintoism from early times to the present-day. It proposes to replace the myth of matriarchy with a more realistic hime-hiko model (joint female/male power).

904 OKANO, H. (1991). Weiblichkeitssymbolik und sexismus in alten und neuen Religionen Japans. Japan-ein Land der Frauen? E. Gössmann. Munchen, Iudicium Verlag: 117–129.
Traces the growth of intolerance towards women's religious activities in both traditional and new religions in Japan.

905 ŌKAWA, R. (1988). Shaka no Honshin (The Essential Message of Shakyamuni). Tokyo, IRH Press.

906 ŌKAWA, R. (1988). Nosutoradamusu no shinyogen (The New Prophecies of Nostradamus). Tokyo, Kōfuku-no-Kagaku Shuppan.

907 ŌKAWA, R. (1989). Utopia Kachi Kakumei (Utopian Value Revolution). Tokyo, Tsuchiya Shoten.

908 ŌKAWA, R. (1989). Shinsetsu Hasshōdō (The Eightfold path). Tokyo, IRH Press.

909 ŌKAWA, R. (1989). Shin shin reikai nūmon (New Guide Book of the Spirit World). Tokyo, IRH Press.

910 ŌKAWA, R. (1989). Jinsei no Hakken (Discovery of Life). Tokyo, IRH Press.

911 ŌKAWA, R. (1989). Jōshō shikō (Ever-victorious thought). Tokyo, IRH Press.
The power of positive thinking and how to avoid defeat and failure as a human being.

912 ŌKAWA, R. (1990). Shinri Yōgo-no Kiso Chishiki 100 (Basic Knowledge About God's Truth Terminology: 100). Tokyo, Kōfuku-no-Kagaku Press.

913 ŌKAWA, R. (1990). Kōfuku-no-Genri (The Principle of Happiness). Tokyo, IRH Press.

A discussion of what constitutes human happiness, looking at love and the human heart and soul.

914 ŌKAWA, R. (1990). Kagirinaku Yasashiku are (Be Gentle Without Limit). Tokyo, IRH Press.

915 ŌKAWA, R. (1990). Yūtopia no Genri (The Principle of Utopia). Tokyo, IRH Press.

916 ŌKAWA, R. (1990). Satori no Genri (The Principle of Enlightenment). Tokyo, IRH Press.

917 ŌKAWA, R. (1990). Kōfuku no Genten (The Origin of Happiness). Tokyo, IRH Kōfuku-no-Kagaku.

918 ŌKAWA, R. (1991). The Laws of the Sun. Tokyo, Japan, IRH Press Co Ltd.
The first in the trilogy of God's Truth, it explains what God, Love and the Ultimate Enlightenment is and presents 'The Golden Age of the Past'.

919 ŌKAWA, R. (1991). *The Laws of Gold.* Tokyo, The IRH Press Co Ltd.
The second volume in the trilogy, this book explains how to establish God's Truth in one's own life, as well as giving a brief historical overview of Buddhism and a glimpse into the future.

920 ŌKAWA, R. (1991). *The Laws of Eternity* (Eien no Hō). Tokyo, IRH Press Co Ltd.
The final volume in the trilogy, this book discusses the multidimensional world and theories of space.

921 ŌKAWA, R. (1991). *The Rebirth of Buddha.* Tokyo, IRH Press.
The messages of the reincarnate Buddha of the present-day to his beloved disciples.

922 ŌKAWA, R. (1991). Ai wa kaze no gotoku (Love is like the Wind). Tokyo, IRH Press.
A poetic spiritual biography of the Greek god, Hermes, incorporating his alleged sayings.

923 ŌKAWA, R. (1991). Nosutoradamusu senritsu no keiji (The terrifying revelations of Nostradamus). Tokyo, Kōfuku-no-Kagaku Shuppan.

924 ŌKAWA, R. (1991). Nosutoradamusu senritsu no keiji: Jinrui no kiki semaru (Frigtening Rrevelations of Nostradamus:The Crisis of Mankind is at Hand). Tokyo, IRH.

925 ŌKAWA, R. (1992). Manga de miru Kōfuku-no-Kagaku. Tokyo, IRH Press Ltd.
Comic-strip of science fiction type explaining the basic concepts of the IRH to young people.

926 ŌKAWA, R. (1992). Satori ni Itaru Michi (The Way to Enlightenment). Tokyo, IRH Press.

927 ŌKAWA, R. (1992). Satori no Kyokuchi towa Nanika (What is the Perfection of Enlightenment). Tokyo, IRH Press.

928 ŌKAWA, R. (1992). Shinri Bunmei no Ruten (The Transition of Truth Civilisation). Tokyo, IRH Press.

929 ŌKAWA, R. (1992). Shinkō to Ai (Faith and Love). Tokyo, IRH Press Ltd.
Faith and love, according to this book are the guiding lights in the fight against the darkness of the present-day world and signs of the dawning of a new civilization.

930 ŌKAWA, R. (1993). Frankly Speaking. Tokyo, Kōfuku no Kagaku Publishing Co.

A series of interviews and discussions with the founder and leader of the Japanese New Religion Kofuko no Kagaku (IRH) including the full tape transcript of the interview taken by The Financial Times.

931 ŌKAWA, R. (1993). *The Challenge of Religion: The Wind of Miracles from Japan.* Tokyo, Japan, The IRH Press Co Ltd.
Discussion of the part religion can and should play in the present world and the necessity of adaptability in all religions.

932 ŌKAWA, R. (1993). Satori no Chōsen (The Challenge of Enlightenment). Tokyo, IRH Press.

933 ŌKAWA, R. (1993). Chinamoku no Buddha (The Silent Buddha). Tokyo, IRH Press.
The secret doctrines and esoteric teachings of Buddhism.

934 ŌKAWA, R. (1993). *Heaven and Hell.* Tokyo, IRH Press.

935 ŌKAWA, R. (1993). Dainamaito Shikō (Dynamite Thinking). Tokyo, IRH Press.
Every human being has the capacity for 'dynamite thinking' and performing miracles inside him or herself. This book reveals how to tap this hidden source.

936 ŌKAWA, R. (1994). *Buddha Speaks.* Tokyo, IRH Press.
The English language version of 'Frankly Speaking'.

937 ŌKAWA, R. (1994). Kokoro no chōsen (Challenge of mind). Tokyo, IRH Press.

938 ŌKAWA, R. (1994). Shōshin Hōgo (The Dharma of the Right Mind). Tokyo, IRH Press.

939 ŌKAWA, R. (1994). Secrets of the Spirit World (A Lecture in Nagaoka, Japan, 14 June 1992 by Ryuho Ōkawa). Tokyo, Kōfuku-no-Kagaku.

940 ŌKAWA, R. (1994). Shin Taiyō no Hō (The New Laws of the Sun). Tokyo, IRH Press.
A revised and updated version of the most famous and popular book of the Kōfuku-no-Kagaku.

941 ŌKAWA, R. (1994). Risō Kokka Nihon no Jōken (The Conditions for an Ideal Japanese State). Tokyo, IRH Press.
A call for a nation-state grounded on religious and moral principles, and guidelines as to how this utopia could be accomplished.

942 ŌKAWA, R. (1995). *Living in the Age of Miracles.* Tokyo, IRH Press.

943 ŌKAWA, R. (1995). Shinsei Nihon no Shishin (Creating a New Japan). Tokyo, IRH Press.
This book was edited from a speech with the same title given at the Tokyo Dome on 10 July 1995. An initial brief criticism of Aum Shinrikyō is followed by a lengthy discussion of Japan's trade and foreign policies, especially towards the United States and suggestions for the improvement of the relationship are given. A condensed English language version is also available.

944 ŌKAWA, R. (1995). Genron no jiyū tai shinkyō no jiyū (Freedom of Speech vs Freedom of Religion). Tokyo, IRH Press.

945 ŌKAWA, R. (1995). Sōka Gakkai Bokokuron (Sōka Gakkai's Threat to the State/Country). Tokyo, IRH Press.

946 ŌKAWA, R. (1995). Ii Shūkyō, Warui Shūkyō (Good Religions, Bad/Wrong Religion). Tokyo, IRH Press.

947 ŌKAWA, R. (1995). *The Age of Choice in Religion.* Tokyo, IRH Press. *English-language version of 3 of the 8 chapters that make up the eponymous Japanese text, 'Shūkyō Sentaku no Jidai'. It talks of the purpose of religion and the secrets of the spirit world.*

948 OKIMOTO, D. I. (1970). *Americans in Disguise*, John Weatherhill.

949 ŌKUBO, A. (1960). '"Counselling" in Tenrikyō.' *Tenri Journal of Religion* 6.

950 ŌKUBO, A. (1969). 'A Study of Social Welfare in Tenrikyō.' *Tenri Journal of Religion* 15.

951 ŌKUBO, A. (1970). 'Social Welfare and Practicality of Hinokishin of Tenrikyō – A Proposal to the International Year of the Disabled Person.' *Tenri Journal of Religion* 16.

952 ŌKUBO, M. (1987). 'Mekishiko ni okeru SGI kannen fukugō juyō katei no shakai-shinrigakuteki bunseki (Socio-Psychological Theories of Acceptance of SGI Conceptual Complexes in Mexico).' Nanbu Mekishiko sonraku ni okeru Katorikku-kei bunka no kenkyū 4: 92–123.

953 ŌKUBO, M. (1987). 'Ibunka ni okeru nikkei shinshūkyō no juyō to henyō (Changing Attitudes and the Acceptance of Japanese New Religions in Foreign Cultures).' Shūkyō kenkyū 273: 25–64.

954 ŌKUBO, M. (1987). 'Mekishiko Nichiren Shōshū ni okeru kuyō-kan to shokuggyōrōdō-kan ni tsuite (Views on Kuyō and Views on Occupational Labour in Nichiren Shōshū of Mexico).' Nishi Nihon shūkyōgaku zasshi 9: 19–27.

955 ŌKUBO, M. (1991). 'The Acceptance of Nichiren Shōshū Sōka Gakkai in Mexico.' Japanese Journal of Religious Studies 18(2–3): 189–212.

956 OLIVER, I. P. (1979). Buddhism in Britain. London, Rider & Co.

957 OLSON, R. (1953). 'Mioshie: A New Messianic Cult.' Papers of the Kroeber Anthropological Society 8(9).

958 OLSON, L. (1971). The Value Creation Society: Sōka Gakkai, A Japanese Religious and Political Phenomenon. Tokyo.

959 OMURA and NISHIYAMA, Eds. (1990). Gendaijin no shūkyō (Contemporary Religion). Tokyo, Yūhikaku.

960 ONO, Y. (1979). Tenshō Kōtai Jingū kyō. Shinshūkyō no Sekai (The World of the New Religions). M. Shimizu. Tokyo, Daizo Shuppan. V: 167–202.

961 ONO, Y. (1980). Seichō-no-Ie. Minzoku Shūkyō to Shakai (Folk Religion and Society). S. Gorai. Tokyo, Kobundo. 5: 212–221.

962 ONO, Y. (1980). Reiyūkai. Minzoku Shūkyō to Shakai (Folk Religion and Society). S. Gorai. Tokyo, Kobundo. 5: 233–243.

963 ŌMOTO (1925). The New Spiritual Movement. Ayabe, Ōmoto Overseas office.

964 ŌMOTO (1952). The Ōmoto Movement, Its Origins, Aims and Objects and the Universal Love and Brotherhood Association. Kameoka, The Ōmoto Headquarters.

965 ŌMOTO (1955). The Basic Teachings of Ōmoto. Kyōto, Jinrui Aizen-kai Kokusaibu.

966 ŌMOTO (1956-). *Ōmoto International.* California, Ōmoto International Department.
Official yearly journal of the Ōmoto Foundation and the Aizenkai (ULBA – Universal Love and Brotherhood Association)

967 ŌMOTO (1958). The Outline of Ōmoto. Kameoka.

968 ŌMOTO (1958). The Fundamentals of the Soul. Ōmoto: 2–3.

969 Ōmoto Hombu Senkyobu (1959). Ōmoto Shinkō no Shiori (The Guide to Ōmoto Belief). Kameoka, Ōmoto Hombu Senkyobu,.

970 Ōmoto Hombu Senkyōbu (1958). Ōmoto no Shinji to Sekai no Shōrai (The Shinto Rites of Ōmoto and the Future of the World). Kameoka, Ōmoto Hombu Senkyōbu.

971 OOMS, H. (1967). 'The Religion of the Household: A case study of Ancestor Worship in Japan.' Contemporary Religions in Japan 8(3–4): 201–333.
Paper based on Oom's fieldwork for his MA degree. A study of household religion in a rural community between Tokyo and Yokohama outlining the social structures within which ancestor worship takes place and its effect on community life.

972 OOMS, H. (1974). Japanese Ancestor Worship as the Religion of the Household. Ancestors. W. H. Newell. Hague, Mouton.

973 OOMS, H. (1974). A Structural Analysis of Japanese Ancestral Rites and Beliefs. Ancestors. W. H. Newell. The Hague, Paris, Mouton Publishers.
Study of ancestor worship in Japan as a religious phenomenon focusing on an analysis of its symbol system and the motivation and religious consciousness of worshippers. Ancestor Rites are seen as 'creating order in the passing of time as experienced in the household'.

974 OOMS, E. G. (1984). Deguchi Nao and Ōmoto-kyo: An Analysis of a Millenarian Cult in Meiji Japan, University of Chicago.

975 OOMS, E. G. (1993). Women and Millenarian Protest in Meiji Japan. Deguchi Nao and ōmotokyō. New York, Cornell University East Asia Program.
Ōmotokyō is a very influential New Religion which has spawned a number of 'world-renewal' New Religions, among them Mahikari, Sekai Kyūseikyō and Seichō-no-Ie. This book is a study of its foundress Deguchi Nao (1836–1918). It also addresses the roles of class and gender in New Religious Movements.

976 OPLER, M. K. (1950). 'Two Japanese Sects.' Southwestern Journal of Anthropology 6.

977 ORO, A. P. (1999). The New Japanese Religions in Brazil: Some Remarks on the Church of World Messianity. *Japanese New Religions in Global Perspective*. P. B. Clarke. Richmond, Surrey, Curzon Press.

978 OSAKA, M. (1930). 'Tenrikyō, One of Japan's new Religions.' *Japan Christian Quarterly* 5.

979 OSAKI, N. (1941). A Study of Interdenominational Cooperation within Each of Three Japanese Religions in Los Angeles: Shinto, Buddhism and Christianity, University of Southern California.

980 OSAKI, K. (1959). Okagebanashi (Stories of Thanksgiving). Kameoka, Ōmoto Hombu Senkyobu.

981 OSAKI, K. (1959). Seishiden (The Biography of a Holy Man). Kameoka, Tenseisha.
Biography of the founder of Ōmoto.

982 OSHIMA, H. (1980). Seinen to Shinshūkyō (The Youth and New Religion). Tokyo, Jiyu Kokuminsha.

983 OSUMI, I. (1987). The Shamanic Healer: The Healing World of Ikuko Osumi and the Traditional Art of Seiki-jutsu. London, Century Hutchinson.
The book looks at a rare form of Japanese traditional medicine, based on shamanic practices of transmitting vital life force from healer to patient. Contains the life story of the healer and a description of rituals and actual cases.

984 OYA, S. (1950). Shinkō Shūkyō (The New Religions). Tokyo, Jeepsha.

985 OZAKI, P. A. M. (1990). 'As religiões japonesas no Brasil.' Missão Japonesa no Brasil.

986 PALMER, A. (1971). Buddhist Politics: Japan's Clean Government Party. The Hague, Martinus Nijhoff.

987 PARKER, K. W. (1983). Okyōsama: Documentation of the founding of Nyorai-kyō, Japan's first 'New Religion', PhD. Pennsylvania University: 221.
Mainly a historical work, it sets the founding of this little-known New Religion in the social and religious context of the time and includes a thorough analysis of the religious texts of the group.

988 PARKS, Y. Y. (1980). 'The Nichiren Shōshū Academy in America: Changes during the 1970s.' Japanese Journal of Religious Studies 7(4): 337–55.
Looks at how Nichiren Shōshū Academy (NSA), a branch of Sōka Gakkai, transformed itself after the 1960s to adapt to a less favourable environment for unorthodox religious groups in 1970s America. Focuses on organizational and membership structure and stages of what she terms 'Americanization'.

989 PEARCE, T. H. (1994). 'Tenchi Seikyō: A Messianic Buddhist Cult.' Japanese Journal of Religious Studies 21(4): 407–424.
Tenchi Seikyō is a small 'new' New Religion of Japan that has converged with the Unification Movement of Rev. Sun Myung Moon. This paper presents the history and nature of Tenchi Seikyō, describes the life of its founder, Kawase Kayo, and outlines Tenchi Seikyō's organization, beliefs and practices. It also explores why the two organizations developed such a relationship.

94

990 PECCEI, A. and IKEDA, D. (1987). Before It Is Too Late. Tokyo, Kōdansha International.
A series of dialogues concerning world peace and education of Sōka Gakkai International and one of the leading figures of the Club of Rome.

991 Perfect Liberty Kyōdan (1951). How to Lead a Happy Life, The PL Order.

992 Perfect Liberty Kyōgakubu (1954). Seichi Rensei Taikenshū (The Experiences of Training at Holy Places). Osaka, PL Shuppansha.

993 Perfect Liberty Kyōgakubu (1958). PL Nōgyō-Taikenshū (The Experience of PL Farming and Agriculture). Tonbayashi, PL Shuppansha.

994 PESSAR, P. R. (1982). 'Millenarian Movements in Rural Brazil: Prophecy and Protest.' *Religion* 12: 187–213.

995 PICONE, M. (1986). Buddhist Popular Manuals and the Contemporary Commercialization of Religion in Japan. Interpreting Japanese Society: Antropological Approaches. J. Hendry and J. Webber. Oxford. *JASO Occasional Papers* No. 5: 157–65.
The purpose of the book is to introduce the social anthropological study of Japan to a wider audience. The article by Mary J. Picone looks at the recent diffusion of religious self-help manuals in order to study the secularization of Japanese modern society and to pinpoint those religious elements which are thought by the author to be the most suitable for commercialization.

996 PIRYNS, E. D. (1984). 'Japan's New Religions: An Interpretation.' *Update: A Quarterly Journal of New Religious Movements* 8(3–4).

997 PIRYNS, E. D. (1985). 'Formative Elements in the Emergence and Growth of the New Religions in Japan.' *Japanese Religions* 13(4).

998 PIRYNS, E. D. (1988). 'Religious Syncretism: The Japanese Case.' *Japanese Religions* 15(1): 49–65.
Outlines the history of religious syncretism in Japan, focusing on the development of Shinto and Buddhism and their merger with elements of Taoism, Confucianism and Christianity. The syncretistic character of the New Religions is briefly discussed.

999 PL KYŌDAN (1950). Essay on the Way of Life, Tondabayashi.

1000 PL KYŌDAN (n.d). Guide to a Happy Life, Tondabayashi.

1001 PLATH, D. (1964). 'Where the Family of God is the Family: The Role of the Dead in Japanese Households.' American Anthropologist 66(2): 300–317.
Plath looks at the underlying social relationships between the living household members and the ancestors focusing on notions of sentiment and emotional expression and on the concept of memorialism.

1002 PLATH, D. W. (1964). The After Hours: Modern Japan and the Search for Enjoyment. Berkeley and Los Angeles, University of California Press.

1003 PLATH, D. W. (1966). 'The Fate of Utopia: Adaptive tactics in Four Japanese Groups.' *American Anthropologist* 68: 1152–62.

1004 PLATH, D. W. (1969). 'Modernization and Its Discontents: Japan's Little Utopias.' *Journal of Asian and African Studies* 4(1): 1–17.

1005 PLUTSCHOW, H. (1983). 'The Fear of Evil Spirits in Japanese Culture.' *Transactions of the Asiatic Society of Japan*: 133–151.

1006 PO, J. K. (1978). *The World of Hawaii's Japanese Americans*. Honolulu, Hawaii, University of Hawaii Press.

1007 PORTER, H. (1968). *The Actors. An Image of the New Japan*. Sydney, Melbourne and London, Angus and Robertson Ltd.
A controversial book focused on aspects of Japanese life.

1008 PUTNAM, G. (1981). 'Tenrikyō: from Japanese Folk Religion to Universal World Religion?' *Japanese Religions* 11(4).

1009 PYE, M. (1973). *Zen and Modern Japanese Religions*. London, Ward Lock.
A brief introduction to Zen Buddhism and its influence on contemporary Japanese religions.

1010 PYE, M. (1977). The Heart Sutra in its Japanese Context. Praj'naparamita and Related Systems: Essays in Honour of Edward Conze. L. Lancaster. Berkeley, California, Berkeley Institute of Buddhist Studies, University of California: 123–34.

1011 PYE, M. (1986). National and International Identity in a Japanese Religion (Byakkō Shinkō Kai). Identity Issues and World Religions. Selected Proceedings of the XVth Congress of the International Association of the History of Religions. V. Hayes, South Australia: Australian Association for the Study of Religion: 234–41.
Tackles issues of nationalism and 'universalism' in reference to Byakkō Shinkō Kai.

1012 PYE, M. (1989). Woran glauben Japans Großindustrielle? Die Religion von Oberschichten. P. Antes and D. Pahnke, Diagonal Verlag.
A brief survey of some of the ways Japanese industrial leaders have been influenced by a range of religious ideas and some of the overtly religious activities observable in Japanese companies. Amongst other influences, notes that of Tenrikyō on Matsushita Konosuke, founder of Matsushita Electric.

1013 PYE, M. (1990). Philology and Fieldwork in the Study of Japanese Religion. Studies on Religions in the Context of Social Sciences; Methodological and Theoretical Relations. W. Tylodi. Warsaw.
Outlines some of the distinctive features of doing fieldwork concerned with the study of religion in Japan, discusses difficulties that may arise, and strategies for dealing with them. Argues for the value of written ephemera produced by religious movements e.g pamphlets, brochures, lists of annual events etc. in studying Japanese religion.

1014 PYE, M. (1994). National and International Identity in a Japanese Religion. *Japanese New Religions in the West*. P. B. Clarke and J. Somers. Folkestone, Kent, Japan Library: 77–87.
A discussion concerning Byakkō Shinkōkai or White Light Association a 'new' religion in Japan.

1015 RAJANA, E. W. (1974). A Sociological Study of New Religious Movements: Chilean Pentecostalism and Japanese New Religions. PhD. London, University of London.

1016 RAJANA, E. W. (1975). New Religions in Japan: An appraisal of two theories. *Modern Japan: Aspects of History, Literature and Society.* W. G. Beasley. Berkeley, University of California Press: 187–197.
This article assesses two alternative theories accounting for the appearance of New Religions in Japan: the 'Emperor-Substitute Theory' and the 'Urban Anomie Theory.' Rajana is critical of both these approaches as being too negative about New Religions and suggests an alternative, that the New Religions are 'intermediate organizations' which 'relate atomised individuals to larger society.'

1017 RAMSEYER, R. (1962). 'Religion in Japan in 1961.' *Contemporary Religions in Japan* III: 18.

1018 RAMSEYER, R. (1963). 'The Sōka Gakkai and the Japanese Elections of 1960 (sic).' *Contemporary Religions in Japan* IV: 287.

1019 RAMSEYER, R. (1965). The Sōka Gakkai, Center forJapanese Studies, Ann Arbor, University of Michigan.

1020 RAMSEYER, R. L. (1972). 'Finances in the New Religions and the Christian Church.' *Japan Christian Quarterly* 37: 84–89.

1021 READER, I. (1985). 'Transformation and Changes in the Teachings of the Sōtō Zen Sect.' *Japanese Religions* 14(1): 28–48.
Looks at the history of the Buddhist Sect, Sōtō Zen focusing on its methods of teaching, publications and educational campaigns over time. Mention is made on page 43 of Sōtō Zen's adoption of the 'hoza' technique from Risshō Kōsei Kai.

1022 READER, I. (1987). 'Back to the Future: Images of Nostalgia and Renewal in a Japanese Religious Context.' *Japanese Journal of Religious Studies* 14(4): 287–303.

1023 READER, I. (1987). 'From Ascetism to the Package Tour: The Pilgrim's Progress in Japan.' *Religion* 17(2): 133–48.

1024 READER, I. (1988). 'The Rise of a Japanese 'New New Religion': Themes in the Development of Agonshū.' *Japanese Journal of Religious Studies* 15(4): 235–61.
Looks at the rapid growth of Agonshū through a discussion of its highly advertized rituals and events. Discusses how Agonshū manages to combine both elements of tradition and the modern to give members a means to deal with contemporary society, while also appealing to concepts of universality. Draws comparisons with other 'new new' religions such as Mahikari, Byakkō Shinkōkai and Shinnyoen.

1025 READER, I. (1988). 'Miniaturization and Proliferation: A Study of Small-Scale Pilgrimages in Japan.' *Studies in Central and East Asian Religions* 1(1): 50–66.

1026 READER, I. (1989). 'Images in Sōtō Zen: Buddhism as a Religion in the Family in Contemporary Japan.' *Scottish Journal of Religious Studies* 10(1): 5–21.

1027 READER, I. (1991). *Religion in Contemporary Japan.* Basingstoke, Macmillan.
This book examines the major areas in which the Japanese participate in religious events, the role of religion in the social system and the underlying views within the

Japanese religious world. It is particularly useful with regard to the developments in Agonshū.

1028 READER, I. (1991). 'Letters to the Gods: The form and meaning of ema.' *Japanese Journal of Religious Studies* 18(1): 23–50.
Discusses the phenomenon of 'prayer tablets' in the Japanese temples.

1029 READER, I., ANDREASON, E., STEFÁNSSON, F. (1993). *Japanese Religions: Past and Present.* Folkestone, Kent, Japan Library.
A general overview of the entire range of contemporary religions including folk religion, Shinto, Buddhism, Christianity and the 'new' religions together with their historical background. The chapter on 'Religion and Politics' is especially interesting putting together a wealth of previously disparate material.

1030 READER, I. (1993). 'Sendatsu and the Development of Contemporary Japanese Pilgrimage.' Nissan Occasional Paper Series No. 17.
The paper is concerned with the nature, activities, roles and responsibilities of the 'sendatsu', or pilgrimage guide and leader of pilgrimage groups, in contemporary Japanese pilgrimage. The main focus is on the formalized system of 'sendatsu' that has been organized and administered by the pilgrimage temples associated with the Shikoku pilgrimage.

1031 READER, I. (1994). Japanese Religions. Insight Japan. 3: 6–9.
A summary of a few of the Japanese Old and New Religions.

1032 READER, I. (1996). A Poisonous Cocktail? Aum Shinrikyō's Path to Violence. Copenhagen, Nordic Institute of Asian Studies.
Daniel Metraux concludes that this article by Ian Reader is the most reasoned and scholarly explanation so far of Aum Shinrikyō's attack on the Tokyo subway in 1995 and that Reader provides a 'superb overview of Aum's history, leadership, ideology, tactics and millenialist views'.

1033 REICHL, C. A. (1993). 'The Okinawan New Religion Ijun-Innovation and Diversity in the Gender of the Ritual Specialist.' *Japanese Journal of Religious Studies* 20(4): 311–330.
Looks at the processes of change that have occurred in Ijun as it has modernized, focusing on the status implications it has had for women leaders as they have come to be replaced by men. A comparison is made with the movements branch in Hawaii where women are still dominant.

1034 REID, D. (1981). 'Remembering the Dead: Change in Protestant Christian Tradition Through Contact with Japanese Cultural Tradition.' *Japanese Journal of Religious Studies* 8(1–2).
Discusses how Japanese Protestantism has been influenced by its contact with the Japanese cultural tradition of ancestor rites and the household system within which it operates.

1035 REID, D. (1984). Japanese Religions. *Handbook of Living Religions.* J. R. Hinnells. Harmondsworth, Middlesex, Penguin: 365–91.

1036 REID, D. (1991). *New Wine: The Cultural Shaping of Japanese Christianity.* Fremont, California, Asian Humanities Press.
Concerns specific issues important for understanding Christianity in contemporary Japan including a study of the role on 'ancestor worship' in Japanese Christianity.

1037 REID, D. (1996). Internationalization of Japanese Religion. *Religion in Japanese Culture*. Tamaru, N. and D. Reid. Tokyo, Kōdansha.

1038 Reiha-no-Hikari (1982). Gosho (Holy Book), Reiha-no-Hikari.

1039 Reiha-no-Hikari (1989). Kami e no Michi (The Road to God). Tokyo, Reiha-no-Hikari.

1040 Reiki (1992). Living Reiki, Takata's Teachings. Mendocino, California, Life Rhythm.
Stories from the life of the founder of Reiki, Hawayo Takata as told to a pupil, Fran Brown.

1041 REISCHAUER, A. K. (1917). Studies in Japanese Buddhism. New York, Macmillan.
Traces the origins, development and spread of Buddhism in Japan. The book discusses the Buddhist canon as known in Japan, outlines the main doctrines of Japanese Buddhism and looks at the place of Buddhism in Japanese life-past, present and future.

1042 REISCHAUER, A. K. (1937). 'Religion in the Japan of Today.' *International Review of Missions* **26**: 322–33.

1043 REISCHAUER, E. O. (1977). *The Japanese*. Cambridge, Massachusetts, The Belknap Press of Harvard University Press.
A view of Japan from a perspective of the late 1970s concentrating on the social organization and values of the Japanese, their political system and on their relationship with the outside world.

1044 REIYŪKAI (1972). Ten No Ongaku (The Life of Kimi Kotani). Tokyo, Reiyūkai.
Life of the Founder.

1045 REIYŪKAI (1985). Zaikeshugi Bukkyō eno Shōtai (Invitation to Lay Buddhism). Tokyo, Reiyūkai.

1046 REIYŪKAI (1986). *The Development of Japanese Lay Buddhism*. Tokyo, The Reiyūkai.
A short book giving an outline of Reiyūkai but particularly useful in its factual appraisal of Sōka Gakkai.

1047 REIYŪKAI, T. (1987). *The Reiyūkai Movement: Buddhism as an Interreligious Philosophy*. Tokyo, The Reiyūkai.

1048 REIYŪKAI, T. (1988). *The Philosophical Foundation of the Lay Buddhist Practice of the Reiyūkai, as depicted in the Lotus Sūtra*. Tokyo, The Reiyūkai.

1049 REIYŪKAI (1991). *The Blue Sutra Guidebook*. Tokyo, Reiyūkai.
Holy Book

1050 REIYŪKAI (n.d). *The Reiyūkai, Its Aims and Practice*. Tokyo, Reiyūkai.

1051 Reiyūkai America (n.d). *Reiyūkai: People Promoting Friendship and Awareness*. Los Angeles, Reiyūkai America.

1052 RENONDEAU, G. (1951). 'Le Traité sue l'Etat'de Nichiren.' *T'oung Pao* XL: 123.

1053 REPP, M. (1995). 'The Earthquake in the Kobe-Osaka Area January 17th 1995. Its impact on religions and their response.' *Japanese Religions* 20(2): 207–229.

1054 Research Association for New Religions (1995). Shinshūkyō Gaidobukku (Guide to the New Religions). Tokyo, Best Books.
A very good starting point for anyone wanting comprehensive but concise information on many of the new and 'new new' religions of Japan including details of the founder and address and phone numbers of the headquarters of each movement.

1055 REYNOLDS, D. K. (1980). *The Quiet Therapies: Japanese Pathways to Personal Growth*. Honolulu, University of Hawaii Press.

1056 RIBEIRO, R. (1962). Brazilian Messianic Movements. *Millenial Dreams in Action*. S.Thrupp. The Hague.

1057 RICCO, M. (1967). Religione della violenza e religione del piacere nel nuovo Giappone. Florence, Saggi.

1058 RICHARDS, E. N. D. (1991). 'The Development of Sekai Kyūseikyō in Thailand.' *Japanese Journal of Religious Studies* 18(2–3): 165–188.

1059 RICHARDSON, J. T. (1978). 'Conversion Careers: In and Out of New Religions.' Sage Contemporary Social Science Issues 47.

1060 RICHARDSON, J. T. (1991). 'Reflexivity and Objectivity in the Study of Controversial New Religions.' Religion 21: 305–318.

1061 Risshō Kōsei Kai (1959). *A Guide to Risshō Kōsei Kai*. Tokyo, Kōsei Publishing Co.

1062 Risshō Kōsei Kai (1966). *Risshō Kōsei Kai*. Tokyo, Kōsei Publishing Co.

1063 Risshō Kōsei Kai. *Dharma World*. Tokyo, Kōsei Publishing Co.
Monthly Magazine.

1064 RISSHŌ KŌSEI KAI (1980). *Risshō Kōsei Kai: An Organization of Buddhist Laymen*. Tokyo, Kōsei Publishing Company.

1065 RISSHŌ KŌSEI KAI (1982). *The Story Of Risshō Kōsei Kai*. Tokyo, Kōsei Publishing Co.

1066 RISSHŌ KŌSEI-KAI (1970). *Risshō Kōsei Kai: A New Buddhist Laymen's Movement in Japan*. Tokyo, Kōsei Publishing Company.

1067 Risshō Kōseikai (1978). Niwano Nikkyō hōwa senshū (A Selection of the Teachings of Niwano Nikkyō). Tokyo, Kōsei Shuppansha.

1068 Risshō Kōsei-kai (1959). Kōsei Kyogaku (The Teaching of Risshō Kōsei-kai), Risshō Kōsei-kai.

1069 Risshō Kōsei-Kai (1966). Risshō Kōsei-Kai. Tokyo, Kōsei Publishing Company.

1070 ROBINSON, J. C. (1969). *Okinawa: A People and Their Gods*. Rutland,Vermont and Tokyo, Japan, Charles E. Tuttle Co.
A short review of the Okinawa people including a description of Okinawa Religion, household religious practice, present trends in religious belief and practice.

1071 ROCHEDIEU, E. (1968). Le Shintoïsme et les Nouvelles Religions du Japan. Paris, Garnier Frères.

1072 ROGGENDORF, J., Ed. (1963). *Studies in Japanese Culture. Tradition and Experiment. Monumenta Nipponica Monographs* No.23. Tokyo, Sophia University.
A collection of twelve scholarly essays on aspects of Japanese religion, philosophy, anthropology, literature, politics, economics, revealing the ingenuity of the Japanese in coping with new ideas and facts whist preserving their cultural identity.

1073 ROHLEN, T. P. (1970). 'Sponsorship of Cultural Continuity in Japan: A Company Training Program.' *Journal of Asian and African Studies* 5(3): 184–192.
Examines the way in which a Japanese company training programme may act as a rite of passage.

1074 ROHLEN, T. P. (1973). 'Spiritual Education in a Japanese Bank.' *American Anthropologist* 75: 1547–62.
Describes a training programme in a Japanese bank which aims to provide 'spiritual education' for new recruits. The programme included meditation in a Zen temple; training at a military base; doing voluntary work without pay in a local community; a weekend doing farm work and sporting activities in the countryside; and an endurance walk. The way in which this programme seeks to modify the 'spirit' of new company recruits is discussed and parallels with religious rituals are noted.

1075 ROHLEN, T. P. (1976). 'The Promise of Adulthood in Japanese Spiritualism.' *Daedalus*(Spring): 125–43.
Examines notions of adulthood in Japan as not a single transition but a process of maturation that continues into old age. Spiritual maturation is the key notion here, in particular the development of 'kokoro' and 'ki'. The importance of the life stories of great leaders as examples to others is discussed, as well as discipline and persistence. Spiritual development is argued in this article to be important in all areas of Japanese life, including those that would be classed as secular in the West.

1076 ROTERMUND, H. O. (1972). 'Einführung zum Shakubuku Kyōten der Sōka Gakkai; Bekehrung auf Biegen und Brechen.' Zeitschrift fur Religions und Geistesgeschichte 24(3): 227–241.
An analysis of the Shakubuku Handbook, previously used by Sōka Gakkai members in converting people, if necessary by forcible persuasion.

1077 ROTERMUND, H. O. (1973). 'Soka-gakkai; ideologie d'une nouvelle secte japonaise.' *Revue de l'Histoire des Religion* 184: 137–157.

1078 ROTERMUND, H. (1976). Les Nouvelles Religions du Japon. *Encyclopédie de la Pléiade: Histoire des religions*. Paris. 3: 520–540.

1079 SAIKI, P. S. (1993). *Early Japanese Immigrants in Hawaii*. Honolulu, Hawaii, University of Hawaii Press.

1080 SAITO, K. (1962). 'Sōka Gakkai: Third Force in Japanese Politics?' *Orient/ West* 7.

1081 SAITO, H. and MAEYAMA, T. (1973). Assimilação e Integração dos Japonêses no Brasil. Petrópolis and São Paulo, Vōzes & Editōria da Universidade de São Paulo.

1082 SAKASHITA, J. (1995). 'Shinnyoen in the U.K.' *Journal of Contemporary Religion* 10(2): 167–179.

1083 SAKI, A. (1955). Kyōso-shomin no kamigami (The Founders – Gods for the People). Tokyo, Aoki shoten.

1084 SAKI, A. (1960). Shinkō-shūkyō: Sore o meguru gendai no jōken (New religions: Their surrounding contemporary conditions). Tokyo, Aoki Shoten.

1085 SAKI, A. (1964). Shinkō Shūkyō (New Religions). Tokyo, Aoki-Shoten.

1086 SAKI, A. (1970). Godai kyōso no jitsuzō (The Founders of Five Religions). Tokyo, Yagumo shoin.

1087 SAKI, A. (1981). Shinkō Shūkyō no Keifu (Geneology of the New Religions). Tokyo, Shiraiwa Shoten.

1088 SAKURAI, Y. (1955). The Basic Teachings of Ōmoto. Kameoka, The Ōmoto Headquarters.

1089 SAKURAI, T. (1973). Minkan shinkō (Folk Beliefs). Shūkyōgaku jiten (Encyclopedia of Religions). Hori Ichirō and E. Oguchi. Tokyo, Tokyo daigaku shuppankai.

1090 SAKURAI, T. (1973). Nihon minkan shinkōron (The theory of Japanese Folk Beliefs). Tokyo, Kōbundō.

1091 SANADA, T. (1979). 'After Prophecy Fails: a Reappraisal of a Japanese Case.' *Japanese Journal of Religious Studies* 6(1–2): 217–237.

1092 SANIEL, J. M. (1965). The Mobilization of Traditional Values in the Modernization of Japan. *Religion and Progress in Modern Asia*. R. N. Bellah. New York, Free Press: 124–49.

1093 SASAKI, Y. (1976). Non-medical Healing in Contemporary Japan: A Psychiatric Study. *Culture-Bound Syndromes, Ethnopsychiatry and Alternative Therapies*. W. P. Lebra. Honolulu, Hawaii University Press.
Analysis of healing practices in two unidentified NRMs on Hachijo island. The author addresses the issue of why non-medical practices are increasing with modernization rather than diminishing through an examination of the efficacy of healing practices of NRMs on a psychological level.

1094 SASAKI, S. (1988). 'Shinshū and Folk Religion: Toward a Post-Modern "Shinshū Theology".' Bulletin of the Nanzan Institute for Religion and Culture 12: 13–35.

1095 SASAKI, R. (1997). On the Use of Novelty and Traditionality in the Japanese New Religions of Japan. Unpublished M.A. thesis. Department of Theology and Religious Studies. London, King's College London.

1096 SATŌ, H. (1953). Kōnkō Daijin, Kōnkō Hombu Kyocho. 1.
2 volume set

1097 SATŌ, K. (1958). *Konkōkyō, A New Religion of Japan*. Konko, General Headquarters of Konkōkyō.

1098 SCALAPINO, R. A. (1964). Ideology and Modernization – The Japanese Case. *Ideology and Discontent*. D. E. Apter. New York, The Free Press of Glencoe.

1099 SCHECTER, J. (1967). *The New Face of Buddha*. New York, Coward-McCann,Inc.

1100 SCHIFFER, W. (1954). Shinkō-Shūkyō: A Social and Religious Phenomenon in Post-War Japan (Proceedings of the Twenty-Third International Congress of Orientalists). Cambridge and London, W. Heffer and Sons.

1101 SCHIFFER, W. (1955). 'New Religions in Post-war Japan.' Monumenta Nipponica 11(1): 1–14.

1102 SCHILLER, E. (1923). 'Ōmotokyō, die neueste Religion Japans.' Zeitschrift für Missionskunde und Religionswissenschaft 38.

1103 SCHILLER, E. (1936). 'Eine neue religiöse Sekte in Japan.' Zeitschrift für Missionskunde und Religionswissenschaft 51.

1104 SCHNEIDER, D. (1961). 'Konkōkyō: A Religion of Meditation.' *Contemporary Religions in Japan* 2(1): 39–.

1105 SCHNEIDER, D. D. B. (1962). *Konkōkyō: A Japanese Religion*. Tokyo, International Institute of the Study of Religions.
This study is an attempt at an appreciation of an old faith, Shinto and a contemporary 'new' religion, Konkōkyō which has its foundation in Shinto. The 'new' is indicative of the religious expressions of the new shape which has become independent in the last decades and represent, if not in fact new religions, then a movement which goes by the name of 'New Religions'.

1106 SCHURHAMMER, G. (1923). *Shinto: The Way of the Gods in Japan. (According to the Printed and Unprinted Reports of the Japanese Jesuit Missionaries in the Sixteenth and Seventeenth Centuries.)*. Bonn.

1107 SEAT, L. (1991). 'Japan's Fastest-Growing New Religions.' *The Japan Christian Quarterly* 57(1): 12–17.

1108 Seichō-no-Ie Truth of Life. Gardena, California, Seichō-no-Ie North American Missionary Headquarters.
Monthly Magazine.

1109 Seichō-no-Ie (1937). Seimei no Jissō (The Truth of Life). Tokyo, Seichō-no-Ie.
One edition in 40 volumes.

1110 Seichō-no-Ie (1941). Shin no chikara (The True Power). Tokyo, Seichō-no-Ie.

1111 Seichō-no-Ie (1953–). Seichō-no-Ie.
Monthly Magazine.

1112 Seichō-no-Ie (1956). Enkan: Seichō-no-Ie Brasil Sōshibu Kaikan Hōdō Kinen Tokushū. São Paulo, Seichō-no-Ie Burajiru Sōshibu.

1113 Seichō-no-Ie (1986–). Lichtquelle. München, Germany, Seichō-no-Ie Lichtquelle.
Bi-monthly magazine for the German-speaking countries.

1114 Seichō-no-Ie Honbu (1980). Seichō-no-Ie gojūnenshi (Fifty Years of Seichō-no-Ie History). Tokyo, Nippon Kyōbusha.

1115 Seichō-no-Ie Latin America Dendō Honbu (1973). Seichō-no-Ie Burajiru Sōshibu Nijū-nen Shi. São Paulo, Igreja Seichō-no-Ie do Brasil.

1116 Seichō-no-Iē Brasil Sōshibu (1973). Seichō-no-Iē Brasil Sōshibu 20 nenshi (Seichō-no-Iē Brasil – História dos 20 anos). São Paulo, Seichō-no Iē Brasil Sōshibu.

1117 Seikyō Times (1972). Nichiren Shōshū and Sōka Gakkai: Modern Buddhism in Action. Tokyo, Seikyō Press.

1118 Seikyō Times (1979). The Major Writings of Nichiren Daishonin. Tokyo, Nichiren Shōshū International Center.

1119 Sekai Bukkyo Kyokai (1962). Sōka Gakkai o Shakubuku suru (Chanting Sōka Gakkai). Tokyo, Jitsugyo no Sekaisha.

1120 Sekai Kyūseikyō (1954–). *The Glory.*
Occasional Newspaper published in English.

1121 Sekai Kyūseikyō (1957). World Messianity and What it Means, Atami.

1122 Sekai Kyūseikyō Kyomubu (1954). Tengoku no Fukuin-sho (The Gospels of Heaven). Atami, Sekai Kyūseikyō to Shuppanbu.

1123 Sekiguschi Sakae (1985). Miyo! mahikari no daikiseki (Look! The Great Miracles of the True Light). Tokyo, Gendai Shorin.

1124 SERED, S. (1994). Priestess, Mother, Sacred Sister: Religions dominated by women. New York, Oxford, Oxford University Press.
A comparative look at what the author calls 'women's religions', with an innovative look at motherhood as a determinant factor in the religious role of women. The Japanese examples are the Ryūkū Islands and the Tenshō-Kotai-Jingū-Kyō.

1125 SERISAWA, K. (1959). Kyōsama (The Foundress). Tokyo, Kadokawa-shoten.

1126 SHARF, R. H. (1995). 'Sanbōkyōdan: Zen and the Way of the New Religions.' *Japanese Journal of Religious Studies* 22(3–4).
An examination of a recently founded Zen sect which has made a disproportionately strong impact in the West compared to the established Japanese Zen sects. Sharf identifies a number of characteristics which Sanbōkyōdan shares with Japanese NRMs and questions how far the division between established and New Religions is valid in Japan and how far it simply reflects an academic division of labour between Buddhologists on the one hand and sociologists, and thropologists and religious studies scholars on the other.

1127 SHELDON, C. (1960). 'Sōka Gakkai and the Nichiren Shū Sect.' *Contemporary Religions in Japan* (March (pp 55–70), June (pp 48–54)).

1128 SHELDON, G. (1986). 'State and Religion in Imperial Japan 1912–1945.' *Japanese Journal of Religious Studies* 12(2): 273–302.

1129 SHIBATA, C. (1983). 'Some Problematic Aspects of Japanese Ancestor Worship.' *Japanese Religions* 13(1): 35–48.

1130 SHIBATA, K. (1993). Daiseishu-Great and Holy Master. Tokyo, Yoko Shuppan.

1131 SHILLONY, B.-A. (1984). 'The Princess of the Dragon Palace: a New Shinto Sect is Born.' *Monumenta Nipponica* 39(2): 177–82.
A brief depiction of a Shinto sect headed by a shamaness, Fujita Himiko. The author presents the vitality of the small sect outlining its characteristics, including its various challenges to the order of Japanese society with its concentration of topics such as feminism, outcasts and Judaism.

1132 SHIMADA, K. (1988). Shūkyō shinjidai (The New Era of Religion). Tokyo, Shūkyō Jiji Kenkyūjo.

1133 SHIMADA, H. (1991). *What's Happening in Religious Organizations*. Tokyo, Kōdansha.

1134 SHIMAZONO, S. (1977). 'Kamigakari kara tasuke made: Tenrikyō no hassei josetsu (From Divine Possession to salvation: An Introduction to the origin of Tenrikyō).' Komazawa daigaku bukkyōgakubu ronshū 8.

1135 SHIMAZONO, S. (1979). 'The Living Kami Idea in the New Religions of Japan.' *Japanese Journal of Religious Studies* 6: 389–412.
Discusses how the New Religions, although often classified as Buddhist or Shinto in origin have emerged from elements of folk belief. Focusing on shamanism and the idea of a 'Parent God' and the 'living kami (god)', the historical development of Tenrikyō and Konkōkyō is discussed.

1136 SHIMAZONO, S. (1981). Shinshūkyō no Shūkyōishiki to Seiten (Religious Consciousness in New Religions and the Scriptures). Nihonjin no Shūkyō no Ayumi (Steps in Japanese Religious History). Hori, I. Tokyo, Daigaku Kyōikusha: 298–312.

1137 SHIMAZONO, S. (1981). 'Religious Influence on Japan's Modernization.' *Japanese Journal of Religious Studies* 8(3–4).

1138 SHIMAZONO, S. (1982). 'Charisma and the evolution of religious consciousness: The rise of the early New Religions of Japan.' *The Annual Review of the Social Sciences of Religion* 6(153–176).

1139 SHIMAZONO, S. (1982). 'Tenrikyō ni Okeru Kyūsaishi Shinwa (The Heilsgeschichte in Tenrikyō).' Tetsugaku Shisō Ronsō University of Tsukuba,(Department of Philosophy) 1: 17–28.

1140 SHIMAZONO, S. (1984). 'Shinshūkyō-kyōdan ni okeru taikendan no ichi: Myōchikai, Risshō Kōseikai, Tenrikyō (The Place of Testimonies in the New Religions: Myōchikai, Risshō Kōsei Kai and Tenrikyō).' Tōkyō-daigaku shūkyōgaku nenpō 2: 1–20.

1141 SHIMAZONO, S. and INOUE, N. (1985). Kaishinron saikō (A New Look at Theories of Conversion). Shūkyōgaku no susume (An exhortation to religious studies). S. Ueda and K.Yanagawa. Tokyo, Chikuma shobō.

1142 SHIMAZONO, S. (1986). The Development of Millennialistic Thought in Japan's New Religions: from Tenrikyō to Honmichi. *New Religious Movements and Rapid Social Change*. J. A. Beckford. London Beverly Hills, Sage Publications: 55–86.

This paper examines millennialistic tendencies in Tenrikyō and its offshoot, Honmichi, through a historical account of the development of these movements.

1143 SHIMAZONO, S. (1986). 'Conversion Stories and their Popularization in Japan's New Religions.' *Japanese Journal of Religious Studies* 13(2–3): 161–175.
Analyses conversion stories in NRMs looking at different time frameworks in conversion stories i.e sudden or gradual, and the factors influencing the formulation of such accounts. The author considers their possible fictional elements, and the factors that may cause them to become standardized, as well as their relationship to other kinds of traditional religious language.

1144 SHIMAZONO, S. (1986). Shūkyō-gengo to shite no taikendan: Reiyūkai kyōdan o rei toshite (Testimonies as Religious Language: The Case of Reiyūkai and its offshoots). Shōwa rokujū-nendo tokutei kenkyū-hōkoku (Report on special research projects during Shōwa 60). Tokyo, Gaikokugo Daigaku Kaigai-jijō Kenkyūsho.

1145 SHIMAZONO, S. (1987). 'Spirit-belief in New Religious Movements and Popular Culture: The Case of Japan's New Religions.' *Journal of Oriental Studies* 26(1): 90–100.
In this article Shimazono considers the dynamism of New Religious movements and their belief in spirits within the setting of the modern urban society. New Religious movements are viewed as 'popular' religion and Shimazono discusses the rise of Japanese new religions and the stress placed on the 'spirit world' from the perspective of the preservation and revival of popular culture in Japan.

1146 SHIMAZONO, S. (1988). Shinshūkyō no taikenshugi: Shoki reiyūkai no bai. Minshū to shakai: Bukkyō to Nihonjin 10. S. Murakami. Tokyo, Shunjūsha.

1147 SHIMAZONO, S. (1991). 'The Expansion of Japan's New Religions into Foreign Cultures.' *Japanese Journal of Religious Studies* 18(2–3): 105–32.
Looks at the history and present state of expansion of Japanese NRMs in Brazil, the US and Asia, discussing also the specific conditions in the host countries that made different aspects of these NRMs appealing.

1148 SHIMAZONO, S. (1992). Gendai kyūsai shūkyōron (Salvation and Virtue: Credal Structure of Shūyōdan-hōseikai). Tokyo, Seikyūsha.

1149 SHIMAZONO, S. (1992). Shin Shinshūkyō to shūkyō būmu (New, New Religions and Religious Boom). Tokyo, Iwanamishoten.

1150 SHIMAZONO, S. (1992). Sukui to toku: Shinshūkyō shinkōsha no seikatsu to shisō (Salvation and Virtue: The Life and Thought of Believers in a New Religious Movement). Tokyo, Kōbundō.

1151 SHIMAZONO, S. (1992). 'Shin Shūkyō no Taishu Jiritsu Shiso to Kenishugi (Thoughts on Self – Reliance for the Public and Authoritarianism of the New Religions).' Rekishi Hyoron(509).

1152 SHIMAZONO, S. (1992). Shūkyō shisō to kotoba (Religious Philosophy and terminology). Gendai Shūkyō gaku 2: Shūkyō shisō to kotoba. W. Tsunega and K. Yanagawa. Tokyo, Tokyo daigaku shuppankai.

1153 SHIMAZONO, S. (1992). 'Seikatsuchi to kindai shūkyō undō: Makiguchi Tsunesaburo no kyōiku shisō to shinkō (Knowledge of Life and Modern Religious Movements: Makiguchi Tsunesaburo's Thoughts and Beliefs on Education).' Shūkyō to shakaijinrugaku(December).

1154 SHIMAZONO, S. (1992). Gendai Kyūsai Shūkyōron (The Study of Contemporary Salvationist Religions). Tokyo, Seikyūsha.

1155 SHIMAZONO, S. (1993). "Mind Rectification' and Language: A Study of the Function of Puns in a New Religion (Kokoro naoshi to kotoba: shinshūkyō ni okeru goro aware no kinō o megutte).' Ibunka Communication Kekyu 6.

1156 SHIMAZONO, S. (1993). Shinshūkyō to haisen senryō: Shūyōdan boku shinkai no baai (New Religions, Defeat and Occupation: The Case of Shūyōdan Bokushinkai). Senryō to Nihon Shūkyō (The Occupation and Japanese Religion). F. Ikado.

1157 SHIMAZONO, S. (1993). Shinshūkyō to Shinto: Kosumo meito to kofuku no Kagaku (New new religions and Shinto: Cosmo mate and Kōfuku-no-Kagaku). Shinto o shiru hon (Get to Know Shinto): 150–154.

1158 SHIMAZONO, S. (1994). Kami to hotoke o koete – Seichō-no-Ie no kyūsai shisō no seisei. Hotoke to kami. Tokyo, Iwanami shoten.

1159 SHIMAZONO, S. (1994). Minshū shūkyō ka, shinshūkyō ka: futatsu no tachiba no tōgō ni mukete (Folk Religion or New Religion? Towards an integration of two standpoints). Hotoke to kami (Buddha and Kami). R. Yasue.

1160 SHIMAZONO, S. (1995). 'New New Religions and This World: Religious Movements in Japan after the 1970s and their Beliefs About Salvation.' *Social Compass* 42(2): 193–206.
Shimazono characterizes beliefs on salvation as presented in two 'new, new' religions in Japan: the God Light Association (GLA) and Kōfuku-no-Kagaku (IRH).

1161 SHIMAZONO, S. (1995). 'In the Wake of Aum: The Formation and Transformation of a Universe of Belief.' *Japanese Journal of Religious Studies* 22(3–4): 381–415.
This paper seeks to situate Aum in the wider context of Japanese religious belief and practice, and to examine the reason for Aum's appeal and the factors contributing to its increasingly isolated and destructive orientation.

1162 SHIMAZONO, S. (1995). Aum Shinrikyō no kiseki. Tokyo, Iwananmi Shoten.
Condensed version in English translation reproduced in Japanese Journal of Religious Studies Vol. 22 No. 3–4, 1995.

1163 SHIMAZONO, S. (1995). 'Aum shinrikyō no shinkō sekai (The World of Belief of Aum Shinrikyō).' Hermes 56 (July 10th).

1164 SHIMAZONO, S. (1996). Aspects of the Rebirth of Religion. *Religion in Japanese Culture*. N. Tamaru and D. Reid. Tokyo, Kōdansha: 171–183.

1165 SHIMAZONO, S. (1996). Seishin Sekai no Yukue (New Spirituality Movements in Global Society). Tokyo, Tokyodo.

1166 SHIMAZONO, S. and K. ISHII, Eds. (1996). Shōhi sareru Shūkyō (Religions as Consumer Products). Tokyo, Shunjūsha.

1167 SHIMAZONO, S. (1997). Gendai shūkyo no kanōsei:Aum Shinrikyō to bōryoku (Possibilities in contemporary religion: Aum Shinrikyō and Violence). Tokyo, Iwanami Shoten.

1168 SHIMIZU, M. (1973). Shinkō Shūkyō (New Religions). Kindai tono Kaiko (Encounter with Modern Times). Tamaru, N. Tokyo, Kōsei Shuppansha. III: 179–236.

1169 SHIMIZU, M., Ed. (1978–9). Shinshūkyō no Sekai (The World of the New Religions). Tokyo, Daizō Shuppan.

1170 SHIMIZU, M. (1979). Shinshūkyō no Keifu (The Geneology of the New Religions). Shinshūkyō no Sekai (The World of the New Religions). M. Shimizu. Tokyo, Daizō Shuppan. I: 6–44.

1171 SHIMIZU, M. (1986). Seikimatsu no Shūkyō (Religion of the End of Century). Tokyo, Ryōhoku Shuppan.

1172 SHINBO, K. (1992). Religious Conversion and Social Integration: Japan's New Religious Movement in Australia. Department of Japanese Studies. Victoria, Australia, Monash University.

1173 Shinnyoen What is Shinnyoen?, Shinnyoen.

1174 Shinnyoen Sono Michi. Honolulu, Hawaii, Shinnyo-en.

1175 Shinnyoen (1977). The Nirvana. Tachikawa, Shinnyoen.Monthly magazine in English language.

1176 Shinnyoen (1992). Pursuing the Way. Tachikawa, Shinnyoen.

1177 Shinnyoen (1994). The Resonating Harmony of Buddha's Law. Tokyo, Shinnyoen.
A book published in commemoration of the Founder's 77th Birthday.

1178 Shinshū Jonganjiha Kangakuryō (1953). Shinkō Shūkyō Kaisetsu (Introduction to New Religions). Kyoto, Hyakkaen.

1179 SHIONOYA, S. (1967). 'Tenrikyō's Future Missionary Work.' *Tenri Journal of Religion* 13.

1180 Shioya, M. (1978). Shūkyō shūdan ni okeru shinkō chiryō (Faith Healing in Religious Groups). Gendai Shūkyō e no shikaku (Perspectives on contemporary religion). Shūkyo Shakaigaku Kenkyūkai-hen. Tokyo, Yūzankaku Shuppan: 159–175.

1181 SHIRAISHI, K., Ed. (1965). Hokubei Senkyō 85 Shūnen Kinenshi (The Eighty-fifth Anniversary of Protestant Work among Japanese in North America 1877–1962), Nanka Kirisutokyō Kyōkai Renmei Shuppanbu.

1182 SHIRAMIZU, H. (1979). 'Organizational Mediums: A Case Study of Shinnyo-en.' *Japanese Journal of Religious Studies* 6(3).
After outlining the founding family and history of Shinnyoen, the author focuses on the role of mediums within the movement and the ways in which they give 'spiritual guidance' to believers.

1183 SHIVELY, D. H. (1969). Nishimura Shigeki: A Confucian view of Modernization. *Changing Japanese Attitudes Toward Modernization*. M. B. Jansen. Princeton, New Jersey, Princeton University Press.

1184 SHUPE, A. D., Jr (1973). 'Toward a structural perspective of modern religious movements.' *Sociological Focus* 6(3): 83–99.
Criticizes the studying of movements like the Japanese New Religions as con-games or cargo-cults.

1185 SHUPE, A. D. (1986). Militancy and Accomodation in the Third Civilization: The Case of Japan's Sōka Gakkai Movement. *Prophetic Religion and Politics (Religion and the Political Order, Volume One)*. J. K. Hadden and A. D. Shupe. New York, Paragon: 235–253.

1186 SHUPE, A. (1991). Globalization versus Religious Nativism: Japan's Sōka Gakkai in the World Arena. Religion and Global Order. R. Robertson and W. R. Garrett. New York, Paragon House: 183–99.

1187 Shūkan Bunshun Magazine (1991). Ōkawa Ryūhō, Furaidē mondai ni 'kotaeru' (Ryūhō Ōkawa answers the 'issues' of Friday). Shūkan Bunshun: 34–39.

1188 Shūkan Bunshun Magazine (1991), Asahara Shōkō, Kageyama Tamio ra ga sanka shite Aum Shinrikyō to Kōfuku no Kagaku ga asa made gekiron (The Heated discussion between Kageyama Tamio (IRH) and Asahara Shōkō (Aum Shinrikyō). Shūkan Bunshun.

1189 SIEVERS, S. L. (1983). Flowers in Salt: The Beginnings of Feminist Consciousness in Modern Japan. Stanford, California, Stanford University Press.
This book analyses the development of feminist consciousness during the Meiji era (1868–1912).

1190 SKELTON, T. L. (1968). Social Movements and Social Change: The Sōka Gakkai of Japan. PhD. Berkeley, University of California at Berkeley.

1191 SMITH, R. J., J. B. Cornell, et al., Eds. (1967). *The Japanese and their Descendants in Brazil: An Annotated Bibliography*. São Paulo, Centro de Estudos Nipo-Brasileiros.

1192 SMITH, R. J. (1970). Acculturation and Assimilation of Urban Japanese in Southern Brazil. Proceedings of the VIIIth International Congress of Anthropological and Ethnological Sciences, Tokyo, Science Council of Japan.

1193 SMITH, R. J. (1970). Buddhism among the Japanese in Southern Brazil. 69th Annual Meeting of the American Anthropological Association, San Diego, California.

1194 SMITH, R. J. (1974). *Ancestor Worship in Contemporary Japan*. Stanford, California, Stanford University Press.
This study includes a historical introduction, a general description of the world of deities and spirits, anthropological descriptions of the rites, sociological data and a psychological picture of the various approaches to the ancestors. A wide variety of material is used in this study and hard quantitative data.

1195 SMITH, R. (1974). Who are the 'Ancestors' in Japan? *Ancestors*. W. H. Newell. Hague, Mouton: 33–59.

1196 SMITH, R. J. (1979). 'The Ethnic Japanese in Brazil.' *Journal of Japanese Studies* 5(1).

1197 SMITH, B. (1988). 'Buddhism and Abortion in Contemporary Japan: Mizuko kuyō and the Confrontation with Death.' *Japanese Journal of Religious Studies* 15(1): 3–24.

1198 SMITH, R., J. (1993). *Japanese Society*. Cambridge, Cambridge University Press.
This is a 'compelling and convincing analysis of contemporary Japanese society.'

1199 SMYERS, S. (1983). 'Women and Shinto: The Relation Between Purity and Pollution.' *Japanese Religions* 12(4).
Smyers examines notions of purity and pollution and also taboos in Shintoism. He endeavours to explain the difference between woman as a 'pollutant' in Shinto and in Buddhism.

1200 SNOW, D. A. (1976). The Nichiren Shōshū Buddhist Movement in America: A Sociological Examination of Its Value Orientation, Recruitment Efforts and Spread. PhD. Los Angeles, University of California.
This Ph.D is based on participant observation and content analysis of movement literature and focuses on recruitment and changes in strategy over time.

1201 SNOW, D. A. (1979). 'A Dramaturgical Analysis of Movement Accomodation: Building Idiosyncrasy Credit as a Movement Mobilization Strategy.' Symbolic Interaction 2(2): 23–44.

1202 SNOW, D. A. (1987). Organization, Ideology and Mobilization: The Case of Nichiren Shōshū of America. *The Future of New Religious Movements*. D. G. Bromley and P. E. Hammond. Macon, Mercer University Press: 153–72.

1203 SNOW, D. (1993). Shakubuku: A Study of the Nichiren Shōshū Buddhist Movement in America, 1960–1975. New York, Garland Publishing.

1204 Sociedade Brasileira de Cultura Japonesa, Ed. (1992). Uma Epopéia Moderna (80 Anos da Imigração Japonesa no Brasil). São Paulo, Dados Internacionais de Catalogação na Publicação.

1205 SOFUE, T. (1981). 'The Psychological Characteristics of the Japanese: An Anthropological Viewpoint.' *Japan Foundation Newsletter*.
Very interesting material on Japanese psychological characteristics which have a bearing on why the Japanese may develop and sustain new religious movements.

1206 Sōka Gakkai (1957). Doctrines of Nichiren Shōshū. Tokyo, Sōka Gakkai.

1207 Sōka Gakkai (1960). The Sōka Gakkai. Tokyo, Sōka Gakkai.

1208 Sōka Gakkai (1960). 'Sōka Gakkai and the Nichiren Shō Sect.' *Contemporary Religions in Japan* 1(1 and 2).

1209 Sōka Gakkai (1966). The Nichiren Shōshū Sōka Gakkai. Tokyo, Sōka Gakkai.

1210 Sōka Gakkai (1979). The Liturgy of Nichiren Shōshū. Tokyo, Nichiren Shōshū Temple.

1211 Sōka Gakkai (1983). Sōka Gakkai. Tokyo, Sōka Gakkai.

1212 Sōka Gakkai (1995–). SGI Quarterly, Sōka Gakkai International.
Replaced the monthly edition of Sōka Gakkai News from June 1995.

1213 Sōka Gakkai International SGI Magazine-UK Express. Taplow Court, Bucks., SGI-UK.
Quarterly Magazine.

1214 Sōka Gakkai International SGI Magazine. Tokyo, Sōka Gakkai International.
Quarterly Magazine.

1215 Sōka Gakkai International (1995). Sōka Gakkai News. Tokyo, SGI Public Relations Bureau.
Monthly News Update replaced by SGI Quarterly in June 1995.

1216 Sōka Gakkai International (1989). Works of Daisaku Ikeda. Tokyo, Sōka Gakkai International.
A catalogue showing the published volumes of Daisaku Ikeda.

1217 Sōka Gakkai International (1991). Issues between the Nichiren Shōshū Priesthood and the Sōka Gakkai (5 Volumes). Tokyo, Sōka Gakkai International.

1218 Sōka Gakkai Overseas Bureau (1965 (approx)). 'This Is the Sōka Gakkai' Series No. 2: No Boundary in True Religion, Sōka Gakkai.

1219 Sōka Gakkai Overseas Bureau (1965 (approx)). 'This Is the Sōka Gakkai' Series No. 3: Sōka Gakkai and Culture Movement, Sōka Gakkai.

1220 Sōka Gakkai Overseas Bureau (1965 (approx)). 'This Is the Sōka Gakkai' Series No. 4: Practices of Believers, Sōka Gakkai.

1221 Sōka Gakkai Overseas Bureau (1965 (approx)). 'This Is the Sōka Gakkai' Series No. 5: Head Temple Taisekiji, Sōka Gakkai.

1222 Sōka Gakkai Overseas Bureau (1965 (approx)). 'This Is the Sōka Gakkai' Series No. 6: Sōka Gakkai and Kōmeitō, Sōka Gakkai.

1223 Sōka Gakkai Overseas Bureau (1965 (approx)). 'This Is the Sōka Gakkai' Series No. 7: The Buddhist Dictionary, Sōka Gakkai.

1224 Sōka Gakkai Overseas Bureau (1965 (approx)). 'This Is the Sōka Gakkai' Series No. 8: What is Shakubuku?, Sōka Gakkai.

1225 Sōka Gakkai Women's Division (1986). Women against War: Personal Accounts of Forty Japanese Women. Tokyo and New York, Kōdansha International.

1226 SOLOMON, T. J. (1977). 'The Response of Three New Religions to the Crisis in the Japanese Value System.' Journal of the Scientific Study of Religion 16(1): 1–14.

1227 SOMERS, J. (1991). 'Japanese Buddhism in Britain.' Religion Today 6(1): 1–4.

1228 SOMERS, J. (1994). Japanese New Religious Movements in Britain. *Japanese New Religions in the West*. P. B. Clarke and J. Somers. Folkestone, Kent, Japan Library: 54–76.

1229 SONOGASHIRA, H. (1991). Ōkawa Ryūhō wa kō yome. Shōbō kara mita 'Kōfuku no Kagaku'. Tokyo, Shōbō Shuppansha.

1230 SONOGASHIRA, H. (1991). Ōkawa Ryūhō wa Buddha de wa nai. Kōfuku-meisō e no keikoku. Tokyo, Shōbō Shuppansha.

1231 SONOGASHIRA, H. (1991). 'Zoku "Ōkawa Ryūhō" wa kō yome. Shōbō kara mita.' Taiyō no hō.

1232 SPAE, J. J. (1955). 'Konkōkyō.' *Missionary Bulletin* 9(8–9).

1233 SPAE, J. J. (1956). 'Ōmotokyō.' *Missionary Bulletin* 10(9).

1234 SPAE, J. J. (1956). 'Seichō-no-Ie.' *Japan Missionary Bulletin* 10(10).

1235 SPAE, J. J. (1958). 'PL Kyōdan: The Perfect Liberty Order.' *Japan Missionary Bulletin* 12(8/ October).

1236 SPAE, J. J. (1958). 'Tenshō Kōtai Jingū Kyō.' *Japan Missionary Bulletin* July.

1237 SPAE, J. J. (1958). 'Odorikyo: The Dancing Religion.' *Japan Missionary Bulletin* 12(6).

1238 SPAE, J. J. (1958). 'Dotoku Kagaku: Moralogy.' *Japan Missionary Bulletin* 12(10).

1239 SPAE, J. J. (1959). 'Sekai Kyūseikyō or Sekai Meshiya-kyō: World Messianity.' *Japan Missionary Bulletin* 13(4): 238–244.

1240 SPAE, J. J. (1959). 'Tenchi Kodo Zenrinkai.' *Japan Missionary Bulletin* 13(8).

1241 SPAE, J. J. (1960). 'Ananaikyo: The Universal Religion.' *Japan Missionary Bulletin* 14(1).

1242 SPAE, J. J. (1960). 'Risshō Kōsei Kai.' *Japan Missionary Bulletin* 14(5).

1243 SPAE, J. J. (1960). 'Reiyūkai.' *The Japan Missionary Bulletin* 14(10).

1244 SPAE, J. J. (1966). 'Popular Buddhist Ethics: Risshō Kōsei Kai.' *Japan Missionary Bulletin* 20.

1245 SPICKARD, J. V. (1977). Shamanistic Renewal in Two Changing Cultures: Sekai Kyūseikyō in Japan and America, Center for the Study of New Religious Movements.

1246 SPICKARD, J. V. (1991). Spiritual Healing Among the Followers of a Japanese New Religion: Experience as a factor in religious motivation. *Research in the Social Scientific Study of Religion*. M. L. Lynn and D. O. Moberg. Greenwich, Connecticut, JAI Press. 3: 135–156.
Based on ethnographic research at Sekai Kyūseikyō's San Francisco mission this study discusses how the experience of 'johrei', a form of spiritual healing attracts members to the movements.

1247 SPICKARD, J. (1995). Body, Nature and Culture in Spiritual Healing. *Studies in Alternative Therapy 2: Body and Nature*. H. Johannessen, S.

Olesen and J. Andersen. Gylling, Denmark, INRAT and Odense University Press: 65–81.
Examines the role of cultural background in the assimilation and reinterpretation of a Japanese NRM in the United States through a case study of the different conceptions of 'johrei' held by three distinct cultural sub-groups within the North American branch of Sekai Kyūseikyō.

1248 SPIER, F. (1986). 'Introducing Agon-shū.' Japanese Religions 14(2): 46–70.
An introductory presentation of Agonshū, discussing the movement's history and leader and detailing its main beliefs and practices.

1249 SPILLUM, L. (1997). Religious Persecution within the Conceptual Framework of State Control. Unpublished M.A. thesis. Department of Theology and Religious Studies. London, King's College London.

1250 STARK, R. (1987). How New Religions Succeed: A Theoretical Model. The Future of New Religious Movements. D. G. Bromley and P. E. Hammond. Macon, Georgia, Mercer University Press.

1251 Stoesz, W. (1986). 'The Universal Attitude of Kōnkō Daijin (Life and Thought of Kawate Bunjirō, Founder of the Konkōkyō; Bibliography).' *Japanese Journal of Religious Studies* 13(1).

1252 STOESZ, W., Ed. (1989). *Kurozumi Shinto: An American Dialogue.* Pennsylvania, Anima Books.
The book contains several essays on Kurozumikyō by scholars such as H. Byron Earhart and Helen Hardacre and also essays by 'insiders' like the Reverend Muneharu Kurozumi.

1253 STOETZEL, J. (1955). *Without the Chrysanthemum and the Sword. A Study of the Attitudes of Youth in Post-War Japan.* London & Paris, William Heinemann.
The book is the outcome of a decision by UNESCO in 1951 to send a French sociologist and a Dutch expert on Japanese civilization to Japan to collect material for a report on the attitudes of Japanese youth.

1254 STONE, J. (1991). 'Re-examining Stereotypes in the Study of Nichiren: Nationalism, Intolerance, and Independence from Tendai.' Supplement to May 1991 Issue of the *Japanese Religions Bulletin.*

1255 STONE, J. (1993). 'Review of Snow 1993 and Hurst 1992.' *Japanese Journal of Religious Studies* 20: 351–59.
A comparison of two books on Sōka Gakkai in America published almost simultaneously and covering a similar period of fieldwork.

1256 STRAELEN, H. v. (1962). 'The Japanese New Religions.' *Numen* 9: 228–40.

1257 STRAELEN, H. V. (1964). 'The Japanese New Religions Are Not New.' *Neue Zeitschrift für Missionswissenschaft* 20: 263–70.

1258 STROUPE, B. (1971). 'Healing in the History of Tenrikyō, the Religion of Divine Wisdom.' *Tenri Journal of Religion* 17: 79–.
Outlines the history of Tenrikyō and the context within which it arose, and examines Tenrikyō notions of disease and healing and the significance of healing in the Tenrikyō world view.

1259 SUBHUTI, D. A. K. (1983). *Buddhism for Today*. Salisbury, Wiltshire, Element Books.
This book is an introduction to the practice of Buddhism in the West as well as a survey of the Friends of the Western Buddhist Order.

1260 SUGAI, T. (1969). 'The Soteriology of New Religions.' *Japanese Religions* 6(2): 23–46.

1261 SUGAI, T. (1971). 'Statistics of Japanese Religions.' *Japanese Christian Quarterly* 37(1): 20–22.

1262 SUGIHARA, Y. and PATH D. W. (1969). Sensei and His People: The Builders of a Japanese Commune. Berkeley, University of California Press.

1263 SUGIMORI, K. (1976). Kenkyū: Sōka Gakkai (A Study: Sōka Gakkai). Tokyo, Jiyūsha.

1264 Sūkyō Mahikari *Sūkyō Mahikari*. Tokyo, Yōkō Shuppan Co. Ltd.

1265 Sūkyō Mahikari (n.d). The Light of Love. Tokyo, Yōkō Shuppan Co. Ltd.

1266 SULLIVAN, L. E. (1988). *Icanchu's Drum: An Orientation to Meaning in South American Religions*. New York, Macmillan.

1267 SUTHERLAND, S. R. and CLARKE, P. B. Eds. (1991). *The Study of Religion, Traditional and New Religions*. London, Routledge.

1268 SUZUKI, P. D. T. (1938). *Japanese Buddhism*. Kyoto, Board of Tourist Industry, Japanese Government Railways.

1269 SUZUKI, S. (1956). 'Gendai Nihon Chūkan Shimin-sō no Shūkyō-Seichō-no-Ie no Shūkyō Shakaigakuteki Kōsatsu (Religion of the Contemporary Japanese Middle Class: A Sociological Analysis of Seichō-no-Ie).' Ritsumeikan Bungaku 130: 181–199.

1270 SUZUKI, H. (1963). 'Toshikasō no shūkyō shūdan-Fukuoka-shi ni okeru Sōka Gakkai (Urban lower-class religious groups: Sōka Gakkai in Fukuoka City).' Shakaigaku kenkyū (Journal of Sociological Studies) 22: 81–102.

1271 SUZUKI, H. (1964). 'Toshikasō no shūkyō shūdan-Fukuoka-shi ni okeru Sōka Gakkai (Urban lower-class religious groups: Sōka Gakkai in Fukuoka City).' Shakaigaku kenkyū (Journal of Sociological Studies) 24–25: 50–90.

1272 SUZUKI, D. T. (1970). *Shin Buddhism. Japan's Major Religious Contribution to the West*. New York, Harper and Row.

1273 SUZUKI, G. (1974). Te no hira ryōji (The Laying-On-Of-Hands Treatment). Tokyo.

1274 SUZUKI, H. (1982). Goseigen: The Holy Words. Tujunga, California, Mahikari.

1275 SUZUKI, K. (1995). An Examination of the Cosmology and Teachings of Kofuku No Kagaku. Unpublished M.A. thesis. Department of Theology and Religious Studies. London, King's College, University of London.

1276 SUZUKI, K. (1995). 'Divination in Contemporary Japan: A General Overview and Analysis of Survey Results.' *Japanese Journal of Religious Studies* **22**(3–4).

This article discusses the main types of fortune-telling currently popular in Japan and the various areas within which it is practised. Young women are identified as the main customers of diviners and the reasons for the appeal of divination practices such as palmistry, tarot cards and Western astrology are discussed.

1277 SWANGER, E. K. (1981). 'A Preliminary Examination of the Omamori Phenomenon.' Asian Folklore Studies **40**(2): 237–252.

1278 SWEARER, D. K. (1972). 'Contemporary Japanese Religion, An Interprative Dilemma.' *Japanese Religions* **7**(4): 35–49.

Discusses the conflicting impressions of Japan as a country with a rich religious history and Japan as a modern secular society. This theme is presented under the notions of immanence/transcendence; relative/absolute; inclusive/exclusive. PL Kyōdan is briefly examined by the author.

1279 SWYNGEDOUW, J. (1978). 'Japanese Religiosity in an Age of Internationalization.' *Japanese Journal of Religious Studies* **5**(2–3): 87–106.

Discusses the changes in Japanese religiosity under the impact of internationalization, tracing the religious tradition of Japan and relating it to modern trends and 'booms'. NRMs are briefly referred to as promoters of universalistic values.

1280 SWYNGEDOUW, J. (1985). 'The Quiet Reversal: A Few Notes on the NHK Survey Of Japanese Religiosity.' *Japan Missionary Bulletin*.

1281 SWYNGEDOUW, J. (1986). Religion in Contemporary Japanese Society.

1282 TAGAMI, M. (1971). 'Tenrikyō kyōso Nakayama Miki no shiseikan (Nakayama Miki: The founder of Tenrikyō – Her view of life and death).' Shintogaku 71: 21–37.

1283 TAJIMA, T. (1996). 'A Comparable Model to Explain the Formation of Japanese Religious Consciousness.' Akenohoshikyō: 103–109.

1284 TAKAGI, H. (1954). 'Shūkyō Kyōdan no Seiritsu Katei – Tenrikyō no Baai (The Process of Formation of a Religious Organization – A Case of Tenrikyō).' Tōyō Bunka Kenkyū-jo Kiyō (Memoirs of the Institute for Oriental Culture, University of Tokyo) 6: 265–338.

1285 TAKAGI, H. (1958). Shinkō Shūkyō: Tai shū o miryō suru mono (New Religions: What Attracts People to Them). Tokyo, Million Books.

1286 TAKAGI, H. (1959). Nippon no shinkō shūkyō: Taishū shisō undō no rekishi to ronri (Japan's New Religions: The History and Logic of Movements Based on the Thought of the Masses). Tokyo, Iwanami Shinsho.

1287 TAKAGI, H. (1959). Nihon no shinkō shūkyō (Japanese New Religions). Tokyo, Iwanami shoten.

1288 TAKAGI, H. (1962). 'Sōka Gakkai Makes Advance into the Political World.' *Japan Socialist Review* (June 16th): 53.

1289 TAKAGI, H. (1964). 'The Rise of the New Religions.' *Japan Quarterly* **11**(3): 283–292.

1290 TAKAHASHI, S. (1971). Kokoro-no Hakken Shinri-hen (Discovery of the Mind-Divine Truth), Sampō Shuppan.

1291 TAKAHASHI, S. (1973). Kokoro-no Hakken Genshō-hen (Discovery of the Mind-Phenomenal Witness), Sampō Shuppan.

1292 TAKAHASHI, S. (1973). Ai-wa Nikushimi-wo Koete (Love Transcends Hatred), Sampō Shuppan.

1293 TAKAHASHI, T. (1988). 'Aperçu de la Prédication de Tenrikyō au Congo-Brazzaville.' *Studies of Worldviews* 1.

1294 TAKAHATATO, T. (1987). Young Man Shinran. Ontario, Wilfred Laurier University Press.

1295 TAKANO, Y. (1962). Tenrikyōshi sankō nenpyō (The Reference History of Tenrikyō). Tenri City, Yotokusha.

1296 TAKANO, T. (1981). The Missionary. Tenri, Japan, Tenrikyō Overseas Mission Department.

1297 TAKASHI, N. (1973). Nichirenshū no seiritsu to tenkai (The Formation and Development of Nichirenshū). Tokyo, Yoshikawa Kōbunkan.

1298 TAKASHI, M. (1983). 'Japanese Religions in Southern Brazil: Change and Syncretism.' *Latin American Studies* 5.

1299 TAKEDA, C. (1957). Sosen sūhai (Ancestor Worship). Tokyo, Heirakuji shoten.

1300 TAKEDA, C. (1959). 'Ancestor Worship in Japanese Folklore and History.' *Japan Science Review* 10.

1301 TAKEDA, C. (1965). Ancestor Worship. III. Japan. *Encyclopedia of Buddhism*. G. P. Malalsekera. Colombo, Government of Ceylon. 1: 593–600 (fasc.4).

1302 TAKEDA, C. (1971). Minzoku bukkyō to sosen shinkō (Folk buddhism and Ancestor Veneration). Tokyo, Tōdai Shuppankai.

1303 TAKEDA, C. (1974). 'Family Religion'in Japan: Ie and Its Religious Faith. *Ancestors*. W. H. Newell. The Hague, Paris, Mouton Publishers: 119–127.

1304 TAKEDA, C. (1974). Recent trends in Studies of Ancestor Worship in Japan. *Ancestors*. W. H. Newell. The Hague, Paris, Mouton Publishers: 129–138.

1305 TAKEDA, C. (1976). Nihonjin no ie to shūkyō (The Family and the Religions of the Japanese). Tokyo, Hyōronsha.

1306 TAKEDA, D. (1991). The Fall of Renmonkyō, and Its Place in the History of Meiji-Period Religions. Contemporary Papers in Japanese Religion(2). N. Inoue. Tokyo, Kokugakuin University: 25–57.

1307 TAKEDA, R. (1994). Akuma no Jabō (The Evil Desires of the Devil). Tokyo, Daiichi Kikaku Shuppan.
From leader of Sōka Gakkai to dictator of Japan: Ikeda Daisaku's leap to power through local elections. The author is a publisher and journalist.

1308 TAKEUCHI, A., S. KOBAYASHI, et al. (1968). The New Religions of Japan: A Panel Discussion. Glimpses of Social Work in Japan. D. Dessau. Tokyo, Social Workers International Club of Japan: 20–27.

1309 TAKI, T. (1956). Kamigami tabō (Gods are Very Busy). Tokyo, Shin'yūkan Shinbunsha.

1310 TAKI, Y. (1968). Mekishiko kokujō taikan-Shokumin nanajūnenshi (An Overview of the Situation in Mexico: A Seventy-year History of Immigration). Mexico City, Shinpōsha.

1311 TAMARU, N. and D. REID, Eds. (1996). Religion in Japanese Culture. Tokyo, Kōdansha.

1312 TAMASHIRO, J. G. (1985). *Konkōkyō, A Japanese Religion in Hawaii,* University of Hawaii.

1313 TANAKA, Y. (1918). Kurozumikyō no kenkyū (Research on Kurozumi-kyō). Tokyo, Tokyodō shoten.

1314 TANAKA, G. (1956). The Brief Outline of the Kurozumikyō, the Most Genuine Japanese Religious Faith. Okayama, Ōmoto.

1315 TANAKA, K. (1982). Dust and Innen (Dust and Fate). Tenri, Tenrikyō Overseas Mission Department.

1316 TANAKA, M. (1986). The Myth of Perfect Motherhood: Japanese Women's Dilemma. Speaking of Faith. *Cross-Cultural Perspectives on Women, Religion and Social Change.* D. L. Eck and D. Jain. New Delhi, Kali for Women.

Although treated unequally, even poorly in the public sphere, Japanese women enjoy a high moral standing within the household. The author considers that this is connected to how women are perceived as a link to the past and future of the family as life-giver and sole care-giver. However, she concludes that real liberation will not be achieved unless Japanese women are willing to relinquish the privileged security of the mother/wife idol and to develop new contexts for defining self.

1317 TANAKA, I. (1986). Shinkō Shūkyō: Kanemōke to Kenryoku Arasoi no Jittai (The Newly Arisen Religions: The Realities of Money-Making and Power Struggle). Tokyo, Seinen Shokan.

1318 TANI, F. (1987). Shinpi kara shūkyō e (From Mystery to Religion). Gendai no kokoro: Sūkyō Mahikari (The Contemporary Mind: Sūkyō Mahikari). S. Hatakenaka. Tokyo, ōbūndo.

1319 TANIGAME, R., Ed. (1985). Nichiren to hokkekyō shinkō (Nichiren and Hokkekyō Belief). Tokyo, Yomiuri Shinbunsha.

1320 TANIGUCHI, M. (1935). Divine Education and Spiritual Training of Mankind. Tokyo, Seichō-no-Ie.

1321 TANIGUCHI, M. (1935). The Power of Faith. Tokyo, Seichō-no-Ie.

1322 TANIGUCHI, M. (1954). Shinri (The Truth). Tokyo, Nihon Kyōbunsha.

1323 TANIGUCHI, M. (1954). Josei no Riso (The Ideal of a Woman). Tokyo, Nippon Kyōbunsha.

Modern and traditional women are presented in contrast and the exaggerations of both tendencies are showed. The founder of Seichō-no-Ie and his wife present a new type of woman, equal to but not identical to man, proud of her nurturing role as wife and mother.

1324 TANIGUCHI, M. (1955). Shinyu e no Michi (The Road to Healing by God). Tokyo, Nihon Kyōbunsha.

1325 TANIGUCHI, M. (1957). Shinjosei Dokuhon (Reading Book for the New Woman). Tokyo, Nippon Kyōbunsha.

Advice to women about how they can surmount difficulties in their family life by being truly grateful and genuinely concerned about others as human beings in their own right rather than as appendages to one's self. Improvement through self-improvement.

1326 TANIGUCHI, M. (1958). Iesu wa jujika no kakarazu (Jesus Was Not Hanged On The Cross). Tokyo, Seichō-no-Ie.

1327 TANIGUCHI, M. (1959). Seimei no Jissō (The Truth of Life). Tokyo, Nihon Kyōbunsha.

The fundamental books of Seichō-no-Ie, in 40 volumes and translated into many languages.

1328 TANIGUCHI, M. (1961). *You Can Heal Yourself: Conquest of Diseases-Cancers, Atomic Diseases through Spitritual Teachings.* Tokyo, Seichō-no-Ie Foundation, Divine Publications Dept.

1329 TANIGUCHI, M. (1961). Onna Ikiru Igi (The Meaning of Being a Woman). Tokyo, Nippon Kyōbunsha.

Another manual for wives and mothers, filled with examples from the everyday life of Seichō-no-Ie followers. Includes discussions of family quarrels, separation and divorce, drinking problems etc.

1330 TANIGUCHI, M. (1962). *Book of Daily Life* (Truth of Life Series). Gardena, California, Seichō-no-Ie, Inc. 7.

1331 TANIGUCHI, S. (1968). 'Bakumatsu ni okeru Kurozumikyō ni tsuite no ichikōsatsu (Kurozumikyō at the Last Days of the Tokugawa Government).' Okayama daigaku kyōikubu kenkyū (6 (March)): 65–81.

1332 TANIGUCHI, M. (1979). Book of Jissō – The Light of Truth (Truth of Life Series). Gardena, California, Seichō-no-Ie Inc. 2.

1333 TANIGUCHI, M. (1983). Erziehung zum Göttlichen (Divine Education and Spiritual Training of Mankind). Heimen, Germany.

1334 TANIGUCHI, M. (1983). Yamato no Kuni Nippon. Tokyo, Nihon Kyōbunsha.

1335 TANIGUCHI, S. (1992). Meditação shinsokan é maravilhosa. São Paulo, Seichō-no-Ie do Brasil.

1336 TANIGUCHI, M. (1993). O que é a Seichō-no-Ie: votos e aprimoramento espiritual dos adeptos da Seichō-no-Ie. São Paulo, Seichō-no-Iē do Brasil.

1337 TATSUKI, Y. (1960). 'PL (Perfect Liberty).' *Contemporary Religions in Japan* 1(3): 20–.

1338 TEBECIS, A. (1977). 'On How Little Is Known About Altered States of Consciousness.' *Japanese Journal of Psychosomatic Medicine* **17**: 256–263.

1339 TEBECIS, A. (1978). Suggestions for Awakened Doctors to the Importance of Mahikari. First International Congress on Spirit-Mind Medical Science, Tokyo.

1340 TEBECIS, A. K. (1982). Mahikari. Thank God for the Answers at Last. Tokyo, Yōkō Shuppan.

1341 TEBECIS, A. (1988). Sagashi motomete kotae wa kokoni: Mahikari. Dickson, A.C.T, Sunrise Press, Dai 5-han nihongoban.

1342 Tenrikyō Tenrikyō Yearbook. Tenri City, Japan, Tenrikyō Headquarters. *Yearly Handbook*

1343 Tenrikyō Tenrikyō Newsletter. Los Angeles, California, Tenrikyō.

1344 Tenrikyō (1952). Tenrikyō gentenshū (The Original Teachings of Tenrikyō). Tenri.

1345 Tenrikyō (1982). The Life of Oyasama, Foundress of Tenrikyō. Tenri, Japan, Tenrikyō Church Headquarters.

1346 Tenrikyō Overseas Mission Department (1978). An Introduction to Tenrikyō and its Teachings. Tenri, Japan, Tenri Jihōsha. *A collection of essays by members and a few foreign scholars.*

1347 Tenrikyō (1930). Tenrikyō. Tambaichi, Dōyūsha.

1348 Tenrikyō (1952). Scriptures of Tenrikyō, Tenri.

1349 Tenrikyō (1958). Oyasato, Guide to Tenrikyō, Tenri.

1350 Tenrikyō (1960). Tenrikyō Kyōkai Honbu (A Short History of Tenrikyō), Tenrikyō.

1351 Tenrikyō (1966). Tenrikyō, Its History and Teachings. Tenri, Japan, Tenrikyō Overseas Mission Department.

1352 Tenrikyō (1985). The Doctrine of Tenrikyō, Tenrikyō Church Headquarters.

1353 Tenrikyō Kyōkai Honbu (1949). Tenrikyō Kyoten (The Canon of Tenrikyō). Tenri, Dōyūsha.

1354 Tenrikyō Kyōkai Hombu (1951). Ofudesaki Sakuin (The Index of Ofudesaki). Tenri, Dōyūsha.

1355 Tenrikyō Kyōkai Hombu (1952). Oyasama no Omokage (The Reminder of Oyasama). Tenri, Dōyūsha.

1356 Tenrikyō Kyōkai Hombu (1955). Tenrikyō Yōran (The Outline of Tenrikyō). Tenri, Dōyūsha.

1357 Tenrikyō Kyōkai Hombu (n.d). Tenrikyō Getenshū (Original Texts of Tenrikyō).

1358 Tenrikyō Kyōkai Honbu (1956). Tenrikyō kyōsoden (The biography of the founder of Tenrikyō). Tenri City, Tenrikyō Dōyūsha.

1359 Tenrikyōgaku Dōgakkai Tenrikyōgaku Kenkyū: Tenrikyō no Gaisetsu (Journal of Tenrikyō Studies: Outline of Tenrikyō). Tenri, Tenrikyō Dōyūsha.

1360 Tenrykyō Brasil Dendō Chō (1958). Tenry-kyō dendō shi (História da Tenry-kyō no Brasil), Tenrykyō sha.

1361 Tenrykyō Brasil Dendō Chō (1985). Tenry-kyō Brasil dendō shi (História da Tenry-kyō no Brasil), Tenrykyō sha.

1362 Tenshō Kōtai Jingū Kyō (1947). Mioshie (The Teachings). Tabuse.

1363 Tenshō Kōtai Jingū Kyō (1951). Seisho (The Unison). Tabuse.

1364 Tenshō Kōtai Jingū Kyō (1952). Mioshie, The Divine Teaching, Tabuse.

1365 Tenshō Kōtai Jingū Kyō (1953). The Paradise of Tabuse. Yamaguchi, Tenshō Kōtai Jingū Kyō.

1366 Tenshō Kōtai Jingū Kyō (1954). The Prophet of Tabuse. Yamaguchi, Tenshō Kōtai Jingū Kyō.
The biography of the founder of Tenshō Kōtai Jingu Kyō, Kitamura Sayō.

1367 Tenshō Kōtai Jingū Kyō (1954-). Tensei (The Voice from Heaven), Tenshō Kōtai Jingū Kyō.
Monthly Magazine.

1368 Tenshō Kōtai Jingū Kyō (1956). Guidance to God's Kingdom, Tabuse.

1369 Tenshō Kōtai Jingū Kyō (1963). Ogamisama Says ... Tabuse, Japan, Tenshō Kōtai Jingū Kyō.

1370 Tenshō Kōtai Jingū Kyō (1970). Divine Manifestation: Ogamisama's Life and Teaching. Tabuse, Tenshō Kōtai Jingu Kyō.

1371 The Institute for Research in Human Happiness (1994). Escallent. Tokyo, Kōfuku-no-Kagaku.
Japanese Language Magazine.

1372 The Institute for Research in Human Happiness (1994). Monthly Miracle. Tokyo, Kōfuku-no-Kagaku.
Monthly Magazine.

1373 The Institute for Research in Human Happiness (1994). What is Kōfuku-no-Kagaku? Tokyo, IRH Press Ltd.

1374 The Institute for Research in Human Happiness (1994-). The Monthly Message. Tokyo, Kōfuku-no-Kagaku.
Monthly Magazine.

1375 The Institute for Research into Human Happiness (1994-). Miracle Wind. Tokyo, Kōfuku-no-Kagaku.

1376 The Institute of Research into Human Happiness (1994). Eternal Buddha. Tokyo, IRH Press Ltd.
Japanese Publication.

1377 The Institute of Research into Human Happiness (1994). Rebirth of Buddha – Messages to His Beloved Disciples. Tokyo, IRH Press Ltd.
Japanese Publication.

1378 The Institute of Research into Human Happiness (1994). The Real Intention of Buddha. Tokyo, IRH Press Ltd.
Japanese Publication.

1379 The Institute of Research into Human Happiness (1994). Firm Stability of Mind – The Way to Overcome Difficulties Through Spirituality. Tokyo, IRH Press Ltd.
Japanese Publication.

1380 The *Japan Times*, S. R. (1995). Terror in the Heart of Tokyo: The Aum Shinrikyō Doomsday Cult. Tokyo, *Japan Times* Ltd.
This is a collection of articles that were written in The Japan Times and The Japan Times Weekly between April and July 1995.

1381 THELLE, N. R. (1984). 'Mediators and Prophets: Founders of Japan's New Religions.' *Update: A Quarterly Journal of New Religious Movements* 8(3–4).

1382 Third Civilization Third Civilization Monthly. Santa Fe, New Mexico.

1383 THOMPSON, S. I. (1968). 'Religious Conversion and Religious Zeal in an Overseas Enclave: The Case of the Japanese in Bolivia.' *Anthropological Quarterly* 41(4): 201–8.

1384 THOMSEN, H. (1959). '"Ise or Daisekiji? Sōka Gakkai".' *Japanese Religions* 1(2).

1385 THOMSEN, H. (1959). 'Ittoen, the Park of One Light.' *Japanese Religions* 1(3).

1386 THOMSEN, H. (1959). 'Japan's New Religions.' *International Review of Missions* 48(July): 283–93.

1387 THOMSEN, H. (1959). Bibliography of the New Religions. Kyoto, Christian Center for the Study of Japanese Religions.

1388 THOMSEN, H. (1959). 'Japan's New Religions.' *Japan Christian Quarterly* 25(4).

1389 THOMSEN, H. (1959). Neue Religionen. Christus Kommt nach Japan. G. Rosenkranz. Bad Salzuflen, Verlag für Missions-und Bibel-Kunde: 39–53.

1390 THOMSEN, H., Ed. (1959). A Religious Map of Japan. Kyoto, Christian Center for the Study of Japanese Religions.

1391 THOMSEN, H. (1960). 'Numerical Strength of the New Religions.' *Japanese Religions* 1(4).

1392 THOMSEN, H. (1963). *The New Religions of Japan.* Tokyo, Tuttle.
The earliest overview of the New Japanese religions. The author gives fairly detailed accounts of the history and doctrines of many of the major and some of the smaller NRM's extant at the time of writing with some translated passages from their 'scriptures'.

1393 TISDALL-YAMADA, Y. (1991). 'The Symbolic Image of Ancestors in the Church of World Messianity.' *Japanese Journal of Religious Studies* 18(2–3): 151–164.

1394 TODA, J. (1958). Shakubuku Kyōten (The Text Book for Shakubuku). Tokyo, Sōka Gakkai.

1395 TODA, J. (1960). 'Preface to Sōka Gakkai and the Nichiren Shō Sect.' Contemporary Religions of Japan (June): 48.

1396 TODA (1992). Ikeda Sōka Gakkai no Shinjitsu (The Truth about Ikeda's Sōka Gakkai). Tokyo, Nisshin Hōdō.
A denunciation of the present leader of Sōka Gakkai.

1397 TOGAWA, I. (1976). Gendai no shinkō shūkyō (New Religions of Today). Tokyo, Taiyō.

1398 TOKORO, S. (1972). Kindai shakai to Nichirenshugi (Modern society and Nichiren-ism). Nihonjin no kōdō to shisō (The Behaviour and Thought of the Japanese). Tokyo, Hyōronsha. **18**.

1399 TOKUCHIKA, M. (1965). 'Reminiscences of Religion in Postwar Japan.' *Contemporary Religions in Japan* **6**(2).

1400 TOMOJI, T. (1981). The Missionary. Tenri, Tenri Overseas Mission Department.

1401 Tosei Shuppansha (1956). Shinkō shūkyō to bukkyo (New Religion and Buddhism). Tokyo, Tosei Shuppansha.

1402 Tosei Shuppansha (1956). Shinkō Shūkyō no kaibō (The Analysis of a New Religion). Tokyo, Tosei Shuppansha.

1403 TOYNBEE, A. J. and D. IKEDA (1976). *The Toynbee-Ikeda Dialogue: Man Himself Must Choose.* Tokyo, Kōdansha International.
Toynbee and Ikeda exchanged written questions and answers and held conversations which were recorded and subsequently edited for publication, revised and approved by Toynbee before his last illness. Man's predicament is considered by these two men in all its aspects: personal and social, political and international, philosophical.

1404 TSUKAMOTO, M. (1994). Minkan shinkō to minshū shūkyō (Local and Folk Religions).

1405 TSUNETADA, M. (1984). Shinto no Sekai. Tokyo, Toki Shobo.
The World of Shintoism.

1406 TSURUFUJI, I. (1939). Kyōha Shintō no kenkyū (Research on Sect Shinto). Tokyo, Rinzan shoten.

1407 TSURUFUJI, I. (1954). Risshō Kōseikai no shinkō (The belief of Risshō Kōsei Kai). Tokyo, Kuretake Shoin.

1408 TSURUMI, S. (1963). 'A Brief History of Sōka Gakkai.' Japanese Religions **3**(3).

1409 TSUSHIMA, M. (1979). 'Shinshūkyō ni okeru seimeishugiteki kyūsai kan (The Vitalistic Concept of Salvation in Japanese New Religions).' Shisō (Thought)(665 (November)): 92–115.

1410 TSUSHIMA, M. (1988). The Relationship between Established and New Religions in Modern Japan. Conflict and Cooperation between Contemporary Religious Groups, Chuō Academic Research Institute.

1411 TSUSHIMA, M. (1991). Emperor and World Renewal in the New Religions: The Case of Shinsei Ryūjinkai. Contemporary Papers in Japanese Religion(2). N. Inoue. Tokyo, Kokukaguin University: 58–92.

1412 TWORKOV, H. (1989). *Zen in America: Profiles of Five Teachers.* San Francisco, North Point Press.

1413 TYLER, S. (1989). 'Honji Suijaku Faith.' *Japanese Journal of Religious Studies* **16**: 227–50.

1414 UCHINO, K. (1986). The Status Elevation Process of Sōtō Zen Sect Nuns in Modern Japan. Speaking of Faith. *Cross-Cultural Perspectives on Women, Religion and Social Change*. D. L. Eck and D. Jain. New Delhi, Kali for Women.
Brief survey of the low status of Buddhist nuns until the Meiji era and the gradual emergence of self-consciousness with the establishment of Sōtō Nuns' Organization in the twentieth century. It discusses the problem of succession and whether it is possible to maintain the traditional ascetic life in the present day and exclude 'unshaved' nuns or widows with children.

1415 UEDA, Y. (1955). The Outline of Tenrikyō Doctrine and its History, Tenri.

1416 UEDA, Y. (1983). The True teaching, Practice and Realization of the Way. Kyoto, Kyoto honwanji International Centre.

1417 UENO, C. (1987). 'The Position of Women in Japan Reconsidered.' *Current Anthropological Supplement: An Anthropological Profile of Japan* **28**(4).

1418 UMEHARA, M. (1975). Shinshūkyō to Sukui (The New Religions and Salvation). Sukui (Salvation). Tokyo, Kōbundo: 173–234.

1419 UMEHARA, M. (1977). Tenkeisha no Shūkyō Honmichi (The Religion of the Revealed: Honmichi). Tokyo, Kōdansha.

1420 UMEHARA, M. (1979). Shinshūkyō no Jidai (The Age of the New Religions). Tokyo, Nisshin Hōdō.

1421 Union of the New Religious Organizations in Japan, Research Office. (1965). Kodo-chi-kyo, a Strange Religion. Reminiscences of Religion in Postwar Japan. Union of the New Religious Organizations in Japan, Research Office.

1422 USARSKI, F. (1988). Die Stigmatisierung Neuer Spiritueller Bewegungen in Der Bundesrepublik Deutschland. Köln, Germany, Böhlau Verlag Köln Wien.

1423 VAN BRAGT, J. (1993). 'An uneven battle: Sōka Gakkai vs. Nichiren Shōshū.' *Bulletin of the Nanzan Institute for Religion and Culture* **17**: 15–31.
Details the breakdown that occurred between Sōka Gakkai and the Buddhist sect Nichiren Shōshū from which it originated. Focuses on passages from Sōka Gakkai's publications to depict the struggle.

1424 VAN STRAELEN, H. (1957). *The Religion of Divine Wisdom: Japan's Most Powerful Religious Movement*. Kyoto, Veritas Shoin.
A coherent study by an outsider of Tenrikyō.

1425 VARLEY, H. P. (1973). *Japanese Culture: A Short History*. London, Faber and Faber Ltd.
An interpretative cultural history tracing the development of Japanese civilization from Neolithic times to the present century highlighting the receptivity to foreign influences that Japan has always shown.

1426 VIOLINN, E. (1985). 'Eastern Meditation Groups: Why Join?' *Sociological Analysis* **46**(2): 147–156.

1427 VOS, G. D. and SOFOE T. (1984). Religion and the Family in East Asia. Osaka, National Museum of Ethnology.

1428 WADA, Y. (1978). 'Women and Her Power in the Japanese Emperor System.' Feminist Japan 1(4).
An article very much in the militant feminist style of the period, it reiterates the belief in a matriarchal origin of Japanese spirituality and politics.

1429 WALDENFELS, H. (1972). 'Moderne religiöse Bewegungen in Japan als Impulse fur eine christliche Theologie?' Verbum 13(1–2): 155–72. Annot Earhart

1430 WALEY, A. (1963). *The Secret History of the Mongols and Other Pieces*. New York, Barnes and Noble.
Contains an article first published as 'Kono Tabi: A Little Known Japanese Religion' in the Bulletin of the Society of Oriental Studies, VII (1933–1935 pp 105–9)

1431 WALLACE, A. (1956). 'Revitalization movements.' *American Anthropologist* 58: 268–281.

1432 WATANABE, U. (1950). Gendai nihon no shūkyō (Religions in Contemporary Japan). Tokyo, Daitō shuppansha.

1433 WATANABE, B. (1957). 'Modern Japanese Religions, Their Success Explained.' *Monumenta Nipponica* 13(April 7th): 153–162.

1434 WATANABE, E. (1968). 'Risshō Kōseikai: A Sociological Observation of its Members, Their Conversion and Their Activities.' *Contemporary Religions in Japan* 9(1–2): 75–151.
Watanabe presents a case study of the new religious movement Risshō Kōsei Kai which at the time celebrated its 30th anniversary. The research presents a detailed survey of RKK members, including distribution by gender, age, occupation, education and the motives, expectations, procedures and activities involved with entering RKK. Research is presented from a sociological perspective, observing how both members needs and expectations as well as RKK doctrinal concerns have developed and adapted in line with social change in postwar Japan.

1435 WATANABE, M. (1978). Shinshūkyō Jūyō ni okeru Jūyō na Tasha no Yakuwari (The Role of the Significant Other in the Acceptance of the New Religions). Hendoki no Ningen to Shūkyō. Tokyo, Miraisha: 29–70.

1436 WATANABE, G. J. and WATANABE W. J. (1989). *The Lotus Sutra in Japanese Culture*. Honolulu, University of Hawaii Press.

1437 WATANABE, M. (1990). 'Brasil ni okeru kyōrei no bunka to nikkey shukyō – São Paulo shi no Inari-kai no jirei o tōshite (Cultura espírita no Brasil e as religiões de origem japonesa – caso da Inari-kai na cidade de São Paulo) (Japanese Religion and the Culture of Possession in Brazil – Through a Case Study of Inari-kai in Saõ Paulo City).' Meiji gakuin ronsō – Shakaigaku-Shakaifukushigaku kenyu (The Meiji Gakuin Sociology and Social Welfare Review) 83(454): 1–52.

1438 WATANABE, M. and IGETA M. (1991). Healing in the New Religions: Charisma and 'Holy Water'. *Contemporary Papers in Japanese Religion* (2). N. Inoue. Tokyo, Kokugakuin University: 162–264.

1439 WATANABE, M. (1991). 'Burajiru ni okeru Risshō Kōsei Kai no tenkai to josei shinja no seikatsu shi (The Development of Risshō Kōsei Kai and the History of Women Followers in Brazil).' Sociology and Social Welfare Research 85.

1440 WATSON, B. (1996). The Lotus Sutra and the Twenty-first Century. Tokyo, Institute of Oriental Philosophy.

1441 WEEKS, J. S. (1974). Risshō Kōsei Kai: A Co-operative Buddhist Sect. Religious Ferment in Asia. R. Miller and K. S. Lawrence. Kansas, University of Kansas Press.

1442 WEISSBROD, L. (1983). 'Religion as National Identity in a Secular Society.' Review of Religious Research 24(3): 188–205.

1443 WERBLOWSKY, R. J. (1966). 'Review of "The New Religions of Japan" by Harry Thomsen.' Journal for the Scientific Study of Religion 5(2): 299–304.

1444 WERBLOWSKY, R. J. (1991). 'Mizuko Kuyō: Notulae on the Most Important "New Religion" of Japan.' Japanese Journal of Religious Studies 18(4): 295–354.

1445 WHITE, J. W. (1964). Militant Religion in Japan: The Sōka Gakkai, Princeton University.

1446 WHITE, J. W. (1966). The Sōka Gakkai in Japanese Politics, Stanford University.

1447 WHITE, J. W. (1967). 'Mass Movements and Democracy: Sōka Gakkai in Japanese Politics.' American Political Science Review 61(September): 744–50.

1448 WHITE, J. W. (1969). Mass Movement, Militant Religion and Democracy: The Sōka Gakkai in Japanese Politics, PhD. Stanford University.

1449 WHITE, J. W. (1970). The Sōka Gakkai and Mass Society. Stanford, California, Stanford University Press.
This 'classic' work is a study of Sōka Gakkai which includes an overview of the organization, context, history, organization, social composition, beliefs and political platform. It then examines the social origins psychological attributes, and political beliefs and behaviour of the Sōka Gakkai leadership and membership which leads on to a look at the 'implications of religio-political movements for Japanese society.'

1450 WILKINSON, S. L. (1975). Nichiren Shōshū Sōka Gakkai in America: An Analysis of Ultimate Concerns Between 1960 and 1965, PhD. University of Iowa.

1451 WILLIAMS, M. A. and COX, C. et al., Eds. (1992). Innovation in Religious Traditions: Essays in the Interpretation of Religious Change. Religion and Society Series 31. Berlin and New York, Mouton de Gruyter.
This collection of essays grew out of a faculty research seminar of the Comparative Religion Program at the University of Washington and covers many subjects. It offers coherent insights into religious innovation in Japan and is a useful adjunct to social science literature on this topic.

1452 WILSON, B. A. (1959). 'An Analysis of Sect Development.' American Sociological Review(February): 3.

1453 WILSON, B. A. (1963). 'Millenialism in Comparative Perspective.' *Comparative Studies in Society and History*(October): 93.

1454 WILSON, B. R. (1971). *Religious Sects: A Sociological Study.* London & New York, Weidenfield & Nicholson & McGraw-Hill.

1455 WILSON, B. (1979). 'The New Religions; Some Preliminary Considerations.' *Japanese Journal of Religious Studies* 6(1–2).

1456 WILSON, B. (1981). The Social Impact of New Religious Movements. Barrytown, New York.

1457 WILSON, B. (1982). Religion in Sociological Perspective. Oxford.

1458 WILSON, B. (1982). The New Religions: Preliminary Considerations. *New Religious Movements: A Perspective for Understanding Society.* E. Barker. New York & Toronto: 16–31.
  This article considers some of the theoretical problems posed by the study of 'New Religions' and attempts to identify some common characteristics of NRMs. He also examines the role of NRMs in society and contrasts the situation in Japan where NRMs mediate between the individual and wider society, and the West where NRMs are more centred on individual needs. Others explored include healing, the role of NRMs in social control and socialisation and the prospects for such movements of having any significant impact on society as a whole.

1459 WILSON, B. (1985). 'The Aims and Vision of Sōka Gakkai.' *Religion Today* 2(1): 7–8.

1460 WILSON, M. (1987). Rebirth and the Western Buddhist. London, Wisdom Publications.

1461 WILSON, B. (1989). 'The Westward Path of Buddhism.' *Journal of Oriental Studies* 2: 1–11.

1462 WILSON, B. (1990). *The Social Dimensions of Sectarianism. Sects and New Religious Movements in Contemporary Society.* Oxford, Clarendon Press.

1463 WILSON, B. and DOBBELAERE, K. (1994). *A Time to Chant: The Sōka Gakkai Buddhists in Britain.* Oxford, Clarendon Press/Oxford University Press.
  Evaluation of detailed questionnaires sent out to the members of the Sōka Gakkai in the U.K with special attention paid to the motivation for joining and staying in the movement.

1464 WIMBERLEY, H. H. (1967). Seichō-no-Ie: A Study of a Japanese Religion-Political Association, Cornell University.

1465 WIMBERLEY, H. H. (1969). 'Some Social Characteristics of a Seichō-no-Ie Congregation in Southern Japan.' *Journal of Asian and African Studies* 4: 186–201.

1466 WIMBERLEY, H. H. (1969). 'Self-Realization and the Ancestors: An Analysis of Two Japanese Ritual Procedures for Achieving Domestic Harmony.' *Anthropological Quarterly* 42(1): 37–51.

1467 WIMBERLEY, H. H. (1972). 'The Knights of the Golden Lotus.' *Ethnology* 11(2): 173–186.

The author examines the aims and activities of a lay group of the political wing of Seichō-no-Ie, and suggests reasons for the pervasiveness of the image of the state as a harmonious family.

1468 WOIRGARDT, R. (1995). Die Neuen Religionen Japans und ihr Sendungsbewusstein im Hinblick auf den Weltfrieden: Eine Analyse am Beispiel der Seichō-no-Ie Bewegung. Frankfurt, Peter Lang.
Based on a detailed analysis of the origin, growth and doctrines of Seichō-no-Ie, the author examines the concept of world peace and the missionary aims of the Japanese NRMs in general, establishing certain similarities of discourse and ideas.

1469 WOODARD, W. P. (1960). 'Understanding Contemporary Japanese Religions.' *Contemporary Religions in Japan* March: 78–83.

1470 WOODARD, W. P. (1960). 'What is a "New Religion".' *Contemporary Religions in Japan* **June**: 70–71.

1471 WOODARD, W. P. (1962). 'Religion in Japan in 1961: New Religions.' *Contemporary Religions in Japan* 3(1): 39–41.

1472 WOODARD, W. P. (1962). 'A Statistical Survey of Religions in Japan.' *Contemporary Religions in Japan.*
Volume 2, No. 4 (December 1961) pp 25–106
Volume 3, No. 1 (March 1962) pp 67–99
Volume 3, No. 2 (June 1962) pp 193–204
Volume 3, No. 3 (Sept 1962) pp 280–90
Volume 3, No. 4 (December 1962) pp 279–88

1473 WOODARD, W. P. (1972). *The Allied Occupation of Japan 1945–52 and Japanese Religions,* E.J.Brill.

1474 WÖHR, U. (1989). Frauen und Neue Religionen. Die Religionsgründer-innen Nakayama Miki und Deguchi Nao. (Women and New Religions. Foundresses Nakayama Miki and Deguchi Nao). Wien, Beiträge zur Japanologie/Institut für Japanologie.
A discussion of the importance a female founder may have on the ideology and aims of a religious movement. Wöhr then goes on to give two examples: the female founders of Tenrikyō and Ōmoto, two of the oldest 'new' religions.

1475 YAJIMA, T. (1985). Agonshū to Kiriyama Seiyū (Agonshū and Kiriyama Seiyu). Tokyo, Akimoto Shobo.

1476 YAKUSHI'IN, T. (1991). Ōkawa Ryūhō & Kōfuku-no-Kagaku. Kyōgi, reigen o kiru! Tokyo, Keibunsha.

1477 YAMADA, Y. (1983). Healing, conversion and ancestral Spirits: Religious Experiences among the Japanese Members of the Church of World Messianity in Los Angeles, California. Japanese Religions in California: A Report on Research Within and Without the Japanese American Community. K. Yamagawa. Tokyo.

1478 YAMADA, Y. (1984). Purifying the Living and Purifying the Dead: Narratives of the Religious Experience of Japanese-American and Caucasian Members of the Church of World Messianity. PhD. Los Angeles, California, University of North Carolina.

1479 YAMADA, Y. (1985). Religious Experiences of Members of the Church of World Messianity in California. Melbourne, Japanese Studies Centre.

1480 YAMADA, M. (1997). Shūkyō teki tagen shakai no kaishin ron: Hokutobu Brazil ni okeru Tenrikyō no Juyo to tenkai (Motives for Conversion in a Religiously Plural Society: Reception and Developments of Tenrikyō in Northeast Brazil), University of Tsukuba: 159.
This dissertation discusses the motives for conversion of Brazilians to Tenrikyō, a Japanese New Religion in what is a religiously plural society. There is also a discussion of Brazilian religiosity in the context of modernity.

1481 YAMAGUCHI, T. (1987). Shinnyoen. Tokyo, Chijinkan.

1482 YAMAMOTO, T. (1961). 'Tenrikyō and Medicine.' *Tenri Journal of Religion* 7.

1483 YAMAORI, T. (1972). 'Sōka Gakkai: A Religious Phoenix.' *Practical Anthropology* 19(4).

1484 YAMAORI, T. (1995). 'The Aum Affair and the Death of Religion in Japan.' Shokun! 27(6): 34–47.

1485 YAMASHITA, A. (1983). 'Modernization and Human Rights: The Historical Significance of the Origin and Development of Tenrikyō.' *Japanese Religions* 12(4).

1486 YAMASHITA, A. (1990). 'Tenrin-ō and Henjō-Nanshi: Two Women Founders of New Religions.' *Japanese Religions* 16(2): 1–23.
Yamashita relates the New Religions boom to the women's liberation movement and feminism in Japan by examining two shamanic women, founders of two New Religions: Nakayama Miki of Tenrikyō and Deguchi Nao of Ōmoto.

1487 YAMASHITA, A. (1997). 'Seikimatsu no mirai shūkyō-Kōfuku-no-Kagaku-ron (Kōfuku no Kagaku – A Future-Oriented "Eschatological" New Religion).' Deai 45 & 46: 66–92.

1488 YAMASHITA, A. (1998). 'The "Eschatology" of Japanese New and New New Religions:From Tenri-kyō to Kōfuku no Kagaku.' *Japanese Religions* 23(1&2): 125–142.

1489 YAMPOLSKY, P. B., Ed. (1990). *Selected Writings of Nichiren*. New York, Columbia University Press.
Nichiren (1222–1282) was a Buddhist Monk who founded Nichiren Buddhism. This book includes 'The Five Major Works', letters to his parishioners and a detailed autobiography.

1490 YANAGAWA, K. and MORIOKA, K. Eds. (1959). Hawaii Nikkei Shūkyō no Tenkai to Genkyō. Tokyo, Tokyo Daigaku Shūkyōgaku Kenkyūshitsu.

1491 YANAGAWA, K. (1968). Nihon ni okeru 'Shūkyō to kindaika-ron' no mondai (The Issue of Religion and Modernization in Japan). Nihon no kindaika no shomondai (Issues Concerning the Modernization of Japan). B. G. Rengo. 2.

1492 YANAGAWA, K. and MORIOKA, K. Eds. (1979). The Current Situation and Future Prospects for Religion Among Hawaii Japanese-Americans. Tokyo, Tōkyō Daigaku Shūkyōgaku Kenkyūshitsu.

1493 YANAGAWA, K. and MORIOKA, K. Eds. (1981). Hawai nikkeijin shakai to nikkei shukyō (Japanese-American society and Japanese-American religion in Hawaii). Tokyo, Tōkyō Daigaku Shūkyōgaku Kenkyūshitsu.

1494 YANAGAWA, K., Ed. (1983). Japanese Religions in California. Tokyo, Department of Religious Studies, University of Tokyo.

1495 YANAGAWA, K. (1983). 'Amerika ni okeru Nihon Bukkyō (Japanese Buddhism in America).' Gakushikai Kaihō 758: 20–24.

1496 YANAGISAKO, S. J. (1985). Transforming the Past. Stanford, California, Stanford University Press.
A study of tradition and kinship among Japanese Americans.

1497 YASUMARU, Y. (1977). Deguchi Nao. Tokyo, Asahi shimbunsha.

1498 YINGER, J. M. (1970). *The Scientific Study of Religion*. New York, Macmillan Co.

1499 YODER, F. R. (1937). 'Rural Missions. A Problem of Culture Inertia in Japan.' Sociology and social research 21(3): 213–216.

1500 YOKOYAMA, M. and NISHIYAMA S. (1988). 'Shin-shinshūkyō būmu: sono shōtai (The New New Religions Boom: Its Real Nature).' Chūō Kōron 103(4).

1501 YONEMOTO, K. (1991). Tōdaide no Buddha, Ōkawa Ryūhō no shinrei semināru. Imadoki no kamisama, Bessatsu Takarajima. Tokyo, JICC. 114: 208–21.

1502 YONEMOTO, K. and SHIMADA H. (1992). Ōkawa Ryūhō no reigen. Tokyo, JICC Shuppankyoku.

1503 YONEMURA, S. (1974). Dōzuku and Ancestor Worship in Japan. Ancestors. W. H. Newell. The Hague, Mouton: 177–203.

1504 YONEYAMA, M. (1978). Risshō Kōsei Kai. Shinshūkyō no Sekai (The World of the New Religions). M. Shimizu. Tokyo, Daizo Shuppan. II: 83–161.

1505 YOSHIDA, T. (1967). 'Mystical Retribution, Spirit Posession, and Social Structure in a Japanese Village.' *Ethnology* 6(3): 237–62.

1506 YOSHIDA, T. (1985). Spirit Possession and Village Conflict. *Conflict in Japan*. E. S. Krauss, T. P. Rholen and P. G. Steinhoff. Honolulu, University of Hawaii Press.

1507 YOSHIHARA, K. (1988). 'Dejiao: A Chinese Religion in Southeast Asia.' *Japanese Journal of Religious Studies* 15(2–3): 199–221.

1508 YOUNG, R. (1988). 'From Gokyō-dōgen to Bankyō-dōkon: A Study in the Self-Universalization of ōmoto.' *Japanese Journal of Religious Studies* 15(4): 263–86.
Young looks at Ōmoto's heraldry of a new age of 'shūsaika' ('interreligious cooperation') based on the historical concept of bankyō-dōkon ('all religions are derived from the same root'). The historical process through which Ōmoto 'universalised' itself is presented.

1509 YOUNG, R. (1989). 'The Little-Lad deity and the Dragon Princess: Jesus in a New World Movement.' *Monumenta Nipponica* 44(1): 31–44.

BIBLIOGRAPHY OF JAPANESE NEW RELIGIONS

A presentation of a little-known Japanese 'new, new' religion Ryuku Kazoku, which combines Shinto, Buddhist and Christian elements, founded by a charismatic female shaman, Fujita Himiko.

1510 YOUNG, R. F. (1989). '"Jesus, the "Christ", and Deguchi Onisaburō: A Study of Aadversarial Syncretism in a Japanese World-Renewal Religion".' *Japanese Religions* 15(4): 26–49.

Discusses the Japanese prototype 'world-renewal' religion Ōmoto and the syncretic function of the 'Christ' motif as formulated by the founder Deguchi Onisaburō. An historical account of Onisaburō's activities and writings along with his perception of and reference to 'Christ' and Christianity is presented.

1511 YOUNG, R. (1990). 'Magic and Morality in Modern Japanese Exorcistic Technologies. A Study of Mahikari.' *Japanese Journal of Religious Studies* 17: 29–50.

The first part of this article analyses notions of possession in Mahikari while the second part examines the expansion of Mahikari outside Japan, specifically in Africa and the Caribbean.

1512 YOUNG, R. F. (1991). 'The "Christ" of the Japanese New Religions.' *Japan Christian Quarterly* 57(1): 18–28, 44–45.

Young argues that concepts of Christianity and in particular Jesus Christ have been widely included in the Japanese New Religious movements alongside traditional, indigenous belief. This phenomenon is discussed with reference to literature and texts of various New Religions and the views and discourse from the founders of movements leading to an overview of how the Christian religion has helped shape several of Japan's New Religions.

1513 YOUNG, R. F. (1995). 'Lethal Achievements: Fragments of a Response to the Aum Shinrikyō Affair.' *Japanese Religions* 20(2): 230–245.

A personal narrative by Young discussing his direct contact as a scholar with a young student who became an Aum Shinrikyō loyalist. Through presentation of this contact, Young reflects on both Aum's early formation and beliefs, how the movement turned sour and also on the overall media handling of the Aum affair as well as implications for scholars in the field of religious studies.

1514 Youth Division of Sōka Gakkai (1982). Peace Is Our Duty: Accounts of What War Can Do To Man. R. L. Gage. Tokyo, The *Japan Times* Ltd.

A collection of eye witness accounts of the horrors of the Second World War in Japan especially concerning the effects war can have on the mind.

1515 Youth Division of Sōka Gakkai (1983). Cries For Peace: Experiences of Japanese Victims of World War II. R. L. Gage. Tokyo, The *Japan Times* Ltd.

A more immediate physical experience of war than its companion piece, this too provides a collection of eye witness accounts and condemnation of war in general.

1516 YUKAWA Y. (1956). 'Tatakarete mo biku tomo shinai-Niwano Nikkyō kaiken ki (Interview with Niwano Nikkyo "No Matter How I am Beaten, I Remain Calm").' Nippon Shūhō 422: 43–47.

1517 YUMIYAMA, T. (1995). 'Varieties of Healing in Present-Day Japan.' *Japanese Journal of Religious Studies* 22(3–4): 267–282.

Examines the growing interest in alternative healing technologies in Japan in the 1990s and compares the notions of 'healing', 'salvation', and 'cure' as found in alternative healing, New Religious movements and traditional medicine.

1518 Zenbōsha (1956). 'Risshō Kōseikai to "Yomiuri" no kettō (The Duel between Risshō Kōseikai and the "Yomiuri" newspaper).' Zenbō **42**: 58–65.

1519 ZIMMERMANN, W. (1954). Licht im Osten. Geistiges Nippon. Munich, Drei Eichen Verlag.

Japanese New Religions Summaries

This section includes 18 summaries of different Japanese New Religions along with a list of academic and denominational publications relevant to each movement. The publications listed here are also listed in the main bibliography, but repeated for ease of reference.

The following movements have been included:

Agonshū

Agon derives from the ancient India Sanskrit word *Agama* meaning 'come', conveying a sense of imparted teaching.

HISTORY

Agonshū was established in 1978 by Kiriyama Seiyū (1921–), the current *Kancho* (leader), although its roots can be said to trace back to an earlier religious group established by Kiriyama in 1954. Kiriyama was born as Tsutsumi Masao but adopted his current name in 1955 after lay ordination in the Shingon Buddhist sect. After a childhood of poverty and several business failures as an adult he spent six months in prison in 1953 for tax offences.

Following his release he attempted to commit suicide and it was during this attempt that he found a copy of the Buddhist text *Junteikannonkyō* detailing the compassions of the deity Kannon. Kiriyama believed himself to have been saved by Kannon and he established the Kannon Jikeikai ('Kannon Worshipping Movement') in 1954. Over the years he began to realize that his earlier misfortunes had been the result of karmic hindrances and in 1970 the deity Kannon was revealed to him in a dream and he was told that his karma had been finally eradicated. The deity instructed him to become a guide for others so that they may also find salvation.

Kiriyama changed the name of the organization to Agonshū in 1978 after reading the Agama Sutras and finding their 'inner truths', which he proclaimed were the essence of original Buddhism and spoken by Sakyamuni himself.

MAIN BELIEFS AND PRACTICES

Agonshū is one of the Buddhist sects, based on the Agon Sutras which are said to have been originally taught by Buddha to his disciples. The main elements in Agonshū comprise the *Shinsei-busshari* (true Buddha relic), the sacred casket where an actual fragment of bone from the Buddha and hence the Buddha spirit resides, and the three esoteric *shugyō* methods of training. The first of these is the *Jōbutsu-hō* which teaches how to acquire the ethical depth and sensitivity required for spiritual enlightenment so as to enable one to cut free from karma. The second is the *Nyoi Hōju-hō*, a secret practice performed with the *Shinsei-busshari*, which gives the ability to achieve happiness and good fortune and the insight to be cut loose from karma (rarely mastered except by Kiriyama Kancho). The third is the *Gumonji Sōmei-hō*, a high-level technique for creating genius and wisdom.

The *busshari* became the main object of worship in Agonshū, because it holds the relic of Buddha and is therefore the manifestation of Buddha himself. When Kiriyama was released from his karma and read the Agama Sutras he realized that established Buddhism was not addressing what he saw to be original Buddhism and the original Buddha. From this time, and with the publication of his central text *Henshin no genri* in 1971, Kiriyama moved towards esoteric Buddhism and claimed to have acquired the five powers of esoteric Buddhism: power of prediction, power of high levels of activity, power to change oneself and one's environment, development of great physical power and the power to realize one's and others' wishes.

Agonshū's cosmology is based on the central idea that, like the founder's experience, all of life's problems and misfortunes are the result of spiritual and karmic hindrances, often inherited from the past and from ancestors. Agonshū members are urged to develop the power of positive thinking and to strive for a happy and positive life. They are also provided with a framework for transforming the suffering of spirits of the dead into Buddhahood (*jōbutsu*), thereby liberating themselves from karmic forces. It is a cosmology based upon ideas of renewal and salvation, put into action for laypeople through the teaching of meditation and various esoteric activities. Members can obtain a smaller version of the *busshari* casket which they can pray before in their homes and by doing so release family members from ancestral hindrance. *Meitoku Kuyō* is a method of training taught by Agonshū which instructs members on how to

136

pray for one's ancestors and involves the cleansing of karmic influences. The Agama texts are used for the purposes of chanting and everyday ritual though members are not expected to read them all.

Agonshū's mission is to save the world from crisis and prevent humankind from committing self-destruction. This is based on the idea that humankind has created powerful levels of science and technology beyond its ability to control and which is causing earth pollution and environmental destruction. Agonshū believes that new social rules and ethics must be created through a core 'religion of wisdom' to bring about world peace and save the earth from moving towards destruction.

MAIN ANNUAL FESTIVALS ARE:

Star Festival	11 February
Flower Festival	8 April (Buddha's birthday)
Obon Festival	13–15 August

(*There is also a fire rite held on the first day of each month.*)

The Star Festival (*Hoshi Matsuri*) is a outdoor *goma* fire ritual on a grand scale when huge pyres of sticks, containing both personal wishes as well as prayers for the ancestors, are burnt while invocations are recited. Agonshū has attracted wide media attention in Japan through this annual festival.

PUBLICATIONS

PERIODICALS INCLUDE:

Dharma Cakra (Japanese monthly magazine for members)
Kaigai Kaihō (Monthly overseas bulletin)
Meitoku Kō News (Club newsletter for those having experienced *Meitoku Kuyō*)

PUBLICATIONS BY AGONSHŪ INCLUDE:

Kiriyama Seiyu, *Henshin no genri* (The principles of transformation), Tokyo, 1971.
Kiriyama Seiyu, *Agon mikkyo ima* (Agon esotericism now), Tokyo, 1978.
Kiriyama Seiyu, *Hito wa donna innen o motsu ka* (What sorts of karma do people have?), Agonshū, 1987.

BRANCHES AND MEMBERSHIP

There is a Kanto Head Office in Tokyo and a Kansai Head Office in Kyoto. The Kansai headquarters is the main religious centre and is near the Heian Shrine area of Kyoto. Membership in 1990 stood at 206,606.

There are the following established overseas branches, though membership is small at this stage:

Country	Branch	Members
Hawaii	Agon Mission of Hawaii	few
USA	Agonshū USA, California	150
Brazil	Agonshū Do Brasil, Sao Paulo	200–250
Taiwan	Taipei Head Office (& Takao Branch Office)	1,000

AGONSHŪ – BIBLIOGRAPHY

1 Agonshū Homa. Tokyo, Agonshu.
Sent to holders of Agonshū monthly good luck charm.

2 Agonshū Dharma Cakra. Tokyo, Agonshū.
Monthly magazine

3 Agonshū Kaigai Kaihō. Kyoto, Agonshū.
Monthly magazine aimed at people overseas.

4 Agonshū Meitoku Kuyō Experience. Tokyo, Agonshū.
A newsletter for those who have experienced Meitoku Kō.

5 Agonshū (1982). Agonshū no shiori. Tokyo, Agonshū Sōhonzan Shuppan-kyoku.
A guidebook to Agonshū.

6 Agonshū (1984). Imakoso Agonshū! Tokyo, Agonshū.

7 Agonshū (1986). Senzo kuyō (Memorial Services for the Ancestors). Tokyo, Shūkyōhōjin Agonshū Kyōgebu.

8 Agonshū (1989). The Agonshū (The Original Teachings of Lord Buddha). Tokyo, Agon Shu.
A pamphlet giving a brief outline of Agonshū teachings in English and Japanese.

9 Agonshū (1992). The Official Foundation Ceremony of the Sōhonzan Sōhonden-Shakazan Daibodaiji. The Main Temple of Agonshū Buddhism, Agonshū.

10 Agonshū (1994). Agonshū. Tokyo, Agonshū International Department.
A booklet introducing the teachings and activities of Agonshū.

11 HAYASHI, M. (1988). Learning from the Japanese New Religions, Fuller Theological Seminary, School of World Mission: 477.

Analyses the growth of 'new religions' from a missological perspective, describing their expansion through social and communicational factors detailing their world view and addressing the missological implications. There are chapters on Ōmoto, Reiyūkai, and Agonshū.

12 KIRIYAMA, S. (1971). Henshin no genri (The Principles of Transformation). Tokyo, Kadokawa Bunsho.

13 KIRIYAMA, S. (1978). Agon mikkyū ima (Agon Esotericism now!). Tokyo, Hirakawa.

14 KIRIYAMA, S. (1981). Ryūjin ga tobu-kaun o yokusuru shugojin shugorei no mochikata (The dragon god flies-the way to acquire protective deities and spirits to improve family fortunes). Tokyo, Hirakawa.

15 KIRIYAMA, S. (1987). Hito wa donna innen o motsu ka (What Types of Karma do People Have?). Tokyo, Agonshū.

16 KIRIYAMA, S. (1994). Hannya Shingyō Meisōhō (Hanya Shingyo Meditation Methods), Agonshū.

17 KIRIYAMA, S. (1995). *Aum Shinrikyō to Agonshū*. Tokyo, Agonshū Press.
The response of Kiriyama, founder of Agonshū, to the Aum Shinrikyō affair.

18 KOBAYASHI, H. (1994). *Agonshū. Shinshūkyō jidai*. M. Shimizu. Tokyo, Daizō Shuppan. **2**: 63–118.

19 MURŌ, T. (1987). *Agonshū Sekai heiwa e no michi* (Agonshū: The Road to World Peace). Tokyo, Seiunsha.

20 READER, I. (1988). 'The Rise of a Japanese "New New Religion": Themes in the Development of Agonshū.' *Japanese Journal of Religious Studies* 15(4): 235–61.
Looks at the rapid growth of Agonshū through a discussion of its highly advertised rituals and events. Discusses how Agonshū manages to combine both elements of tradition and the modern to give members a means to deal with contemporary society, while also appealing to concepts of universality. Draws comparisons with other 'new new' religions such as Mahikari Byakko Shinkōkai and Shinnyoen.

21 READER, I. (1991). *Religion in Contemporary Japan*. Basingstoke, Macmillan.
This book examines the major areas in which the Japanese participate in religious events, the role of religion in the social system and the underlying views within the Japanese religious world. It is particularly useful with regard to the developments in Agonshū.

22 READER, I. (1994). Japanese Religions. *Insight Japan*. 3: 6–9.
A summary of a few of the Japanese Old and New Religions

23 SPIER, F. (1986). 'Introducing Agonshū.' *Japanese Religions* 14(2): 46–70.
An introductory presentation of Agonshū, discussing the movement's history and leader and detailing its main beliefs and practices.

24 YAJIMA, T. (1985). *Agonshū to Kiriyama Seiyū* (Agonshū and Kiriyama Seiyu). Tokyo, Akimoto Shobō.

Byakkō Shinkō Kai

'White Light Association'

HISTORY

Byakkō Shinkō Kai was founded in 1951 by Goi Masahisa (1916–80). After devoting years of his life to rigorous spiritual training, in 1949 he is said to have reached enlightenment at which time his body was released from all karmic bonds. He then began to search for a way to alleviate human suffering. Goi prayed to God for a simple spiritual practice and was given an answer in the prayer words: 'May Peace Prevail on Earth'.

Goi believed that words and thoughts are waves vibrating at different frequencies, shaping the world, and he began a study of light wave science. The Peace Prayer, which is said to vibrate at the highest possible level, is believed to have a purifying effect on people and the planet and is dedicated to the attainment of peace, harmony and world salvation.

Following his death in 1980, Goi Masahisa's adopted daughter Saionji Masami became the spiritual leader, although it is believed that Goi still talks through her, using her as a medium. Saionji conducts lectures throughout Japan, the content of which, along with articles written by the late founder, form the basis for the monthly member's magazine.

MAIN BELIEFS AND PRACTICES

'*Byakkō* is a Japanese word meaning "white light". It is the clear and free-flowing light emitted from the deepest and highest condition of a human being. This publication is for people who wish to call forth this pure light in their daily lives, letting it create a bright future for humanity and the planet earth.' (Inside flap of *Byakkō* Magazine)

Byakkō Shinkō Kai is a religious spiritual organization centred around the main activity of praying for world peace and the central prayer of 'May Peace Prevail On Earth'. Members believe that the world is divided into the physical realm and the Divine Realm and that mankind must free itself from the karmic cycle and revitalize its intrinsic divinity. The movement is also involved with the study of cosmic wave light physics. Byakkō Shinkō Kai's fundamental concern is to spread the universal prayer for peace through the spiritual development of followers, who are urged to develop and express their divinity, harmony and true selves as the children of God.

Byakkō Shinkō Kai believes that world peace cannot be accomplished unless the whirlpool of karmic waves circulating the planet are harmonized and purified through the peace prayer and the earth is safely anchored in the fourth dimension. Because every person's energy is believed to come from one universal source, collective effort through faith can transform the physical realm into the Divine Realm and mankind will be eternally associated with God.

The Prayer for World Peace is as follows:

May peace prevail on earth
May peace be in our homes and countries
May our missions be accomplished
We thank thee, Guardian Deities
and Guardian Spirits

Illness or suffering is believed to be caused because light from the Divine Realm can be obscured or intercepted by karmic deposits in the mental realm. That is, a person can become ill because of the waves emitted from the discontented souls of ancestors or people around one. Goi believed that medical science must research into and accept the view that mental influences from outside the physical realm can cause sickness.

PUBLICATIONS

Byakkō (Quarterly in English)
Heywa (Quarterly in Japanese)

PUBLICATIONS BY THE MOVEMENT INCLUDE:

Goi Masahisa, *God and Man*, Byakkō Press, 1983.
Goi Masahisa, *The Future of Mankind*, Byakko Press, 1985.

BRANCHES AND MEMBERSHIP

The headquarters of Byakkō Shinkō Kai are in Chiba Prefecture, Japan, where there is a holy centre named *Hijirigaoka* ('holy man hill'). The organization is supported by members who contribute a yearly membership. Membership in Japan as of 1996 is around 20,000.

There is one branch at present in London. The number of members overseas, is believed to be around 1,000.

BYAKKŌ SHINKŌ KAI – BIBLIOGRAPHY

1 READER, I. (1988). 'The Rise of a Japanese "New New Religion": Themes in the Development of Agonshū.' *Japanese Journal of Religious Studies* 15(4): 235–61.
   Looks at the rapid growth of Agonshū through a discussion of its highly advertised rituals and events. Discusses how Agonshū manages to combine both elements of tradition and the modern to give members a means to deal with contemporary society, while also appealing to concepts of universality. Draws comparisons with other 'new new' religions such as Mahikari Byakkō Shinkōkai and Shinnyoen.

Honmichi

'True Path'   'Original Way'

HISTORY

H onmichi honours Nakayama Miki (1798–1887), foundress of Tenrikyō, as its own foundress, but from 1913 a new revelatory leader, Ōnishi Aijiro (1881–1958), emerged and is often viewed as the founder of Honmichi itself. When several members of his family fell ill to various afflictions Ōnishi joined Tenrikyō and came to believe they were afflicted with bad karma and that he as a believer had to work to eliminate this purpose of proselytization. On 15 August 1913 he achieved an 'ultimate state of bliss' and believed he had been possessed by the prophet and revelator Kanrodai-Sama. He claimed he had been chosen as the 'revealed one' (*tenkeisha*), the mediator of divine revelation, chosen to express God's will and to lead the Tenrikyō organization.

He expressed his revelations and was initially dismissed from Tenrikyō, but did return to the church later. However, after gradually gathering followers from Tenrikyō he left the movement in 1924 to devote himself full-time to his own religious activities. He established *Tenri Kenkyūkai* ('Tenri Study Association') in 1925 and attracted more followers, especially young military men. In 1926 he issued material denying the emperor's divinity and right to lead the nation. Ōnishi believed Japan was heading for war and disaster and that the only hope was to follow his teachings. He was arrested and sentenced to penal servitude along with many of his followers. He was released in 1935 but after issuing further material in 1938 his organization was disbanded in 1939 and he was again imprisoned until 1946.

Upon his release the group reorganized under the name Tenri Honmichi ('Original way of Heavenly Truth'), later becoming simply Honmichi. At this time he also designated his first daughter Ōnishi Aiko as *kyoshu* (teaching head) and his second son Ōnishi Masanori as *kanshu* (superintendent) and they subsequently took over the leadership when he died in 1958. When they later died in 1966 and 1971 respectively they were succeeded by Masanori's first and second sons, Motooki and Masataka. At this time a splinter group emerged under the leadership of Ōnishi's second daughter Tama who established a separate movement under the name of *Honbushin* ('True Construction'). Soon after this it was proclaimed that Masanori's sixth son Yasuhiko (1960–) was in fact the *Kanrodai-Sama* ('reborn again') and he assumed the leadership.

MAIN BELIEFS AND PRACTICES

Honmichi which derives from Tenrikyō is Shinto in origin. (Tenrikyō used to belong to the Shinto Sect Organizations but its category was transferred to 'Other Religions' in 1970). Honmichi worships a group of ten *kami* centred around the deity *Tenri Ō no Mikoto* and also follows the writings of Tenrikyō's foundress Nakayama Miki.

Honmichi emphasizes that people must be of a proper state of mind. Misfortune, sickness and personal calamities are believed to be the result of improper use of the mind that God has given. Continued efforts to 'right-mindfulness' with the help of *Kanrodai-Sama* as leader, will result in the establishment of *Kanrodaisekai* (Heaven on Earth). *Hinokishin* ('Construction of Mind') is the selfless service to express one's gratitude to God and the practice of Honmichi's teachings.

Honmichi has a tradition of systematic millennial development. It is concerned with a coming 'catastrophe', future world war and grave crisis, when people will be saved through prayer and by following the human *Kanrodai* which will usher in the coming of the divine world of the *Kanrodai*. Honmichi advocates that the construction of the *Kanrodai*, that is the construction of paradise in this world under the leadership of the reborn human *Kanrodai* with all the people globally united as one, is the purpose for which God created humankind. Disease and human suffering is seen as evil power obstructing God's benevolent powers and must be alleviated through prayer.

144

PUBLICATIONS

PUBLICATIONS BY THE MOVEMENT INCLUDE:

Kyōgi Ippan (*The Outline of the Doctrine*), by Ōnishi Aijirō, 1950.
Honmichi Kyogibu (*An Outline of Honmichi*), Honmichi, 1972.

BRANCHES AND MEMBERSHIP

Honmichi has its headquarters in Takaishi City, Osaka, where the Main Sanctuary is situated, a wooden structure of traditional Japanese design, built in 1953. There are an additional two branches and four chapters of Honmichi in Japan.

Honmichi members as of 1990 numbered 316,825.

There is one overseas branch in Los Angeles, USA, which was established in 1984.

HONMICHI – BIBLIOGRAPHY

1 SHIMAZONO, S. (1986). 'The Development of Millennialistic Thought in Japan's New Religions: from Tenrikyō to Honmichi.' *New Religious Movements and Rapid Social Change*. J. A. Beckford. London
   This paper examines millennialistic tendencies in Tenrikyō and its offshoot, Honmichi, through a historical account of the development of these movements.

2 UMEHARA, M. (1977). *Tenkeisha no Shūkyō Honmichi* (The Religion of the Revealed: Honmichi). Tokyo, Kōdansha.

Kōdō Kyōdan

A Buddhist lay order, Kōdō-Kyōdan was founded on 18 October 1936 by President Okano Shōkō (1900–78) and his wife Kimiko. Okano Shōkō had entered the priesthood at the 'Naka-In' Temple, Kawagoye, Saitama-ken, of the Tendai Sect in 1918, and then joined Reiyūkai in 1934. After studying Buddhism and the teachings of the Lotus Sutra, he went on to establish a branch organization called *Kodokai*, which was later established as an independent juridical person under the name of Kōdō Kyōdan in 1948. Okano advocated a new interpretation of the Lotus Sutra, the 'Fully Ripened Dharma of the Lotus Sutra'. He continued to hold the title of Bishop (Gon-Dai-Sojo) in the Tendai Sect while he was President of Kōdō-Kyōdan.

The second president, Okano Shokan, succeeded his father on New Years Day, 1975 and the founder died a few years later on 15 August 1978.

The next in line to succeed, the founder's grandson, Okano Shōjun, received his PhD. in the field of Sociology in Religion from St Antony's College, Oxford University, in 1991.

MAIN BELIEFS AND PRACTICES

The main scripture of Kōdō Kyōdan is the teachings of the 'Fully Ripened Dharma of the Lotus Sutra', also known as 'The Ripe Lotus Sutra, The Mature Religion'. This is concerned with the opening and revealing of the Lotus Sutra's original message. It has three aspects: firstly, 'to open what is near and reveal what is far away' which means to understand the significance of the history of Sakyamuni

146

Buddha and through his birth the reality of the Original Buddha as the source of the universe; secondly, 'to open *shaku* (trace) and reveal *hon* (basic)', meaning to gain an insight into the original Buddha through the activities of the historical Buddha; and thirdly, 'to open the provisional and reveal the true', meaning to realize the true teaching of the Lotus Sutra by studying the provisional teaching of the Mahayana. Kōdō Kyōdan belongs to the Japan Buddhist Federation and has had a close historical relationship with the Temple of Tendai Sect, Enryakuji on Mt Hiei.

The spirit of filial piety is an essential practice and thanksgiving services, especially to the late founder, are held throughout the year. True filial piety preached by Kōdō Kyōdan involves the vertical relations between parents and children as well as an extension of this affection and compassion horizontally to society in general. Kōdō Kyōdan believes that it is more important to honour the forbears, rather than to worship an image or deity, as honouring the ancestors brings protection and happiness to the family. Acts of filial piety should be performed regularly in the home and within society.

Major festivals include the 'Hana Matsuri' in April in celebration of the birth of Sakyamuni Buddha and the Obon Festival for the ancestors in the summer.

PUBLICATIONS

PERIODICALS:

Kōdō Shimbun (Japanese monthly newspaper)
Kōdō News (Overseas quarterly edition of the above)

PUBLICATIONS BY THE MOVEMENT:

There have been several books written by the founder Archbishop Shōdō Okano and his wife Lady Kimiko Okano including:

An Introduction to Kōdō Kyōdan Buddhism, Archbishop Shodo Okano, Kōdō Kyōdan, Yokohama, 1967
The Heart of a Bodhisattva, Lady Kimiko Okano, Kōdō Kyōdan, 1970

Kōdō Kyōdan conducts weekly radio broadcasts on several Japanese networks, as well as a regular short-wave programme to Brazil

BRANCHES AND MEMBERSHIP

The present headquarters of Kōdō Kyōdan are located on a hill named Kodo-san, overlooking Yokohama City. They include the Main Hall (*Hombutsu-Den*), the Secretariat Annex (*Jimukyoku Shinkan*) and the Buddha Relics Tower (*Busshari-Den*), enshrining a portion of the sacred relics of Sakyamuni Buddha brought to Japan long ago from Mt Tendai in China and presented to Kōdō Kyōdan in 1952 by the head temple of the Tendai Sect.

Membership in Japan is around 450,000 followers as of 1996. There are no overseas branches at present.

KŌDŌ KYŌDAN – BIBLIOGRAPHY

1 OKANO, A. S. (1967). An Introduction to Kōdō Kyōdan Buddhism. Yokohama, Kōdō Kyōdan.
   Written by the founder of Kōdō Kyōdan, this book sets out the teachings, faith and practice of the religion.

2 OKANO, K. L. (1970). The Heart of a Bodhisattva. Yokohama.
   Written by Lady Okano, the wife of the founder of Kōdō Kyōdan, this book discusses the principles and teachings of Buddha and the application of these practices in the context of daily life as a Mahayana Bodhisattva.

Kōfuku-no-Kagaku

The Institute for Research in Human Happiness (IRH)

By Masaki Fukui[1]

HISTORY

Kōfuku-no-Kagaku, the Institute for Research in Human Happiness, was established in Tokyo by a former businessman, Ryuho Ōkawa (30 years of age then), in October 1986.[2]

Ōkawa was born on 7 July 1956, in Tokushima Prefecture, Japan. He did not consider himself a particularly religious person in his youth, though he did believe in the existence of the spirit world. He was very successful as a student in terms of academic achievement, and after graduating from the University of Tokyo in law, he started his first career as a businessman at *Tōmen*, one of Japan's major trading houses.

On 23 March 1981, while still a student at university, Ōkawa experienced his first discourse with a high spirit. Through continuous religious experiences, Ōkawa gradually became aware that he was an incarnation of the highest spiritual being, called *El Cantare*[3] which was revealed to him by the consciousness of Gautama Siddhartha (or Shakyamuni the Buddha). From this he realized that he had a great mission of salvation for all living creatures through spreading the Truth on earth.

Ōkawa started his movement in October 1986 with only a few other members as staff, and a number of members but no followers as such. However, the movement's growth was quite phenomenal, and after the third anniversary of its establishment, Kōfuku-no-Kagaku's headquarters was moved to one of Tokyo's most expensive business buildings in Kioichō, Shinjuku, the area for business and politics, the rent for which was over 100,000 pounds (25 million yen) a month.

In 1991 Kōfuku-no-Kagaku's growth and activities gave rise to a social phenomenon, known as the 'Kōfuku-no-Kagaku Phenomenon', and suddenly caught everybody's attention. It is now come classified as a Japanese 'new' new religion.[4] Let us briefly review its 12 year-history.

□

Ōkawa appeared in public for the first time in October 1986, and gave his first sermon in Tokyo, in front of some 80 guests. In March 1987 he gave his first official public lecture, entitled The Principles of Happiness, to an audience of about 400 people, and this marked the beginning of his Institute's activities.

The period from 1987 to 1989 was one of intensive study of the teachings of the Master. During this two-year period, Kōfuku-no-Kagaku concentrated on educating future teachers, and training the management of the movement (p. 32). It should be noted here that in 1989 Ōkawa started to emphasize the importance and significance of 'faith', that is, Buddhist 'Devotion to the Three Treasures', for the first time in his Institute. (p. 36).

Kōfuku-no-Kagaku's spirit of evangelism was declared shortly before the beginning of 1990 the year known within the Institute as 'Sunrise 90'. During this year the objective was to raise 'the Sun of Truth' all over Japan. In other words, it marked the official beginning of a campaign to make Kōfuku-no-Kagaku's name known throughout Japan. In this same year the size of the Institute greatly expanded; from just over 10,000 in January, to 30,000 by the end of May, and to 60,000 by the end of June, and reached 77,000 by the end of July (p. 43).

'The Miracle Three-Year Project' was begun in 1991. With this project Kōfuku-no-Kagaku aimed to establish a great religious revolution in Japan and become Japan's most influential and largest religion. Kōfuku-no-Kagaku succeeded in obtaining its official status as a religious body (Shūkyō Hōjin) in March 1991. During that year, a number of articles appeared on Kōfuku-no-Kagaku, including articles in The Financial Times and The Wall Street Journal. A first 'Birthday Festival (Goseitan-sai)' was held, too, in the Tokyo Dome (one of Japan's main indoor baseball stadiums) with 50,000 members attending. Ryuho Ōkawa for the first time declared his identity as El Cantare one of whose titles is 'the Buddha of Mahāyāna' (p. 46).

Shortly after the Festival, however, Kōfuku-no-Kagaku entered into long dispute with *Kōdansha*, one of the largest publishing companies in Japan, to protest over one of its weekly magazines (*the Friday* and *Shūkan-Gendai*) which carried a series of critical articles on Kōfuku-no-Kagaku and Ōkawa. The Institute immediately protested against the articles for carrying fabricated stories about Kōfuku-no-Kagaku, and also accused the publisher of selling magazines by means of, 'religion bashing'. High profile members of Kōfuku-no-Kagaku, namely, Tamio Kageyama (writer) and Tomoko Ogawa (actress), led several demonstrations and marched in Tokyo's streets in September 1991 in protest. A number of court cases followed between the members of the Institute and the publishing company (some of which are still in progress). The Institute itself sued the publisher, the writers, and the commentators, including some academics in departments of religious studies.

During 1992, Ōkawa's teaching became more Buddhist as he claimed that traditional Buddhist teachings had become distorted over the last 2,600 years, Ōkawa, as the reincarnated Buddha, was now correcting these (p. 52). From 1992 onwards, Kōfuku-no-Kagaku began to hold religious ceremonies and rituals including the services for ancestors. The Group also introduced *'Gohonzon'*, a religious icon for worship at home (p. 54). In 1993, Ōkawa declared that a religious war had begun (p. 54).

The so-called 'Big-Bang Three-Year Project' began in 1994–96 and with it Kōfuku-no-Kagaku started a full-scale programme of missionary work. During one of his early lectures in 1994, Ōkawa emphasized that the Buddha they believed in was El Cantare, whose mission was more than that of Gautama the Buddha and of Jesus Christ. Ōkawa taught that he, as the Buddha, descended to earth to guide his followers, to make humankind happy, to set humankind free, and to open the door to the twenty-first century (pp. 56–7).

1994 was also significant for the Institute in terms of its doctrine. In the April issue of the monthly Kōfuku-no-Kagaku magazine, Ōkawa indicated a new direction. Until then the movement had mentioned a considerable amount of other religious/historical figures in their teaching, such as Jesus, Moses, Confucius, Nichiren, Amaterasu-Omi-Kami (the Shinto Sun goddess), and so on, and for this reason some people criticized the movement for what they saw as a mixture of doctrines from different religions. Kōfuku-no-

Kagaku, however, changed its approach to illustrate that this criticism was unjustified, and more emphasis was placed on a single high spirit, that is, El Cantare, (pp. 50–60). At this very point the concept of 'Devotion to the Three Treasures', namely, the Buddha, the Dharma, and the Sangha[5] was considered to be of supreme importance.

In terms of its international mission, Kōfuku-no-Kagaku opened its first overseas office in New York (Kōfuku-no-Kagaku USA) in January 1994, which was followed by other official branches in Los Angeles, London, and São Paulo.

It should be noted here that Kōfuku-no-Kagaku's first feature film, *The Terrifying Revelations of Nostradamus*, with Ōkawa himself as the executive producer, was released in September 1994 and was allegedly based on truths from the spirit world. This film was shown at cinemas all over Japan.

It was also in 1994 that Kōfuku-no-Kagaku's social activities achieved a higher profile. For instance, members of the Institute organized several demonstrations against *Kōdansha* protesting over what they considered to be their strong pornographic magazine publications. Some 31,000 people in Tokyo, and 35,000 people in Osaka marched in the main streets.

When the Great Earthquake of Osaka and Kobe took place (17 January 1995), Ōkawa sent 20,000 people from Kōfuku-no-Kagaku to the stricken area to assist with rescue activity. This included supplying doctors, providing food, building public baths, and so on (p. 65).

Kōfuku-no-Kagaku's appearance in the public domain continued with another demonstration; this time (1995) against *Aum Shinrikyō*. The Aum Group had already had trouble with the public and the police, but soon after the kidnapping of Mr Kariya occurred (28/2/95), Kōfuku-no-Kagaku started to reveal to politicians, the mass media and other public bodies, that Aum was behind the kidnapping. About 10,000 members of Kōfuku-no-Kagaku took part in a demonstration and distributed leaflets in Tokyo's streets naming Aum as the criminal (p. 67). Two days after this (20/3/95) the Aum members spread Sarin gas in the Tokyo underground system seemingly in order to divert police attention away from the kidnapping case. Ironically, however, this incident triggered the police's investigation two days later – all their facilities were raided simultaneously and most of the core members arrested. The trial continues.

Kōfuku-no-Kagaku's critical stance against such 'heretical' reli-gions[6] continued. It was during 1995 that the Group's extremely critical messages against other NRMs were published, including, the Unification Church, Jehovah's Witnesses, Cosmo Mates (or World Mates), the God Light Association (GLA), and Sōka Gakkai. Kōfuku-no-Kagaku gave as one of the main reasons for their direct criticism the necessity to underline the criteria of right and wrong religion for the benefit of the people in the future.[7]

One of the other features of Kōfuku-no-Kagaku's activities in 1995 was that Ōkawa addressed a large number of political as well as economic issues. In terms of missionary activities on the international stage, some new overseas offices were opened in Korea (Seoul), Australia (Melbourne), Canada (Toronto), Hawaii, and San Francisco. At the same time the Institute started to publish its monthly journals in English, French, Korean, Chinese, and Portuguese. The Group's first monthly opinion magazine, *The Liberty*, which was targeted at the general public rather than exclusively at members, appeared in local bookshops in this same year (pp. 69–71).

Kōfuku-no-Kagaku regarded the year 1996, the final year of the Group's Big-Bang Project, as a difficult period for religions in Japan, since people's views about religion were becoming more cynical because of the incidents and troubles caused by some 'anti-social' NRMs (pp. 72–3). Ōkawa, however, criticized the opinion held by some critics that religion was an unnecessary thing. He said that this was the age when the right religion was needed to enlighten the people (pp. 72–3).

1996 was also the year in which Kōfuku-no-Kagaku declared that it had entered a new era, known as *'Daijō no Jidai* (the Age of *Mahāyāna)'*. Kōfuku-no-Kagaku's first major temple, *Shōshin-Kan*, was also built in 1996, and in this same year one of Ōkawa's principle books, *The Laws of the Sun*, was for the first time published in English and in Portuguese by non-Japanese publishers. Also in 1996 the headquarters was moved to a new nine-storey building in *Shinagawa*, Tokyo.

In 1997 Kōfuku-no-Kagaku entered its new phase called 'The New Hope Three-year Project', which was to last until the end of 1999. Ōkawa says that a dark age might come soon. However, Kōfuku-no-Kagaku is optimistic about the new century, and his Institute is preparing for this new era.[8]

Probably one of the Group's most conspicuous activities in 1997 was the release of their second feature film *Hermes – The Winds of Love*. This film was shown for a month at 114 cinemas across Japan. The film was fully animated with computer graphics based on the life of the Greek hero, Hermes, who is also believed by the members of Kōfuku-no-Kagaku to be one of Ōkawa's past existences.

□

It follows from what has been said so far, therefore, that Kōfuku-no-Kagaku's twelve-year-activities can be divided mainly into four chronological phases. The first phase was the study period between 1987–89, during which time Kōfuku-no-Kagaku concentrated on the members' studies of the doctrine, and the phase was concluded with a declaration of their commitment to evangelism.

The second phase was the period of evangelism which officially started in 1990 followed by the full-scale missionary project from 1991 to 1993 ('the Miracle Three-Year Project'). During this period the Institute officially became a 'religion' by being legally recognized as a religious body by the metropolitan government of Tokyo, and the teachings of Ōkawa were more in keeping with Buddhism.

The Institute then entered its third phase of the 'Big-Bang Three-Year Project' from 1994 to 1997 to spread its message to the world, and several overseas centres as well as local liaison offices were opened in main cities of the world.

Kōfuku-no-Kagaku's fourth and current phase of 'the New-Hope Project' started in 1997.

As already stated, their first temple, *'Shōshin-Kan'* (the House of the Right Mind), was officially opened on 4th August 1996 in *Utsunomiya* City in Tochigi Prefecture (about 100 kilometres north east of Tokyo), and the other training centre, *'Mirai-Kan'* (the House of the Future), was opened on 2 November 1997, also in Utsunomiya City. Both these facilities are now collectively regarded as *'Sō-Honzan'* (the Head Temple). *Shōshin-Kan*, for example, is a modern building of great size, which has the appearance of a white, Ancient Greek temple, which is open to the public. According to Kōfuku-no-Kagaku, these temples have been designed to provide an environment where visitors are able to receive religious training, such as meditation, in relaxing surroundings away from the distractions of the outside, secular world.

Kōfuku-no-Kagaku is now planning to build three more training centres in Japan; one in *Nikkō*, (Tochigi Prefecture), one in *Kyūshū,*and another one in the *Kansai* region. Their first temple outside Japan was opened in Jundiai (São Paulo, Brazil) on 1 March 1998.

MAIN BELIEFS & PRACTICES

Kōfuku-no-Kagaku's teachings embrace a wide range of religious issues. These span from, for example, practical advice on how to solve everyday domestic problems, to cosmology, and the secrets of the universe. The teachings, however, all point towards a prime purpose, that is, to obtain 'real' happiness and 'soul-training' in each person's own particular circumstances.

One of the fundamental parts of the teaching is called 'Quest for the Right Mind'. In order to quest or pursue the 'Right Mind' the members practise the core teaching of the Institute, 'The Fourfold Path', which consists of 'Love', 'Knowledge', 'Self-Reflection', and 'Development'. These four categories are collectively called 'the Principles of Happiness' the practice of which can bring 'real' happiness.

However, this 'real' human happiness cannot be realized without 'faith'. Faith is the most important thing for human beings, says Kōfuku-no-Kagaku, because all humans are considered to be children of the Buddha/God.[9] Kōfuku-no-Kagaku's opposition to materialism, atheism, and beliefs in *genze-riyaku* (or this-worldly benefit)[10] is regarded as proof that the Institute distinguishes a 'right' form of faith from a 'wrong' one or wrong ideology. According to the Institute, the foundation of right faith is knowing that all human beings have an eternal life and that they come and go between two realms, namely this world and the other world; in other words they are reincarnated.

KŌFUKU-NO-KAGAKU'S VIEW OF HAPPINESS AND UTOPIA

As we have seen, Kōfuku-no-Kagaku can be directly translated to mean the 'science of happiness'. The reason why this Institute calls itself a 'science' is that the human mind tends to work according to certain rules (*hōsoku*), and by researching these rules or laws it is believed that any individual can move in a certain direction, for example the direction towards happiness.[11]

The Institute has a clear definition of the word 'happiness'. Happiness, which is understood within the context of the 'Happiness of the Individual', is to know the Truth (or the teaching of the Buddha). In other words, the wisdom or the 'spiritual food' which one can attain by practising the Buddha's teaching constitutes 'happiness'. Thus, individual happiness is considered in the Institute to be the same as a state of enlightenment,[12] and the higher your state of enlightenment becomes, the greater the happiness you will attain.

Kōfuku-no-Kagaku's other views of 'happiness' is called the 'Happiness that penetrates this world and the other world'. This 'real' happiness is based on the 'spiritual outlook upon life (*reiteki jinsei-kan*)' which is considered to be of supreme importance in Kōfuku-no-Kagaku. Ōkawa teaches that what one can bring back to the other world after death, that is the 'real world', is mind only, not your expensive car, your title, your money, and so on. Nonetheless, if your mind is full of anger, hatred, jealousy, anxiety, and attachment to 'this-worldly' things, then that is what you will bring back to the other world. However, Ōkawa teaches, you cannot enter the heavenly world with this kind of mind, because Heaven is full of heavenly energy, such as love and compassion which are polar opposites to the negative mind just described. For this reason, therefore, Kōfuku-no-Kagaku, teaches that Heaven and Hell already exist in this world, and not only in the world after death. In other words, as long as you live with the mind full of love and compassion, then you will be full of happiness, and this happiness is what you can bring back 'home'. This is how the 'Happiness that penetrates this world and the other world' is to be understood.

Individual happiness has to be spread – that makes for 'the Happiness of Society', namely, the Utopia that Kōfuku-no-Kagaku is in pursuit of. Utopia is often considered to be the Kingdom of God, Paradise on earth, which is to come after the Apocalypse, in many, so called, millenarian movements. However, Kōfuku-no-Kagaku's millennium is not considered to be dramatically different from the world as we know it in a physical sense. Kōfuku-no-Kagaku's Utopia is simply a world in which everybody can say 'I am happy',[13] in the sense defined above. Kōfuku-no-Kagaku's Utopia begins with a little utopia in the mind of each individual, and not by apocalyptic events.

This is the main part of the belief system within Kōfuku-no-Kagaku. Its wider doctrine, such as history since the creation of the universe and the multidimensional structure of the universe, that is the explanations of the universe in terms of time and space, overlay this main part.

'KŌFUKU-NO-KAGAKU'S SPIRITUAL OUTLOOK UPON LIFE'

I have mentioned that the term 'real' happiness is based on the 'spiritual outlook upon life (*reiteki jinsei-kan* in Japanese)'. From this starting point, Ōkawa emphasizes the importance of knowing that 'life is eternal' as well as the importance of understanding the mechanism of 'reincarnation'. These are the movement's two most fundamental beliefs necessary to achievement of 'real' happiness. 'Eternal life' does not mean an everlasting physical life on earth, but life as a spirit. This spirit with an eternal life reincarnates on earth from time to time (on average about once every three hundred years) in order to experience 'soul-training' that is, to allow one's soul to evolve, for the development of oneself. This notion seems to be one of the most important concepts of Kōfuku-no-Kagaku theology, (see: Kōfuku-no-Kagaku Sōgō-Honbu, 1994, pp. 155–161).

Kōfuku-no-Kagaku regards materialism and atheism as evil, because these ideologies cause people to think that death is the end of everything. As long as people think that life is experienced only once, they will live a life pursuing gratification in this world with the consequent attachment to material goods, such as money, property, social status, and so on. According to Kōfuku-no-Kagaku, however, the greatest task for all humans on earth is to polish the mind, something many of them have forgotten, thereby generating suffering for themselves by attachment to earthly desires.

By realizing the truth of eternal life and understanding the mechanism of reincarnation, Kōfuku-no-Kagaku says, people can comprehend why it is necessary to live virtuously; to act well; to love and respect others, and so on. Understanding reincarnation is the beginning of enlightenment and of a life with 'real' happiness.

□

As mentioned before, Kōfuku-no-Kagaku's main teaching, the Principles of Happiness, consists of Love, Knowledge, Development, and Self-Reflection. Each one of these is an important task which all the Kōfuku-no-Kagaku followers are supposed to practise in order to attain the Right Mind. Here, I would like to focus mainly on two principles, namely 'Love' and 'Self-Reflection'.

'The Principle of Love' is considered to be the most important of the four principles.[14] Ōkawa teaches his followers to choose Love if they have to choose one of the four principles. He goes on to say that many people do not realize that love is for giving, and, instead, are preoccupied with taking from others. Such people tend to think that someone else is going to make them happy, but the idea of this 'taking love' is in fact the very cause of unhappiness. Such people suffer because they cannot always get the love they are craving for from others. Kōfuku-no-Kagaku emphasises that 'giving love' is the beginning of happiness. It teaches that 'You do not have to worry about losing something by giving love, because the love you give becomes yours, because this is the Law.' The reward of the love one gives is believed to come from the Buddha/God. The more love you give the closer to the Buddha/God you are, and this is 'real' happiness for all human beings. When the world is filled with people who want to give love to others, it will turn into a Utopia.

Kōfuku-no-Kagaku teaches that love has several stages (see: *'The Laws of the Sun'*, 1994 & 1996, Ch.3, sections 6 & 7), which are:

☐ Instinctive love (4th dimension)
☐ Fundamental love (5th dimension)
☐ Spiritually nurturing love (6th dimension)
☐ Forgiving love (7th dimension)
☐ 'Existence' as love (8th dimension)
☐ God's love (9th dimension)
   (See: *'The Laws of the Sun'*, p. 61)

Kōfuku-no-Kagaku has much to say about the nature of the universe in this connection, as is evident in Ōkawa's main book, *The Laws of the Sun*. Briefly, the universe consists of several dimensional layers. Beyond the third dimension (i.e. this physical world) is the spirit world, and the highest realm for the human consciousness is the ninth dimension, where only 10 high spirits live, such as the spirits of Jesus, Confucius, Moses, and the Buddha. Thus, the supreme form of love for humankind is love of the ninth dimension. The distinctive teaching of this 'development of love' is regarded as original to Kōfuku-no-Kagaku. In *The Laws of the Sun* (Ch.3, section 9), Ōkawa explains the relationship between the Buddhist traditional doctrine 'the Noble Eightfold Path' and his 'Development of Love'. Kōfuku-no-Kagaku also declares that Christianity and Buddhism, though these historical religions have often been considered to have completely different orientations, share much in common in this respect. In Kōfuku-no-Kagaku, it is understood that pursuing enlightenment means aiming at a higher stage of love. The level of enlightenment achieved and the level of love you give to others is therefore proportionate. Kōfuku-no-Kagaku strongly believes that this thought is the key to their religious reformation and aims to integrate 'Love' and 'Enlightenment', as well as oriental and occidental civilizations.[15]

The following phrase sums up the essence of Kōfuku-no-Kagaku's teaching: 'without self-reflection there is no enlightenment'. In this sense, practising self-reflection, the third principle of the *Principles of*

Happiness, is regarded as highly important. Self-reflection is considered to be necessary for human beings in order to live happy lives.

This principle is a condition of going back to the heavenly world, says Kōfuku-no-Kagaku. One has to correct his/her wrong deeds and tendencies, either after death or while still alive, according to the mind of the Buddha or God. This is done only by the individual herself or himself, not by the Buddha. As long as the person possesses the wrong thoughts which are against the will of the Buddha, then he/she cannot go through Heaven's door.

Importantly, however, if a person does not know where the mind of the Buddha is, that person cannot correct his/her wrong thoughts. For this reason all humans must study the Truth. As I mentioned earlier, mind is the only thing one can bring back to the world after death; therefore, how much you have polished it while on earth by studying the Truth, is the crucial question. Kōfuku-no-Kagaku insists that this material world on earth is the best place for this spiritual training.[16]

THE SIGNIFICANCE OF 'HELL'

According to Ōkawa, in this modern age over 50% of the dead go to one of the dark realms, which are collectively called 'Hell'. This is often because of a variety of wrong thoughts and ideologies (such as materialism and atheism) as well as of wrong religious teachings.

Ōkawa says that all human beings are given free will, and it is completely up to them how to use it. For this reason one can decide to become a highly respectable being, like an angel or a bodhisattva, but at the same time it is also possible for a person to go to Hell, depending on how they use that free will. Hell, therefore, is considered to be realms to which souls who made wrong use of free will while on earth go, to reflect upon their wrong deeds and actions. Wrong thoughts are such things as anger, jealousy, pessimism, hatred, lust, egoticism, lies, materialism, atheism, and various desires for this-worldly things, such as anger, money and social status.

Souls in Hell are considered to be ill, because they are in a state of malnutrition from lack of 'love', and crave for more love from others without knowing that love is for 'giving'. In this sense Hell was not created by the Buddha or God, it was created by humans or by their wrong thoughts, to be exact. Kōfuku-no-Kagaku, therefore, regards Hell as a hospital for souls in which they stay temporarily not the world of eternal judgement,[17] and when the soul has managed to complete his/her self-reflection, he/she can return to a heavenly world until his/her next opportunity of reincarnation on earth.

I have introduced several theoretical aspects of Kōfuku-no-Kagaku's teachings so far. Here, I would like to refer to more practical parts of its teaching.

Kōfuku-no-Kagaku's view on 'happiness' has a lot to do with its outlook on life. For Kōfuku-no-Kagaku believers, the meaning of life is 'soul-training' and the 'creation of utopia'. They claim that if you start looking at life from the perspective that 'this world is a place which is provided for us to develop our souls', your life will start to look completely different. In this Institute it is believed that people choose their own parents and their life-environment before birth in order to correct their *karma,* or the tendency of their soul; to get rid of bad karma and create good karma. Kōfuku-no-Kagaku considers, therefore, that humans have chosen the most appropriate life environment in order to practise their own 'soul-training'. In this sense, their view on life on earth is quite different from that of the Judao-Christian tradition, for example.

Life on earth, however, is known to have many problems. Humans are preoccupied by everyday things. Kōfuku-no-Kagaku teaches that all these anxieties are the most appropriate 'exam-questions' for the soul. Once a person has managed to give the correct answer to the questions he will not have to take the same examination in the next life.

This is how the students of this Institute see the world. It is, thus, considered to be incorrect to attribute unhappiness or dissatisfaction with things to other people or the environment one is living in; it is necessary to reflect and to come to realize this truth. For this reason it is said: 'Without self-reflection there is no enlightenment'.

Many members of Kōfuku-no-Kagaku over its twelve-year history believe their leader, Ōkawa to be *Buddha,* and the incarnation of the Lord El Cantare.[18] As such, he is the central figure of worship in Kōfuku-no-Kagaku. For this reason, the Group's *Gohonzon,* the object of worship, carries a photograph of Ōkawa as the Lord El Cantare. He is believed to have descended on Earth with a mission to bring a new age in the twenty-first century.

Why did El Cantare have to descend on Earth now? Kōfuku-no-Kagaku believes that the modern world is in a state of crisis, caused by wrong thoughts, wars, and so on. As a result the contemporary world is covered with dark thoughts which may trigger all kinds of cataclysmic disasters.[19] Hence, his descent.

Under his guidance, his followers practise the Buddha's teaching, *the Dharma*, and the 'Principles of Happiness'. With its slogan, 'Quest for the Right Mind', that is, the mind of the Buddha/God, every single follower of the Institute tries to achieve his or her own self-transformation. Kōfuku-no-Kagaku is, thus, regarded as *the Sangha*, the community of people who have transformed, or are now trying to transform themselves. In the Sangha, namely Kōfuku-no-Kagaku, their common aim is to form people who can contribute to the performance of the Buddha's will and create happiness. The Buddha, the Dharma, and the Sangha, that is the Buddhist 'Three Treasures (*tri-ratna*)', are, therefore, regarded to be of supreme importance for the Kōfuku-no-Kagaku believers whose aim is to achieve this objective.

PUBLICATIONS

THE GROUP'S PERIODICALS

Monthly *'Kōfuku-no-Kagaku'* (the Group's official monthly journal)
'The Dendō'
'The Hermes Angels' (Journal for children)
'The Liberty' (monthly magazine targeted non-members too)

RYŪHŌ ŌKAWA'S MAIN PUBLICATIONS

'The Laws of the Sun'
'The Laws of Gold'
'The Laws of Eternity'
'The Rebirth of Buddha'
'The Challenge of Enlightenment' Vol.1 & 2 (Japanese version only)[20]
'A Revolution of Happiness' (Japanese version only)[21]

BRANCHES AND MEMBERSHIP: FIGURES OVERSEAS

Kōfuku-no-Kagaku's overseas activities expanded rapidly especially during their three-year 'Big-Bang Project' from 1994 to 1997. After opening its very first branch in New York (Kōfuku-no-Kagaku USA), the Institute has opened a few other branch offices in the world's main cities. Up until now, March 1998, there are four branch offices within the United States (Los Angeles, San Francisco, Hawaii, and New York as the head office), as well as offices in Canada (Toronto), Brazil (São Paulo), Korea (Seoul), Australia (Melbourne), and Europe (London), and there are several local liaison offices in many locations of the world.

Kōfuku-no-Kagaku's membership system has changed a few times since its first establishment. At each change of the system, entry to the Group was opened more widely, and as a result many more people were able to join the Institute. At first, for instance, Ōkawa limited the size of the membership by insisting on an entrance examination. The candidates of this period had to read at least ten pieces of literature written by Ōkawa, and submit an essay which was examined by Ōkawa himself.

After a change in the system, the membership came to consist of two kinds. Whilst the reading of ten books was still the minimum requirement for the applicants for 'Full Membership (Sei-Kaiin)', who pledged themselves to the 'Quest for the Right Mind', a new type of member, called 'Friendship Member (Shiyū-Kaiin)' was also accepted. The latter were sympathizers of the Group and subscribed to its monthly journals. With this new system and as a result of its full-scale evangelism, after 1990, Kōfuku-no-Kagaku declared a membership of 5.6 million worldwide at the end of 1991, the Institute's fifth year. Kōfuku-no-Kagaku, then entered a new phase called their three-year missionary project, 'Miracle Three-Year Project', from 1991 to 1994.

There has been a further change in the definition of member in the sense that the Institute no longer uses the term 'member' (kaiin), and instead uses the term 'believer' (shinja). In order to become an official member of Kōfuku-no-Kagaku, the applicant still has to fill in a form and be accepted by the Group in the same way as before, though this is now easier. However, Kōfuku-no-Kagaku believers are not necessarily official members.

There are seven types of believer now.[22] According to this classification, those who attend the Institute's lecture-sessions, or those who believe in Ōkawa's teaching by reading his literature, are considered to be believers, whether registered as members or not. The Institute introduced this wider view of believership because the original definition of membership had become inadequate, as it excluded sympathizers. Understood in this sense the number of the Kōfuku-no-Kagaku believers members was about ten million worldwide which included 40,000 in the United States, 20,000 in Brazil, around 6,000 in Korea, and 10,000 in Europe.[23]

NOTES

1 This entry was written by Masaki Fukui who would like to thank Kōfuku-no-Kagaku Headquarters' International Division for providing a large amount of information. He would especially like to thank Miss Nina Hakkarainen and Mr Yasunari 'Rocky' Uchimura.

2 Most information detailed here regarding the history of Kōfuku-no-Kagaku is from the Group's Ten-Year Anniversary Book (Page numbers given in the text without a footnote refer to this book), and their official monthly journal, 'Kōfuku-no-Kagaku' No.113 (July 1996), pp. 32–35.

3 'El Cantare' means 'the beautiful land of light Earth'. This spirit is believed to be 'the supreme grand spirit of the terrestrial group'. See: 'The Laws of the Sun', 1994 & 1996, p. I & p. 19.

4 Shimazono observes that religious organizations/movements that flourished during the 1970s and 1980s are all 'new' new religions. The year the group was founded is thus not relevant. See: Inoue, 1992, p. 228.

5 The Buddha (El Cantare/Ōkawa), the Dharma (the teaching of Ōkawa), and the Sangha (the community of disciples, that is, Kōfuku-no-Kagaku).

6 By 'heresy' the Group means wrong teachings which can misguide followers, and anti-social behaviour.

7 Hikaku-Shūkyō Kenkyū-Kai (ed.), 'Machigai Darake no Shūkyō Erabi', Vol.1, 1995, p. 202.

8 Monthly 'Kōfuku-no-Kagaku', No.119 (1/97), pp. 23–4.

9 Kōfuku-no-Kagaku Sōgō-Honbu (ed.), Tokyo 1994, p. 12.

10 Kōfuku-no-Kagaku does not reject the idea of genze-riyaku as such, as the Group also teaches the importance of happiness in this world, too; for example, they have prayers to achieve success in this world, economic prosperity, traffic safety, and so on. However, when it is solely for utilitarian, selfish purposes, the Institute regards this as evil, as it is not 'real' happiness but egotism.

11 'Samsāra', December 1991, pp. 46–7.

12 Kōfuku-no-Kagaku Sōgō-Honbu (ed.),1994, p. 115.

13 Ibid., p. 115.

14 Kōfuku-no-Kagaku Sōgō-Honbu (ed.), 1994, pp. 64–5.

15 Kōfuku-no-Kagaku Sōgō-Honbu (ed.), 1994, pp. 84–5.

16 See: Kōfuku-no-Kagaku Sōgō-Honbu (ed.), 1994, Ch.2, Section 6.

17 See: Ibid., Ch.3, Section 4.

18 Ōkawa is believed to have been previously reincarnated several times on Earth. For example, part of El Cantare's consciousness appeared on Earth as La Mu (Mu: c.17,000 years ago), as Thoth (Atlantis: c.12,000 years ago), as Rient Arl Croud (Inca Empire: c.7,000 years ago), as Ophealis (Greece: c.6,500 year ago), as Hermes (Greece: c.4,300 years ago), as Gautama Siddhartha (India: c.2,600 years ago), and as Ryūhō Ōkawa (Japan: 1956–). See: Ōkawa, 'The Laws of the Sun' p. 142

19 Kōfuku-no-Kagaku Sōgō-Honbu (ed.), 1994, pp. 32–3.

20 *'Satori no Chōsen'* in Japanese.
21 *'Kōfuku no Kakumei'* in Japanese.
22 I was told this by Mr Yasunari Uchimura, the manager of the European branch office.
23 The figures stated here are in accordance with a report from Kōfuku-no-Kagaku's International Division in February 1998.

KŌFUKU-NO-KAGAKU – BIBLIOGRAPHY

1 ASTLEY, T. (1995). 'The Transformation of a Recent Japanese New Religion.' *Japanese Journal of Religious Studies* **22**(3–4).
   Examines the rise to prominence of Kōfuku-no-Kagaku, the way in which its organization, teachings and public profile have changed in the course of the movement's development.

2 BERTHON, J.-P. (1991). 'Kofuku no kagaku ou la Science du bonheur:la naissance d'une nouvelle religion japonaise.' *France-Japan Eco.*

3 KOBAYASHI, A. (1994). A Study of a Japanese New Religion: The Institute for Research into Human Happiness. M.A. dissertation *Theology and Religious Studies*. London, King's College.
   A study of a Japanese New Religion which includes interviews with some members in the UK.

4 Kōfuku-no-Kagaku Kōhō-Kyoku (1995). Daishinsai sabaibaru manyuaru. Kore de anata wa sukuwareru (Survival manual for the Great Earthquake: This is How You Will Be Saved). Tokyo, IRH.

5 Kōfuku-no-Kagaku (1989). The No Shi (Brain Death is No Death). Tokyo, IRH Press.

6 Kōfuku-no-Kagaku (1994). Love is for Giving. Tokyo, IRH Press.

7 Kōfuku-no-Kagaku (1995). Sōka Gakkai Ruining Japan. Tokyo, Kōfuku-no-Kagaku General Headquarters.

8 Kōfuku-no-Kagaku (1995). Genron no Jiyū tai Shinkyō no Jiyū (Freedom of Speech vs. Freedom of Religion). Tokyo, Kōfuku-no-Kagaku General Headquarters.

9 MULLINS, M. R. (1992). *Japan's New Age and Neo-New Religions:Sociological Interpretations*. Perspectives on the New Age. J. R. Lewis and J. G. Melton. Albany, New York, State University of New York Press: 232–46.
   Gives brief historical account of the emergence of NRMs in Japan from the Meiji restoration onwards, divided into four periods of growth. The main focus is on the last of these periods, beginning in the late 1970s when the influence of the New Age Movement began to appear in Japan. The neo-New religion Kōfuku-no-Kagaku is cited in this context as an example of a Japanese New Age Movement. In addition to tracing New Age influences on the Japanese neo-New Religions, this article strongly emphasizes the importance of indigenous folk beliefs in these movements, in particular shamanism and magical practices.

10 ŌKAWA, R. (1988). Nosutoradamusu no shinyogen (The New Prophecies of Nostradamus). Tokyo, Kōfuku-no-Kagaku Shuppan.

11 ŌKAWA, R. (1989). Utopia Kachi Kakumei (Utopian Value Revolution). Tokyo, Tsuchiya Shoten.

12 ŌKAWA, R. (1989). *Jōshō shikō (Ever-ictorious thought)*. Tokyo, IRH Press.
   The power of positive thinking and how to avoid defeat and failure as a human being.

13 ŌKAWA, R. (1990). Shinri Yōgo-no Kiso Chishiki 100 (Basic Knowledge About God's Truth Terminology: 100). Tokyo, Kōfuku-no-Kagaku Press.

14 ŌKAWA, R. (1990). Kōfuku-no-Genten (The Origin of Happiness). Tokyo, IRH Kōfuku-no-Kagaku.

15 ŌKAWA, R. (1991). The Laws of the Sun. Tokyo, Japan, IRH Press Co Ltd.
The first in the trilogy of God's Truth, it explains what God, Love and the Ultimate Enlightenment is and presents 'The Golden Age of the Past'.

16 ŌKAWA, R. (1991). The Laws of Eternity (Eien no Hō). Tokyo, IRH Press Co Ltd.
The final volume in the trilogy, this book discusses the multidimensional world and theories of space.

17 ŌKAWA, R. (1991). The Laws of Gold. Tokyo, The IRH Press Co Ltd.
The second volume in the trilogy, this book explains how to establish God's Truth in one's own life, as well as giving a brief historical overview of Buddhism and a glimpse into the future.

18 ŌKAWA, R. (1991). Ai wa kaze no gotoku (Love is like the Wind). Tokyo, IRH Press.
A poetic spiritual biography of the Greek god, Hermes, incorporating his alleged sayings.

19 ŌKAWA, R. (1991). Nosutoradamusu senritsu no keiji (The Terrifying Revelations of Nostradamus). Tokyo, Kōfuku-no-Kagaku Shuppan.

20 ŌKAWA, R. (1992). Manga de miru Kōfuku-no-Kagaku. Tokyo, IRH Press Ltd.
Comic-strip of science fiction-type explaining the basic concepts of the IRH to young people.

21 ŌKAWA, R. (1992). Shinkō to Ai (Faith and Love). Tokyo, IRH Press Ltd.
Faith and love, according to this book are the guiding lights in the fight against the darkness of the present-day world and signs of the dawning of a new civilization.

22 ŌKAWA, R. (1993). Frankly Speaking. Tokyo, Kōfuku no Kagaku Publishing Co.
A series of interviews and discussions with the founder and leader of the Japanese new religion Kōfuko no Kagaku (IRH) including the full tape transcript of the interview taken by The Financial Times.

23 ŌKAWA, R. (1993). The Challenge of Religion: The Wind of Miracles from Japan. Tokyo, Japan, The IRH Press Co Ltd.
Discussion of the part religion can and should play in the present world and the necessity of adaptability in all religions.

24 ŌKAWA, R. (1993). *Dainamaito Shikō* (Dynamite Thinking). Tokyo, IRH Press.
Every human being has the capacity for 'dynamite thinking' and performing miracles inside him or herself. This book reveals how to tap this hidden source.

25 ŌKAWA, R. (1994). Secrets of the Spirit World (A Lecture in Nagaoka, Japan, June 14th1992 by Ryuho Ōkawa). Tokyo, Kōfuku-no-Kagaku.

26 ŌKAWA, R. (1994). Shin Taiyo no Hō (The New Laws of the Sun). Tokyo, IRH Press.
A revised and updated version of the most famous and popular book of the Kōfuku-no-Kagaku.

27 ŌKAWA, R. (1994). *Risō Kokka Nihon no Jōken* (The Conditions for an Ideal Japanese State). Tokyo, IRH Press.
A call for a nation-state grounded on religious and moral principles, and guidelines as to how this utopia could be accomplished.

28 ŌKAWA, R. (1995). Genron no jiyū tai shinkyō no jiyū (Freedom of Speech vs Freedom of Religion). Tokyo, IRH Press.

29 ŌKAWA, R. (1995). Sōka Gakkai Bōkokuron (Sōka Gakkai's Threat to the State/ Country). Tokyo, IRH Press.

30 ŌKAWA, R. (1995). Ii Shūkkyō, Warui Shūkkyō (Good Religions, Bad/Wrong Religion). Tokyo, IRH Press.

31 ŌKAWA, R. (1995). The Age of Choice in Religion. Tokyo, IRH Press.
English-language version of 3 of the 8 chapters that make up the eponymous Japanese text, 'Shūkyō Sentaku no Jidai'. It talks of the purpose of religion and the secrets of the spirit world.

32 SHIMAZONO, S. (1993). Shinshūkyō to Shinto: Kosumo meito to kofuku no Kagaku (New New religions and Shinto: Cosmo mate and Kōfuku-no-Kagaku). *Shinto o shiru hon (Get to know shinto)*: 150–154.

33 Shūkan Bunshun Magazine (1991). Ōkawa Ryūhō, Furaide mondai ni 'kotaeru' (Ryūhō Ōkawa answers the 'issues' of Friday). Shūkan Bunshun: 34–39.

34 Shūkan Bunshun Magazine (1991). Asahara Shōkō, Kageyama Tamio ra ga sanka shite Oumu Shinrikyō to Kōfuku-no-Kagaku ga asa made gekiron (The Heated Discussion between Kageyama Tamio (IRH) and Asahara Shōkō (Aum Shinrikyō). Shūkan Bunshun.

35 SUZUKI, K. (1995). An Examination of the Cosmology and Teachings of Kōfuku-no-Kagaku.
M.A. dissertation. Department of Theology and Religious Studies. London, King's College, University of London.

36 The Institute for Research in Human Happiness (1994). Escallent. Tokyo, Kōfuku-no-Kagaku.
Japanese Language Magazine.

37 The Institute for Research in Human Happiness (1994). Monthly Miracle. Tokyo, Kōfuku-no-Kagaku.
Monthly Magazine.

38 The Institute for Research in Human Happiness (1994). What is Kōfuku-no-Kagaku? Tokyo, IRH Press Ltd.

39 The Institute for Research in Human Happiness (1994–). The Monthly Message. Tokyo, Kōfuku-no-Kagaku.
Monthly Magazine.

40 The Institute for Research into Human Happiness (1994–). Miracle Wind. Tokyo, Kōfuku-no-Kagaku.

41 The Institute of Research into Human Happiness (1994). Eternal Buddha. Tokyo, IRH Press Ltd.
Japanese Publication.

42 The Institute of Research into Human Happiness (1994). Rebirth of Buddha – Messages to His Beloved Disciples. Tokyo, IRH Press Ltd.
Japanese Publication.

43 The Institute of Research into Human Happiness (1994). The Real Intention of Buddha. Tokyo, IRH Press Ltd.
Japanese Publication.

44 The Institute of Research into Human Happiness (1994). Firm Stability of Mind – The Way to Overcome Difficulties Through Spirituality. Tokyo, IRH Press Ltd.
Japanese Publication.

45 YONEMOTO, K. (1991). *Tōdaide no Buddha, Ōkawa Ryūhō no shinrei seminâru. Imadoki no kamisama, Bessatsu Takarajima.* Tokyo, JICC. **114**: 208–21.

46 YONEMOTO, K. and H. SHIMADA (1992). *Ōkawa Ryūhō no reigen.* Tokyo, JICC Shuppankyoku.

Konkōkyō

'Golden Light Teachings'   'Religion of Golden Light'

HISTORY

K onkōkyō was founded by Kawate Bunjiro (1814–83). A peasant farmer in Okayama Prefecture Kawate Bunjiro became very ill in 1855, according to tradition, because he had offended the deity Konjin (the malevolent golden *kami*). Kawate then began to pray to Konjin, which led to him being called upon by Konjin on 15 November 1859 to pray and search for peace and happiness for humanity. He received several divine messages from this deity and was asked to retire from farming to perform *toritsugi*-mediation full-time, build a place of worship (*hiromae*) and teach others. Kawate who did not believe the deity Konjin to be malevolent began to refer to him as *Tenchi Kane No Kami* ('The Golden Kami of Heaven and Earth') or Kōnkō Daijin ('The Great Kami of Golden Light'). From this date in 1859 Kawate believed that this deity had actually taken possession of his body and he was actually Kōnkō Daijin. He became the mediator between the people and the *kami*. This date in 1859 is therefore viewed as Konkōkyō's founding day.

From 1870 to 1884, Kōnkō Daijin's son Hagio, who was officially installed as the founder's successor in 1900, became a *kyodoshoku* ('national evangelist') under the Meiji state's promotion of Shinto. He and his main disciple, Satō Norio, were influential in aligning Konkōkyō with State Shinto and having it authorized by the government as a sect in 1900, despite Kōnkō Daijin's assertion throughout his life that it was not a another version of Shinto.

Since the early 1980s Konkōkyō has rejected Shinto and the part the movement played in prewar State Shinto. There has been a move to return to the true spirit of the founder's teachings.

MAIN BELIEFS AND PRACTICES

The name 'golden light teachings' refers to the belief that member's lives will shine brightly and light up humanity if they follow the teachings of Kōnkō Daijin. The central concept is the reciprocity between God and humanity, which leads to the fulfilment of both. People and society are believed to suffer because they ignore the principles of the universe as advocated by *Tenchi Kami No Kami*, that is, a world where *Kami* and man maintain each other's well-being through interdependence of *aiyo kakeyo*. God is believed to be benevolent and believers can receive spiritual counsel (*toritsugi*) from a priest who is in direct contact with God. Konkōkyō followers thus worship the deity 'Tenchi Kane No Kami' (lit: 'Principle Parent of the Universe'), believed to be the parent of all humanity, that is, everything in the universe originates from the *Kami*. Life is bestowed upon an individual from *Kami* and it is linked with all lives.

Konkōkyō is concerned with solutions to problems such as pollution, suffering and prejudice. People are urged to follow *Kami's* teachings in every aspect of daily life. *Kami* will give followers the power to overcome human sorrow and pain. Konkōkyō emphasizes the importance of tolerance and respect for different religions and cultures. There is an overall wish for world peace and human happiness.

Toritsugi-mediation (or 'intermediation') is the fundamental element of the Konkōkyō faith and functions to connect individuals with *Kami*. Konkōkyō mediators are able to convey both worshipper's requests to *Kami* and the wishes of *Kami* to humans. At the same time mediators share both the feelings of the worshippers and the feelings of *Kami*. Worshippers can pray to Kami at any time of the day during their daily schedules. Members visit Kōnkō churches to sit with ministers who will talk and pray with them, all the time mediating between the members and the Principle Parent.

Konkōkyō is recognized officially as Shinto in religious tradition, because Kōnkō Daijin obtained a Shinto licence early in the movement's history to avoid persecution from officials and powerful religious figures. However, *Tenchi Kane no Kami* was not a recognized Shinto deity and *toritsugi* was not a Shinto practice.

The key instruction in Konkōkyō teachings is the *Tenchi Kakitsuke* ('Divine Reminder'), as follows:

Ikigami Kōnkō Daijin,
Tenchi Kane no Kami, isshin ni negae.
Okage wa waga kokoro ni ari.
Kongetsu konnichi de tanomei

Through Ikigami Kōnkō Daijin,
To Tenchi Kane no Kami,
Pray with a single heart.
The divine favour depends
Upon one's own heart.
On this very day pray

Main festivals are:

New Year Festival	1 January
Spring Festival	Vernal Equinox
Grand Festival	4, 7, 10 April
Foundation of Church Festival	10 June
Autumn Festival	Autumn Equinox
Festival of Founder's Birthday	29 September
Foundation Memorial Day	15 November
Mission Day	10 December

(Also minor festivals are on the 10th and 22nd of each month)

PUBLICATIONS

PERIODICALS INCLUDE:

Kōnkō Kyoho (monthly)
Konkōkyōto (3 times monthly)
Konkōkyō Seinen (monthly)
Wakaba (monthly)
Tsuchi (bi-weekly)
Hotsume Shimbun (bi-weekly)
Yatsunami (5 times a year)
Toritsugi (semi-annually)
Face to Faith, Quarterly Newsletter from Konkōkyō International Centre, Tokyo

PUBLICATIONS BY THE MOVEMENT INCLUDE:

Kōnkō Daijin: A Biography, published by Kōnkō Churches of America, San Francisco, 1981. (A shortened translation of the official biography of the founder)

Konkōkyō kyoten, (Revised version of sacred scriptures), published by Konko-machi, 1983.

Tenchi Wa Kataru: Konkōkyō Kyoten-sho, published by Konkōkyō Headquarters, 1989. (Collection of about 400 passages selected from the Konkōkyō Kyoten, Sacred Scriptures of Konkōkyō. A version is also published in English, *The Voice of the Universe*, Konkōkyō, 1996).

BRANCHES AND MEMBERSHIP

Konkōkyō Headquarters are in Okayama, Japan and there is a Konkōkyō International Centre in Bunkyo-ku, Tokyo, Japan. Konkōkyō is divided into administrative districts throughout Japan with local churches. The *kyoshu* or spiritual leader is chosen from the founder's descendants and the *kyokan* or administrative heads are chosen from the leaders of churches in the district.

As of 1996, the number of Konkōkyō believers in Japan is about 400,000.

Konkōkyō has the following overseas branches:

Branch	Location	Established	Members
Kōnkō Churches of North America	San Francisco, USA	April, 1939	800 (incl. Canada)
Kōnkō Missions in Hawaii	Honolulu, Hawaii		700
Igreja Kōnkō Do Brasil De Birigui	Birigui, Brasil		500
Centro De Actividades De Konkōkyō En Asuncion	Asuncion, Paraguay		'several'

Total number of Konkōkyō believers overseas is about 2,000. (Includes USA, Canada, Hawaii, Brazil, Paraguay, and 'a few' in South Korea).

KONKŌKYŌ – BIBLIOGRAPHY

1 ARAKI, M. (1982). Kōnkō Daijin and Konkō-Kyō: A Case Study of Religious Meditation. Chicago, University of Chicago.

2 FUKUDA, Y. (1955). *Outline of Sacred Teaching of Kōnkō Religion*. San Francisco, Kōnkō Missions of North America.

3 FUKUDA, Y. (n.d). Hand Book of the Kōnkō Mission. San Francisco, Kōnkō Mission.

4 HAMMER, R. (1961). The Idea of God in Japan's New Religions – with Special Reference to Tenrikyō, Konkōkyō, Sekai Kyūseikyō, Ōmotokyō, Reiyūkai, Risshō Kōsei Kai, PL Kyōdan, Seichō-no-Ie and Annaikyo. *University of London*, London.

5 HARDACRE, H. (1986). 'Creating State Shinto:The Great Promulgation Campaign and the New Religions.' *Japanese Journal of Religious Studies* 12(4): 29–64.
   The first part of this paper examines the way in which the Japanese state attempted to create a state religion through the Great Promulgation Campaign of 1870–1884. The latter part of the paper analyses the effect of this campaign on two of the New Religions, Kurozumikyō and Konkōkyō.

6 INOUE, N. (1982). 'Hokubei ni okeru Konkōkyō no Tenkai (Jyō) (The History of Kōnkō Church in North America).' *Shinto Shūkyo* 107: 26–53.
   Also additional articles in Shinto Shūkyō Nos. 109 and 110.

7 INOUE, N. (1991). 'The Dilemma of Japanese-American Society – A Case Study of Konkōkyō in North America.' *Japanese Journal of Religious Studies* 18(2–3): 133–150.

8 KAMSTRA, J. H. (1994). *Japanese Monotheism and New Religions. Japanese New Religions in the West*. P. B. Clarke and J. Somers. Folkestone, Kent, Japan Library: 103–116.

9 Konkōkyō KŌNKŌ Review. Los Angeles, California, Konkōkyō.

10 Konkōkyō (1933). The Sacred Scriptures of Konkōkyō. Konko-cho, Japan, Konkōkyō Hombu.

11 Konkōkyō (1954). Konkōkyō kyogi (Konkōkyō Doctrines), Kōnkō Honbu Kyōchō.

12 Konkōkyō (1959). Konkōkyō Kyoten (Konkōkyō Scriptures), Kōnkō Hombu Kyōchō.

13 Konkōkyō (1971). Daily Service Book. San Francisco, Ministerial Staff of Kōnkō Churches of America.

14 Konkōkyō (1976). Konkōkyō's 50 Years in America. San Francisco, Kōnkō Churches of America.

15 Konkōkyō (1981). Kōnkō Daijin, A Biography. San Francisco, Kōnkō Churches of America.

16 Konkōkyō (1996). Voice of the Universe: Selected Teachings of Konkōkyō. Tokyo, Konkōkyō.

17 KYŌCHŌ, K. H. (1953). *Kōnkō daijin* (The Great God Kōnkō). Okayama, Konkōkyō Honbu Kyōchō.

18 KYŌCHŌ, K. H. (1972). *Gaisetsu: Konkōkyō* (The Explanation: Konkōkyō). Okayama, Konkōkyō Honbu Kyōchō.

19 LANDE, A. and CLARKE, P. B. (1988). 'Japan (New Religious Movements).' *The World's Religions*. S.Sutherland, L. Houlden, P. B. Clarke and F. Hardy. London, Routledge: 932–944.

20 MCFARLAND, H. N. (1967). *The Rush Hour of the Gods: A Study of new Religious Movements in Japan.* New York, Macmillan.
   One of the first books to give a general review which encompasses relevant Japanese history as well as socio-religious background. The author, a professor of the history of religion examines five new religions, Konkōkyō, PL Kyōdan, Seichō-no-Ie, Risshō Kōsei Kai, and Sōka Gakkai.

21 MORIKAWA, M. (1982). Honkyo josei fukyōsha ni tsuite no ichishiron, toku ni shodai josei kyōkaichō ni tsuite. (A Comment on Missionaries of Our Religion Particularly About the First Female Founder.). *Konkōkyōgaku*, Konkōkyō. **22**: 76–95.

22 MURAKAMI, S. (1972). *Kōnkō daijin no shōgai* (The Life of Kōnkō Daijin). Tokyo, Iwanami shoten.

23 NISHIMURA, S. (1956). Manual of Konkōkyō, Kōnkō Hombu Kyōchō.

24 RAMSEYER, R. L. (1972). 'Finances in the New Religions and the Christian Church.' *Japan Christian Quarterly* 37: 84–89.

25 REPP, M. (1995). 'The Earthquake in the Kobe-Osaka Area January 17th 1995. Its Impact on Religions and Their Response.' *Japanese Religions* 20(2): 207–229.

26 SATO, H. (1953). Kōnkō Daijin, Kōnkō Hombu Kyōchō. **1**.
   2 volume set

27 SATO, K. (1958). Konkōkyō, A New Religion of Japan. Konko, General Headquarters of Konkōkyō.

28 SCHNEIDER, D. (1961). 'Konkōkyō: A Religion of Meditation.' *Contemporary Religions in Japan* 2(1): 39–.

29 SCHNEIDER, D. D. B. (1962). *Konkōkyō: A Japanese Religion.* Tokyo, International Institute of the Study of Religions.
   This study is an attempt at an appreciation of an old faith, Shinto and a contemporary 'new' religion, Konkōkyō which has its foundation in Shinto. The 'new' is indicative of the religious expressions of the new shape which has become independent in the last decades and represent, if not in fact new religions, then a movement which goes by the name of 'New Religions'.

30 SHIMAZONO, S. (1979). 'The Living Kami Idea in the New Religions of Japan.' *Japanese Journal of Religious Studies* 6: 389–412.
   Discusses how the New Religions, although often classified as Buddhist or Shinto in origin have emerged from elements of folk belief. Focusing on shamanism and the idea of a 'Parent God' and the 'living kami (god)', the historical development of Tenrikyō and Konkōkyō is discussed.

31 SPAE, J. J. (1955). 'Konkōkyō.' *Missionary Bulletin* 9(8–9).

32 STOESZ, W. (1986). 'The Universal Attitude of Kōnkō Daijin (Life and Thought of Kawate Bunjiro, Founder of the Konkōkyō; Bibliography).' *Japanese Journal of Religious Studies* 13(1).

33 TAMASHIRO, J. G. (1985). *Konkōkyō, A Japanese Religion in Hawaii*, University of Hawaii.

Kurozumikyō

HISTORY

Kurozumikyō was founded by Kurozumi Munetada (1780–1850) on 11 November 1814 after a revelation in which he believed himself to have been possessed by the sun goddess Amaterasu. A Shinto priest of the Imamura Shrine, he had lost both parents in an epidemic and had himself become critically ill for three years during which time he had prayed to Amaterasu. In his revelation he received the knowledge that the divine and human are essentially one and that the whole universe was a living being in him. He called this revelation *'tenmei jikiju'* ('direct reception of the will of heaven').

Kurozumi recovered from his illness and resumed his priestly duties. He also began to teach the meaning of his revelation, attracting a considerable number of believers, many of whom were influential samurai. During the 1840s he established a formal religious body under the name of Kurozumikyō, which later received official recognition as an independent Shinto sect from the government in 1872.

The present 6th generation head is Kurozumi Muneharu.

MAIN BELIEFS AND PRACTICES

Kurozumikyō teaches that the sun goddess Amaterasu is the supreme deity of the universe. It is Shintoistic in its teaching and traditions, but tends towards monotheism in its worship of the Sun Goddess. All people are believed to originate from the *kami* and may become one with the *kami* (*ikitoshi*) through spiritual practice.

The movement places emphasis on healthy living and healing and encourages followers to lead a 'cheerful' life. Believers worship the Sun Goddess in their homes or at the shrine by offering prayers and purification rites. Particular to the movement is the *nippai* ('Sun-Swallowing Rite'), when members inhale the fresh air while worshipping as if to swallow the sun and thereby the spirit of God. This rite is believed to bring health and happiness.

Disease and evil are believed to be curable by the Sun Goddess and by therapeutic and purifying rituals, often involving the use of consecrated water and holy rice, which are used to heal ailing parts of the body. *Majinai* is a form of healing used by ministers which involves blowing upon the area of the body infected by disease or illness. The blowing releases the essence of divinity (*yoki*) derived from the Sun.

In its early history the movement had strong elements of magic and mystic healing rituals, but it has gradually come to place emphasis on virtues such as diligence, filial piety and harmony. Spiritual practice has become the central way to cultivate such virtues and is believed to lead to popular salvation. Emphasis is placed upon *kokoro* and the powers it possesses for self-cultivation and the attainment of harmony.

Kurozumikyō followers do not regard death as polluting as does Shrine Shinto, but as the start of a new life in heaven when one becomes a *kami*. Ancestor worship is practised and most branch churches of Kurozumikyō in Japan provide sacred space for ancestral tablets to be enshrined.

Kurozumikyō uses the Founder's writings as its sacred scripture. Three main festivals are held each year:

Founder's Festival	17–18 April
Purification Festival	30 July
Winter Solstice Festival	

PUBLICATIONS

PERIODICALS INCLUDE:

Kuni no hikari (prewar)
Keisei zasshi (prewar)
Nisshin (monthly)
Omichizure (monthly)

PUBLICATIONS BY THE MOVEMENT INCLUDE:

Tanaka, Gorō, *The Brief Outline of the Kurozumi-kyō, the most Genuine Japanese Religious Faith*, Ōmoto, Okayama, 1956.
Nobuhara, T., *The Brilliant Life of Munetada Kurozumi: A Philosopher and Worshipper of the Sun*, PMC Publications, Tokyo, 1980.
Taiyō Amaneku (The Sun Sheds its Blessing Universally), Kurozumikyō Nisshinsha, Okayama, 1981.

BRANCHES AND MEMBERSHIP

The organization's headquarters are in Okayama City, where a large *kami* hall (*Shintozan*) was built in 1974. There are two Munetada Shrines, dedicated to the Founder, one in Kyoto and the other in Okayama.

Kurozumikyō was at its strongest during the 1880s when it had a membership of six-to-seven hundred thousand. After World War II it became more of a provincial religion based in western Japan (mainly Okayama and Kyoto). Many of its followers are farming people. By the 1970s its membership had dropped to around 400,000. Membership as of 1990 was 295,225.

KUROZUMIKYŌ – BIBLIOGRAPHY

1 HARA, K. (1960). *Kurozumi Munetada* (The founder of Kurozumikyō). Tokyo, Yoshikawa kōbunkan.

2 HARA, K. (1970). 'Kōmei tennō to Kurozumikyō.' *Kokoro* 23 (9 (September)): 65–71.

3 HARDACRE, H. (1986). *Kurozumikyō and the New Religions of Japan*. Princeton, Princeton University Press.
   Though a detailed analysis of a particular new religion, this book also discusses the shared assumptions and world view of the majority of Japanese NRMs.

4 HARDACRE, H. (1986). 'Creating State Shinto:The Great Promulgation Campaign and the New Religions.' *Japanese Journal of Religious Studies* 12(4): 29–64.
   The first part of this paper examines the way in which the Japanese state attempted to create a state religion through the Great Promulgation Campaign of 1870–1884. The latter part of the paper analyzes the effect of this campaign on two of the New Religions, Kurozumikyō and Konkōkyō.

5 HEPNER, C. W. (1935). The Kurozumi Sect of Shinto. Tokyo, Meiji Japan Society.
   The author states that the object of his dissertation is to show the relationship of the Kurozumi-Sect to Shinto, and to present a complete study of the Sect and to place a valuation on its teachings and practical work.

6 HIROTA, M. (1974). 'Bakumatsu, isshin-ki no Kurozumikyō (Kurozumikyō at the Last Days of the Tokugawa Government and the Meiji Restoration).' *Okayama daigaku hōbungakubujutsu kiyō* (*Okayama University Hobungakubujutsu bulletin*) (34 (October)): 13–25.

7 IKADO, F. (1972). 'Genze riyaku-sono ronri to shinri (This-Worldly Benefits: The Logic and Ethic).' *Nihon Bukkyō* (*Japanese Buddhism*) (34 (February 1972)): 1–23.

8 INOUE, N. (1981). *Hamamatsu ni okeru Kurozumikyō no juyō to tenkai* (The acceptance and development of Kurozumikyō in Hamamatsu). *Toshi shakai no shūkyō* (Religions in urban society). N. Tamaru. Tokyo, Tokyo daigaku shūkyōgaku kenkyūshitsu.

9 KODERA, M. (1971). 'Kurozumikyō no rekishiteki seikaku (Kurozumikyō in history).' *Okayama shigaku* (24 (September)): 39–64.

10 KŌMOTO, K. (1976). Kyōsosama no oitsuwa (Tales of the Founder). Okayama, Kurozumikyō Nisshinsha.

11 KUROZUMI, M. (1974). Kurozumikyō kyōso (The Founder of Kurozumikyō). Okayama, Kurozumikyō Nisshinsha.

12 KUROZUMI, T. (1976). Kurozumikyō kyōsoden (Tales of the Founder of Kurozumikyō). Okayama, Kurozumikyō Nisshinsha.

13 Kurozumikyō (1957). Kurozumikyō. Okayama, Ōmoto.

14 Kurozumikyō (1981). Taiyō Amaneku (The Sun Sheds Its Blessing Universally). Okayama, Kurozumikyō Nissinsha.

15 MIYAKE, H. et al (1972). 'Genze riyaku kankei bunken mokuroku (Bibliography of This-Worldly benefits).' *Nihon Bukkyō* (Japanese Buddhism) (34 (February)): 46–47.

16 NOBUHARA, T. (1980). *The Brilliant Life of Munetada Kurozumi: A Philosopher and Worshipper of the Sun*. Tokyo, PMC Publications.

17 STOESZ, W., Ed. (1989). *Kurozumi Shinto: An American Dialogue*. Pennsylvania, Anima Books.
    The book contains several essays on Kurozumikyō by scholars such as H. Byron Earhart and Helen Hardacre and also essays by 'insiders' like the Reverend Muneharu Kurozumi.

18 TANAKA, Y. (1918). *Kurozumikyō no kenkyū* (Research on Kurozumikyō). Tokyo, Tokyodō shoten.

19 TANAKA, G. (1956). *The Brief Outline of the Kurozumikyō, the Most Genuine Japanese Religious Faith*. Okayama, Ōmoto.

20 TANIGUCHI, S. (1968). 'Bakumatsu ni okeru Kurozumikyō ni tsuite no ichikōsatsu (Kurozumikyō at the last days of the Tokugawa government).' *Okayama daigaku kyōikubu kenkyū shūroku* (Okayama University kyoikubu kenkyu shuroku) (6 (March)): 65–81.

Mahikari

'True Light'

HISTORY

Mahikari was founded in 1959 by Okada Yoshikazu (1901–74), who is said to have received divine revelations from God which form the fundamental teachings and principles of the movement. These detail how to attain health, harmony and happiness through purification of the mind, body and soul with True Light. After serving in the Imperial Guards during the Pacific War where he suffered a serious back injury the founder was told by physicians that he had tuberculosis of the spine and only had three more years to live. At this point he realized that his real parent was God and began to devote himself to the service of God and mankind. His disease began to disappear and he became a successful business-man until his companies were destroyed by bombing at the end of the World War. II

On his birthday, 27 February 1959, he suddenly became ill and fell into unconsciousness in which state he was transported to the astral world and told by God to become the bearer of the True Light of God. He was told to change his name to Okada Kotama (Kotama: 'Jewel of Light'). He officially established the movement on 28 August 1960 and it came to be formally known as Sekai Mahikari Bunmei Kyōdan ('Church of the World True-Light Civilization').

Following his death in 1974 there was a split in the movement over the leadership and two branch organizations have emerged under the names Sūkyō Mahikari and Sekai Mahikari Bunmei Kyōdan.

Sūkyō Mahikari (Sūkyō: 'Reverent Teachings') is led by Okada's daughter, Okada Sachiko, known by the spiritual name of *Keijusama* ('Blessed Jewel'). As the second spiritual leader she is referred to as *Oshienushisama* ('Master of Teaching') and Okada after his death became known as *Sukuinushisama* ('Great Saviour'). Keiju was the adopted daughter of Okada and seen by many followers as the natural successor. Approximately 80% of Mahikari members aligned themselves with her and Sūkyō Mahikari remains the larger organization today.

Sekai Mahikari Bunmei Kyōdan is led by Sekiguchi Sakae one of the first believers who said to have been officially chosen by Okada as the second leader before his death. After several years of litigation in the Japanese courts Sekiguchi was legally established as the leader of the original Mahikari movement in 1978, although the majority of members had already aligned with Sūkyō Mahikari. The doctrine for both branches has remained essentially the same.

MAIN BELIEFS AND PRACTICES

Mahikari, 'True Light', is a purifying spiritual energy that is used to attain health and well-being in everyday life. The main practice is the radiating of this True Light to parts of the body, especially forehead, back of head, neck and kidneys, in order to eliminate impurities and spiritual, mental and physical difficulties. Members can begin to radiate this True Light after attending a three-day seminar (*kenshu*) and receiving a Divine pendant known as *omitama*. The practice of radiating light through the hands is known as *Mahikari no waza* or *okiyome* (transmission of light). Before radiating light, the Divine World Prayer, *Amatsu Norigoto*, is chanted, which is believed to purify and awaken spirits and souls to truth or the 'original power as children of God'.

Most Mahikari Centres have an altar in which the *Goshintai* ('Divine Object') is held, a physical object through which a person can communicate with the spirit of God. It takes the form of a framed scroll with a comma-like symbol on a golden disc, through which the light of God is believed to emanate.

Ideas of reincarnation and karma are central in the movement. Mahikari teaches that many of life's problems, such as illness and other personal misfortunes are caused by evil or unhappy spirits that disturb or possess the living. The purification technique of radiating True Light can therefore help not only the living but also remove spirits who may have attached themselves to a person.

As well as providing spiritual healing centres, Mahikari has set up farms in several countries to grow vegetables and fruit under True Light, thereby avoiding chemical toxins and pollutants. Sūkyō Mahikari also has its own Health Centre in Takayama, Japan.

Sūkyō Mahikari sponsors Yoko Civilization International Conferences which are nonsectarian gatherings of scholars of all disciplines and nationalities to discuss contemporary social problems. The conferences aim to promote prosperity in the twenty-first century and ensure that technology is kept in balance with the natural environment. The movement urges that the coming civilization should make the best use of the cultures and traditions of each region, without conflict between religious sects, races and nations. Many believers see Mahikari not as a religion, but more as a form of science and therapy.

PUBLICATIONS

CENTRAL TEXTS:

Goseigen (The Book of Holy Words)
Norigotoshū (The Book of Prayers)

PUBLICATIONS BY THE MOVEMENT INCLUDE:

Tebecis, A.K., *Mahikari: Thank God for the Answers at last*, Yoko Shuppan, Tokyo, 1982.
Gendai no kokoro: Sūkyō Mahikari (The Spirit of Today: Sūkyō Mahikari), Mahikari, Tokyo, 1985.

BRANCHES AND MEMBERSHIP

SŪKYŌ MAHIKARI

The headquarters of Sūkyō Mahikari is in Takayama City, Gifu prefecture, Japan. There are approximately 650,000 members in Japan (over 800,000 including overseas members).

Sūkyō Mahikari has spread to 75 countries and 90 ethnic groups. The main branches are as follows:

Regional Office	Major Centres	Established
Sūkyō Mahikari Australia & Oceania HQ, Canberra, Australia	Canberra	Feb 1977
	Adelaide	Dec 1977
	Sydney	Dec 1977
Sūkyō Mahikari Asia Region HQ, Singapore	Kuala Lumpur	Sep 1984
Sūkyō Mahikari Shidobu Europe-Afrique, HQ Luxembourg	Paris	Feb 1972
	Marseilles	April 1974
	Gudadeloupe	Nov 1974
	Martinique	Nov 1974
	Nice	May 1975
	Toulouse	Nov 1979
	St. Nazaire	June 1975
	Milan	April 1974
	Turin	Nov 1976
	Abidjan	Oct 1975
	Kinshasa	July 1976
Sūkyō Mahikari North American Region HQ, California, USA	Los Angeles	Feb 1974
	San Francisco	Feb 1974
	New York	May 1975
	Hawaii	March 1975
Sūkyō Mahikari Sede de Orientacao para a America, HQ Sao Paulo, Brasil	Caracas	June 1982
	Mexico City	Sept 1977
	Lima	June 1976
	Trujillo	Sept 1978
	Sao Paulo	April 1974
	Rio De Janeiro	Aug 1975
	Londrina	Aug 1975
	Brasilia	July 1980
	Curitiba	July 1989

SEKAI MAHIKARI BUNMEI KYŌDAN

The main headquarters of Sekai Mahikari Bunmei Kyōdan are in Shizuoka Prefecture, Japan. As of February 1996 there are around 100,000 members worldwide (including Japan). Foreign branches are as follows:

Country	Branch	Established
Philippines	Manila	Jan 1990
	Baguio	Jan 1993
Canada	Port Moody	Dec 1985
USA	Irvine	Nov 1988
	Seplveda	Oct 1991
	Mission Viejo	Oct 1995
	Lebanon	Oct 1991
	Lexington	Nov 1994
Uruguay	Montevideo	Jul 1991
Germany	Freiburg	Jan 1994
Indonesia	Jakarta	Jul 1991
Thailand	Chiangmai	Jul 1989
Korea	Seoul	Jun 1988
	Pusan	Jan 1987
Taiwan	Taizhong	Feb 1990
	Taipei	Mar 1988
	Pingdong	Jul 1989
	Wuqi	May 1991
	Tianmu	Jul 1988
	Gaoxiong	Jun 1988
	Huanglin	Jul 1992

MAHIKARI – BIBLIOGRAPHY

1 BOUMA, G., W. SMITH, et al. (1998). Japanese Religion in Australia: Mahikari and Zen in a Multicultural Society. *Japanese New Religions in Global Perspective*. P. B. Clarke. Richmond, Surrey, Curzon Press.

2 CORNILLE, D. C. (1991). *The Phoenix Flies West. The Dynamics of Mahikari in Northern Europe*. 5th International Conference on 'New Religions in a Global Perspective', Santa Barbara, California.
This paper is valuable in helping to understand how Mahikari functions in Europe and how it is being received in Europe. It describes the new dynamics of interaction between Mahikari and the new culture in which it is becoming established. The new religion no longer spontaneously emerges in answer to existing needs, but is superimposed upon a tradition in which it must either cater for different needs or bring about a redefinition of needs within its own context.

3 CORNILLE, D. C. (1992). *Sekte of Kunst? Mahikari, een nieuwe Japanse godsdienst in de Nederlanden*. Religieuze Bewegingen in Nederland 24. R. Kranenborg. Amsterdam, VU Uitgeverji.

4 CORNILLE, D. C. (1994). *Different forms of Spirit Meditation in Mahikari and Shinnyo-en: Shamanism East and West. Le Défi Magique.* J.-B. Martin, Presses Universitaires de Lyon. 2.

This contribution was a paper given at the CESNUR Conference of 1992 in Lyon concerning 'Magic and Occultism in Contemporary Societies'. It focuses on Mahikari and Shinnyo-en, new religions having similar worldviews and consideration of different forms of shamanism as a factor for their expansion.

5 CORNILLE, C. (1994). Jesus in Japan: Christian Syncetism in Mahikari. Japanese New Religions in the West. P. B. Clarke and J. Somers. Folkestone, Kent, The Japan Library: 88–102.

A discussion of the syncretism of Christian elements in one of the 'new, new' religions, Mahikari.

6 DAVIS, W. (1980). *Dojo: Magic and Exorcism in Modern Japan.* Stanford, California, Stanford University Press.

An ethnographic description and theoretical analysis of he history, teachings and practices of Sūkyō Mahikari with particular focus on possession and healing through exorcism.

7 DAVIS, W. (1991). *Fundamentalism in Japan: Religious and Political. Fundamentalisms Observed.* M. E. Marty and R. S. Appleby. Chicago and London, University of Chicago Press: 782–813.

Davis analyses Japan's society, politics and religion under the concept of fundamentalism. He discusses prewar political fundamentalism in terms of 'civil religion' and gives an historical outline of the state's use of both Buddhism and Shinto in national development and the way in which religion and government were unified to enforce a structure of national identity. Davis then looks at political fundamentalism in the postwar concentrating on Japan's new religions, especially Risshō Kōsei Kai, Mahikari and Sōka Gakkai. He outlines their theology and activities including political activity. Finally he discusses whether the New Religions can be termed fundamentalist, how they relate to Japan's socio-political and cultural realities and the contemporary influence of historical fundamentalism.

8 DEVOS, G. (1982). *Afterward. The Quiet Therapies: Japanese Pathways to Personal Growth.* D. Reynolds. Honolulu, University of Hawaii Press.

9 HATANAKA, S. (1987). *Gendai no Kokoro: Sūkyō Mahikari.* Tokyo, Obunsha.

10 HEISIG, J. (1990). 'Magic and Morality in Modern Japanese Exorcistic technologies – A Study of Mahikari.' *Japanese Journal of Religious Studies* 17(1): 29.

11 HURBON, L. (1980). 'La Double Fonctionnement des sectes aux Antilles. Le Cas du Mahikari en Guadeloupe.' *Archives de sciences sociales des religions* 25: 50–1.

12 HURBON, L. (1986). New Religious Movements in the Caribbean, in *New Religious Movements and Rapid Social Change.* J. A. Beckford. Newbury Park, California, Sage: 145–176.

This article looks at a range of new religious movements in the Caribbean including Mahikari. It draws a contrast between Mahikari and some Christian sects, especially Jehovah's Witnesses and Seventh Day Adventists, in that Mahikari validates and strengthens African ideas of spirit possession. Mahikari is seen here as offering an alternative to Western based models of modernity and that is more supportive of Caribbean Africans' sense of ethnic identity.

13 HURBON, L. (1991). 'Mahikari in the Caribbean.' *Japanese Journal of Religious Studies* 18(2–3): 243–264.

An examination of the way in which Mahikari has found widespread acceptance in the Caribbean cultural context because of the way in which Mahikari teachings are perceived by the movement's members to echo Caribbean folk beliefs regarding the ancestors and spirit possession.

14 KASHIO, N. (1996). *Gendai Furansu toshi to shinshūkyō undo: Pari Mahikari no jirei* (The Modern French City and New Religious Movements:the Case of Mahikari in Paris). *Cities and Civilization*. T. Makoto, Mineruva Shobō.

15 KNECHT, P. and S. HATANAKA (1993). 'Dentō o kumu shinshūkyō: Mahikari.' *Academia (Jinbun-Shakaikagakuhen)* 57(7–271).

16 KNECHT, P. (1995). 'The Crux of the Cross: Mahikari's Core Symbol.' *Japanese Journal of Religious Studies* 22(3–4).
   Explores the symbolism of the cross in both sects of Mahikari (sekai mahikari Bunmei Kyōdan and Sūkyō Mahikari). it also discusses the importance of japan in mahikari's teachings, and identifies some of the sources drawn upon by the founder of Mahikari.

17 KOEPPING, K. P. (1967). 'Sekai Mahikari Bunmei Kyōdan: A preliminary discussion of a recent religious movement in Japan.' *Contemporary Religions in Japan* 8(2): 101–134.

18 LANDE, A. and CLARKE, P. B. (1988). Japan (New Religious Movements). *The World's Religions*. S.Sutherland, L. Houlden, P. B. Clarke and F. Hardy. London, Routledge: 932–944.
   A short summary of the features of several Japanese New Religious Movements including Sōka Gakkai, Nichiren Shōshū, Sekai Kyūseikyō, Ōmotokyō, PL Kyōdan, Risshō Kōsei Kai, Konkōkyō, Tenrikyō, Mahikari, Seichō-no-Ie and Reiyūkai.

19 Mahikari Primary Training Reference Textbook. Takayama Gifu Prefecture:- Sūkyō Mahikari H.Q, L.H Yōkōshi no Tomo.
   There is also an Intermediate and Advanced Training Reference Textbooks.

20 Mahikari (1977). Yokoshi Norogoto Shu. Los Angeles, California, Sekai Mahikari Bunmei Kyōdan of America.

21 Mahikari (1985). Gendai no kokoro: Sūkyō Mahikari (The Spirit of Today: Sūkyō Mahikari). Tokyo, Ohbunsha.

22 Mahikari (1985–). Mahikari. Tokyo, Yōkō Shuppan.
   Monthly Magazine.

23 Mahikari (1989). Mahikari Mondō. Tokyo, L.H. Yōkōshi Shuppan.

24 MATSUNAGA, L. (1998). Spirit First, Mind Follows, Body Belongs: Notions of Health, Illness and Disease in Sūkyō Mahikari U.K. *Japanese New Religions in Global Perspective*. P. B. Clarke. Richmond, Surrey, Curzon Press.

25 McVEIGH, B. (1991). Gratitude, obedience and humility of heart: The cultural construction of belief in a Japanese New Religion. Princeton, Princeton University.
   The dissertation has three main purposes: to present the ideology of Sūkyō Mahikari as a coherent, though syncetistic whole; to delineate the group's theory of human nature and to discuss the social construction of mind and spirit.

26 McVEIGH, B. (1991). 'Gratitude, Obedience, and Humility of Heart: The Morality of Dependency in a New Religion.' *Journal of Social Science (International Christian University, Tokyo)* 30(2): 107–125.

27 McVEIGH, B. (1992). 'The Vitalistic Conception of Salvation as expressed in Sūkyo Mahikari.' *Japanese Journal of Religious Studies* 19(1): 41–68.
   This article seeks to apply to Mahikari the argument of Tsushima et al. (1979) that Japanese NRMs do possess a distinctive concept of spiritual salvation. McVeigh proposes a four aspect paradigm for understanding Mahikari and possibly other Japanese NRMs. In this paradigm, the

crucial aspects of the movement are subsumed under the headings: Divine Source; Divine Power; Divine Personage; and Divine Practice.

28 McVEIGH, B. (1992). 'The Master Metaphor of Purity: The Symbolism of Authority and Power in Sūkyō Mahikari.' *Japanese Religions* 17(2): 98–125.
This article examines the notions of purity in Mahikari, and suggests that purity forms a master metaphor running through all Mahikari ideology. It pays particular attention to the rituals designed to maintain purity.

29 McVEIGH, B. (1992). 'The Authorization of Ritual and the Ritualization of Authority: The Practice of Values in a Japanese New Religion.' *Journal of Ritual Studies* 6(2): 39–58.

30 McVEIGH, B. (1993). 'Building Belief through the Body: The Physical Embodiment of Morality and Doctrine in Sūkyō Mahikari.' *Japanese Religions* 18(2): 140–161.
McVeigh outlines the main ideas on the body held by Sūkyō Mahikari members, reflecting on notions of the body as a physical, moral and spiritual entity and how this manifests itself in the movement's activities and rituals.

31 McVEIGH, B. (1995). 'Learning Morality Through Sentiment and the Senses: The Role of Emotional Experience in Sūkyō Mahikari.' *Japanese Religions* 20(1): 56–76.
Discusses how the religious organization Sūkyo Mahikari strategically use sentiment and emotion to reinforce belief among their followers. McVeigh outlines fundamental principles and ethnomorality of Mahikari centring on the notion of dependency and then examines how emotional experience is utilised through the ritual practice of exorcism, testimonials and ceremonies.

32 McVEIGH, B. (1996). 'Spirit Possession in Sūkyō Mahikari: A Variety of Sociopsychological Experience.' *Japanese Religions* 21(2): 283–297.
An attempt to describe and explain spirit possession in Sūkyō Mahikari in sociopsychological terms.

33 MIYANAGA, K. (1983). Social Reproduction and Transcendence: An Analysis of the Sekai Mahikari Bunmei Kyōdan, a Heterodox Religious Movement in Contemporary Japan., University of British Columbia.

34 OKADA, H. (1987). Gendai no kokoro: Sūkyō Mahikari (The Spirit of Today: Sūkyō Mahikari). Tokyo, Obunsha.

35 OOMS, E. G. (1993). *Women and Millenarian Protest in Meiji Japan. Deguchi Nao and Ōmotokyō.* New York, Cornell University East Asia Program.
Ōmotokyō is a very influential New Religion which has spawned a number of 'world-renewal' New Religions, among them Mahikari, Sekai Kyūseikyō and Seichō-no-Ie. This book is a study of its foundress Deguchi Nao (1836–1918). It also addresses the roles of class and gender in New Religious Movements.

36 READER, I. (1988). 'The Rise of a Japanese "New New Religion": Themes in the Development of Agonshū.' *Japanese Journal of Religious Studies* 15(4): 235–61.
Looks at the rapid growth of Agonshū through a discussion of its highly advertised rituals and events. Discusses how Agonshū manages to combine both elements of tradition and the modern to give members a means to deal with contemporary society, while also appealing to concepts of universality. Draws comparisons with other 'new new' religions such as Mahikari Byakko Shinkōkai and Shinnyoen.

37 READER, I. (1994). 'Japanese Religions.' *Insight Japan.* 3: 6–9.
A summary of a few of the Japanese Old and New Religions.

38 Sekiguschi Sakae (1985). Miyo! mahikari no daikiseki (Look! The Great Miracles of the True Light). Tokyo, Gendai Shorin.

39 SHIBATA, K. (1993). *Daiseishu-Great and Holy Master.* Tokyo, Yoko Shuppan.

40 SOMERS, J. (1994). Japanese New Religious Movements in Britain. *Japanese New Religions in the West.* P. B. CLarke and J. Somers. Folkestone, Kent, Japan Library: 54–76.

41 Sūkyō Mahikari (n.d). Tokyo, Yoko Shuppan Co. Ltd.

42 Sūkyō Mahikari (n.d). The Light of Love. Tokyo, Yoko Shuppan Co. Ltd.

43 SUZUKI, G. (1974). Te no hira ryōji (The Laying-On-Of-Hands Treatment). Tokyo.

44 SUZUKI, H. (1982). *Goseigen: The Holy Words.* Tujunga, California, Mahikari.

45 TANI, F. (1987). *Shinpi kara shukyō e* (From Mystery to Religion). *Gendai no kokoro: Sūkyō Mahikari* (The Contemporary Mind: Sūkyō Mahikari). S. Hatakenaka. Tokyo, Kōbūndo.

46 TEBECIS, A. (1977). 'On How Little is Known about Altered States of Consciousness.' *Japanese Journal of Psychosomatic Medicine* **17**: 256–263.

47 TEBECIS, A. (1978). *Suggestions for Awakened Doctors to the Importance of Mahikari.* First International Congress on Spirit-Mind Medical Science, Tokyo.

48 TEBECIS, A. K. (1982). *Mahikari. Thank God for the Answers at Last.* Tokyo, Yōkō Shuppan.

49 TEBECIS, A. (1988). *Sagashi motomete kotae wa kokoni: Mahikari.* Dickson, A.C.T, Sunrise Press, Dai 5-han nihongoban.

50 YOUNG, R. (1990). 'Magic and Morality in Modern Japanese Exorcistic Technologies. A Study of Mahikari.' *Japanese Journal of Religious Studies* **17**: 29–50.

The first part of this article analyses notions of possession in Mahikari while the second part examines the expansion of Mahikari outside Japan, specifically in Africa and the Caribbean.

Ōmoto (Ōmotokyō)

'Great Foundation'   'Great Origin'

HISTORY

Ōmoto was founded by Deguchi Nao (1836–1918), a poverty-stricken peasant women who had a series of divine revelations beginning in 1892. Nao met Ueda Kisaburo (1871–1948), a mystic and spiritualist, around 1897 and he became her adopted son-in-law, marrying her daughter Sumi (1883–1952) and changing his name to Deguchi Onisaburō. With the help of both Sumi and Onisaburō, Nao began to record her revelations and develop her teachings based upon a reconstruction of an ideal society and world. She began to gather followers and established a centre of worship in Ayabe City, Kyoto and a training centre in Kameoka City, Kyoto.

Ōmoto's ideology, with its opposition to capitalism, war and the landlord system, rapidly became popular with dissident peasant farmers and intellectuals and by the early 1930s had attracted around 2,000,000 members. In 1925 Onisaburō founded the *Aizenkai* ('Universal Love and Brotherhood Association' – ULBA). In both 1921 and 1935 Onisaburō was arrested and imprisoned because of his beliefs that he should become the leader of Japan and Ōmoto's challenge to the myth of the deity Amaterasu as the divine ancestor of the imperial line. Ōmoto buildings were destroyed and the movement was dissolved by the government in 1935. Onisaburō remained in prison from 1935 until his release in 1942.

In January 1946 Onisaburō reorganized Ōmoto and registered it as a religious juridical person under the name Aizenen ('Community of Love and Virtue'). The name was changed to Ōmoto Aizenen ('Grand Source of the Community of Love and Virtue') in 1950 and then in 1952 it adopted the present name Ōmoto. After Onisaburō's death in 1948 Sumi became the second leader of Ōmoto. Sumi revitalized Ōmoto and reorganized many of its former associations for the promotion of agriculture, art and education, including the re-establishment of the *Aizenkai* in 1949.

Deguchi Nao is venerated as the spiritual founder (*kaiso*) and Onisaburō as the doctrinal founder (*kyoso*). Ōmoto has continued to be headed by a female descendant of the foundress. Following Sumi's death in 1952, Deguchi Naohi (1915–1990) granddaughter of the foundress and daughter of Onisaburō and Sumi became the third leader of Ōmoto. Naohi strove to bring about an awareness of the unity of art and religion in everyday life as well as the recognition of the fundamental unity of all religions. Following Naohi's death in 1990, her daughter Kiyoko became the current leader.

MAIN BELIEFS AND PRACTICES

Ōmoto is Shinto by classification and has been categorized as a 'world renewal' religion. During her initial revelatory experiences Nao Deguchi was heavily influenced by the teachings of Konkōkyō and their faith in the *kami* (god) Konjin. She is said to have written *Ofudesaki* ('The Tip of the Divine Writing Brush'), the sacred scriptures of Ōmoto, under the direction of this deity *Ushitora-no-Konjin,*(Great Father God) while she herself was illiterate. She gradually moved away from Konkōkyō and developed her own teachings while writing. In *Ofudesaki* she predicted the destruction of humanity and called for a return to traditional society and for the construction of an age of world renewal and peace, the Kingdom of *Miroku*.

Ōmoto's anti-government and anti-war stance prior to and during World War II, culminated in their primary mission to establish an age of world peace, during the reconstruction period following Japan's defeat. Onisaburō claimed that the *kami* had allowed him to survive the war in order to establish this new world.

The doctrines of Ōmoto are based on the revelations of Nao Deguchi, essentially the writings in *Ofudesaki*, and the teachings of Onisaburō. Although Shinto by classification, Ōmoto is a sect rooted in mystical Shinto, and the Buddhist and folk traditions of Japan. It is a religion which is devoted to the traditional arts of Japan and the link between art and religion. Onisaburō Sumi and Naohi were artists. Onisaburō particularly made numerous ink-paintings, calligraphy and ceramics throughout his life, including more than 3,000 tea bowls. Ōmoto views art as a spiritual discipline as well as a form of mediation, self-expression and prayer.

Believers pray daily in front of their household altars and also practice *chinkon kishin*, Ōmoto's discipline of meditation that leads to union with God. A communal service is usually held once a month. Main annual festivals are: the great Setsubun or Spring Festival which also commemorates the day God revealed himself to Nao Deguchi; the Miroku Festival in April and the Harvest Festival when a pilgrimage is made to the hill of Ten'nodaira ('Imperial Flat Hill') where Nao, Onisaburō and Sumi are buried.

PUBLICATIONS

PERIODICALS INCLUDE:

Ōmoto (in Japanese, English and Esperanto, issued bi-monthly since 1956)
Aizen-en (monthly)
Jinrui Aizen Shimbun (every ten days)
Ōmoto International (Journal of the Ōmoto Foundation and the Aizenkai – English)

MAIN PUBLICATIONS BY THE MOVEMENT INCLUDE:

Ofudesaki, by Deguchi Nao, (Translated by Hino Iwao as *Ofudesaki, the Holy Scriptures of Ōmoto*, copyright 1974)
Iwao, Hino ed., *The Outline of Ōmoto*, Kyoto, 1970
Deguchi, Kyotaro, *The Great Onisaburō Deguchi*, Ōmoto Foundation, Kyoto, 1973.
Nao Deguchi: A Biography of the Foundress of Ōmoto, Ōmoto Foundation, 1982.
In Search of Meaning, by Hidemaru Deguchi, (Translated by William Gilkey and Masamichi Tanaka) Ōmoto Foundation, 1994.

BRANCHES AND MEMBERSHIP

Ōmoto has its headquarters in Kameoka City, Kyoto Prefecture, Japan, where it has established the *Ten-onkyo* (holy grounds) and the *Bansho-den* ('Hall of a Million Beatitudes'). The spiritual centre is in Ayabe where the main sanctuary *Miroku-den* ('Hall of the Future Buddha Maitreya') and the *Choseiden* sanctuary are located.

Although extremely popular in the prewar period, Ōmoto never regained its former strength after WWII. However, several other new religions have grown out of Ōmoto in the postwar period, notably Sekai Kyūseikyō and Seichō-no-Ie, becoming more successful than the parent movement itself.

There are currently around 170,000 Ōmoto members in Japan.

Ōmoto has one overseas branch in Brazil, which was established in Autumn 1957. There are approximately 1,000 members in Brazil.

ŌMOTO – BIBLIOGRAPHY

1 BOBILIN, R. T. (1968). *Japanese Peace Movements.* The Religious Situation: 1968. D. R. Cutler. Boston, Beacon Press.

2 DEGUCHI, O. (1957). *A Guide to God's Way.* Kameoka, Ōmoto Central Office.

3 DEGUCHI, N. (1957). *Scripture of Ōmoto by Deguchi Nao*, Ōmoto Central Office.

4 DEGUCHI, I. (1963). 'Ōmoto (Great Foundation).' *Contemporary Religions in Japan* **4**(3): 230–247.

5 DEGUCHI, K. (1973). The Great Onisaburō Deguchi. Kyoto, Japan, Ōmoto Foundation: 266.
   This book is the English translation of a biographical portrait of Onisaburō Deguchi, the driving force behind the Ōmoto sect written by his grandson.

6 FRANCK, F. (1975). *An Encounter with Ōmoto. 'The Great Origin', a faith rooted in the ancient mysticism and the traditional arts of Japan.* New York.

7 FRANK, F. (1975). An Encounter with Ōmoto. West Nyack, New York, Cross Currents/Ōmoto Foundation.

8 GRAY, W. (1974). 'Ōmoto and Teihard de Chardin: Two Case Studies in Revitalization.' *Japanese Religions* **8**.

9 HAMMER, R. (1961). The Idea of God in Japan's New Religions – with Special Reference to Tenrikyō, Konkōkyō, Sekai Kyūseikyō, Ōmotokyō, Reiyūkai, Risshō Kōsei Kai, PL Kyōdan, Seichō-no-Ie and Annaikyo. *University of London*, London.

10 HARDACRE, H. (1988). 'Gender and the Millennium in Ōmoto Kyōdan: the Limits of Religious Innovation.' *Innovation in Religious Traditions: Essays in the Interpretation of Religious Change.* M. Williams, C. Cox and M. S. Jaffe. Berlin and New York, Mouton de Grutyer.
   The founders of Ōmotokyo, Deguchi Nao and her son-in-law, Deguchi Onisaburō, practised a gender-role reversal in which she was a male spirit in a female body and he was a female spirit in a male body. The author examines the Buddhist antecedents for this reversal and its relation to millenarian thought, but argues that the challenge the founders represented to the traditional gender system was never extended to their followers.

11 HIBBARD, E. L. (1962). 'Interview with Leaders of Ōmotokyo.' *Japan Christian Quarterly* **28**.

12 *Hidemaru*, D. (1994). In Search of Meaning. Kyoto, The Ōmoto Foundation.

13 HINO, I. P. (1964). 'Comments by a Disciple of the Master Onisaburō Deguchi on 'Modern Japanese Religions' by Offner and Van Straelen and 'The New Religions of Japan' by H. Thomsen.' *Contemporary Religions of Japan* 5(1): 75f.

14 HINO, I. P. (1970). *The Outline of Ōmoto*. Kameoka, Japan, Ōmoto Foundation.

15 HINO, I. P. (1974). Ofudesaki: The Holy Scriptures of Ōmoto. Kameoka, Ōmoto.
This is a translation of the holy scriptures by Hino.

16 IKEDA, A. (1982). *Ōmoto shiryō shūsei* (Collected Historical Works on Ōmoto). Tokyo, San'ichi Shobō.

17 KAMSTRA, J. H. (1994). Japanese Monotheism and New Religions. Japanese New Religions in the West. P. B. Clarke and J. Somers. Folkestone, Kent, Japan Library: 103–116.
Polytheism, the belief in myriads of deities has been one of the pillars of Shinto in particular and of Japanese religion in general. This article highlights the contrast with the new religions such as Tenrikyō, Konkōkyō and Ōmotokyō which believe in deities with monotheistic qualities. Kamstra analyses the impact of Christian theistic qualities on Japanese new religions.

18 KERR, A. (1982). 'Ōmoto and other Religions.' *Ōmoto International* April–June: 30–34.

19 KERR, A. (1983). 'Ōmoto and other Religions.' *Ōmoto International* January–June: 9–13.

20 KOBAYASHI, S. (1960). 'Ōmoto: A Religion of Salvation.' *Japanese Religions* 2(April): 38–50.

21 LANDE, A. and CLARKE, P. B. (1988). *Japan (New Religious Movements). The World's Religions*. S.Sutherland, L. Houlden, P. B. Clarke and F. Hardy. London, Routledge: 932–944.
A short summary of the features of several Japanese New Religious Movements including Sōka Gakkai, Nichiren Shōshū, Sekai Kyūseikyō, Ōmotokyō, PL Kyōdan, Risshō Kōsei Kai, Konkōkyō, Tenrikyō, Mahikari, Seichō-no-Ie and Reiyūkai.

22 MAEYAMA, T. (1983). *Japanese Religions in Southern Brazil: Change and Syncretism*, The University of Tsukuba.
This article discusses the religious life of the Japanese in southern Brazil by presenting ethnographical case studies of religious organizations. It begins with an outline of Japanese emigration and how this influenced the general absence of traditional Shinto religion in Brazil. This leads to the central discussion of new religions, first focusing on the activities of six movements: Ōmoto, Tenrikyō, Seicho-no-Ie, Sekai-Kyūsei-Kyō, P.L Kyōdan and Sōka Gakkai. The next section presents five Nippo-Brazilian new religions, groups originating in Brazil but rooted in Japanese cultural and religious tradition: Shirei-kyō, Fudō Myō, inari Daimyōjin, Kaminoya Yaoyorozukyō and Nossa Senhora de Kannan.

23 MAEYAMA, T. and SMITH, R. J. (1983). *Ōmoto: A Japanese 'New Religion' in Brazil*, University of Tsukuba.

24 MURAKAMI, S. (1979). *Ōmoto Shinyu: Ten no Maki* (Ōmoto Divine Oracles: The Book of Heaven). Tokyo, Heibonsha.

25 NADOLSKI, T. (1973). *Ōmoto and the Japanese Imperial Government. Nihon bunka kenkyū (Studies in Japanese Culture)*. 2: 26–32.

26 NADOLSKI, T. P. (1975). The Socio-Political Background of the 1921 and 1935 Ōmoto Suppressions in Japan, University of Pennsylvania.

27 NAKAHARA, Z. (1950). 'Ōmoto no kenkyū (A Study of Ōmoto).' *Minzokugaku Kenkyū* **15**.

28 NAKAMURA, T. (1920). *Ōmotokyō no Kaibō*. Tokyo, Nihon Seishin Igakkai.

29 NAKAMURA, T. (1932). 'Kokusai-shūkyō ōmoto-kyō (Ōmoto, the International Religion).' *Kami no kuni* (December): 44–49.

30 Ōmoto (1925). The New Spiritual Movement. Ayabe, Ōmoto Overseas office.

31 Ōmoto (1952). The Ōmoto Movement, Its Origins, Aims and Objects and the Universal Love and Brotherhood Association. Kameoka, The Ōmoto Headquarters.

32 Ōmoto (1955). The Basic Teachings of Ōmoto. Kyōto, Jinrui Aizen-kai Kokusaibu.

33 Ōmoto (1956–). Ōmoto International. California, Ōmoto International Department.
Official yearly journal of the Ōmoto Foundation and the Aizenkai (ULBA – Universal Love and Brotherhood Association).

34 Ōmoto (1958). The Outline of Ōmoto. Kameoka.

35 Ōmoto (1958). The Fundamentals of the Soul. *Ōmoto*: 2–3.

36 Ōmoto Hombu Senkyobu (1959). Ōmoto Shinkō no Shiori (The Guide to Ōmoto Belief). Kameoka, Ōmoto Hombu Senkyobu,.

37 Ōmoto Hombu Senkyōbu (1958). Ōmoto no Shinji to Sekai no Shōrai (The Shinto Rites of Ōmoto and the Future of the World). Kameoka, Ōmoto Hombu Senkyōbu.

38 OOMS, E. G. (1984). Deguchi Nao and Ōmoto-kyo: An Analysis of a Millenarian Cult in Meiji Japan, University of Chicago.

39 OOMS, E. G. (1993). *Women and Millenarian Protest in Meiji Japan. Deguchi Nao and ōmotokyō*. New York, Cornell University East Asia Program.
Ōmotokyō is a very influential New Religion which has spawned a number of 'world-renewal' New Religions, among them Mahikari, Sekai Kyūseikyō and Seichō-no-Ie. This book is a study of its foundress Deguchi Nao (1836–1918). It also addresses the roles of class and gender in New Religious Movements.

40 OSAKI, K. (1959). Okagebanashi (Stories of Thanksgiving). Kameoka, Ōmoto Hombu Senkyobu.

41 OSAKI, K. (1959). Seishiden (The Biography of a Holy Man). Kameoka, Tenseisha.
Biography of the founder of Ōmoto.

42 READER, I. (1994). Japanese Religions. Insight Japan. **3**: 6–9.
A summary of a few of the Japanese Old and New Religions.

43 REPP, M. (1995). 'The Earthquake in the Kobe-Osaka Area January 17th 1995. Its impact on religions and their response.' *Japanese Religions* **20**(2): 207–229.

44 SAKURAI, Y. (1955). The Basic Teachings of Ōmoto. Kameoka, The Ōmoto Headquarters.

45 SCHILLER, E. (1923). 'Ōmotokyō, die neueste Religion Japans.' *Zeitschrift für Missionskunde und Religionswissenschaft* **38**.

46 SPAE, J. J. (1956). 'Ōmotokyō.' *Missionary Bulletin* **10**(9).

47 SUGAI, T. (1969). 'The Soteriology of New Religions.' *Japanese Religions* 6(2): 23–46.

48 TANAKA, G. (1956). *The Brief Outline of the Kurozumikyō, the Most Genuine Japanese Religious Faith*. Okayama, Ōmoto.

49 WÖHR, U. (1989). *Frauen und Neue Religionen. Die Religionsgründerinnen Nakayama Miki und Deguchi Nao*. (*Women and New Religions. Foundresses Nakayama Miki and Deguchi Nao*). Wien, Beiträge zur Japanologie/Institut für Japanologie.
A discussion of the importance a female founder may have on the ideology and aims of a religious movement. Wöhr then goes on to give two examples: the female founders of Tenrikyō and Ōmoto, two of the oldest 'new' religions.

50 YAMASHITA, A. (1990). 'Tenrin-ō and Henjō-Nanshi: Two Women Founders of new religions.' *Japanese Religions* 16(2): 1–23.
Yamashita relates the new religions boom to the women's liberation movement and feminism in Japan by examining two shamanic women, founders of two new religions: Nakayama Miki of Tenrikyō and Deguchi Nao of Ōmoto.

51 YASUMARU, Y. (1977). *Deguchi Nao*. Tokyo, Asahi shimbunsha.

52 YOUNG, R. (1988). 'From Gokyō-dōgen to Bankyō-dōkon: A Study in the Self-Universalization of Ōmoto.' *Japanese Journal of Religious Studies* 15(4): 263–86.
Young looks at Ōmoto's heraldry of a new age of 'shūsaika' ('interreligious cooperation') based on the historical concept of bankyō-dōkon ('all religions are derived from the same root'). The historical process through which Ōmoto 'universalized' itself is presented.

53 YOUNG, R. F. (1989). 'Jesus, the "Christ", and Deguchi Onisaburō: A Study of Adversarial Syncetism in a Japanese World-renewal Religion'. *Japanese Religions* 15(4): 26–49.
Discusses the Japanese prototype 'world-renewal' religion Ōmoto and the syncretic function of the 'Christ' motif as formulated by the founder Deguchi Onisaburō. An historical account of Onisaburō's activities and writings along with his perception of and reference to 'Christ' and Christianity is presented.

P L Kyōdan

Perfect Liberty Kyōdan: 'Church of Perfect Liberty'

HISTORY

The First Founder (*Oshieoya*) was the Rev. Miki Tokuharu (1871–1938), who was a Zen Buddhist priest of the *Obaku* Sect. In 1912 he met Rev. Kanada Tokumitsu who cured his asthma by performing the Sacred Rite of *Ofurikae* (power of temporarily curing illness). Miki Tokuharu and his son Miki Tokuchika (1900–83) became Kanada's disciples, learning the precepts of his Tokumitsu Church as well as the sacred rite of *Ofurikae*. Before his death Kanada urged Tokuharu to pray for the remaining three precepts of his teachings to be revealed and to then establish a church devoted to people and society. Tokuharu duly established new Tokumitsu Kyōkai in 1924, which changed its name to the Hitonomichi Kyōkai ('The Way of Man Society') in 1931.

Hitonomichi was ordered to disband by the military government in April 1937 because of its beliefs that man was of the same spirit as deity and for treating the Imperial Rescript on Education as a religious text and worshipping Amaterasu as its chief deity. Both Tokuharu and Tokuchika were imprisoned. Tokuharu died in prison but Tokuchika re-established the organization after his release on 29 September 1946 under the new name of the Church of Perfect Liberty, becoming the second founder. After his death in 1983, he was succeeded by the Third Founder, his adopted son, Rev. Miki Takahito (1957–). It is believed he becomes *oshieoyasama* (patriarch or spiritual leader of PL) and each leader receives God's revelations

194

allowing him to teach and guide people. Moreover, in each *oshieoyasama* the spiritual power is believed to increase because of the spiritual resources passed on through the generations.

MAIN BELIEFS AND PRACTICES

PL Kyōdan's motto is 'Life is Art': 'If you can master a way of life by practising the teachings of this philosophy, you can attain a state of mind that parallels Perfect Liberty – total mental freedom. Life can then become a continuous, conscious self-expression; hence life is art.' (from *The Power of Perfect Liberty*, by Dr Marcus Bach).

The basic precept of PL Kyōdan expresses a unity of Self (mind) and the World (society). True freedom and a fulfilling life is believed to be achieved when both social and personal freedom co-exist. Life, like art, must be lived in a balanced, creative and aesthetically expressive manner. PL is concerned with a 'Divine Universal Scheme' and the correct mental attitude to live one's life within the global environment and rules of the universe. It claims to be independent and not related to other religions, but at the same time does not contradict the teachings of other religions. However, it has been identified as having been indirectly influenced in ideology and practice by Ōmoto in the early years.

There is no holy book as such, but there are the PL 21 Precepts which were received from God by the Founder and succeeding *Oshieoyasama*. There are also the 21 Principles which support these Precepts and teach how to lead fulfilled lives. The 21 Precepts provide a set of guidelines for the arranging of one's life into a series of self-expressions that ultimately form a masterpiece of art. They are available in written form or on video or cassettes for members to learn from. There are also daily peace prayers available in written form on a PL calendar for members to follow. Members are urged to practice *Oyashikiri* prayer (*Oya* = parent; *Shikiri* = strong faith and promise) during which they chant to *Mioya Ōkami* (God, creator of the universe) while looking at the centre of the PL prayer symbol. The prayer symbol has 21 petals representing the PL 21 Precepts and a centre which represents the window to God. The symbol is placed in a portable *omitama* for use at home or at work, and during prayer an offering of money (*hōshō*) is given to the *omitama*. The attitude of mind needed to implement the artistic elements of life is *makoto* (sincerity). Members who achieve *mdkoto* achieve a life which has become a work of art and are therefore living in 'Perfect Liberty'.

PL followers see illness, injury or misfortune as *mishirase* (divine warning) and a need for *mioshie* (divine instruction). This instruction teaches the cause of the *mishirase* which is based on negative or unnatural mental habits. *Mioshie* is not for the curing of illness or problems, but a guide to how to change ones state of mind and become more positive. There are PL Health Check-up Centres in Tokyo and Osaka and a PL Hospital. A medical clinic has also been opened in Sao Paulo, Brazil. Both modern medicine and counselling on mental causes of illness are combined in the treatment. There are also PL Botanical Research Institutes in Osaka, Japan and Aruja, Brazil which work to develop virus free plants and vegetables, as well as carry out cancer research and projects with NASA space programmes.

It is believed that 'Children are a Mirror of their Parents' and emphasis is placed on the art of rearing children as well as respect for parents. There is a PL Gakuen School system, beginning with a kindergarten and ending with a women's junior college as well as a hygiene and nurses' training school. PL Gakuen was established in 1953.

PL Kyōdan's public worship centres around both stylish and liturgical rituals of prayer accompanied by bowing, sermons, testimonials and offerings. The 21st day of each month is a Thanksgiving Day Service to show appreciation to *Oshieoyasama* for his personal sacrifice and also to thank God for the blessings received in the previous month. The main festival is the Founders Day Ceremony on 1 August of each year, when PL believers gather at the PL Holy Land to show their appreciation and pray to the first and second founders. On this day the Oshieoya purifies all the participants through the Rite of Blessing in front of the altar of the main temple and then a huge display of fireworks is held as a symbol of the hope for world peace. Other ceremonies are: New Year's Day on January 1st; PL Establishment Day on 29 September; and Oshieoyasama's Birthday on 2 December. Other monthly ceremonies include: Day of Peace on the 1st of each month and Ancestors' Day on the 11th of each month.

PUBLICATIONS

PERIODICALS INCLUDE:

Perfect Liberty Magazine (English)
PL News

PL Seinen (monthly)
Geijutsu Seikatsu (monthly)
Tanka Geijutsu (monthly)

PUBLICATIONS BY THE MOVEMENT INCLUDE:

Perfect Liberty: How to Lead a Happy Life, PL Order, Tondabayashi, 1951.
The PL Handbook, PL Order, Tondabayashi, 1964.
Perfect Liberty: Guide to Perfect Liberty, PL North American Headquarters, Glendale, CA, 1975.

BRANCHES AND MEMBERSHIP

The present PL Headquarters are at Tondabayashi, Osaka, Japan, and were constructed in 1953. There is a holy PL Peace Tower at the centre of Habikino Hills close to the headquarters. The tower is 590 feet high and was completed on 1 August 1970. It is dedicated to all those in human history who have died in war.

There are around 300,000 members in Japan.

According to the headquarters, there are over 500 churches in ten different countries and a total membership of more than 1,000,000 members. There are overseas churches in the U.S.A., Hawaii, Canada, Brazil, Argentina, Paraguay, Peru, Paris and Australia.

There are the following main branches overseas:

Branch	Country	Established	Members
Church of Perfect Liberty	California, USA	June 1960	1,200
Church of Perfect Liberty	Ottawa, Canada		
Inst. Religiosa Perfect Liberty	Sao Paulo, Brazil	Sept. 1957	360,000
Inst. Religiosa Perfecta Libertad	Buenos Aires, Argentina	July 1976	15,000
Perfect Liberty	Paris, France	1978	100

P L KYŌDAN – BIBLIOGRAPHY

1 BACH, M. (1971). *The Power of Perfect Liberty. Out of Japan: A Creative Breakthrough in Humanity's Quest for a New Man in a New Age*, Englewood Cliffs, USA.
Details the author's personal contact with Perfect Liberty, discussing its teachings and values, its leader and members, and its vision of world peace.

2 ELLWOOD, R. S. (1974). *The Eagle and the Rising Sun: Americans and the New Religions of Japan.* Philadelphia, Westminster Press.
   Ellwood examines the impact of five 'new religions' in America: Tenrikyō, Sōka Gakkai, Sekai Kyūseikyō, Seichō-no-Ie and Perfect Liberty. The cultural exchange between East and West as presented by the development of these movements in America is discussed.

3 FUJIKURA, Y. (1992). Alguns Aspectos de Inculturação no Trabalho Missionário da Perfect Liberty Kyōdan no Brasil (Some Aspects of Inculturation in the Missionary Work of PL in Brazil). M.A. Dissertation, São Paulo, Pontificia Universidade Católica.

4 HAMMER, R. (1961). The Idea of God in Japan's New Religions – with Special Reference to Tenrikyō, Konkōkyō, Sekai Kyūseikyō, Ōmotokyō, Reiyūkai, Risshō Kōsei Kai, PL Kyōdan, Seichō-no-Ie and Annaikyo. *University of London,* London.

5 HAMMER, R. J. (1963). 'The Scriptures of Perfect Liberty Kyōdan: A Translation with a Brief Commentary.' *Japanese Religions* 3(1).

6 KITAMURA, T. (1958). Oyashikiri Taikenshū (Experiences of Oyashikiri). Tondabayashi, PL Shuppansha.

7 LANDE, A. and CLARKE, P. B. (1988). *Japan (New Religious Movements). The World's Religions.* S. Sutherland, L. Houlden, P. B. Clarke and F. Hardy. London, Routledge: 932–944.
   A short summary of the features of several Japanese New Religious Movements including Sōka Gakkai, Nichiren Shōshū, Sekai Kyūseikyō, Ōmotokyō, PL Kyōdan, Risshō Kōsei Kai, Konkōkyō, Tenrikyō, Mahikari, Seichō-no-Ie and Reiyūkai.

8 MCFARLAND, H. N. (1967). *The Rush Hour of the Gods: A Study of New Religious Movements in Japan.* New York, Macmillan.
   One of the first books to give a general review which encompasses relevant Japanese history as well as socio-religious background. The author, a professor of the history of religion examines five new religions, Konkōkyō, PL Kyōdan, Seichō-no-Ie, Risshō Kōsei Kai, and Sōka Gakkai.

9 MORI, Y. (1979). *Perfect Liberty Kyōdan. Shinshūkyō no Sekai* (The World of the New Religions). M. Shimizu. Tokyo, Daizo Shuppan. V: 83–124.

10 NAKAMAKI, H. (1991). 'The Indigenization and Multinationalization of Japanese Religion-Perfect Liberty Kyōdan in Brazil.' *Japanese Journal of Religious Studies* **18**(2–3): 213–242.
   Describes the history of PL Kyōdan in Brazil and analyses the way in which it has transformed itself into a multinational organization. Nakamaki seeks to show parallels between multinational religions and multinational enterprises and also argues for a link between the overseas expansion of Japanese enterprises and that of Japanese religions.

11 Perfect Liberty Kyōdan (1951). How to Lead a Happy Life, The PL Order.

12 Perfect Liberty Kyogakubu (1954). Seichi Rensei Taikenshū (The Experiences of Training at Holy Places). Osaka, PL Shuppansha.

13 Perfect Liberty Kyogakubu (1958). PL Nōgyō-Taikenshū (The Experience of PL Farming and Agriculture). Tonbayashi, PL Shuppansha.

14 PL Kyōdan (1950). Essay on the Way of Life, Tondabayashi.

15 PL Kyōdan (n.d.). Guide to a Happy Life, Tondabayashi.

16 SPAE, J. J. (1958). 'PL Kyōdan: The Perfect Liberty Order.' *The Japan Missionary Bulletin* 12(8/ October).

17 SWEARER, D. K. (1972). 'Contemporary Japanese Religion, An Interpretive Dilemma.' *Japanese Religions* 7(4): 35–49.

Discusses the conflicting impressions of Japan as a country with a rich religious history and Japan as a modern secular society. This theme is presented under the notions of immanence/ transcendence; relative/absolute; inclusive/exclusive. PL Kyōdan is briefly examined by the author.

18 TATSUKI, Y. (1960). 'PL (Perfect Liberty).' *Contemporary Religions in Japan* 1(3): 20–.

Reiha-no-Hikari Kyōkai

'Light of Divine Power'   'Society of the Light of Spiritual Wave'

HISTORY

Reiha-no-Hikari was founded in 1954 by Hase Yoshio (1914–1984) in Matsudo City, Chiba Prefecture, Japan, under the name *Hase-sensei Sangyo no kai* ('Teacher Hase's Association of Truth Seeking'). Having been sickly since childhood, Hase contracted tuberculosis while in Manchuria as a soldier in 1936 and was sent back to Japan and hospitalized. While in hospital he developed further illnesses and was given one month to live by his doctor. He left hospital and undertook a religious pilgrimage, during which he received a revelation from God telling him to become the messenger of God. He recovered from his illness and in 1943 married and set up a small business.

On 7 March 1954, Hase Yoshio reached enlightenment and the realization that he was the emissary of the God of the Macrocosms, a messiah born to save humankind through the divine power of *reiha* (spirit waves) generated through his own body. He began to 'save' people with his spirit waves and in that year founded the *Hase-sensei Sangyo no kai*. On 7 March 1969, the movement changed to its present name when it received recognition as a religious juridical person and relocated to Noda City, Chiba Prefecture.

Members refer respectfully to the founder as *Goshugojin-sama* (The Guardian God of Humanity). After his death in 1984 Hase is believed to have become an eternal wave of spiritual energy. The current leader is Hase Keiji, the founder's son, referred to as *Nidai-sama* ('The Second Generation').

MAIN BELIEFS AND PRACTICES

Reiha no Hikari teaches that the *Goshugojin-sama*, as the son of God the Creator, can save with his supernatural power (divine power) all people who are suffering in this 'degenerate' age. This essentially refers to all people as it is believed that the human race, having lost God, is leading itself to extinction. The movement teaches that God knows of the coming of the third world war. Believers are to prepare for the coming of the new world.

Reiha-no-Hikari is concerned with giving relief to people suffering from various ailments and diseases, a doctrine originating from the founder's personal suffering from tuberculosis and pleurisy, which he overcame by practising *zazen*. The movement preaches that human beings are connected to God through the 'spiritual wave' (the founder became this wave upon his death) but that humans break this connection through sin. Individuals can regain the power of life and purify the connection to God through Reiha-no-Hikari practice. This practice involves a person receiving *o-tsunagari* (connection) when he/she must pray a special purification prayer to heal the soul for two weeks followed by a prayer for healing disease. During this process sacred sake is placed on the person's head and neck and a talisman with the person's name, sex and prayer written on it is floated on the pond of Holy God. The person also refers a wooden talisman *Go-Shintai Ofuda* ('Divine Emblem Plaque') and is encouraged to pray at home. This process ensures that a person has established a 'divine link' (*mitsunagari*) with the Church so that they can then receive the spirit waves and with it salvation.

The main scriptures are the *Gosho* (Writing) and *Seikun* (Oath Instructions). The main prayer is: '*Goshugojin-sama, nidai-sama, please help us follow the path to the salvation of mankind*'.

MAIN FESTIVALS ARE:

Go seijin sai (Feast for Holy God)	7 March (Anniversary of Founding)
Go seiryō sai (Feast for Pure Journey)	June
Go seitan sai (Feast for Birthday)	July
Hō reiha kansha sai (Thanksgiving Day)	March

BRANCHES AND MEMBERSHIP

Tenshi Kaku is the 'Castle of Salvation' or 'Angel Tower' modelled after a Japanese castle tower and constructed in 1975 in Noda City, Chiba Prefecture. The current leader, Hase Keishi, lives there.

Membership as of 1990 was 761,175.

REIHA-NO-HIKARI KYŌKAI – BIBLIOGRAPHY

1 Reiha-no-Hikari (1982). Gosho (Holy Book), Reiha-no-Hikari.
2 Reiha-no-Hikari (1989). Kami e no Michi (The Road to God). Tokyo, Reiha-no-Hikari.

Reiyūkai Kyōdan

'Society of Friends of the Spirits'

HISTORY

Reiyūkai is believed to be the oldest of the major modern Nichiren sects. It was founded as an informal association in 1924 by Kubo Kakutarō (1892–1944). His sister-in-law, Kotani Kimi (1901–1971), was co-foundress. She married Kubo's brother Kotani Yasukichi (1895–1927) in 1925.

Kubo, formerly an employee of the Imperial Household Ministry, regarded himself as the Nichiren of the Taishō era. Like the medieval saint Kubo set out to bring Buddhism to the masses. In 1919 Kubo began studying the Lotus Sutra and practising *senzo-kuyō*, the remembering and honouring of one's ancestors. Japan at this time was experiencing a period of rapid change. Western culture was making an impact, there was rapid industrialization, social liberalism, economic crisis and the destruction caused by the Kanto Earthquake of 1924. Kubo believed that in order to cope with social reform and confusion people needed some form of mental, spiritual and ethical guidance. He also saw changes in Japan at that time as a threat to traditional values and therefore felt a religious response centred around the tradition of ancestor worship and return to family values to be necessary. His beliefs centred around lay Buddhism and his vision was a harmonious lay Buddhist society where people could actively seek to improve their lives by putting Buddhist teachings into practice in their daily lives, rather than relying on priests to perform rituals. Kubo began to formulate and elaborate Reiyūkai doctrine and ritual, while Kotani Kimi began to gather followers.

Kotani was a shamanistic foundress. Her childhood was spent in severe poverty following the death of her father and at the age of 17 she went to Tokyo to work as a maid where she met Yasukichi. Yasukichi became ill early on in their marriage and Kubo urged Kimi to convert to his teachings and worship the ancestors in order to heal Yasukichi, which she did. She became a devoted preacher of Kubo's message following this. By sharing the poverty of migrant workers and slum-dwellers in the poorer sections of Tokyo, and nursing them through faith healing, she gained converts. Even after her death she continued to be widely regarded as a 'living Buddha'.

Reiyūkai was formally inaugurated in Tokyo in July 1930, and was incorporated as a religious juridical person in March 1946. The current President: is Dr Tsugunari Kubo (1936–), the son of Kubo Kakutaro, who became president following the death of Kotani Kimi in 1971. Tsugunari gained his PhD. in Buddhist Sanskrit Literature from the University of Tokyo.

MAIN BELIEFS AND PRACTICES

Reiyūkai is based on two primary ideas: the virtue of the Lotus Sutra and the importance of ancestor worship. It is a Buddhist lay organization based on Nichiren Buddhism and Kubo formulated his philosophy based upon the teachings of Sakyamuni Buddha and the Lotus Sutra scripture. In 1928 Kubo and Kotani compiled the Blue Sutra, a short sutra including several selections from the Three-Fold Lotus Sutra. This was made in order that members could recite sutra in less than half an hour every morning and evening. The Blue Sutra was expanded in 1933 with other selections from Lotus Sutra and remains the main sutra to be recited daily by members today.

In 1971 Reiyūkai began to promote their 'Inner Trip Movement', which aimed at people becoming aware of the necessity to know one's inner self and included a missions campaign directed at North and South America. This was followed in 1981 with the 'Inner Self-Development Movement', which encourages individuals to improve themselves while being aware that they are connected with everyone around them. Thus, individuals must not only develop themselves but form positive relationships with others. This was expanded upon in 1990 under the slogan of 'Life – A Dynamic Exchange', which encourages people to understand that they are just one of the myriad life forms existing on earth, living amidst innumerable human relationships sustained by nature. All their campaigns have conveyed a quality of 'universality', seen to be relevant to the twenty-first century.

Reiyūkai's main beliefs are employed in daily life through the central practices of recitation of the Blue Sutra, *senzo-kuyo* and *michibiki*. Informal groups *hōza* employ methods of teaching and group counselling.

Senzo-kuyo is lay ancestor rites, which is central to Reiyūkai belief. Reiyūkai's development of lay ancestor ritual without the need for rites to be performed by a priest was an innovation in Japanese religious history. Reiyūkai believes in honouring not only patrilineal ancestors but also matrilineal ancestors. *Senzo-kuyō* is a duty for all members of the family and not the sole duty of the first-born son, as is the traditional custom in Japan. Worshipping of the ancestors is not advocated, that is, they are not considered to be divine beings. Rather, members should recognize that ancestors are the source of life and that they have an ongoing connection to them as well as an obligation to thank and remember them. Similarly, people gain karma from their ancestors. Neglect of the ancestral spirits thus causes misfortune. People are advised to gather together as many of their ancestors' mortuary tablets (*ihai*) as possible and revere the spirits they represent, as social upheavals are a sign of ancestral distress and lack of human care towards ancestors. The ancestral spirits are offered food, drink and worship and one is expected to recite the sutras twice daily before the home altar.

'Healing' also plays a part in Reiyūkai in the sense that there is a belief in faith healing, rather than the healing of illness. An individual's conversion to the movement is often based upon having received some form of healing of a personal problem, and a member's rise through the ranks centres around the healing through faith and proselytization of others. The practice of healing in Reiyūkai is also linked to ancestor worship, as inherited karma and lack of respect to one's ancestors is believed to cause social disorder.

Michibiki, a fundamental practice of Reiyūkai, is the act of convincing others of the merit of 'Inner Self Development', by guiding them and practising it with them. Stemming from 'Dependent Origination', it stresses the interconnectedness of people's lives and seeks the further improvement of relationships with others. It is believed that *michibiki* enables an individual to meet various types of people thereby becoming aware of his/her own shortcomings and good points. It is believed that improving oneself can lead to an improved world.

Overall, Reiyūkai sees itself as a 'universal spiritual teaching' which is compatible with other religions. That is, people can combine Reiyūkai with their own spiritual beliefs without the necessity to convert. Reiyūkai believes its role is not to offer direct answers, but provide methods whereby people can discover and improve themselves, thereby discovering answers. It is stressed that the path to individual identity is through the framework of human relationships.

Main services are held on the 8th, 18th and 28th of each month.

PUBLICATIONS

PERIODICALS INCLUDE:

Circle (The international Reiyūkai Magazine)
Reiyūkaiho (monthly bulletin)
Myōhō (monthly youth journal)

PUBLICATIONS BY THE MOVEMENT INCLUDE:

Kotani Kimi, *A Guide to Reiyūkai*, Reiyūkai Kyōdan, 1958.
The Reiyūkai Shakaden Completion Ceremony, November 9, 1975, Reiyūkai, 1975.

OTHER PUBLICATIONS:

The most comprehensive scholarly work on Reiyūkai to date is Helen Hardacre (1984) *Lay Buddhism in Contemporary Japan: Reiyūkai Kyōdan*, Princeton University Press. In her study Hardacre looks at the contemporary activities of the movement, especially its relationship to the family, the importance of ancestor worship and the role of women. She describes how the Reiyūkai ritual of ancestor worship in the home brings the husband, wife and children together in collective activity and gives a positive religious significance to marriage and the family. In addition, she details how Reiyūkai women are active as branch leaders, creating independent and responsible roles for themselves in the public domain, while still paradoxically maintaining the traditional idea of 'a woman's place is in the home'. The central notion of filial piety reflects Reiyūkai's concern with the breakdown of the family in modern society and women especially are exhorted to be diligent in their daily worship of the ancestors in the home and in their role as a stable linchpin of the family.

BRANCHES AND MEMBERSHIP

Reiyūkai has its central headquarters in Minato-ku, Tokyo. It's main meeting hall, the Shakaden ('the dwelling of Sakyamuni Buddha') was completed in 1975. Reiyūkai also has a training retreat Mirokusan ('the mountain of Maitreya Bodhisattva') on Mt. Togasa on the Izu peninsula, established in 1964. Meihō Junior and Senior High Schools were also founded that year in Higashi-Murayama, Tokyo by Kotani Kimi.

Reiyūkai is active in social programmes and has contributed extensively to rehabilitation centres for the physically handicapped and the Red Cross as well as donated a large hall to the City of Tokyo for welfare work in 1958. The Ise City Plaza, built by Reiyūkai in 1984, was also donated to Ise City for use as a civic centre. Reiyūkai also sponsors annual International Youth Speech Festivals.

Among present membership in Japan, 70% reside in urban areas and 30% in rural areas. Reiyūkai employs a pyramid structure of organization where a person rises in rank through 'converting' others who become the 'spiritual children' of that person who is then the 'spiritual parent'. A member will attend *hōza* meetings held by his/her 'parent', and groups of *hōza* form branches (*shibu*). This person-to-person based organizational structure rather than regional basis is because of the main practice of *michibiki*. *Oya-ko* (parent-child)-based relationships are central, but there is also a concept of equality of all members, despite this hierarchical nature. Members in Japan in 1996 number 3,070,000.

Reiyūkai began to take its teaching outside of Japan in 1972. There are currently branches in 17 foreign countries, as follows:

Country	No. Members	Established
Brazil	70,000	1975
Canada	500	1975
Darjeeling (India)	1,000	
England	500	1978
France	4,000	1979
India	2,000	1983
Italy	300	1977
Korea	5,000	1974
Mexico	3,000	1977
Nepal	80,000	1983
Paraguay	2,000	1983
Peru	1,000	1979

Country	No. Members	Established
Philippines	2,000	1976
Spain	300	1984
Taiwan	5,000	1977
Thailand	3,000	1979
U.S.A.	1,000	1972

Reiyūkai's organizational structure based on personal links between the converter and the converted has meant that there have been several splinter groups that have emerged from Reiyūkai, throughout its history. The main movements are as follows:

Movement	Members (1988)	Established
Risshō Kōsei Kai,	6,248,419	1938
Myōdōkai Kyōdan,	219,380	1951
Myōchikai Kyōdan,	903,028	1950
Bussho Gonenkai,	1,980,993	1950
Hosshikai Kyōdan,	123,003	1950
Shōgikai Kyōdan,		1951
Kōdō Kyōdan,	401,452	1935
Shishinkai	136,376	1938
Daiekai Kyōdan	178,762	1951

REIYŪKAI KYŌDAN – BIBLIOGRAPHY

1 HAMMER, R. (1961). The Idea of God in Japan's New Religions – with Special Reference to Tenrikyō, Konkōkyō, Sekai Kyūseikyō, Ōmotokyō, Reiyūkai, Risshō Kōsei Kai, PL Kyōdan, Seichō-no-Ie and Annaikyo. PhD. University of London, London. Annot Earhart

2 HARDACRE, H. (1979). 'Sex-role Norms and Values in Reiyūkai.' *Japanese Journal of Religious Studies* 6: 445–60.
Based on concrete examples, Hardacre presents a full picture of the roles women are expected to fulfil in one of the Japanese New Religious Movements.

3 HARDACRE, H. (1984). *Lay Buddhism in Contemporary Japan: Reiyūkai Kyōdan.* Princeton, Princeton University Press.

4 HARDACRE, H. (1988). *Maitreya in Modern Japan. Maitreya, the Future Buddha.* A. Sponberg and H. Hardacre. Cambridge, Cambridge University Press: 270–284.
The author makes a study of the significance of Maitreya in Reiyūkai Kyōdan.

5 HAYASHI, M. (1988). Learning from the Japanese New Religions, Fuller Theological Seminary, School of World Mission: 477.
Analyses the growth of 'new religions' from a missiological perspective, describing their expansion through social and communicational factors detailing their world view and addressing the missological implications. There are chapters on Ōmoto, Reiyūkai, and Agonshū.

6 INOUE, N., Ed. (1991). *New Religions: Contemporary Papers in Japanese Religion.* Tokyo, Institute for Japanese Culture and Classics, Kokugakuin University.
A collection of five essays which amount to a general survey in Japanese New Religions and include the following movements: Renmonkyō, Shinsei Ryūjinkai, Reiyūkai-derived groups, and Tenshō Kōtai Jingūkyō.

7 KOHLER, W. (1962). *Die Lotus-Lehre und die modernen Religionen in Japan.* Zurich, Atlantis Verlag.

8 KOMOTO, M. (1988). 'The Place of Ancestors in the New Religions: The Case of Reiyūkai-derived Groups.' *Transaction of the Institute for Japanese Culture and Classics* 62.

9 KOTANI, K. (1958). A Guide to Reiyūkai. Tokyo.

10 KOTANI, K. (1958). Watakushi no Shūgyō Seikatsu Sanjū nen (My Thirty Years Practice). Tokyo, Reiyūkai Kyōdan.

11 KOTANI, K. (1958). Watakushi no shugyō seikatsu, sanjūgo nen. (My Religious Life of 35 Years). Tokyo, Reiyūkai.

12 KŌMOTO, M. (1991). *The Place of Ancestors in the New Religions: The Case of Reiyūkai Derived Groups. Contemporary Papers in Japanese Religion* (2). N. Inoue. Tokyo, Kokagakuin University: 93–124.

13 LANDE, A. and CLARKE P. B. (1988). Japan (New Religious Movements). *The World's Religions.* S. Sutherland, L. Houlden, P. B. Clarke and F. Hardy. London, Routledge: 932–944.
A short summary of the features of several Japanese New Religious Movements including Sōka Gakkai, Nichiren Shōshū, Sekai Kyūseikyō, Ōmotokyō, PL Kyōdan, Risshō Kōsei Kai, Konkōkyō, Tenrikyō, Mahikari, Seichō-no-Ie and Reiyūkai.

14 MONTGOMERY, D. (1991). *Fire in the Lotus: The Dynamic Buddhism of Nichiren.* London, Mandala.
Contains a brief general history of Buddhism and its introduction to Japan, followed by a description of the development of Nichiren Buddhism in Japan. The founding of Sōka Gakkai is then described, and its subsequent expansion in Japan and later in the United States is outlined. A brief account of Reiyūkai, Risshō Kōsei Kai, and other smaller Nichiren groups abroad is also given. Appendix One contains Nichiren Buddhist prayers and sutras.

15 NAWATA, S. (1978). *Reiyūkai. Shinshūkyō no Sekai (The World of the New Religions).* Tokyo, Daizo Shuppan. II: 5–81.

16 NAWATA, S. (1979). *Reiyūkai. Shinshūkyō no sekai (The World of New Religions).* Tokyo, Daizōkan. 2: 6–81.
This volume contains information concerning Reiyūkai, Risshō Kōsei Kai and Sōka Gakkai.

17 OGASAWARA, K. (1985). Nihon-teki senzo saishi no Brasil – teki tenkai- Risshō Kōsei-kai to Reiyūkai no hikaku o tōshite (Desenvolvimento brasileiro do culto ao antepassado de estilo japonēs – pela comparação entre Risshō Kōsei-kai e Reiyūkai). Sān Paulo, Centro de Estudos Nipo-Brasileiros.

18 ONO, Y. (1980). *Reiyūkai. Minzoku Shūkyō to Shakai* (Folk Religion and Society). S. Gorai. Tokyo, Kobundo. 5: 233–243.

19 READER, I. (1994). Japanese Religions. *Insight Japan.* 3: 6–9.
A summary of a few of the Japanese Old and New Religions.

20 Reiyūkai (1972). Ten No Ongaku (The Life of Kimi Kotani). Tokyo, Reiyūkai.
Life of the Founder.

21 REIYŪKAI (1985). Zaikeshugi Bukkyo eno Shotai (Invitation to Lay Buddhism). Tokyo, Reiyūkai.

22 REIYŪKAI (1986). The Development of Japanese Lay Buddhism. Tokyo, The Reiyūkai.
A short book giving an outline of Reiyūkai but particularly useful in its factual appraisal of Sōka Gakkai.

23 REIYŪKAI (1987). The Reiyūkai Movement: Buddhism as an Interreligious Philosophy. Tokyo, The Reiyūkai.

24 REIYŪKAI (1988). The Philosophical Foundation of the Lay Buddhist Practice of the Reiyūkai, as ddepicted in the Lotus Sūtra. Tokyo, The Reiyūkai.

25 Reiyūkai (1991). The Blue Sutra Guidebook. Tokyo, Reiyūkai.
Holy Book.

26 Reiyūkai (n.d). The Reiyūkai, Its Aims and Practice. Tokyo, Reiyūkai.

27 Reiyūkai America (n.d). Reiyūkai:People Promoting Friendship and Awareness. Los Angeles, Reiyūkai America.

28 SHIMAZONO, S. (1986). *Shūkyō-gengo to shite no taikendan: Reiyūkai kyōdan o rei toshite* (Testimonies as Religious Language: The Case of Reiyūkai and Its Offshoots). Shōwa rokujū-nendo tokutei kenkyū-hōkoku (Report on Special Research Projects during Shōwa 60). Tokyo, Gaikokugo Daigaku Kaigai-jijō Kenkyūsho.

29 SHIMAZONO, S. (1988). *Shinshūkyō no taikenshugi: shoki Reiyūkai no bai. Minshū to shakai: Bukkyō to Nihonjin 10.* S. Murakami. Tokyo, Shunjūsha.

30 SPAE, J. J. (1960). 'Reiyūkai.' *The Japan Missionary Bulletin* 14(10).

Risshō Kōsei Kai

'Society Establishing Righteousness and Harmony in accordance with Buddhist principles'

HISTORY

Risshō Kōsei Kai is one of the largest new religions in contemporary Japan. It split from Reiyūkai of which its founders Niwano Nikkyo (1906–) and Naganuma Myoko (1889–1957) were both former members.

Niwano was a shopkeeper, and when his daughter became ill with 'sleeping sickness' in 1934 he turned to Reiyūkai for advice and became convinced that the Lotus Sutra provided answers to the problems of suffering. However by 1938 he believed that Reiyūkai was not placing enough emphasis on the Lotus Sutra and so in March 1938 he established the movement Dainihon Risshō Kōsei Kai, which was later incorporated as a religious juridical person under the name Risshō Kōsei Kai in August 1948.

Naganuma Myoko was a shaman. A sickly woman she was regarded by followers as a 'living Buddha'.

MAIN BELIEFS AND PRACTICES

The word *rissho* is an allusion to Nichiren's famous remonstrance of 1260, the *Rissho ankoku ron* ('establish true Buddhism to secure peace in our country'), and is intended to hold before people the ideal of a true faith that involves a concern for society as a whole. The word *kosei* indicates an aim to be a faith-oriented fellowship of harmoniously related believers who seek perfection of character, enlightenment and eventual Buddhahood. Risshō Kōsei Kai define themselves in one of their publications as a *'society organized by people of the same faith in order to realize a happy world by making efforts to perfect men's personality through mutual communication and encouragement on the basis of the true teaching proclaimed by Sakyamuni'*.

Risshō Kōsei Kai is a lay Buddhist organization of the Nichiren tradition. It adopts the Three Hokke Sutras (Muryogi Sutra, Lotus Sutra and Kanfugen Sutra) as its basic sutras and makes the teaching of Fundamental Buddhism the foundation of the doctrine. The main chant is *'Namu Myoho Renge-kyo'* meaning 'To take refuge in the Lotus Sutra'. The main object of worship is the 'Great Beneficent Teacher and Lord Sakyamuni, the Eternal Buddha' (*Go-honzon*) and founder of Buddhism. Worship of Sakyamuni is not based upon him as a human being or actual Buddha with human form, rather through veneration of him is the basis of devotion to the 'law' (universal truth) he brought. Importance is placed on 'Devotion to the three treasures': *'We take refuge in the Buddha, We take refuge in the Law, We take refuge in the Sangha* (close connection or people in harmony).'

Risshō Kōsei Kai describes its purpose as an organization for the learning of everlasting universal truth as preached by Sakyamuni and for the practising of this in family and society in order to achieve a happy home life, good society and a peaceful world.

Risshō Kōsei Kai employs the *hōza* system: small gatherings and daily group sessions in which people of both sexes meet with a leader to discuss problems of faith or concerns of daily life. The participants are seated (*za*) usually in a circle and endeavour to find solutions to the problems presented by considering them in relation to Buddhist principles (*hō*). This is 'group therapy' but within a defined religious framework. People can discuss topics such as personal problems, politics and education and the central aim lies in teaching individuals the true way of life. It is believed that listening to an individual's suffering is based on one of the Four Noble Truths. Spiritual progress is made using suffering as a stepping stone.

The movement encourages pilgrimages by local groups to the Tokyo centre, home visiting, group lectures, pamphlet handouts and other projects for propagating the faith. As well as group counselling, there are sermons, missionary visits, group worship, study of the doctrine as well as sporting events such as baseball and martial arts.

Many followers join Risshō Kōsei Kai because of sickness or personal misfortune. Followers are urged to 'Make the self the light' ie: depend upon themselves and practice their spirituality. The establishment of Kōsei Hospital where it is stressed that 'the diseases of the mind' are healed by faith and the 'the diseases of the body' are cured by medical treatment highlights the importance placed upon illness and healing.

Ancestor Worship and filial piety are also encouraged, as means of eliminating negative karmic effects. Emphasis is placed on the perfection of the personality and the realisation of peace on earth as well as on religious training for personal discipline. Risshō Kōsei Kai stresses that everyone can follow the path to Buddhahood through living the life of moral and spiritual wisdom and by delaying Nirvana, like a bodhisattva, in order to serve a suffering humanity. A 'perfect life' can break the laws of karma and reincarnation.

In 1970 Risshō Kōsei Kai launched the 'Brighter Society Movement', a public-spirited movement bringing together secular, religious, and governmental organisations to create a better society, and an international movement for the attainment of world peace through interreligious cooperation. The movement emphasizes family relationships and exhibits positive ecumenical concern, and has contributed greatly to the work of the World Conference of Religions and Peace.

MAIN FESTIVALS ARE:

Foundation Festival	March 5
Flower Festival	April 8
Grand Festival	October 12

PUBLICATIONS

PERIODICALS INCLUDE:

The Kōsei (monthly)
The Kōsei Shimbun (weekly)
The Kōsei Graphic (monthly to all members)
The Yakushin (monthly for youth groups)
The Kōsei Times (monthly in English)
Dharma World (monthly in English)

There are numerous books and guides on the movement published by Risshō Kōsei Kai's publishing company, Kōsei Publishing Co., Tokyo, as well as several publications by President Niwano. Main publications include:

Risshō Kōsei Kai, Kōsei Publishing Co., Tokyo, 1966.
Risshō Kōsei Kai shi, (*The history of Risshō Kōsei Kai*), 5 Volumes, Kyōdanshi Hensan Iinkai, Tokyo, 1984.

MAIN PUBLICATIONS BY PRESIDENT NIWANO ARE:

Travel to Infinity, 1968.
Buddhism for Today: A Modern Interpretation of the Threefold Lotus Sutra, 1976.
A Buddhist Approach to Peace, 1977.
Lifetime Beginner: An Autobiography, 1978.

BRANCHES AND MEMBERSHIP

Risshō Kōsei Kai's central headquarters are in Suginami-ku, Tokyo. The Great Sacred Hall, which was completed in 1964 and is located in the Tokyo Headquarters is the holy centre for the movement. There are many branch churches and additional training halls throughout Japan. Organisationally it divides Japan into a network of eleven districts with a centre in each. It maintains churches in most of the large cities.

Risshō Kōsei Kai has several welfare institutions for members – a hospital, library, schools, a retirement home and a cemetery. Their dates of establishment are as follows:

Kōsei-gakuen High School & Kōsei-gakuen Middle School (boys) (1956)
Kōsei-gakuen Girl's High School & Kōsei-gakuen Girl's Middle School (1955)
Kōsei-gakuen Kindergarten (1955)
Kōsei Library (1953)
Kōsei Hospital (1952)
Kōsei Nursery School (1949) Postwar efforts to rescue war orphans
Kōsei Aged People's Home (1958)
Kōsei Park Cemetery (1951)
Fukui Kōsei Gakuen (branch church's kindergarten)

Masutomi Kōsei Villa (1957) (recreational and health spa)
Kōsei Scholarship Association (1958) (educational grants to youth)

Membership in Risshō Kōsei Kai is based on the household as a primary unit, but members are divided into organisational groups such as the Men's Division, the Women's Division, and the Young People's division (under 30 years).

In 1990 Risshō Kōsei Kai membership was 6,348,120.

As of 1982, there were 224 branches in Japan as well as branches in Korea, Brazil, mainland U.S.A. and Hawaii.

RISSHŌ KŌSEI KAI – BIBLIOGRAPHY

1 ANDERSON, R. W. (1994). 'Risshō Kōseikai and the Bodhisattva Way.' *Japanese Journal of Religious Studies* 21(2–3): 311–337.
   This article concerns conflicts that arise in families associated with Risshō Kōsei Kai as a result of the sect's emphasis on 'following the bodhisattva way.'

2 DALE, K. J. (1969). 'Authority in Risshō Kōsei Kai.' *Japan Missionary Bulletin* **23**(8).

3 DALE, K. J. (1970). An Investigation of the Factors Responsible for the Impact of Hōza of Risshō Kōsei Kai as a Means of Religious Propagation and Education in Contemporary Japan. City of New York, Union Theological Seminary.

4 GERLITZ, P. (1975). 'Kathartische und therapeutische Elemente in der Seelsorge der Risshō Kōsei Kai.' *Zeitschrift für Religions-und Geistesgeschichte* **27**(4).

5 HAMMER, R. (1961). The Idea of God in Japan's New Religions – with Special Reference to Tenrikyō, Konkōkyō, Sekai Kyūseikyō, Ōmotokyō, Reiyūkai, Risshō Kōsei Kai, PL Kyōdan, Seichō-no-Ie and Annaikyo. *University of London*, London.

6 INABA, K. ('998). 'Altruism in the Contemporary Religions and the network of altruistic practice: A case study of Risshō Kōsei-Kai.' *Journal of the Japanese Association for the study of Religion and Society* 4: 151–177.
   This article deals with altruism in Japanese contemporary religions including an examination of two concepts namely 'Harmony Ethics' described by Shimazono (1992) and 'Vitalism' suggested by Tsushima et al. (1979) as the common structure and the world view of the beliefs and teachings of Japanese NRMs. There is an overview of altruism in Risshō Kōsei-Kai.

7 KAMOMIYA, J. (1952). Shinkō Taikenshū (Faith Experiences). Tokyo, Risshō Kōseikai Shūgaku Kenjō.

8 KAMOMIYA, J. (1961). 'Risshō Kōsei Kai.' *Contemporary Religions in Japan* 2(1): 30.

9 KISALA, R. (1994). 'Etica sociale e attività di welfare delle nouve religioni. Il caso del Tenrikyō e del Risshō Kōsei Kai.' *Religioni e Società* **17**.

10 KISALA, R. (1994). *Social ethics and the Japanese New Religions: the Social Welfare Activities of Tenrikyō and Risshō Kōseikai. New Religious Movements in Asia and the Pacific Islands: Implication of Church and Society*. R. C. Salazar. Manila, De La Salle University.

11 KISALA, R. (1994). 'Contemporary Karma-Interpretations of Karma in Tenrikyō and Risshō Kōsei Kai.' *Japanese Journal of Religious Studies* 21(1): 73–92.

12 KOHLER, W. (1962). *Die Lotus-Lehre und die modernen Religionen in Japan.* Zurich, Atlantis Verlag.

13 LANDE, A. and CLARKE, P. B. (1988). Japan (New Religious Movements). *The World's Religions.* S. Sutherland, L. Houlden, P. B. Clarke and F. Hardy. London, Routledge: 932–944.
    A short summary of the features of several Japanese New Religious Movements including Sōka Gakkai, Nichiren Shōshū, Sekai Kyūseikyō, Ōmotokyō, PL Kyōdan, Risshō Kōsei Kai, Konkōkyō, Tenrikyō, Mahikari, Seichō-no-Ie and Reiyūkai.

14 MATSUNO, J. (1976). *Gendai Shakkai to Risshō Kōsei Kai* (Contemporary Society and Risshō Kōsei Kai). *Gendai Bukkyō* (Contemporary Buddhism). H. Nakamura, K. Kasahara and H. Kaneoka. Tokyo, Kōsei Shuppansha. 9: 209–295.

15 MORIOKA, K. (1989). *Shinshūkyō no kōgeki, ōsen to kiketsu – Risshō Kōseikai no 'Yomiuri jiken'* (The Offence, Accepting Challenge and Conclusion Towards New Religions – Risshō Kōseikai's 'Yomiuri' Newspaper Case). Shinshūkyō undō no tenkai katei. K. Morioka. Tokyo, Sōbunsha.

16 MORIOKA, K. (1994). 'Attacks on New Religions: Risshō Kōseikai and the "Yomiuri Affair".' *Japanese Journal of Religious Studies* 21(2–3): 281–310.
    Risshō Kōseikai, one of Japan's most successful New Religions faced a crisis in the mid-1950's when the 'Yomiuri Shinbun' published a series of articles criticising its activities. This essay examines the circumstances of the affair, analyses the response by Risshō Kōseikai and investigates how the incident affected the society's development.

17 NAWATA, S. (1979). *Reiyūkai. Shinshūkyō no sekai* (The World of New Religions). Tokyo, Daizōkan. 2: 6–81.
    This volume contains information concerning Reiyūkai, Risshō Kōsei Kai and Sōka Gakkai.

18 NEHRING, A. (1992). *Risshō Kōsei Kai. Eine neubuddhistische religion in Japan.* Erlangen, Verlag der Ev.-Luth Mission.

19 NISHIO, H. K. (1967). 'Comparative Analysis of the Risshō Kōseikai and the Sōka Gakkai.' *Asian Survey* 7(11): 776–790.
    This article traces the historical development of the Risshō Kōsei Kai and the Sōka Gakkai religious movements, comparing and contrasting their membership, composition, their doctrinal orientations, recruitment methods, organizational structure, political activity and their general historical rivalry.

20 NIWANO, N. (1959). Hokkekyō no atarashii kaishaku (The New Interpretation of Hokkekyo). Tokyo.

21 NIWANO, N. (1976). Niwano Nikkyō jiden (The Biography of Niwano Nikkyō). Tokyo, Kōsei Shuppansha.
    Niwano Nikkyō was a recent president of Risshō Kōseikai

22 NIWANO, N. (1977). A Buddhist Approach to Peace. Tokyo, Kōsei Publishing Company.

23 NIWANO, N. (1978). Lifetime Beginner: An Autobiography. Tokyo, Kōsei Publishing Co.

24 NIWANO, N. (1982). *My Father, My Teacher: A Spiritual Journey.* Tokyo, Kōsei Publishing Co.

25 NIWANO, N. (1989). Kokoro no naka no Sampomichi (The Inward Path). Tokyo, Kōsei Publishing Company.

26 READER, I. (1985). 'Transformation and Changes in the Teachings of the Sōtō Zen Sect.' *Japanese Religions* 14(1): 28–48.
Looks at the history of the Buddhist Sect, Sōtō Zen focusing on its methods of teaching, publications and educational campaigns over time. Mention is made on page 43 of Sōtō Zen's adoption of the 'hōza' technique from Risshō Kōsei Kai.

27 READER, I. (1994). Japanese Religions. *Insight Japan.* 3: 6–9.
A summary of a few of the Japanese Old and New Religions.

28 REPP, M. (1995). 'The Earthquake in the Kobe-Osaka Area January 17th 1995. Its impact on religions and their response.' *Japanese Religions* 20(2): 207–229.

29 Risshō Kōsei Kai (1959). A Guide to Risshō Kōsei Kai. Tokyo, Kōsei Publishing Co.

30 Risshō Kōsei Kai (1966). Risshō Kōsei Kai. Tokyo, Kōsei Publishing Co.

31 Risshō Kōsei Kai (1979?–). Dharma World. Tokyo, Kōsei Publishing Co.
Monthly magazine.

32 Risshō Kōsei Kai (1980). Risshō Kōsei Kai: An Organization of Buddhist Laymen. Tokyo, Kōsei Publishing Company.

33 Risshō Kōsei Kai (1982). The Story Of Risshō Kōsei Kai. Tokyo, Kōsei Publishing Co.

34 Risshō Kōsei-Kai (1970). Risshō Kōsei Kai: A New Buddhist Laymen's Movement in Japan. Tokyo, Kōsei Publishing Company.

35 Risshō Kōseikai (1978). Niwano Nikkyō hōwa senshū (A Selection of the Teachings of Niwano Nikkyō). Tokyo, Kōsei Shuppansha.

36 Risshō Kōsei-kai (1959). Kōsei Kyogaku (The Teaching of Risshō Kōsei-kai), Risshō Kōsei-kai.

37 Risshō Kōsei-Kai (1966). Risshō Kōsei-Kai. Tokyo, Kōsei Publishing Company.

38 SHIMAZONO, S. (1984). 'Shinshūkyō-kyōdan ni okeru taikendan no ichi: Myōchikai, Risshō Kōseikai, Tenrikyō (The Place of Testimonies in the New Religions: Myōchikai, Risshō Kōsei Kai and Tenrikyō).' *Tōkyō-daigaku shūkyō-gaku nenpō* 2: 1–20.

39 SPAE, J. J. (1960). 'Risshō Kōsei Kai.' *Japan Missionary Bulletin* 14(5).

40 SPAE, J. J. (1966). 'Popular Buddhist Ethics: Risshō Kōsei Kai.' *The Japan Missionary Bulletin* 20.

41 TSURUFUJI, I. (1954). *Risshō Kōseikai no shinkō* (The belief of Risshō Kōsei Kai). Tokyo, Kuretake Shoin.

42 WATANABE, E. (1968). 'Risshō Kōseikai: A Sociological Observation of Its Members, Their Conversion and Their Activities.' *Contemporary Religions in Japan* 9(1–2): 75–151.
Watanabe presents a case study of the new religious movement Risshō Kōsei Kai which at the time celebrated its 30th anniversary. The research presents a detailed survey of RKK members, including distribution by gender, age, occupation, education and the motives, expectations, procedures and activities involved with entering RKK. Research is presented from a sociological perspective, observing how both members needs and expectations as well as RKK doctrinal concerns have developed and adapted in line with social change in postwar Japan.

43 WATANABE, M. (1991). 'Burajiru ni okeru Risshō Kōsei Kai no tenkai to josei shinja no seikatsu shi (The Development of Risshō Kōsei Kai and the History of Women Followers in Brazil).' *Sociology and Social Welfare Research* **85**.

44 YONEYAMA, M. (1978). *Risshō Kōsei Kai. Shinshūkyō no Sekai (The World of the New Religions)*. M. Shimizu. Tokyo, Daizo Shuppan. II: 83–161.

45 YUKAWA Y. (1956). 'Tatakarete mo biku tomo shinai-Niwano Nikkyō kaiken ki (Interview with Niwano Nikkyō "No Matter How I am Beaten, I Remain Calm").' Nippon Shūhō **422**: 43–47.

46 Zenbōsha (1956). 'Risshō Kōseikai to 'Yomiuri' no kettō (The Duel Between Risshō Kōseikai and the 'Yomiuri' newspaper).' *Zenbō* **42**: 58–65.

Seichō-no-Ie

'House of Growth' 'Home of Infinite Life, Wisdom and Abundance'

HISTORY

Seichō-no-Ie was founded by Taniguchi Masaharu (1893–1985) in 1930. A graduate of Waseda University, Taniguchi was an avid reader of both Western and Eastern philosophy and had been a member of Ōmoto for four years. He was deeply concerned with what he saw as contradictions in life and the suffering of mankind. In 1928 he read a book by the American New Thought teacher Fenwicke Holmes, which helped him form the system of thought that later came to be Seichō-no-Ie. In 1930 while in deep meditation the new light – the Truth, was revealed to him and he published his first issue of *Seichō-no-Ie*.

Taniguchi supported government policies during WWII and Seichō-no-Ie continues to be identified with right wing causes. Following Taniguchi's death in 1985, his son Reverend Seicho Taniguchi became the current president.

MAIN BELIEFS AND PRACTICES

Seichō-no-Ie is a mix of Japanese spiritual tradition and American New Thought. Its beliefs are centred around the 'Truth of Life' Movement. The movement is non-denominational and the Seichō-no-Ie badge is said to symbolise the unity of all religions. There is a fundamental belief that all religions emanate from one universal god and that man is a child of God and therefore divine in nature and capable of developing the creative powers of God. One needs to be awakened to the God-like divinity and divine attributes of God that all already possess. All sufferings and difficulties are believed to be either the symbolic reflection of one's erroneous thinking or the results of self-punishment and can be overcome through self-reflection. Evil phenomena is believed to be the result of delusive thoughts and feelings which must be overcome.

The movement's main theme is that all people can attain spiritual fulfilment through the realisation of the God-consciousness within all of us. Through the power of the mind ones physical condition can be improved through the replacing of negative with positive thoughts and beliefs. The movement teaches the fundamental practice of a form of meditation known as *shinsokan* (Meditation to Visualise God) as well as several chants. While meditating the main invocation is recited:

> *It is the life of God who permeates the universe*
> *My acts are not my own to claim*
> *They are the acts of God who permeates the universe*
> *May the Lord or Seichō-no-Ie who has appeared to teach us the*
> *way of God, the Parent of heaven and earth*
> *Guide and protect us*

This is followed by meditative thought on the six attributes of God:

> *God's sea of infinite wisdom*
> *God's sea of infinite love*
> *God's sea of infinite abundance*
> *God's sea of infinite joy*
> *God's sea of infinite harmony*
> *God's infinite life of power*

Seichō-no-Ie is concerned with the concept of healing in that it places emphasis on the power of thought to heal the physical body. However, it encourages treatment by a medical doctor. The basic principles of the movement centre around the affirmation that everything in life is a manifestation of God and therefore perfect. Its four basic principles are: (1) one truth, one God, one religion; (2) man is a child of God; (3) reconciliation to everything in the universe achieves perfect harmony; (4) gratitude to everybody and everything.

The main scripture of Seichō-no-Ie is the *Holy Sutra, Nectarean Shower of Holy Doctrine*, which was delivered to the founder while he was in meditation in 1931. There are no main religious festivals throughout the year, though the founder's birthday is usually observed. In some ways, Seichō-no-Ie is, more a philosophy of life than a religious organization, a movement of people who subscribe to its literature and attend lectures and classes.

PUBLICATIONS

PERIODICALS INCLUDE:

Seichō-no-Ie (monthly)
Shitohato (monthly)
Risosekai (monthly)
Seishin Kagaku (monthly)
Hikari no Izumi (monthly)
Truth of Life Magazine (monthly in English, Spanish, Japanese, Portuguese and German)

PUBLICATIONS BY THE MOVEMENT INCLUDE:

Truth of Life, 40 volume series, Seichō-no-Ie, (1961–).
Seichō-no-Ie is on the internet at: http://www.snitruth.org

BRANCHES AND MEMBERSHIP

The main headquarters of Seichō-no-Ie are located in Shibuya, Tokyo, Japan and there is a spiritual headquarters and Grand shrine in Nagasaki. As of December 31, 1994 members in Japan numbered 877,110 and members outside of Japan numbered 1,542,970, making a total membership of 2,420,080.

MAIN OVERSEAS BRANCHES ARE AS FOLLOWS:

Regional Centres	Country	Established
Seichō-no-Ie North American Missionary Headquarters*	Gardena California, USA	August 1940
Seichō-no-Ie Truth of Life Center	Toronto, Canada*	May 1964
Seichō-no-Ie Do Brasil	Sao Paulo, Brasil	August 1952
Seichō-no-Ie R.O.C. Missionary Headquarters	Taipei, Taiwan	December, 1993

Other branches include Mexico, Peru, Korea and parts of Europe.

* There are additional Truth of Life Centres in Hawaii, Chicago, Florida, Houston, New York, Portland, San Francisco, San Jose, Seattle, Winnipeg and Vancouver.

SEICHŌ-NO-IE – BIBLIOGRAPHY

1 BECKFORD, J. (1984). 'Holistic Imagery and Ethics in New Religious and Healing Movements.' *Social Compass* **31**(2–3).

2 CARPENTER, R. T. and ROOF, W. C. (1995). 'The Transplanting of Seichō-no-Ie from Japan to Brazil: Moving Beyond the Ethnic Enclave.' *Journal of Contemporary Religion* **10**(1): 41–54.
Analyses the growth of Seichō-no-Ie in Brazil and how it has been successfully transplanted from Japan, focusing on a framework centred on ideology, practice, environment and organization.

3 CHAPEL, G. W. (1989). 'Synthesizing Eastern and Western Religious Traditions: The Rhetoric of Japan's Seichō-no-Ie Movement.' *The Journal of Communication and religion* 12 -March.

4 CLARKE, P. B. (1994). Japanese 'Old', 'New' and 'New, New' Religious Movements in Brazil. *Japanese New Religions in the West*. P. B. Clarke and J. Somers. Folkestone, Kent, Japan Library: 149–160.
This article considers the nature of appeal and the impact of two Japanese new religions in Brazil: Seichō-no-Ie and Sekai Kyūsei Kyō.

5 ELLWOOD, R. S. (1974). *The Eagle and the Rising Sun: Americans and the New Religions of Japan*. Philadelphia, Westminster Press.
Ellwood examines the impact of five 'new religions' in America: Tenrikyō, Sōka Gakkai, Sekai Kyūseikyō, Seichō-no-Ie and Perfect Liberty. The cultural exchange between East and West as presented by the development of these movements in America is discussed.

6 HAMMER, R. (1961). The Idea of God in Japan's New Religions – with Special Reference to Tenrikyō, Konkōkyō, Sekai Kyūseikyō, Ōmotokyō, Reiyūkai, Risshō Kōsei Kai, PL Kyōdan, Seichō-no-Ie and Annaikyo. *University of London*, London.

7 LANDE, A. and CLARKE, P. B. (1988). Japan (New Religious Movements). *The World's Religions*. S. Sutherland, L. Houlden, P. B. Clarke and F. Hardy. London, Routledge: 932–944.
A short summary of the features of several Japanese New Religious Movements including Sōka Gakkai, Nichiren Shōshū, Sekai Kyūseikyō, Ōmotokyō, PL Kyōdan, Risshō Kōsei Kai, Konkōkyō, Tenrikyō, Mahikari, Seichō-no-Ie and Reiyūkai.

8 MARRACH, L. (1978). Seichō-no-Ie: Um Estudo de sua penetração entre os Brasileiros. Master's dissertation. São Paulo, Pontificia Universidade Católica: 166.

9 ONO, Y. (1980). *Seichō-no-Ie. Minzoku Shūkyō to Shakai* (Folk Religion and Society). S. Gorai. Tokyo, Kobundo. 5: 212–221.

10 OOMS, E. G. (1993). *Women and Millenarian Protest in Meiji Japan. Deguchi Nao and Ōmotokyō*. New York, Cornell University East Asia Program.
Ōmotokyō is a very influential New Religion which has spawned a number of 'world-renewal' New Religions, among them Mahikari, Sekai Kyūseikyō and Seichō-no-Ie. This book is a study of its foundress Deguchi Nao (1836–1918). It also addresses the roles of class and gender in New Religious Movements.

11 RICCO, M. (1967). *Religione della violenza e religione del piacere nel nuovo Giappone*. Florence, Saggi.

12 Seichō-no-Ie Truth of Life. Gardena, California, Seichō-no-Ie North American Missionary Headquarters.
Monthly Magazine

13 Seichō-no-Ie (1937). Seimei no jisso (The Truth of Life). Tokyo, Seichō-no-Ie.
One edition in 40 volumes

14 Seichō-no-Ie (1941). Shin no chikara (The True Power). Tokyo, Seichō-no-Ie.

15 Seichō-no-Ie (1953–). Seichō-no-Ie.
Monthly magazine

16 Seichō-no-Ie (1956). Enkan: Seichō-no-Ie Brasil Sōshibu Kaikan Hōdō Kinen Tokushū. São Paulo, Seichō-no-Ie Burajiru Sōshibu.

17 Seichō-no-Ie (1986–). Lichtquelle. München, Germany, Seichō-no-Ie Lichtquelle.
Bi-monthly magazine for the German-speaking countries.

18 Seichō-no-Ie Honbu (1980). *Seichō-no-Ie gojūnenshi* (Fifty years of Seichō-no-Ie History). Tokyo, Nippon Kyōbusha.

19 Seichō-no-Ie Latin America Dendō Honbu (1973). Seichō-no-Ie Burajiru Sōshibu Nijū-nen Shi. São Paulo, Igreja Seichō-no-Ie do Brasil.

20 Seichō-no-Ie Brasil Sōshibu (1973). Seichō-no-Iē Brasil Sōshibu 20 nen-shi (Seichō-no-Ie Brasil – História dos 20 anos). São Paulo, Seichō-no Iē Brasil Sōshibu.

21 SHIMAZONO, S. (1994). *Kami to hotoke o koete – Seichō-no-Ie no kyūsai shisō no seisei. Hotoke to kami.* Tokyo, Iwanami shoten.

22 SOMERS, J. (1994). *Japanese New Religious Movements in Britain. Japanese New Religions in the West.* P. B. CLarke and J. Somers. Folkestone, Kent, Japan Library: 54–76.

23 SPAE, J. J. (1956). 'Seichō-no-Ie.' *Missionary Bulletin* 10(10).

24 SUZUKI, S. (1956). 'Gendai Nihon Chūkan Shimin-sō no Shūkyō-Seichō-no-Ie no Shūkyō Shakaigakuteki Kōsatsu (Religion of the Contemporary Japanese Middle Class: A Sociological Analysisof Seichō-no-Ie).' *Ritsumeikan Bungaku* 130: 181–199.

25 TANIGUCHI, M. (1935). The Power of Faith. Tokyo, Seichō-no-Ie.

26 TANIGUCHI, M. (1954). Shinri (The Truth). Tokyo, Nihon Kyōbunsha.

27 TANIGUCHI, M. (1954). Josei no Risō (The Ideal of a Woman). Tokyo, Nippon Kyōbunsha.
Modern and traditional women are presented in contrast and the exaggerations of both tendencies are showed. The founder of Seichō-no-Ie and his wife present a new type of woman, equal to but not identical to man, proud of her nurturing role as wife and mother.

28 TANIGUCHI, M. (1955). Shinyu e no Michi (The Road to Healing by God). Tokyo, Nihon Kyōbunsha.

29 TANIGUCHI, M. (1957). Shinjosei Dokuhon (Reading Book for the New Woman). Tokyo, Nippon Kyōbunsha.
Advice to women about how they can surmount difficulties in their family life by being truly grateful and genuinely concerned about others as human beings in their own right rather than as appendages to one's self. Improvement through self-improvement.

30 TANIGUCHI, M. (1958). Iesu wa jujika no kakarazu (Jesus was not hanged on the cross). Tokyo, Seichō-no-Ie.

31 TANIGUCHI, M. (1959). Seimei no Jissō (The Truth of Life). Tokyo, Nihon Kyōbunsha.
The fundamental books of Seichō-no-Ie, in 40 volumes and translated in many languages.

32 TANIGUCHI, M. (1961). You Can Heal Yourself: Conquest of Diseases-Cancers, Atomic Diseases through Spitritual Teachings. Tokyo, Seichō-no-Ie Foundation, Divine Publications Dept.

33 TANIGUCHI, M. (1961). Onna Ikiru Igi (The Meaning of Being a Woman). Tokyo, Nippon Kyōbunsha.
Another manual for wives and mothers, filled with examples from the everyday life of Seichō-no-Ie followers. Includes discussions of family quarrels, separation and divorce, drinking problems etc.

34 TANIGUCHI, M. (1962). Book of Daily Life (Truth of Life Series). Gardena, California, Seichō-no-Ie, Inc. 7.

35 TANIGUCHI, M. (1979). Book of Jisso – The Light of Truth (Truth of Life Series). Gardena, California, Seicho- no-Ie Inc. 2.

36 TANIGUCHI, M. (1983). Erziehung zum Göttlichen (Divine Education and Spiritual Training of Mankind). Heimen, Germany.

37 TANIGUCHI, M. (1983). Yamato no Kuni Nippon. Tokyo, Nihon Kyōbunsha.

38 TANIGUCHI, S. (1992). Meditação shinsokan é maravilhosa. São Paulo, Seichō-no-Iē do Brasil.

39 TANIGUCHI, M. (1993). O que é a Seichō-no-Ie: votos e aprimoramento espiritual dos adeptos da Seichō-no-Ie. São Paulo, Seichō-no-Iē do Brasil.

40 WIMBERLEY, H. H. (1967). *Seichō-no-Ie: A Study of a Japanese Religion-Political Association*, Cornell University.

41 WIMBERLEY, H. H. (1969). 'Some Social Characteristics of a Seichō-no-Ie Congregation in Southern Japan.' *Journal of Asian and African Studies* 4: 186–201.

42 WIMBERLEY, H. (1972). 'The Knights of the Golden Lotus.' *Ethnology* 11(2): 173–186.
The author examines the aims and activities of a lay group of the political wing of Seichō-no-Ie, and suggests reasons for the pervasiveness of the image of the state as a harmonious family.

43 WOIRGARDT, R. (1995). *Die Neuen Religionen Japans und ihr Sendungsbewusstein im Hinblick auf den Weltfrieden: Eine Analyse am Beispiel der Seichō-no-Ie Bewegung.* Frankfurt, Peter Lang.
Based on a detailed analysis of the origin, growth and doctrines of Seichō-no-Ie, the author examines the concept of world peace and the missionary aims of the Japanese NRMs in general, establishing certain similarities of discourse and ideas.

Sekai Kyūseikyō

'Church of World Messianity'

HISTORY

Sekai Kyūseikyō was founded in 1935 by Okada Mokichi (1882–1955), who was formerly active in Ōmoto but broke away to form his own theories on healing practices. In 1926 Okada received a revelation from the Buddhist Goddess of Mercy, Kannon, instructing him to become a prophet and giving him divine light (*jorei*) to heal disease and illness. In February 1928 Okada had established a new religious organization Dainihon Kannonkai ('Great Japan Association for the Worship of the Bodhisattva Kannon'), which was based on two goals: the religious goal of communion with divine beings and the therapeutic goal of healing disease through the laying on of hands. Ordered by government officials to choose one or the other, Okada and his followers chose the healing goal, changing the name of their group to the Nihon Jōka Ryōhō ('Japanese Association for Therapy through Purification').

After World War II Okada revived the religious dimension of his activities, incorporating his group as a religious juridical person in March 1947 under the name Nihon Kannon Kyōdan ('Japan Organization for the worship of the Bodhisattva Kannon'). In 1950 a split within this group led Okada to form the Sekai Meshiya Kyo ('Messianic Religion of the World'), later changing its name to Sekai Kyūseikyō.

During his life Okada identified himself as the Bodhisattva Kannon and later the Messiah. He placed great importance on healing practices and related illness to spiritual clouds and prescribed his own ways for removing them. Notable among his treatments were applications of finger pressure, hand pressure and herbal medicines. After his death his wife Yoshi became the head of the movement until her death in 1962 when their daughter Okada Itsuki became the leader. Yōichi has been the current leader since 1992.

MAIN BELIEFS AND PRACTICES

A development of the eschatological wing of Ōmoto, Sekai Kyūseikyō's main teachings emphasise the coming of a paradise on earth through an accelerating impouring of divine light. Disasters and suffering in this world are caused by God, who is a universal God, destroying the old and making way for this new world. Preparation for this paradise is through the two main practices and activities of jōrei (channelling of divine light through a cupped upraised hand to a body or object to cleanse it of evil), which heals and purifies the mind and body, and *shizen nōhō* (agriculture that follows the way of nature).

Jōrei is concerned with healing and involves the idea that the human body accumulates impurities that sometimes lead to illness. The practice of jōrei is central to all Church gatherings. Meaning spiritual purification, jōrei is a faith-healing technique in which the palm of the believer is held a few inches away from the affected area of the patient's body. The member channelling the light wears an *ohikari* ('sacred focal point') around their neck allowing them to channel jōrei. A mystic ray of purifying power will radiate from the believer's palm and begin to heal the sufferer. This power is believed to derive from the founder, himself regarded as a living deity (*ikigami*), and becomes available to those who join the sect and adhere to its principles. Jōrei is viewed as a form of healing that can not only heal disease and illness, but also bring good fortune, spiritual purification and solutions to personal problems. Praying and chanting accompanies jōrei. The main prayer is the *Amatsunor-igoto* (Divine World Prayer). Karma from one's ancestors can also cause distress and problems in this life, and jōrei and prayers is the means of alleviating this.

Shizen nōhō involves the idea that chemical fertilizers are injurious. It is a food-growing technique which depends on the belief that nature has a power of its own to bring forth healthy plants and wholesome food. Plants are only weakened and made susceptible to disease when men use artificial or animal fertilisers.

Sekai Kyūseikyō urges that farmers avoid the use of fertilisers and use the natural way thereby devoting their efforts to the raising of pure and natural crops. Jōrei, as 'God's light' is applied to the soil to purify the earth and give nourishment to plants.

Spiritual training sessions help people through the jōrei technique and there are also pilgrimages to the Atami centre. The main God, as revealed to Okada, is the 'True God of the Marvellous Light'. Festivals are held at the Spring Equinox and at the Autumn Equinox.

PUBLICATIONS

PERIODICALS:

Eiko (newspaper)
Chijo Tengoku (monthly)
The Glory (English)

PUBLICATIONS BY THE MOVEMENT INCLUDE:

Okada, Mokichi, *Jōrei: divine light of salvation*, The Society of Jōrei, 1984.

MEMBERSHIP AND BRANCHES

Sekai Kyūseikyō's headquarters are located in Shizuoka-ken, Japan, and there are also three holy centres, the Atami Centre, the Hakone Centre and the Saga/Kyoto Centre. The main centre in Atami is a model for the ideal of 'paradise on earth' (*chijō tengoku*). The grounds have abundant trees, grass, rocks and flowering shrubs. In addition there are two museums in Atami and in Hakone with collections of art objects. (Okada was the son of a dealer in antiques).

After WWII Okada sent followers to USA. There are now missionaries in Europe, Pacific Islands, Nth/Latin America, Korea, Taiwan and a large expansion in Brazil and Thailand. When Sekai Kyūseikyō moved to Europe, it moved away from magical practices and focused on the advancement of Japanese culture and language, natural farming and the promotion of arts. It's cultural arm is the MOA Foundation (MOA: Mokichi Okada Association) which focuses on cross-cultural awareness and international exchange through the fields of art, education and scientific research. Activities in Japan include the establishment of the MOA Museum of Art in Atami in 1982, and the funding of the MOA Interdisciplinary Environmental

Research Institute in Kyoto which researches into pollution and agricultural-related sciences. Activities abroad include funding an elementary school in Peru, the establishment of an agricultural training school in Thailand, the building of a ceramics school in Mexico as well as several centres for cultural classes on Japan and Japanese language schools worldwide including Brazil, Argentina, U.S.A., France, Belgium, Portugal, the U.K., Taiwan and Southeast Asia.

Sekai Kyūseikyō membership as of 1990 numbered 835,756.

SEKAI KYŪSEIKYŌ – BIBLIOGRAPHY

1 Church of World Messianity World Messianity Newsletter. Long Beach, California, The Church of World Messianity.

2 Church of World Messianity MOA Newsletter. Long beach, California, Mokichi Okada Association (MOA).

3 Church of World Messianity (1965). Fragments from the Teachings of Meishu-sama. Atami, Japan, Church of World Messianity.

4 Church of World Messianity (1976). Ohikari. Los Angeles, California, Church of World Messianity. 1.

5 Church of World Messianity (1976). *Introductory Course of World Messianity and Joining the Church*. Los Angeles, California, Church of World Messianity.

6 Church of World Messianity (1977). *Sampai*. Los Angeles, California, Church of World Messianity.

7 Church of World Messianity (1978). *Foundation of Paradise on Earth*. Los Angeles, California, Church of World Messianity.

8 Church of World Messianity (1983). The Light from the East. Atami, Japan, MOA Productions.

9 Church of World Messianity (n.d). Member's Handbook. Atami, Japan, Church of World Messianity.

10 Clarke, P. B. (1994). *Japanese 'Old', 'New' and 'New, New' Religious Movements in Brazil. Japanese New Religions in the West*. P. B. Clarke and J. Somers. Folkestone, Kent, The Japan Library: 149–160.
   This article considers the nature of appeal and the impact of two Japanese new religions in Brazil: Seichō-no-Ie and Sekai Kyūsei Kyō

11 DERRETT, E. M. A. (1984). The International Face of a Japanese 'New Religion' – the Beliefs and Expansion of Sekai Kyūseikyō. Theology and Religious Studies. PhD. London, King's College.
   In this thesis, while initially placing the teachings of Sekai Kyūseikyō's founder, Okada, in the cultural context of late nineteenth-century Japan, the author then examines and contrasts the expansion of this religion in Brazil and Thailand and the degree of receptiveness of the foreign members to its most distinctive teachings and practices.

12 DERRETT, E. M. (1984). 'A Japanese "New" Religion in Britain: Sekai Kyūseikyō.' *Religion Today One* (2/3): 12–13.

An introduction to the movement Sekai Kyūseikyō describing its founding and teachings and how it is establishing itself in Britain.

13 DERRETT, E. M. A. (1987). Signs Along a Better Way: The Methods of Evangelization of a Japanese 'New Religion' in Brazil and Thailand. In *The New Evangelists: Recruitment Methods and Aims of New Religious Movements*. P. B. Clarke. (Ed.) London, Ethnographica.
Derrett examines evangelistic methods used by Sekai Kyūsei Kyō (SKK) in Brazil and Thailand. Four methods are examined: miracles, heightening of pleasurable emotion, teachings and guidance and the example of the faithful, and their appeal to and interpretation by members in both countries is compared and contrasted. Derrett's theme is that these methods are interpreted by members as 'signs' of a religious success and determine a religion's authority and thus expansion.

14 ELLWOOD, R. S. (1974). *The Eagle and the Rising Sun: Americans and the New Religions of Japan*. Philadelphia, Westminster Press.
Ellwood examines the impact of five 'new religions' in America: Tenrikyō, Sōka Gakkai, Sekai Kyūseikyō, Seichō-no-Ie and Perfect Liberty. The cultural exchange between East and West as presented by the development of these movements in America is discussed.

15 FUJIEDA, M. (1960). 'The Church of World Messianity.' *Contemporary Religions in Japan* 1(4): 24.

16 HAMMER, R. (1961). The Idea of God in Japan's New Religions – with Special Reference to Tenrikyō, Konkōkyō, Sekai Kyūseikyō, Ōmotokyō, Reiyūkai, Risshō Kōsei Kai, PL Kyōdan, Seichō-no-Ie and Annaikyo. *University of London*, London.

17 LANDE, A. and CLARKE, P. B. (1988). Japan (New Religious Movements). *The World's Religions*. S. Sutherland, L. Houlden, P. B. Clarke and F. Hardy. London, Routledge: 932–944.
A short summary of the features of several Japanese New Religious Movements including Sōka Gakkai, Nichiren Shōshū, Sekai Kyūseikyō, Ōmotokyō, PL Kyōdan, Risshō Kōsei Kai, Konkōkyō, Tenrikyō, Mahikari, Seichō-no-Ie and Reiyūkai.

18 MATSUOKA, H. (1993). 'Nikkei Shūkyō no Kaishin (Conversion to Japanese New Religion: The Case of Church of World Messianity).' *Journal of Religious Studies* 17(2): 122–144.

19 NAKAMURA, I. and T. TADA, Eds. (1984). *Jōrei: Divine light of Salvation: Okada Mokichi*. Kyoto, Japan, Society of Jōrei.

20 OKADA, M. (1947). Tengoku no fukuin (Gospels from Heaven). Atami, Sekai Kyūseikyō Shuppanbu.

21 OKADA, M. (1953). Amerika o Sukuu (Saving America). Atami, Sekai Kyūseikyō Shuppanbu.

22 OKADA, M. (1953). Sekai Kyūseikyō Kisekishū (The Miracles of Sekai Kyūseikyō). Atami, Sekai Kyūseikyō Shuppanbu.

23 OKADA, Y. (n.d). Guse no Hikari (The Light of the Messiah). Atami, Sekai Kyūseikyō Hombu.

24 OOMS, E. G. (1993). Women and Millenarian Protest in Meiji Japan. Deguchi Nao and Ōmotokyō. New York, Cornell University East Asia Program.
Ōmotokyō is a very influential New Religion which has spawned a number of 'world-renewal' New Religions, among them Mahikari, Sekai Kyūseikyō and Seichō-no-Ie. This book is a study of

its foundress Deguchi Nao (1836–1918). It also addresses the roles of class and gender in New Religious Movements.

25 ORO, A. P. (1999). *The New Japanese Religions in Brazil: Some Remarks on the Church of World Messianity. Japanese New Religions in Global Perspective.* P. B. Clarke. Richmond, Surrey, Curzon Press.

26 Sekai Kyūseikyō (1954–). The Glory.
Occasional Newspaper published in English

27 Sekai Kyūseikyō (1957). World Messianity and What it Means, Atami.

28 Sekai Kyūseikyō Kyomubu (1954). Tengoku no Fukuin-sho (The Gospels of Heaven). Atami, Sekai Kyūseikyō to Shuppanbu.

29 SOMERS, J. (1994). *Japanese New Religious Movements in Britain. Japanese New Religions in the West.* P. B. Clarke and J. Somers. Folkestone, Kent, Japan Library: 54–76.

30 SPAE, J. J. (1959). 'Sekai Kyūseikyō or Sekai Meshiya-kyo: World Messianity.' *Japan Missionary Bulletin* 13(4): 238–244.

31 SPICKARD, J. V. (1977). *Shamanistic Renewal in Two Changing Cultures: Sekai Kyūseikyō in Japan and America*, Center for the Study of New Religious Movements.

32 SPICKARD, J. V. (1991). *Spiritual Healing Among the Followers of a Japanese New Religion: Experience as a Factor in Religious Motivation. Research in the Social Scientific Study of Religion.* M. L. Lynn and D. O. Moberg. Greenwich, Connecticut, JAI Press. 3: 135–156.
Based on ethnographic research at Sekai Kyūseikyō's San Francisco mission this study discusses how the experience of 'johrei', a form of spiritual healing attracts members to the movements.

33 SPICKARD, J. (1995). *Body, Nature and Culture in Spiritual Healing. Studies in Alternative Therapy 2: Body and Nature.* H. Johannessen, S. Olesen and J. Andersen. Gylling, Denmark, INRAT and Odense University Press: 65–81.
Examines the role of cultural background in the assimilation and reinterpretation of a Japanese NRM in the United States through a case study of the different conceptions of 'johrei' held by three distinct cultural sub-groups within the North American branch of Sekai Kyūseikyō.

34 TISDALL-YAMADA, Y. (1991). 'The Symbolic Image of Ancestors in the Church of World Messianity.' *Japanese Journal of Religious Studies* 18(2–3): 151–164.

35 YAMADA, Y. (1983). *Healing, Conversion and Ancestral Spirits: Religious Experiences among the Japanese Members of the Church of World Messianity in Los Angeles, California. Japanese Religions in California: A Report on Research Within and Without the Japanese American Community.* K. Yamagawa. Tokyo.

36 YAMADA, Y. (1984). Purifying the Living and Purifying the Dead: Narratives of the Religious Experience of Japanese-American and Caucasian Members of the Church of World Messianity. Los Angeles, California, University of North Carolina.

37 YAMADA, Y. (1985). *Religious Experiences of Members of the Church of World Messianity in California.* Melbourne, Japanese Studies Centre.

Shinnyoen

'Garden of Absolute Reality'

HISTORY

Shinnyoen was founded in 1936 by Itō Shinjō (1906–1989) and his wife Itō Tomoji (1912–1967) when they formed a religious association called Risshōkaku in a suburb of Tokyo, Tachikawa. Before that Shinjō had studied and mastered the science of divination called *Byōzeishō*, which had been passed down in his family. In December, 1935 Shinjō and Tomoji enshrined the image of Achala and they began the 30-day winter training from the beginning of the New Year in 1936. Tomoji succeeded to *Reinō* (the Spiritual Faculty) from her aunt on 4 February 1936. From that time, Tomoji and Shinjō began a new career together entirely devoted to religion, serving as 'mediums of salvation' to people who came to have their fortunes told.

The number of followers increased and they soon established an organization. On the other hand, Shinjō trained at Daigoji, the head temple of Daigo school of Shingon esoteric Buddhism. There, he mastered all the trainings and gained the title of Great Acharya (Great Master). Although first affiliated with an already established sect (Shingonshū Daigoha) to gain legal recognition, it seceded in January 1948 to become a religious organization in its own right taking the name Makoto Kyōdan, which was later changed to Shinnyoen in June 1951. It became a religious juridical person in May 1953.

231

Two sons of the founders died from illness during childhood, but it is said that they opened the spiritual path to unite this world and the invisible world and that *Bakku Daiju* (the great power of salvation) was established. They are known as the *ryōdoji sama* (holy brothers) in Shinnyoen doctrine. The current leader is Itō Shinsō (known as Keishu-sama among followers), a daugther of Shinjō (Kyōshu-sama) and Tomoji (Shōjuin-sama).

MAIN BELIEFS AND PRACTICES

Shinnyoen is a Buddhist sect that is based on the *Great Nirvana Sutra*, said to be Gautama's last teachings. Its aim is to realize happiness for humankind; to pursue genuine world peace; and to seek *jōraku gajō* (eternal joy and purity ie: lifting of karmic burdens) as taught in the Nirvana Sutra.

There is a strong belief in a spirit world where the deceased members of the founding family dwell. Shinnyoen leaders (both family members and other organizational leaders) are mediums who have acquired their positions through the practice of Buddha's Nirvana teachings. They spiritually guide followers to teach them how to be reborn into the realm of joy and develop their buddha-nature. The 'secrets of the Buddha' are expressed through the mediums to the followers. All mediums are believed to gain support and power from the members of the founder's family already existing in the spirit world. They also receive solace and salvation from the venerated dead members of the founding family.

Shinnyoen members can rise through four spiritual ranks: (1) *Daijō* (Mahayana) (2) *Kangi* (Happiness) (3) *Daikangi* (Great Happiness) (4) *Reinō* (Spiritual Faculty). Promotion through the ranks is based upon a member's practice of Shinnyoen faith, service to the movement and proselytization.

Mediums carry out four kinds of spiritual guidance (*sesshin*): *kōjō sesshin*, ('spiritual guidance for the sake of improvement') and *kōjō sōdan sesshin*, ('spiritual guidance and consultation for the sake of improvement), both for followers' general self-improvement, though the former is a more regular monthly guidance; and *sōdan sesshin* ('spiritual guidance and consultation') and *kantei sesshin* ('spiritual guidance and expert opinion'), for followers who need to solve specific problems. In Zen Buddhism, there is also a meditation called *sesshin*. However, in Shinnoyen *sesshin* is practised in a relatively short time with the aid of *reinōsha* (spiritual mediums).

232

PUBLICATIONS

PERIODICALS:

Nirvana (monthly, English)
Naigai Jihō (monthly)
Kangi Sekai (quarterly)

PUBLICATIONS BY THE MOVEMENT:

Ichinyo no Michi (The way to Nirvana) 1957, 1968, 1972, 1979.
Fuji no Hanabusa, 1969.
Tomoshibi Nen Nen, 1976.

BRANCHES AND MEMBERSHIP

The Grand Holy Temple and headquarters of Shinnyoen are in Tachikawa, Tokyo.
 Membership in 1990 stood at 679,414.

THERE ARE THE FOLLOWING OVERSEAS BRANCHES OF SHINNYOEN:

Country	*Branch*
USA	Shinnyoen USA
	California Headquarters
	Los Angeles Branch
	Seattle Branch
	New York Branch
Hawaii, USA	Shinnyoen Hawaii, Honolulu
France	Shinnyoen France, Paris
Belgium	Shinnyoen Belgium, Schoten
Italy	Shinnyoen Italia, Milano
UK	Shinnyoen UK, Surrey
Taiwan	Shinnyoen Taiwan, Taipei
Hong Kong	Shinnyoen Hong Kong
Singapore	Shinnyoen Singapore

SHINNYOEN – BIBLIOGRAPHY

1 AKIBA, Y. (1991). 'Shinnyoen ni okeru 'reinō'.' *Bukkyō* **16**: 56–66.

2 HIROTA, M. (1990). Shinnyōen: sono gendaisei to kakushinsei. Tokyo.

3 Itō Shinjō (n.d). Tomoshibi Nen Nen (Buddha's Light Everlasting), Shinnyoen.

4 Itō Tomōji Shōjuin (1992). A Wisteria Cluster. Tokyo, Shinnyoen.
Two volume set of sermons by the wife of the founder of Shinnyoen

5 NAGAI, M. (1992). 'Shinnyoen ni okeru reinō sōshō.' *Daigaku shūkyōgaku nenpō* 9: 101–15.

6 NAGAI, M. (1993). 'Shin-shūkyō ni okeru shūyōsei to jujutsusei: Shinnyoen o jirei to shite.' Nenpō shakaigaku ronshū 6(167–78).

7 NAGAI, M. (1995). 'Magic and Self-Cultivation in a New Religion: The Case of Shinnyoen.' *Japanese Journal of Religious Studies* 22(3–4).
Analyses the role of magical practices and their relationship to self-cultivation in the teachings of Shinnyoen through an examination of reports of the transmission of spiritual power and through narratives of followers.

8 NAGATANI, C. (1995). *Shinnyoen no sesshin shugyō to shinja no sekaikan henyō ni tsuite. Kyūshū Daigaku Bungakubu Hikaku Shūkyōgaku Kenkyūshitsu.* N. Sakai and S. Takezawa, Fukuoka.

9 NUMATA, K. (1990). 'Shinnyoen no kenkyū.' *Shakaigaku ronshū* 24(1): 55–86.

10 READER, I. (1988). 'The Rise of a Japanese "New New Religion": Themes in the Development of Agonshū.' *Japanese Journal of Religious Studies* 15(4): 235–61.
Looks at the rapid growth of Agonshū through a discussion of its highly advertised rituals and events. Discusses how Agonshū manages to combine both elements of tradition and the modern to give members a means to deal with contemporary society, while also appealing to concepts of universality. Draws comparisons with other 'new new' religions such as Mahikari Byakkō Shinkōkai and Shinnyoen.

11 SAKASHITA, J. (1995). 'Shinnyoen in the U.K.' *Journal of Contemporary Religion* 10(2): 167–179.

12 Shinnyoen What is Shinnyoen?, Shinnyoen.

13 Shinnyoen Sono Michi. Honolulu, Hawaii, Shinnyo-en.

14 Shinnyoen (1977). The Nirvana. Tachikawa, Shinnyoen.
Monthly magazine in English language.

15 Shinnyoen (1992). Pursuing the Way. Tachikawa, Shinnyoen.

16 Shinnyoen (1994). The Resonating Harmony of Buddha's Law. Tokyo, Shinnyoen.
A book published in commemoration of the Founder's 77th Birthday.

17 SHIRAMIZU, H. (1979). 'Organizational Mediums: A Case Study of Shinnyo-en.' *Japanese Journal of Religious Studies* 6(3).
After outlining the founding family and history of Shinnyoen, the author focuses on the role of mediums within the movement and the ways in which they give 'spiritual guidance' to believers.

18 YAMAGUCHI, T. (1987). *Shinnyoen.* Tokyo, Chijinkan.

Sōka Gakkai

'Value Creation Society'

HISTORY

Sōka Gakkai was founded on 18 November 1930 by Makiguchi Tsunesaburo (1871–1944), a follower of Nichiren Shōshū since 1928, and his student Toda Josei (1900–58). Makiguchi was a teacher and wrote on what he called 'value-creating education' based on Nichiren doctrine. Establishing a society under the name Soka Kyoiku Gakkai ('Value Creating Educational Society'), its name was changed to Sōka Gakkai in 1937. In its early days the society was concerned with educational reform in line with Makiguchi's value-creating theories.

Both Makiguchi and Toda, along with others, were imprisoned in 1943 as 'thought criminals' for advising their followers not to purchase amulets from the Grand Shrine of Ise. Makiguchi died in prison, but Toda was released in 1945 and began to reconstruct the organization, creating a dynamic and highly organized movement. Sōka Gakkai grew rapidly in the early postwar period. It was incorporated as an independent religious juridical person in 1952 and by 1960 had claimed membership in around 750,000 households. Its aggressive proselytism in the 1950s and 60s led to much criticism, especially its political aim of uniting religion and politics which led to the creation of the political party Kōmeitō ('Clean Government Party'), which has been influential in Japanese politics since its inception in 1964.

Following Toda's death in 1958, leadership passed to Ikeda Daisaku (1928–) two years later in 1960. Under Ikeda's leadership

235

Sōka Gakkai expanded to reach over ten million households in Japan and over one million abroad by the mid-1980s. During this time it shifted to become less overtly militant and severed its official links with Kōmeitō. It has shifted its focus to more universalistic ideals. As president of Sōka Gakkai International (SGI), founded in 1975, Ikeda is now a prominent figure both in Japan and abroad speaking publicly on human development, world peace and current political issues. Nichiren Shōshū and Sōka Gakkai separated completely in 1991.

MAIN BELIEFS AND PRACTICES

Sōka Gakkai is a lay Buddhist association related to the Nichiren Shōshū group. The organization has two fundamental aims: the realization of individual happiness through the practice of Nichiren Buddhism and the realisation of a peaceful society through the application of Buddhism to culture and education. This is based on the doctrine *Risshō ankoku ron* ('On securing peace of the land'). Sōka Gakkai teaches of the coming of the 'Third Civilization', when true faith will spread over the world, bringing an era of peace and plenty.

There are 'three great secret laws' in Sōka Gakkai: the *Kaidan* (place of instruction and worship – Taisekiji near Mt. Fuji), the *Gohonzon* (sacred mandala scroll inscribed with the names of many Buddhas and Bodhisattvas, enshrined at Taisekiji and believed to hold the universal power of all Buddhas) and the *Daimoku* (phrase '*Namu-Myōhō-renge-kyō*' invoking the Lotus Sutra, which is chanted morning and evening). Daily chanting is an important ritual, believed to bring wisdom, happiness and health to individuals and to be the source of salvation and world peace for all mankind. The practice is claimed to alleviate the accumulated effects of the past and bring a beneficial future. The ultimate goal is human revolution out of which will emerge world peace.

Sōka Gakkai believes that religion should be the moral basis of society and as such focuses on the 'reformation' of all human activities by creating values in everyday life based on Buddhism. Religion is viewed as being able to overcome human discontent and to lead to happiness and harmony, and therefore is essential to all areas of society. Accordingly, Sōka Gakkai is involved in a wide range of activities including political activities, such as world peace and human welfare, and cultural and educational activities, including the establishment of several schools and a university and the sponsoring of various academic and cultural groups. These include:

Soka University (1971)
Soka Schools System (Japan and Abroad)
Tokyo Fuji Art Museum (1983)
Min-On Concert Association (1963)
Institute of Oriental Philosophy (1962)
Boston Research Center for the 21st Century (1993)

Annual religious activities and festivals observed by the movement are as follows:

New Year's *Gongyō* (Prayer) Service	January
Coming of Age Day *Gongyō* Service	15 January
Nichiren Daishonin's Birthday *Gongyō* Service	16 February
Spring Memorial Service for the deceased	March
Commemoration of the Establishment of Nichiren Buddhism	28 April
Sōka Gakkai Day	3 May
Sōka Gakkai's Memorial Gongyō Service for the deceased	July
Prayers for World Peace and War Dead	August
Respect for the Aged Day	15 September
Autumn Memorial Service for the deceased	September
Commemoration of the Inscription of the Object of Worship	October
Commemoration of Nichiren's Passing	October
Seven-Five-Three Children's Festival	15 November
Sōka Gakkai Foundation Day	18 November

PUBLICATIONS

There are numerous publications about Sōka Gakkai, but some of the main ones are as follows:

PERIODICALS INCLUDE:

Daibyaku Renge (monthly)
Seikyō Shimbun (weekly)
The Seikyō Times (monthly)
Seikyō Gurafu (weekly pictorial)
SGI Quarterly (English)
Boston Research Center for the 21st Century Newsletter (English)

PUBLICATIONS BY THE MOVEMENT INCLUDE:

The Buddhist Democracy, Sōka Gakkai Series, Tokyo.
Culture and Religion, Sōka Gakkai Series, Tokyo.
Ikeda, Daisaku, *The Human Revolution*, Volume Series, 1965–.
Ikeda, Daisaku, *The Living Buddha*, 1976.
Ikeda Daisaku, *Dialogue on Life*, 2 Vols., 1977.
Ikeda, Daisaku, *A Lasting Peace*, 2 Vols., 1987.

Internet Address: http://www.infoweb.or.jp/SOKAGAKKAI/

BRANCHES AND MEMBERSHIP

Sōka Gakkai has its headquarters in Shinjuku, Tokyo and its main temple Taiseiki-ji at the foot of Mt Fuji. It is vertical in organisational structure, with the President and Executive Committee at the head and regional and prefectural organisations below. There are also horizontal divisions based on age and sex groupings. Membership is predominantly urban based.

There are 76 Sōka Gakkai organizations worldwide that are incorporated under Sōka Gakkai International (SGI). There are SGI members in 128 countries and regions.

Statistics on Membership in Japan (as of 1 November 1995):

Households: 8,120,000
Youth Division:
  Young Men's Division: 2,700,000
  Young Women's Division: 1,650,000
Study Dept. Membership: 2,440,000

Main SGI Headquarters Overseas are:

Country	Branch Name	Established
USA (Santa Monica, California)	SGI – USA Headquarters	mid 1960s
Canada (Toronto)	Sōka Gakkai International Association of Canada	late 1970s
Brazil (Sao Paulo)	Associacao Brasil SGI	mid 1960s
Mexico (Mexico City)	SGI – Mexico	

Country	Branch Name	Established
UK (Maidenhead, Berkshire)	Sōka Gakkai International of the United Kingdom	mid 1970s
France (Paris)	Sōka Gakkai France	late 1960s
Italy (Firenze)	Associazione Italiana Sōka Gakkai	late 1970s
Germany (Morfelden-Walldorf)	SFI Deutschland E.V.	late 1960s
Belgium (Brussels)	SGI – Belgium	
Denmark (Copenhagen)	SGI – Denmark	
Netherlands (Zeist)	SGI – Netherlands	
Hong Kong (Kowloon)	Sōka Gakkai International of Hong Kong	mid 1960s
Singapore	Singapore Sōka Association	late 1960s
India (New Delhi)	Bharat Sōka Gakkai	late 1970s
Malaysia (Kuala Lumpur)	Sōka Gakkai Malaysia	
Thailand (Bangkok)	Sōka Gakkai Thailand	
Australia (Sydney)	SGI – Australia	
New Zealand (Wellington)	SGI – New Zealand	

Official membership Statistics are by continent as follows (as of 1 November 1995):

North America	338,000
Central America	12,000
South America	205,000
Asia/Oceania	779,000
Europe	19,000
Middle East/Africa	7,000
Total Overseas Members of SGI	1,360,000

SŌKA GAKKAI – BIBLIOGRAPHY

1 ABE, N. (1992). 'Sōka Gakkai kai'in ni tsugu.' *Bungei Shunjū* 70(2): 167–75.
A proclamation to the members of Sōka Gakkai

2 ASTLEY, T. (1992). 'A Matter of Principles: A Note on the Recent Conflict Between Nichiren Shōshū and Sōka Gakkai.' *Japanese Religions* 17: 167–75.

3 AZUMI, K. (1967). Functions of Sōka Gakkai Membership (Unpublished Paper), Columbia University.

4 BABBIE, E. T. (1966). 'The Third Civilization: An Examination of Sōka Gakkai.' *Review of Religious Research* 7: 101–121.
Babbie presents a case study of Sōka Gakkai as an international religious movement, reflecting on the factors determining its success as a world-proselytizing religion. Briefly tracing the origins and growth of the movement, Babbie then reviews the literature on the study of religious organizations using this as a basis to present the main theme of his paper: a developmental model of a successful world-proselytizing religion. Babbie's model contains four elements: field, message, initial group, and expansion phase which he applies to the case of Sōka Gakkai.

5 BASABE, F. M., Anzai, S. and Alphonso M. Nebreda (1967). *Japanese Youth Confronts Religion: A Sociological Survey.* Tokyo, Sophia University Press.

6 BETHEL, D. M. (1973). *Makiguchi-The Value Creator.* New York, John Weatherhill Inc.
The book traces the development of Tsunesaburo Makiguchi's philosophy and its influence on his educational theories. The author draws on new research, personal interviews, and Makiguchi's own writings to give a clear picture of the magnitude and revolutionary quality of his theories and the role these theories played in the development and growth of Sōka Gakkai. (from flaptext)

7 BLACKER, C. (1964). 'Le Sōka Gakkai japonais; l'activisme politique d'une secte bouddhiste.' *Archives de sociologie des religions* 17.

8 BLOOM, A. (1965). 'Observations in the Study of Contemporary Nichiren Buddhism.' *Contemporary Religions of Japan* VI(1): 58–74.
This article reflects on the myriad of organizations deriving their doctrines and activities from Nichiren Buddhism. Following interviews, the author depicts the nature of thought in these Nichiren organizations, in particular Sōka Gakkai.

9 BOCKING, B. (1981). 'Reflections on Sōka Gakkai.' *The Scottish Journal of Religious Studies* 2(1): 38–52.

10 BOCKING, B. (1994). Of Priests, Protests and Protestant Buddhists: the Case of Sōka Gakkai International. *Japanese New Religions in the West.* P. B. Clarke and J. Somers. Folkestone, Kent, The Japan Library: 117–131.
This article discusses Sōka Gakkai, the most well known and most successful of the post-war Japanese lay religious movements. It considers the direction of development of Sōka Gakkai International following the split between the Sōka Gakkai organizations and the Nichiren Shōshū sect of which it was a lay movement.

11 BRANNEN, N. (1961). 'A Visit to Taisekiji, Head Temple of Sōka Gakkai.' *Contemporary Religions in Japan* II(2/June): 13–30.

12 BRANNEN, N. (1961). 'A Visit to Sōka Gakkai Headquarters.' *Contemporary Religions in Japan* 2(1 March): 55–62.

13 BRANNEN, N. (1962). 'The Teaching of Sōka Gakkai.' *Contemporary Religions in Japan* 3(3): 247.

14 BRANNEN, N. (1964). 'False Religions, Forced Conversions, Iconoclasm.' *Contemporary Religions in Japan* V: 232.

15 BRANNEN, N. (1964). 'Sōka Gakkai: New Religious Sect or Third World Power?' *Japan Studies* 1(2).

16 BRANNEN, N. (1964). 'Sōka Gakkai's Theory of Value.' *Contemporary Religions of Japan* 5(2): 143–54.
This article discusses Tsunesaburo Makiguchi's 'theory of life' from which Sōka Gakkai derived its name, depicting how this philosophy of utilitarianism was utilised as a fundamental basis for the teachings of the Nichirenshū sect, and the inconsistencies it has exposed.

17 BRANNEN, N. S. (1966). 'Religion and Politics: Sidelights on Sōka Gakkai.' *Japanese Religions* 4(4).

18 BRANNEN, N. S. (1967). 'Happiness and Life's Objective (Chapter 4 of Shakubuku Kyōten).' *Contemporary Religions of Japan* 8(2).

19 BRANNEN, N. (1968). *Sōka Gakkai: Japan's Militant Buddhists.* Richmond, Virginia, John Knox Press.

20 BRETT, C. (1979). 'The Kōmeitō and local Japanese Politics.' *Asian Survey* 19: 366–78.

21 CAUSTON, R. (1988). *Nichiren Shōshū Buddhism.* London, Rider & Co. Ltd.
The author who was chairman of Nichiren Shōshū Buddhism UK (Sōka Gakkai) explains the teachings and practice of the movement and gives examples of how individuals and families have overcome problems through practicing the teaching.

22 CHANDRA, L. (1996). The Lotus Sutra and the Present Age: The Philosophy of SGI President Daisaku Ikeda. Tokyo, Institute of Oriental Philosophy.

23 CLARK, E. T. (1949). *The Small Sects in America.* New York.

24 COWAN, J. (1982). *The Buddhism of the Sun.* Richmond, Surrey, Nichiren Shōshū of the United Kingdom.
Essays by various members of the movement discussing teaching and practices.

25 DATOR, J. (1965). 'The Sōka Gakkai: A Socio-Political Interpretation.' *Contemporary Religions in Japan* 6(3): 205–242.
Examines why Sōka Gakkai has been sucessful as a social and political force. There is discussion about its establishment as 'organizational group' within Japan's social environment, the appeal of its teachings in contemporary society and the organization's political strategy. The last section examines the dangers facing the Sōka Gakkai and offers suggestions for its future.

26 DATOR, J. (1967). 'The Sōka Gakkai in Japanese Politics.' *A Journal of Church and State* IX: 211.

27 DATOR, J. (1968). Demographic and Attitudinal Data on Sōka Gakkai Members (Unpublished paper prepared for presentation at annual convention of Association for Asian Studies), Association for Asian Studies (also published by Stanford University, California).

28 DATOR, J. A. (1969). *Sōka Gakkai- Builders of the Third Civilization.* Seattle and Washington, University of Washington Press.
An examination of Sōka Gakkai from a sociological and political perspective, detailing the movement's organization and expansion, the composition of both its American and Japanese members and its appeal as a religious and ideological group.

29 DELIKHAN, G. A. (1964). 'Sōka Gakkai's Starting Success.' *The Asia Magazine* **4**(42 (October 18th)): 4–5.

30 DUMOULIN, H. (1963). *Sōka Gakkai, eine moderne Volksreligion: ein Besuch im Haupttempel Taisekiji*. Das Moderne Japan: Einführende Aufsätze. J. Roggendorf.

31 DUMOULIN, H. (1964). 'Sōka Gakkai.' *Die Katholischen Missionen* **83**.

32 DUMOULIN, H. (1969). 'Buddhismus im modernen Japan.' *Saeculum* **20**: 291–351.

33 EARHART, H. B. (1976). 'Recent Publications on Sōka Gakkai.' *History of Religions* **15**(3): 264–88.

34 ELLWOOD, R. S. (1974). *The Eagle and the Rising Sun: Americans and the New Religions of Japan*. Philadelphia, Westminster Press.
Ellwood examines the impact of five 'new religions' in America: Tenrikyō, Sōka Gakkai, Sekai Kyūseikyō, Seichō-no-Ie and Perfect Liberty. The cultural exchange between East and West as presented by the development of these movements in America is discussed.

35 ENDO, Y. (1964). 'Sōka Gakkai, the Study of a Society for the Creation of Value.' *Anglican Theological Review* **46**: 131–141.

36 ENDŌ, T. (1996). The Lotus Sutra and the Philosophy of Sōka Gakkai. Tokyo, Institute of Oriental Philosophy.

37 EPP, R. (1980). 'Some Aspects of Daisaku Ikeda's Thought.' *Japan Christian Quarterly* **46**.

38 FUJIWARA, H. (1970). *I Denounce Sōka Gakkai*. Tokyo, Nisshin Hōdō.

39 GARRIGUES, S. L. (1975). 'The Sōka Gakkai Enshrining Ceremony: Ritual Change in a Japanese Buddhist Sect in America.' *Eastern Anthropologist* **28**(2).

40 GITTINGS, J. A. (1967). 'Politics of Mercy in Sōka Gakkai.' *Japan Christian Quarterly* **33**: 197–99.

41 GROSS, C. H. (1970). *Sōka Gakkai and Education*, Michigan State University, College of Education, Institute for International Studies.

42 HASHIMOTO, H. and W. MCPHERSON (1976). 'Rise and Decline of Sōka Gakkai: Japan and the United States.' *Review of Religious Research* **17**: 82–92.

43 HASHIMOTO, H. and W. MCPHERSON (1976). 'Rise and Decline of Sōka Gakkai: Japan and the US.' *Review of Religious Research* **17**(2).

44 HELTON, W. R. (1965). 'Political Prospects of the Sōka Gakkai.' *Pacific Affairs* **38**(314): 231–244.

45 HESSELGRAVE, D. J. (1965). A Propagation Profile of the Sōka Gakkai, University of Minnesota.

46 HESSELGRAVE, D. J. (1965). 'Resurgent Buddhism of the Sōka Gakkai.' *Christianity Today* **9**((May 7th 1965)): 45–46.

47 HESSELGRAVE, D. J. (1978). *Nichiren Shōshū Sōka Gakkai: The Lotus Blossom in Modern Japan. Dynamic Religious Movements*. D. J. Hesselgrave. Grand Rapids, Michigan, Baker Book House.

48 HOLTZAPPLE, V. R. (1977). Sōka Gakkai in Midwestern America: A Case Study of a Transpositional Movement. St. Louis, University of Washington.

Participant observation and study in a midwestern American city in which movement elite and local members were in conflict over recruitment practices

49 HOURMANT, L. (1989). 'Ascèse, rationalité, modernité en contexte oriental: le bouddhisme de la Sōka Gakkai.' Social Compass **36**(1): 83–94.

50 HOURMANT, L. (1990). *'Transformer le poison en élixir.' L'alchimie du désir dans un culte néo-bouddhique, la Sōka Gakkai française. De L'Emotion en Religion.* F. Champion and D. Hervieu-Léger. Paris, Centurion: 71–119.

51 HOURMANT, L. (1993). *La relation à l'objet sacré dans un culte néo-bouddhique: la Sōka Gakkai française. Systèmes de pensée en Afrique noire (Fétiches II. Puissance des objets, charme des mots 12.)*: 145–171.

52 HURST, J. D. (1980). The Nichiren Shōshū Sōka Gakkai in America: The Ethos of a New Religious Movement, Temple University: **401**.
This dissertation examines Nichiren Shōshū of America (NSA) and its history as an international movement and its development in America. The implications of its ethos and world view for American culture are analysed.

53 HURST, J. (1992). *Nichiren Shōshū Buddhism and the Sōka Gakkai in America: The Ethos of a New Religious Movement.* New York, Garland Publishing Inc.
One of the most recent and complete accounts of the development and spread of the movement within the US with particular reference to the ethos (as opposed to 'world view') of the group.

54 IKEDA, D. (1961). Sōka Gakkai. Tokyo, Seikyō Shimbunsha.

55 IKEDA, D. (1965). Science and Religion. Tokyo, Sōka Gakkai.

56 IKEDA, D. (1966). Guidance Memo. Tokyo, Seikyō Press.

57 IKEDA, D. (1972). The Human Revolution. New York and Tokyo, John Weatherhill Inc. **1**.
A thinly disguised 'fictional' account of the appearance, spread and persecution of Sōka Gakkai.

58 IKEDA, D. (1973). Yesterday, Today, Tomorrow. Santa Monica, California, World Tribune Press.

59 IKEDA, D. (1975). Guidance Memo. Santa Monica, California, World Tribune Press.

60 IKEDA, D. (1976). Dialogue on Life. Tokyo, Nichiren Shōshū International Center. **2**.
Explores the nature and expression of life from Buddhist perspectives and with reference to scientific and philosophical analyses. Ikeda hopes to illustrate a clear path to human happiness and prosperity, a revolutionary change in individual spiritual values.

61 IKEDA, D. (1976). Buddhism: The Living Philosophy. Tokyo, The East Publications Inc.
The book is a clear and general account of the way the Buddhist life philosophy can help man understand his true place in the universe and live in harmony and happiness with the universal laws governing all life. Ikeda discusses the nature and goals of the Sōka Gakkai.

62 IKEDA, D. (1976). The Living Buddha: An Interpretive Biography. Tokyo, Japan, John Weatherhill Inc.

63 IKEDA, D. (1976). Advice to Young People. Los Angeles, World Tribune Press.

64 IKEDA, D. (1976). Daily Guidance. Los Angeles, World Tribune Press.

65 IKEDA, D. (1977). Buddhism, The First Millenium. Tokyo, Kōdansha International.

66 IKEDA, D. (1977). Heritage of the Ultimate Law of Life. Santa Monica, California, World Tribune Press.

67 IKEDA, D. (1977). On Requital for the Buddha's Favor. Santa Monica, California, World Tribune Press.

68 IKEDA, D. (1978). Songs from My Heart. New York and Tokyo, John Weatherhill Inc.
Poems and photographs of Daisaku Ikeda

69 IKEDA, D. (1978). The True Object of Worship. Santa Monica, California, World Tribune Press.

70 IKEDA, D. (1979). On the Japanese Classics. New York and Tokyo, John Weatherhill Inc.
A series of conversations between Daisaku Ikeda and Makoto Nemoto in which they discuss the great works of Japanese literature.

71 IKEDA, D. (1979). Glass Children and Other Essays. Tokyo, Kōdansha International.
Essays on a wide variety of subjects concerning the application of Buddhism in everyday life: socialization of children, family life, world peace etc.

72 IKEDA, D. and Y. INOUE (1980). Letters of Four Seasons. Tokyo, Kōdansha International.

73 IKEDA, D. and R. HUYGHE (1980). La Nuit Appelle L'Aurore. Dialogue Orient-Occident sur la crise contemporaine. France, Flammarion.

74 IKEDA, D. (1980). Shinpan Ikeda kaichō zenshū 10, Kōgihen (Collected works of President Ikeda, New Edition). Tokyo, Seikyō Shinbunsha. **10.**

75 IKEDA, D. (1981). A Lasting Peace. New York and Tokyo, John Weatherhill Inc. **1.**
In his second collection of addresses the honorary president of Sōka Gakkai confronts the most pressing issues of today: nuclear disarmament and environmental destruction, the polarization of the globe into east and west, north and south, education, cultural pluralism, and the need for human spiritual renewal. His remarks on all these themes are well considered and well reasoned, but what makes them remarkable is his deep commitment to the resolution of these problems from the standpoint of religious conviction and the transformation of the self. (from flaptext)

76 IKEDA, D. (1982). The Human Revolution. New York and Tokyo, John Weatherhill Inc.
Five volumes

77 IKEDA, D. (1982). Life: An Enigma, a Precious Jewel. 1982, Kōdansha International.

78 IKEDA, D. and B. WILSON (1984). *Human Values in a Changing World: A Dialogue on the Social Role of Religion.* London & Sydney, Macdonald.
This is series of conversations-recorded and edited between Daisaku Ikeda-Japanese leader of Sōka Gakkai and Professor Bryan Wilson of All Souls College, Oxford, Britain's foremost sociologist of religion. A wide range of issues are discussed including the social role of religion, ethics of the modern age, the character of nationalism etc.

79 IKEDA, D. (1985). Buddhism and the Cosmos: Daisaku Ikeda in conversation with Masayoshi Kiguchi and Eiichi Shimura. London, Macdonald.
A series of conversations between the leader of Sōka Gakkai, Daisaku Ikeda and a respected astronomer (Kiguchi) and journalist (Shimura). In this wide-ranging and controversial series of

conversations Ikeda presses both science and mysticism into the service of the Human Revolution and the delineation of the way forward. He explores the implication of recent astronomical and cosmological findings, clarifying their meaning for the world in the light of Buddhist wisdom.

80 IKEDA, D. (1986). The Flower of Chinese Buddhism. New York and Tokyo, John Weatherhill Inc.
The fascination of the story of introduction of Buddhism to China lies in the meeting of two great civilizations in Asia: India, the cradle of Buddhism, and China where Buddhism was transformed and transported to Korea and Japan. Ikeda traces the history of Buddhism in China, including discussion of the translations of Buddhist scriptures and the scholarly activity in China.

81 IKEDA, D. (n.d). Sōka Gakkai-Its Ideals and Traditions.

82 IKEDA, D. (n.d). A Historical View of Buddhism.

83 INGRAM, P. (1969). 'Sōka Gakkai and the Kōmeito: Buddhism and Political Power in Japan.' *Contemporary Religions in Japan* 10(3–4): 155–.

84 International Institute for the Study of Religions (1960). 'Sōka Gakkai and the Nichiren Shū Sect.' *Contemporary Religions in Japan* 1(1).

85 IONESCU-DUCARU, S. (1999). Adapt or Perish: The Story of Sōka Gakkai in Germany. *Japanese New Religions in Global Perspective.* P. B. Clarke. Richmond, Surrey, Curzon Press.

86 ISHIMOTO, B. S. (1935). *Facing Two Ways: The Story of My Life.* London, Toronto, Melbourne and Sydney, Cassell & Company Ltd.
A brief and candid chapter on the author's own search for a meaningful religion, with references to Pure Land, Zen and Nichiren Buddhism.

87 ITALIAANDER, R. (1973). *Soka gakkai: Japans Neue Buddhisten.* Erlangen, Verlag Der Evangelisch-Lutheran Mission.

88 *Japan Times* (1979). Ikeda Quits Presidency of Sōka Gakkai Group. *Japan Times Weekly.* Tokyo.

89 KAMSTRA, J. H. (1960). 'Japans grosste-Gefahr-die Sōka Gakkai(1).' *Zeitschrift fur Missionwissenschaft und Religionswissenschaft* 44(1): 41–51.

90 KAMSTRA, J. H. (1960). 'Japans grosste-Gefahr-die Sōka Gakkai(2).' *Zeitschrift fur Missionwissenschaft und Religionswissenschaft* 44(2): 98–106.

91 KASAHARA, K. (1976). *Gendai Shakai to Sōka Gakkai (Modern Society and Sōka Gakkai). Gendai Bukkyo (Contemporary Buddhism).* N. Hajime. Tokyo, Kōsei Shuppansha. 20: 123–207.

92 KASAI, M. (1983). 'Mekishiko genchijin ni okeru Nihon bunka juyō no ichi keitai-Nichiren Shōshū dendō ni kansuru jirei kenkyū (One Form of Acceptance of Japanese Culture among Native Mexicans: A Case Study of Nichiren Shōshū proselytization).' *Nanbu Mekishiko sonraku ni okeru Katorikku-kei bunka no kenkyū* 2.

93 KIRIMURA, Y. (1977). *Fundamentals of Buddhism.* Tokyo, Nichiren Shōshū Center.

94 KIRIMURA, Y., Ed. (1982). *Outline of Buddhism.* Tokyo, Nichiren Shōshū International Center.

95 KIRIMURA, Y. (1982). The Life of Nichiren Daishonin. Tokyo, Nichiren Shōshū International Center.

96 KISALA, R. (1994). 'Sōka Gakkai, Kōmeitō and the Separation of Religion and State in Japan.' *Nanzan Bulletin* **18**.

97 KLEIN, N. H. (1968). 'On the Doctrine of Sōka Gakkai.' *Japanese Religions* **5**(3).

98 KNOTT, K. (1988). *New Religious Movements. The British: Their Religious Beliefs and Practices* 1800–1986. T. Thomas. London, Routledge.
An account of the growth of new religious movements in the UK. A number of movements are discussed, including Baha'i, the Unification Church, ISKCON, Scientology and the Rajneesh Movement. Sōka Gakkai, Sōtō Zen, and Nichiren Shōshū are also mentioned, but are not discussed in detail.

99 KOBAYASHI, S. (1958). 'Sōka Gakkai, a Strange Buddhist Sect.' *Japan Christian Quarterly* **24**(April): 104–111.

100 KODAIRA, Y. (1958). Sōka Gakkai. Tokyo, Nihon Hōsō Shuppansha.

101 KOEPPING, K.-P. (1969). 'Sōka Gakkai, eine kämpferische neue Religion Japans.' *Indo- Asia* **3**: 247–258.

102 Kōfuku-no-Kagaku (1995). Sōka Gakkai Ruining Japan. Tokyo, Kōfuku-no-Kagaku General Headquarters.

103 KOHLER, W. (1962). *Die Lotus-Lehre und die modernen Religionen in Japan.* Zurich, Atlantis Verlag.

104 KUDO, T. (1961). 'The Faith of Sōka Gakkai.' *Contemporary Religions of Japan* **2**(2): 1–12.

105 KUMASAKA, Y. (1966). 'Sōka Gakkai: Group Psycholoic Study of a New Religio-Political Organization.' *American Journal of Psychotherapy* **20**(July): 462–70.

106 LANDE, A. and CLARKE, P. B. (1988). Japan (New Religious Movements). *The World's Religions.* S. Sutherland, L. Houlden, P. B. Clarke and F. Hardy. London, Routledge: 932–944.
A short summary of the features of several Japanese New Religious Movements including Sōka Gakkai, Nichiren Shōshū, Sekai Kyūseikyō, Ōmotokyō, PL Kyōdan, Risshō Kōsei Kai, Konkōkyō, Tenrikyō, Mahikari, Seichō-no-Ie and Reiyūkai.

107 LAUER, H. (1975). 'A Study of the Nichiren Shōshū Academy of America.' *CCNY Journal of Anthropology* **1**(1): 7–26.

108 Look (1963). A New Face Called Sōka Gakkai Raises Old Problems in Modern Japan. Look: **18**.

109 MACIOTI, M. I. (1996). *Il Buddha che è in noi (The Buddha Within Ourselves).* Rome.
Dr Macioti's Study of Sōka Gakkai in Italy.

110 MAKIGUCHI, T. (1937). Sōka Kyōikuhō no Kagakuteki Chōshūkyōteki Jikken Shōmei (Practical Experimentation in Value-Creating Educational Methods Through Science and Supreme Religion). Tokyo, Sōka Kyōiku Gakkai.

111 MAKIGUCHI, T. (1943). Kachi Sōzō (The Creation of Value). Tokyo, Soka Kyoiku Gakkai.

112 MAKIGUCHI, T. (1953). The Theory of Value. Tokyo, Sōka Gakkai.

113 MAKIGUCHI, T. (1953). Kachiron (A Discussion of Value). Tokyo.

114 MAKIGUCHI, T. (1964). The Philosophy of Value. Tokyo, Seikyō press.

115 MCCRIMMON, M. (1964). 'From Christianity to Sōka Gakkai.' *The Japan Missionary Bulletin* 18(July): 397–402.

116 MCFARLAND, H. N. (1967). *The Rush Hour of the Gods: A Study of new Religious Movements in Japan.* New York, Macmillan.
One of the first books to give a general review which encompasses relevant Japanese history as well as socioreligious background. The author, a professor of the history of religion examines five new religions, Konkōkyō, PL Kyōdan, Seichō-no-Ie, Risshō Kōsei Kai, and Sōka Gakkai.

117 MÉTRAUX, D. A. (1978). The Religious and Social Philosophy of Sōka Gakkai, Columbia University.

118 MÉTRAUX, D. (1979). 'The Sōka Gakkai's Philosophy of Life.' *Proceedings of First International Symposium on Asian Studies.*

119 MÉTRAUX, D. (1980). 'Why Did Ikeda Quit?' *Japanese Journal of Religious Studies* 7(1).
An attempt to explain the reason for Ikeda's abrupt resignation from his post as the president of Sōka Gakkai in 1970 and subsequent move to Sōka Gakkai International, the overseas development branch of the movement. This explanation reveals tensions between the priesthood and the lay organisation. The 1991 split between the two may show that Métraux's interpretation is correct.

120 MÉTRAUX, D. (1986). 'The Sōka Gakkai's Search for the Realization of the World of Rissho Ankokuron.' *Japanese Journal of Religious Studies* 13(1): 31–61.
Métraux discusses Sōka Gakkai's claim to be Nichirens' successor and focuses on the movements' emphasis of its peace movement which is based on Nichiren's treatise Risshō Ankokuron. ('Establishment of Righteousness and Security in the Country').

121 MÉTRAUX, D. (1988). *The History and Theology of Sōka Gakkai.* New York, Edwin Mellen Press.
A more up-to-date account of Sōka Gakkai both at home and abroad. Critical but by no means hostile. Includes a chapter on the success of Nichiren Shōshū in America.

122 MÉTRAUX, D. (1992). 'The Dispute between the Sōka Gakkai and the Nichiren Shōshū Priesthood: A Lay Revolution Against a Conservative Clergy.' *Japanese Journal of Religious Studies* 19(4): 325–36.
Outlines the confrontation between Sōka Gakkai and the Nichiren Shōshū sect, describing the claims on both sides and the steps taken during the dispute. Métraux reflects on the ability of a new religious movement to prosper without an organized clergy.

123 MÉTRAUX, D. A. (1994). *The Sōka Gakkai Revolution.* Lanham, New York, London, University Press of America.
Métraux examines the activities of the Sōka Gakkai movement, including its history, relationship with politics, its concern with education, its conflict with the Nichiren Shōshū sect and its internationalization. His theme is 'revolution' based on the movement's own use of the word to describe the human experience that members of Sōka Gakkai attain.

124 MIZOGUCHI, A. (1978). *Sōka Gakkai.* Shinshūkyō no Sekai (*The World of the New Religions*). Nawata Sanae et al. Tokyo, Daizō Shuppan. II: 164–240.

125 MONTGOMERY, D. (1991). *Fire in the Lotus:The Dynamic Buddhism of Nichiren.* London, Mandala.
Contains a brief general history of Buddhism and its introduction to Japan, followed by a description of the development of Nichiren Buddhism in Japan. The founding of Sōka Gakkai is then described, and its subsequent expansion in Japan and later in the United States is outlined.

A brief account of Reiyūkai, Risshō Kōsei Kai, and other smaller Nichiren groups abroad is also given. Appendix One contains Nichiren Buddhist prayers and sutras.

126 MOOS, F. (1963). 'Religion and Politics in Japan: The Case of Sōka Gakkai.' *Asian Survey* 3(3).

127 MORI, K. (1977). Study of Makiguchi Tsunesaburo:The Founder of Sōka Gakkai. *Theology Department*, Graduate Theological Union: **242**.

128 MORRIS, I. (1960). *Nationalism and the Right Wing in Japan.* New York.

129 MURATA, K. (1959). Sōka Gakkai, Communist Envy. *Japan Times.* Tokyo.

130 MURATA, K. (1969). *Japan's New Buddhism – An Objective Account of Sōka Gakkai.* New York and Tokyo, Walker/Weatherhill.
An introductory book presenting basic teachings, history and organizational framework of the movement as well as an outline of its educational and social welfare activities. Deliberate contrast to the generally negative view of Sōka Gakkai at the time.

131 MURATA, K. (1971). *Japan's New Buddhism.* New York, John Weatherhill Inc.
An account of Sōka Gakkai by a Japanese journalist.

132 NAKABA, T. (1968). *Nihon no choryu: Sōka Gakkai hatten no ayumi* (A Japanese Trend: The History of Sōka Gakkai's Development).

133 NAKABA, T. (1972). *Amerika no Nichiren Shōshū* (Nichiren Shōshū in America). Tokyo, Senzeki Press.

134 NAKANO, T. (1992). 'Sōka Gakkai and its Peace Movements: The making of the counter communism?' *Religion Today* 7(2): 5–8.

135 NAWATA, S. (1979). *Reiyūkai. Shinshūkyō no sekai* (The World of New Religions). Tokyo, Daizōkan. 2: 6–81.
This volume contains information concerning Reiyūkai, Risshō Kōsei Kai and Sōka Gakkai.

136 NAYLOR, C. (1991). 'Nichiren, Imperialism and the Peace Movement.' *Japanese Journal of Religious Studies* 18(1): 51–78.

137 Nichiren Shōshū International Center, Ed. (1979). *The Major Writings of Nichiren Daishonin.* Tokyo, Nichiren Shōshū International Center.
Three volume set of books containing English translations of the doctrinal writings and letters of Nichiren Daishonin (1222–1282).

138 Nichiren Shōshū International Center (1987). *Buddhism and the Nichiren Shōshū Tradition.* Tokyo, Nichiren Shōshū International Center.

139 NISHIO, H. K. (1967). 'Comparative Analysis of the Risshō Kōseikai and the Sōka Gakkai.' *Asian Survey* 7(11): 776–790.
This article traces the historical development of the Risshō Kōsei Kai and the Sōka Gakkai religious movements, comparing and contrasting their membership, composition, their doctrinal orientations, recruitment methods, organizational structure, political activity and their general historical rivalry.

140 NORMAN, W. H. H. (1970). 'Sōka Gakkai, Kōmeitō and Freedom of Speech.' *Japan Christian Quarterly* 36: 258–265.

141 OFFNER, C. B. (1969). 'Sōka Gakkai.' *Japan Christian Quarterly* 35(3).

142 OGUCHI, I. and A. SAKI (1957). *Sōka Gakkai.* Tokyo, Aoki-shoten.

143 Oh, J. K.-c. (1972). 'Fusion of Politics and Religion in Japan: The Sōka Gakkai Kōmeitō.' *Journal of Church and State* 14: 59–74.

144 Oh, J. K. (1973). 'The Nichiren Shōshū of America.' *Review of Religious Research* **14**: 169–177.

145 OKAMOTO, R. (1963). Japan: A New Faith Called Sōka Gakkai Raises Old Problems in Modern Japan. *Look*. **27**: 15–26.

146 ŌKAWA, R. (1995). Sōka Gakkai Bokokuron (Sōka Gakkai's Threat to the State/ Country). Tokyo, IRH Press.

147 ŌKUBO, M. (1987). 'Mekishiko ni okeru SGI kannen fukugō juyō katei no shakai-shinrigakuteki bunseki (Socio-Psychological Theories of Acceptance of SGI Conceptual Complexes in Mexico).' *Nanbu Mekishiko sonraku ni okeru Katorikku-kei bunka no kenkyū* **4**: 92–123.

148 ŌKUBO, M. (1987). 'Mekishiko Nichiren Shōshū ni okeru kuyō-kan to shokuggyōrōdō-kan ni tsuite (Views on Kuyō and Views on Occupational Labour in Nichiren Shōshū of Mexico).' *Nishi Nihon shūkyōgaku zasshi* **9**: 19–27.

149 ŌKUBO, M. (1991). 'The Acceptance of Nichiren Shōshū Sōka Gakkai in Mexico.' *Japanese Journal of Religious Studies* **18**(2–3): 189–212.

150 OLSON, L. (1971). *The Value Creation Society: Sōka Gakkai, A Japanese Religious and Political Phenomenon*. Tokyo.

151 PARKS, Y. Y. (1980). 'The Nichiren Shōshu Academy in America: Changes during the 1970s.' Japanese Journal of Religious Studies **7**(4): 337–55.
Looks at how Nichiresn Shōshū Academy (NSA), a branch of Sōka Gakkai, transformed itself after the 1960s to adapt to a less favorable environment for unorthodox religious groups in 1970s America. Focuses on organizational and membership structure and stages of what she terms 'Americanization'.

152 PECCEI, A. and D. IKEDA (1987). Before It Is Too Late. Tokyo, Kōdansha International.
A series of dialogues concerning world peace and education of Sōka Gakkai International and one of the leading figures of the Club of Rome.

153 RAMSEYER, R. (1962). 'Religion in Japan in 1961.' *Contemporary Religions in Japan* **III**: 18.

154 RAMSEYER, R. (1963). 'The Sōka Gakkai and the Japanese Elections of 1960 (sic).' *Contemporary Religions in Japan* **IV**: 287.

155 RAMSEYER, R. (1965). *The Sōka Gakkai*, Center for Japanese Studies, Ann Arbor, University of Michigan.

156 RAMSEYER, R. L. (1972). 'Finances in the New Religions and the Christian Church.' *Japan Christian Quarterly* **37**: 84–89.

157 READER, I. (1994). Japanese Religions. *Insight Japan*. **3**: 6–9.
A summary of a few of the Japanese Old and New Religions.

158 REIYŪKAI (1986). The Development of Japanese Lay Buddhism. Tokyo, The Reiyūkai.
A short book giving an outline of Reiyūkai but particularly useful in its factual appraisal of Sōka Gakkai.

159 RENONDEAU, G. (1951). 'Le Traité sue l'Etat'de Nichiren.' *T'oung Pao* **XL**: 123.

160 REPP, M. (1995). 'The Earthquake in the Kobe-Osaka Area January 17th 1995. Its Impact on Religions and Their Response.' *Japanese Religions* **20**(2): 207–229.

161 RICCO, M. (1967). *Religione della violenza e religione del piacere nel nuovo Giappone*. Florence, Saggi.

162 ROTERMUND, H. O. (1972). 'Einführung zum Shakubuku Kyōten der Sōka Gakkai; Bekehrung auf Biegen und Brechen.' *Zeitschrift fur Religions und Geistesgeschichte* **24**(3): 227–241.
An analysis of the Shakubuku Handbook, previously used by Sōka Gakkai members in converting people, if necessary by forcible persuasion.

163 ROTERMUND, H. O. (1973). 'Soka-gakkai; ideologie d'une nouvelle secte japonaise.' *Revue de l'Histoire des Religion* **184**: 137–157.

164 SAITO, K. (1962). 'Sōka Gakkai: Third Force in Japanese Politics?' *Orient/ West* **7**.

165 Seikyō Times (1972). Nichiren Shōshū and Sōka Gakkai: Modern Buddhism in Action. Tokyo, Seikyō Press.

166 Seikyō Times (1979). The Major Writings of Nichiren Daishonin. Tokyo, Nichiren Shōshū International Center.

167 Sekai Bukkyo Kyokai (1962). Sōka Gakkai o Shakubuku suru (Chanting Sōka Gakkai). Tokyo, Jitsugyo no Sekaisha.

168 SHELDON, C. (1960). 'Sōka Gakkai and the Nichiren Shū Sect.' *Contemporary Religions in Japan* (March (pp 55–70), June (pp 48–54)).

169 SHUPE, A. D. (1986). Militancy and Accommodation in the Third Civilization: The Case of Japan's Sōka Gakkai Movement. *Prophetic Religion and Politics (Religion and the Political Order, Volume One)*. J. K. Hadden and A. D. Shupe. New York, Paragon: 235–253.

170 SHUPE, A. (1991). Globalization versus religious nativism: Japan's Sōka Gakkai in the world arena. *Religion and Global Order*. R. Robertson and W. R. Garrett. New York, Paragon House: 183–99.

171 SKELTON, T. L. (1968). Social Movements and Social Change: The Sōka Gakkai of Japan. Berkeley, University of California at Berkeley.

172 SNOW, D. A. (1976). The Nichiren Shōshū Buddhist Movement in America: A Sociological Examination of Its Value Orientation, Recruitment Efforts and Spread. Los Angeles, University of California.
This Ph.D is based on participant observation and content analysis of movement literature and focuses on recruitment and changes in strategy over time.

173 SNOW, D. A. (1979). 'A Dramaturgical Analysis of Movement Accommodation: Building Idiosyncrasy Credit as a Movement Mobilization Strategy.' *Symbolic Interaction* **2**(2): 23–44.

174 SNOW, D. A. (1987). Organization, Ideology and Mobilization: The Case of Nichiren Shōshū of America. *The Future of New Religious Movements*. D. G. Bromley and P. E. Hammond. Macon, Mercer University Press: 153–72.

175 Sōka Gakkai (1957). Doctrines of Nichiren Shōshū. Tokyo, Sōka Gakkai.

176 Sōka Gakkai (1960). The Sōka Gakkai. Tokyo, Sōka Gakkai.

177 Sōka Gakkai (1960). 'Sōka Gakkai and the Nichiren Shū Sect.' *Contemporary Religions in Japan* **1**(1 and 2).

178 Sōka Gakkai (1966). The Nichiren Shōshū Sōka Gakkai. Tokyo, Sōka Gakkai.

179 Sōka Gakkai (1979). The Liturgy of Nichiren Shōshū. Tokyo, Nichiren Shōshū Temple.

180 Sōka Gakkai (1983). Sōka Gakkai. Tokyo, Sōka Gakkai.

181 Sōka Gakkai (1995–). SGI Quarterly, Sōka Gakkai International.
Replaced the monthly edition of Sōka Gakkai News from June 1995.

182 Sōka Gakkai International SGI Magazine-UK Express. Taplow Court, Bucks., SGI-UK.
Quarterly Magazine.

183 Sōka Gakkai International SGI Magazine. Tokyo, Sōka Gakkai International.
Quarterly Magazine.

184 Sōka Gakkai International (1986?–1995). Sōka Gakkai News. Tokyo, SGI Public Relations Bureau.
Monthly News Update replaced by SGI Quarterly in June 1995.

185 Sōka Gakkai International (1989). Works of Daisaku Ikeda. Tokyo, Sōka Gakkai International.
A catalogue showing the published volumes of Daisaku Ikeda.

186 Sōka Gakkai International (1991). Issues between the Nichiren Shōshū Priesthood and the Sōka Gakkai (5 Volumes). Tokyo, Sōka Gakkai International.

187 Sōka Gakkai Overseas Bureau (1965 (approx)). 'This Is the Sōka Gakkai' Series No. 2: No Boundary in True Religion, Sōka Gakkai.

188 Sōka Gakkai Overseas Bureau (1965 (approx)). 'This Is the Sōka Gakkai' Series No. 3: Sōka Gakkai and Culture Movement, Sōka Gakkai.

189 Sōka Gakkai Overseas Bureau (1965 (approx)). 'This Is the Sōka Gakkai' Series No. 4: Practices of Believers, Sōka Gakkai.

190 Sōka Gakkai Overseas Bureau (1965 (approx)). 'This Is the Sōka Gakkai' Series No. 5: Head Temple Taisekiji, Sōka Gakkai.

191 Sōka Gakkai Overseas Bureau (1965 (approx)). 'This Is the Sōka Gakkai' Series No. 6: Sōka Gakkai and Kōmeitō, Sōka Gakkai.

192 Sōka Gakkai Overseas Bureau (1965 (approx)). 'This Is the Sōka Gakkai' Series No. 7: The Buddhist Dictionary, Sōka Gakkai.

193 Sōka Gakkai Overseas Bureau (1965 (approx)). 'This Is the Sōka Gakkai' Series No. 8: What is Shakubuku?, Sōka Gakkai.

194 Sōka Gakkai Women's Division (1986). Women against War: Personal Accounts of Forty Japanese Women. Tokyo and New York, Kōdansha International.

195 SOMERS, J. (1994). *Japanese New Religious Movements in Britain. Japanese New Religions in the West.* P. B. Clarke and J. Somers. Folkestone, Kent, Japan Library: 54–76.

196 STONE, J. (1991). 'Re-examining Stereotypes in the Study of Nichiren: Nationalism, Intolerance, and Independence from Tendai.' *Supplement to May 1991 Issue of the Japanese Religions Bulletin.*

197 STONE, J. (1993). 'Review of SNOW 1993 and HURST 1992.' *Japanese Journal of Religious Studies* **20**: 351–59.

A comparison of two books on Sōka Gakkai in America published almost simultaneously and covering a similar period of fieldwork.

198 SUGIMORI, K. (1976). *Kenkyū: Sōka Gakkai* (A Study: Sōka Gakkai). Tokyo, Jiyūsha.

199 SUZUKI, H. (1963). 'Toshikasō no shūkyō shūdan-Fukuoka-shi ni okeru Sōka Gakkai (Urban Lower-Class Religious Groups: Sōka Gakkai in Fukuoka City).' *Shakaigaku kenkyū* (*Journal of Sociological Studies*) 22: 81–102.

200 SUZUKI, H. (1964). 'Toshikasō no shūkyō shūdan-Fukuoka-shi ni okeru Sōka Gakkai (Urban Lower-Class Religious Groups: Sōka Gakkai in Fukuoka City).' *Shakaigaku kenkyū* (*Journal of Sociological Studies*) **24–25**: 50–90.

201 TAKAGI, H. (1962). 'Sōka Gakkai Makes Advance into the Political World.' *Japan Socialist Review*(June 16th): **53**.

202 TAKASHI, N. (1973). *Nichirenshū no seiritsu to tenkai* (The Formation and Development of Nichirenshu). Tokyo, Yoshikawa Kōbunkan.

203 TAKEDA, R. (1994). *Akuma no Jabō* (The Evil Desires of the Devil). Tokyo, Daiichi Kikaku Shuppan.
From leader of Sōka Gakkai to dictator of Japan: Ikeda Daisaku's leap to power through local elections. The author is a publisher and journalist.

204 THOMPSON, S. I. (1968). 'Religious Conversion and Religious Zeal in an Overseas Enclave: The Case of the Japanese in Bolivia.' *Anthropological Quarterly* **41**(4): 201–8.

205 THOMSEN, H. (1959). "Ise or Daisekiji? Sōka Gakkai'.' *Japanese Religions* 1(2).

206 TODA, J. (1958). Shakubuku Kyōten (The Text Book for Shakubuku). Tokyo, Sōka Gakkai.

207 TODA, J. (1960). 'Preface to Sōka Gakkai and the Nichiren Shū Sect.' *Contemporary Religions of Japan* (June): **48**.

208 TODA (1992). *Ikeda Sōka Gakkai no Shinjitsu* (The Truth about Ikeda's Sōka Gakkai). Tokyo, Nisshin Hōdō.
A denunciation of the present leader of Sōka Gakkai.

209 TOYNBEE, A. J. and IKEDA, D. (1976). The Toynbee-Ikeda Dialogue: Man Himself Must Choose. Tokyo, Kōdansha International.
Toynbee and Ikeda exchanged written questions and answers and held conversations which were recorded and subsequently edited for publication, revised and approved by Toynbee before his last illness. man's predicament is considered by these two men in all its aspects: personal and social, political and international, philosophical

210 TSURUMI, S. (1963). 'A Brief History of Sōka Gakkai.' *Japanese Religions* 3(3).

211 VAN BRAGT, J. (1993). 'An uneven battle: Sōka Gakkai vs. Nichiren Shōshū.' *Bulletin of the Nanzan Institute for Religion and Culture* 17: 15–31.
Details the breakdown that occurred between Sōka Gakkai and the Buddhist sect Nichiren Shōshū from which it originated. Focuses on passages from Soka gakkai's publications to depict the struggle.

212 WATSON, B. (1996). The Lotus Sutra and the Twenty-first Century. Tokyo, Institute of Oriental Philosophy.

213 WHITE, J. W. (1964). Militant Religion in Japan: The Sōka Gakkai, Princeton University.

214 WHITE, J. W. (1966). The Sōka Gakkai in Japanese Politics, Stanford University.

215 WHITE, J. W. (1967). 'Mass Movements and Democracy: Sōka Gakkai in Japanese Politics.' *American Political Science Review* 61(September): 744–50.

216 WHITE, J. W. (1969). Mass Movement, Militant Religion and Democracy: The Sōka Gakkai in Japanese Politics, Stanford University.

217 WHITE, J. W. (1970). *The Sōka Gakkai and Mass Society.* Stanford, California, Stanford University Press.
This 'classic' work is a study of Sōka Gakkai which includes an overview of the organization, 'its context, history, organization, social composition, beliefs and political platform. It then examines the social origins psychological attributes, and political beliefs and behaviour of the Sōka Gakkai leadership and membership' which leads on to a look at the 'implications of religio-political movements for Japanese society.'

218 WILKINSON, S. L. (1975). Nichiren Shōshū Sōka Gakkai in America: An Analysis of Ultimate Concerns Between 1960 and 1965, University of Iowa.

219 WILSON, B. A. (1959). 'An Analysis of Sect Development.' *American Sociological Review*(February): 3.

220 WILSON, B. A. (1963). 'Millenialism in Comparative Perspective.' *Comparative Studies in Society and History*(October): 93.

221 WILSON, B. (1985). 'The Aims and Vision of Sōka Gakkai.' *Religion Today* 2(1): 7–8.

222 WILSON, B. and DOBBELAERE, K. (1994). *A Time to Chant: The Sōka Gakkai Buddhists in Britain.* Oxford, Clarendon Press/Oxford University Press.
Evaluation of detailed questionnaires sent out to the members of the Sōka Gakkai in the U.K with special attention paid to the motivation for joining and staying in the movement.

223 YAMAORI, T. (1972). 'Sōka Gakkai: A Religious Phoenix.' *Practical Anthropology* 19(4).

224 Youth Division of Sōka Gakkai (1982). Peace Is Our Duty: Accounts of What War Can Do To Man. R. L. Gage. Tokyo, The *Japan Times* Ltd.
A collection of eye witness accounts of the horrors of the Second World War in Japan especially concerning the effects war can have on the mind.

225 Youth Division of Sōka Gakkai (1983). Cries For Peace: Experiences of Japanese Victims of World War II. R. L. Gage. Tokyo, The *Japan Times* Ltd.
A more immediate physical experience of war than its companion piece, this too provides a collection of eye-witness accounts and condemnation of war in general.

Tenrikyō

'Religion of Heavenly Wisdom'

HISTORY

Tenrikyō was founded by a charismatic woman, Nakayama Miki (1798–1887) in 1838, when she began to have revelatory experiences. Nakayama, a farmer's wife, was possessed during a shamanistic rite by the deity *Tenri-O-no-Mikoto* ('Lord of Heavenly Reason') who was revealed to her as the true original god. The deity revealed scripture and gave her healing gifts. She began to work miracles, teaching that a life of sincere piety would lead to divine protection.

Nakayama formed a group in 1838 which was recognized by the government as a member of the Shinto Sect Organizations. Following her death, God began to speak through her disciple Iburi Izō (1833–1907), who went on to develop a structured church system.

In 1941 Tenrikyō became a religious juridical person. In April 1970 Tenrikyō removed itself from the Association of Shinto Sects and was transferred to the 'Other Religions' classification because it saw itself as having a universal mission.

MAIN BELIEFS AND PRACTICES

Believers worship the deity *Tenri-Ō-no-Mikoto*, believed to be the creator of the universe and of mankind, also known as Oyagami ('God the Parent'). It is believed that the deity revealed himself to Nakayama to deliver people from suffering and evil and prepare for

254

the coming of a *kanrodai sekai* ('perfect divine kingdom'), when humankind will enjoy *yoki-gurashi*('joyous and blissful life') in union with *Tenri-O-no-Mikoto*. This deity also made known to Nakayama a special plot of land (*jiba*), believed to be where man was originally born and it is on this land that the main worship centre is built and the sacred pillar (*kanrodai*) erected.

Nakayama wrote two of the central three Tenrikyō texts, *Mikagurauta* ('Songs for the Sacred Dance' written 1866–1875) and *Ofudesaki* ('Tip of the Divine Writing Brush' written 1869–82), and also taught the movement's main Tenrikyō rite, the *Kagura Zutome* ('salvation dance service'). Izō Iburi, the channel for God's message after Miki's death, later wrote the third text *Osashizu* ('Divine Directions' written 1887–1907). On 26 January 1887, while performing the salvation dance service, Nakayama died and is believed to have ascended to a spiritual state. Her ascension, teachings, and 'model life' became the focal points of the Tenrikyō faith. Tenrikyō holds that the revelation to Nakayama was God's way of amending human selfishness, and her life and teachings are therefore held as living for others.

Tenrikyō believers follow the teachings of Nakayama, who taught that one must rid oneself of envy, desire, hatred and other evil thoughts. Leading a harmonious and cheerful life will be rewarded with 'strange and wonderful help' (*fushigi na tasuke*). Life is believed to be something lent from God and progressive purification of the human soul through reincarnation can lead to a state of makoto-shinjitsu ('sincere piety'). Salvation can be attained through receiving *osazuke* ('holy grant'), performing *hinokishin* ('daily service') and making pilgrimages to the *jiba*.

Tenrikyō teaches that illness requires not just medical attention but also spiritual action, as it is a sign from God that life has become out of balance and requires some sort of self reform to overcome a personal problem or misfortune.

After World War II, in 1947, Tenrikyō launched the movement *Fukugen* ('Restoration of the Original Teachings'), a purification of the movement's teachings, believed to have become distorted under state nationalism and state Shinto. Tenrikyō gradually became distinct from Sect Shinto under this movement. Its current movement emphasizes the slogan 'The Path to the Joyous Life'.

In the postwar era, Tenrikyō has established various social and cultural institutions, including Tenri University (1925), Tenri Sankōkan Museum, Tenri Library, a publishing house, a hospital and an orphanage.

Main festivals are:

New Year Festival	1 January
Great Vernal Festival	26 January*
Vernal Commemoration of the Dead	27 March
Anniversary of the Foundress	18 April*
Holy Labour Day	18 May
Apostolate of the Press Day	4 August
Day of Wayside Preaching	18 August
Autumnal Commemoration of the Dead	21 September
Great Autumnal Festival	26 October*

* Three Grand Festivals

Monthly services are held at the headquarters on the 26th day of each month.

PUBLICATIONS

There have been numerous publications about Tenrikyō, but some of the main ones are as follows:

PERIODICALS INCLUDE:

Tenri Journal of Religion, 1955–
Tenrikyō (Los Angeles), 1955–
Tenrikyō Hawaii Monthly, (Honolulu), 1957–

THE THREE CENTRAL TEXTS:

Osashizu, 7 vols., Tenri, 1966
Ofudesaki, the Tip of the Divine Writing Brush, sponsored by Tenrikyō Church Headquarters, Tenri, 1971
Mikagura-uta: The Songs for the Tsutome, translated by Tenrikyō Church Headquarters, Tenri, 1972

PUBLICATIONS BY THE MOVEMENT IN ADDITION TO THE THREE CENTRAL TEXTS INCLUDE:

Guide to Faith, Pamphlet Series, 1959–
Nakayama Shozen, *On the Idea of God in Tenrikyō Doctrine*, Tenri, 1962
Tenrikyō: Its History and Teaching, Tenrikyō Church Headquarters, Tenri, 1966

Fukaya Tadamasa, *Fundamental Doctrines of Tenrikyō*, Tenri, 1973
Tenrikyō Yearbook, 1975–
Ellwood, Robert S., *Tenrikyō: A Pilgrimage Faith*, Tenri, 1982
The Teachings and History of Tenrikyō, Tenrikyō Overseas Mission
   Department, 1986
Tenrikyō is on the internet at: http://www.mahoroba.or.jp/~kaiden/

BRANCHES AND MEMBERSHIP

Tenrikyō's Headquarters are in Tenri City, Nara, Japan, and are referred to as *Oyasato* (Parental Home). The *Oyasato's* main buildings are the Main Sanctuary, which houses the Inner Sanctuary containing the *jiba*, the Foundress' Sanctuary and the Memorial Hall, all connected by a corridor.

No registration takes place when people become followers of Tenrikyō, but figures refer to those followers who have taken a further step by completing a special doctrinal course in Tenri and have become *Yōboku*, 'timber for the construction of the Joyous Life World'. *Yōboku* members in Japan are 1,053,960 in 1996.

Tenrikyō's missionary work overseas has the greatest scope of the new religious movements and it established the Tenrikyō Overseas Mission Department in 1927. Churches and Missions Overseas with numbers of *Yōboku* members are as follows: (as of February 1996)

Country	No. Churches	No. Stations	No. Yoboku
*USA (Mainland) (est.1934)	58	67	} 2,864
*Hawaii (est.1954)	37	36	
Canada	4	9	176
*Brazil (est.1951)	74	308	4,826
*Mexico (est.1985)	2	3	156
*Colombia (est.1972)		5	58
Paraguay	2	5	65
Argentina		10	69
Peru	1		49
Chile		1	6
Ecuador		1	4
*Singapore (est.1972)		3	100
*Thailand (est.1982)		7	679
India	1	1	125
Nepal			136
Indonesia		7	123

Country	No. Churches	No. Stations	No. Yoboku
Malaysia		1	190
Laos		1	10
Philippines		3	143
*South Korea (est.1908)	78	68	4,389
*Taiwan (est.1934)	15	60	6,667
China			140
*Hong Kong (est.1978)		2	123
*Congo (est.1975)	1	2	22
Kenya			14
Italy		1	12
United Kingdom		2	37
*France (est.1970)	1	2	151
Germany			29
Spain		2	4
Switzerland		1	13
Australia	1	3	65
New Zealand		1	5
Samoa		1	
Total:	275	613	1,085,730[1]

1 Total figure of 1,085,730 for *Yoboku* members includes the 1,053,960 members in Japan, as well as 10,268 members recorded as 'unknown' in terms of area, and small numbers of members in other countries, including North Korea (3), Myanmar (1), Cambodia (1), Sri Lanka (1), Pakistan (1), Turkey (1), Palestine (1), Egypt (2), Algeria (1), Ethiopia (3), Ghana (2), Nigeria (1), Tanzania (1), Madagascar (2), Ukraina (2), Kazakhstan (1), Austria (2), Netherlands (2), Denmark (2), Greece (2), Norway (4), Costa Rica (1), Panama (1), Uruguay (1), Bolivia (4), Venezuela (3). These figures are all supplied by the Overseas Mission Department, Tenrikyō H.Q., Tenri, Nara, Japan and are as of 26 February 1996.
* Chief Tenrikyō Missions Abroad

TENRIKYŌ – BIBLIOGRAPHY

1 BALET, L. (1909). 'Le Tenrikyō, religion de la raison celeste.' *Melanges Japonais* 6: 23–24.

2 BECKER, C. B. (1995). 'Mechanisms and Features of Religious Healing.' *Tenri Journal of Religion* 23(March): 105–116.
A description and assessment of experiments performed to measure the efficacy of different types of religious healing.

3 CHINNERY, T. E. (1971). *Religious Conflict and Compromise in a Japanese Village: A First-Hand Observation of the Tenrikyō Church.* Vancouver, The University of British Columbia.

4 Dōyūsha (ed) (1953). Kyōgikōshūkairoku (Record of Teaching Lectures). Tenri, Dōyūsha.

5 ELLWOOD, R. S. J. (1969). 'Models, Metaphors and Religious Movements.' *Tenri Journal of Religion* **15**.

6 ELLWOOD, R. S. (1974). *The Eagle and the Rising Sun: Americans and the New Religions of Japan.* Philadelphia, Westminster Press.
Ellwood examines the impact of five 'new religions' in America: Tenrikyō, Sōka Gakkai, Sekai Kyūseikyō, Seichō-no-Ie and Perfect Liberty. The cultural exchange between East and West as presented by the development of these movements in America is discussed.

7 ELLWOOD, R. S. (1982). *Tenrikyō: A Pilgrimage Faith, The Structure and Meanings of a Modern Japanese Religion.* Nara, Tenri University.
In the forewood, Ellwood states that this study is intended to be a description and an interpretation along the lines of empathetic phenomenology of Tenrikyō.

8 FARR, K. (1935). *Tenrikyō: Teaching of the Heavenly Reason,* University of Washington.

9 FUKAYA, T. (1955). 'The Fundamental Doctrines of Tenrikyō.' *Tenri Journal of Religion* **1**.

10 FUKAYA, T. (1956). Tenrikyō Nyūmon. Tenri, Dōyūsha.
The introductory text of Tenrikyō.

11 FUKAYA, T. (1956). Yōkigurashi e no Michi (The road to the Yōkigurashi – a way of joyous life). Tenri, Dōyōsha.

12 GOWEN, H. (1935). 'Tenrikyō, the Religion of Heavenly Reason.' *The Journal of the Society for the Study of Religions* **12**.

13 GUARIGLIA, G. (1959). *Prophetismus und Heilserwartungs-Bewegungen als völkerkundliches und religionsgeschichtliches Problem.* Horn and Vienna, Verlag Ferdinand Berger. Annot Earhart

14 HAAS, H. (1900). *Tenrikyō order ein neues synkretistische Religionsgebilde in Japan unserer Tage.*

15 HAAS, H. (1910). *'Tenrikyō: Ein neues synkretistisches Religionsgebilde in Japan unserer Tage.'* Zeitschrift für Missionskunde und Religionswissenschaft **25**.

16 HAAS, H. (1910). 'Die Tanzpsalmen der Tenrikyō-kwai.' *Zeitschrift für Missionskunde und Religionswissenschaft* **25**.

17 HAMADA, T. (1990). Tenrikyō: Zonmei no kyoso Nakayama Miki (The Living Founder of Tenrikyō-Nakayama Miki). Tokyo, Kōdansha.

18 HAMMER, R. (1961). The Idea of God in Japan's New Religions – with Special Reference to Tenrikyō, Konkōkyō, Sekai Kyūseikyō, Ōmotokyō, Reiyūkai, Risshō Kōsei Kai, PL Kyōdan, Seichō-no-Ie and Annaikyo. *University of London,* London.

19 HAYASAKA, M. (1972). 'Issues Surrounding the Official Recognition of Tenrikyō and Konkōkyō.' *Tenri Journal of Religion* **18**.

20 HIRASAWA, H. (1963). 'Tenrikyō Followers' Views of Disease Seen From Patients with Malignant Tumours.' *Tenri Journal of Religion* **9**.
Contrasts views of disease from a medical and religious perspective, and discusses the varying ways in which followers of Tenrikyō being treated at Tenri hospital for malignant tumours, accommodated these two perspectives.

21 HUANG, C.-h. (1989). 'Tenrikyō no Taiwan ni okeru dendō to juyō.' *Minzokugaku kenkyū* **54**(3): 292–306.

A discussion of evangelism and acceptance of Tenrikyō in Taiwan.

22 IIDA, T. (1958). 'Tenrikyō and Humanism.' *Tenri Journal of Religion* 4.

23 IIDA, T. (1986). 'Shūkyō to kezai-Tenrikyō no baai(Religion and economics: The Case of Tenrikyō).' *Tenri Daigaku gakuhō* 151: 15–38.

24 IKOMA, F. (1950). Tenrikyō Yōgi (The Tenrikyō Textbook). Tenri, Dogensha.

25 IKOMA, F. (1955). Kyōsama Goshōden (A Small Biography of the Founder). Tenri, Dōyūsha.

26 IMAMURA, E. (1955). Tenrikyō Nyūmon (The Introductory Textbook of Tenrikyō). Tenri, Dōyūsha.

27 INAGAKI, S. (1953). *Shinkō Shūkyo no Hihan* (Criticism of New Religions). Kyoto, Nagata Bunshodo.

28 INOUE, A. and M. EYNON (1987). A Study of Ofudesaki. Tenri, Tenrikyō Dōyūsha.

29 IWAI, T. (1932). *The Outline of Tenrikyō*, Tenrikyō Dōyūsha.

30 KAMSTRA, J. H. (1994). 'Japanese Monotheism and New Religions'. *Japanese New Religions in the West*. P. B. Clarke and J. Somers. Folkestone, Kent, Japan Library: 103–116.
Polytheism, the belief in myriads of deities has been one of the pillars of Shinto in particular and of Japanese religion in general. This article highlights the contrast with the new religions such as Tenrikyō, Konkōkyō and Ōmotokyō which believe in deities with monotheistic qualities. Kamstra analyses the impact of Christian theistic qualities on Japanese new religions.

31 KISALA, R. (1994). 'Etica sociale e attività di welfare delle nouve relgioni. Il caso del Tenrikyō e del Risshō Kōsei Kai.' *Religioni e Società* 17.

32 KISALA, R. (1994). *Social ethics and the Japanese New Religions: the Social Welfare Activities of Tenrikyō and Risshō Kōseikai. New Religious Movements in Asia and the Pacific Islands: Implication of Church and Society*. R. C. Salazar. Manila, De La Salle University.

33 KISALA, R. (1994). 'Contemporary Karma-Interpretations of Karma in Tenrikyō and Risshō Kōsei Kai.' *Japanese Journal of Religious Studies* 21(1): 73–92.

34 KOUAME, N. (1995). 'Tenri: les trois visages d'une ville religieuse.' *Etudes Japonaises* 8: 57–75.

35 LANDE, A. and CLARKE, P. B. (1988). Japan (New Religious Movements). *The World's Religions*. S. Sutherland, L. Houlden, P. B. Clarke and F. Hardy. London, Routledge: 932–944.
A short summary of the features of several Japanese New Religious Movements including Sōka Gakkai, Nichiren Shōshū, Sekai Kyūseikyō, Ōmotokyō, PL Kyōdan, Risshō Kōsei Kai, Konkōkyō, Tenrikyō, Mahikari, Seichō-no-Ie and Reiyūkai.

36 LOFTIN, M. T. (1951). Japanese in Brazil: A Study in Immigration and Acculturation, Vanderbilt University.

37 MATSUMOTO, S. (1976). In Quest of the Fundamental. Tenri, Japan, Tenrikyō Overseas Mission Department.

38 MATSUMOTO, S. (1981). Modern Society and Spiritual Maturity. Tenri, Japan, Tenrikyō Overseas Mission Department.

39 MORI, K. (1985). Brasil ni okeru Tenrikyō no tenkai to soshikika no tokushitsu (Desenvolvimento da Tenrikyō no Brasil e a peculiaridade do seu processo de organizaçao). São Paulo, Centro de Estudos Nipo-Brasileiros.

40 MORI, S. (1995). 'Historical Trends in Religious Studies: Methodological Change in the Studies of tenrikyo Religion by Christian Missionaries and Western Scholars of Religion.' *Tenri Journal of Religion* 23(March): 67–104.

41 MOROI, M. (1954). Shinjitsu no Michi (The True Road). Tenri, Dōyūsha.

42 MOROI, Y. (1964). 'Tenrikyō: Some Misconceptions Corrected.' *Contemporary Religions of Japan* 4(4): 304–324.

43 MOROI, Y. (1972). Contemporary Thought and Tenrikyō, Tenri: Tenrikyō Overseas Mission Department.

44 NAKAJIMA, H. (1956). 'The Conception of Death in Tenrikyō.' *Tenri Journal of Religion* 2.

45 NAKAJIMA, H. (1957). 'The fundamentality of Tenrikyō's view of the salvation.' *Tenri Journal of Religion* 3.

46 NAKAJIMA, H. (1961). 'The Basic Structure of the Idea of Salvation in Tenrikyō.' *Tenri Journal of Religion* 7.

47 NAKAJIMA, H. (1962). 'A Basic Structure of Revelation in Tenrikyō Doctrine.' *Tenri Journal of Religion* 8.

48 NAKAJIMA, H. (1964). 'The Divine Model of the Foundress of Tenrikyō.' *Tenri Journal of Religion* 10.

49 NAKAMURA, K. (1951). *A Talk on the Tenrikyō Scriptures*. Tenri, Dōyūsha.

50 NAKAMURA, K. (1953). Kyososama no Hinagata (A Model of the Founder). Tenri, Dōyūsha.

51 NAKAYAMA, S. (1954). The Doctrine of Tenrikyō. Tokyo, Tenrikyō.
    The standard guide to the Tenrikyō faith.

52 NAKAYAMA, S. (1954). On the idea of God in the Tenrikyō Doctrine, Tenri.

53 NAKAYAMA, S. (1957). On the Doctrine of Tenrikyō, Tenri.

54 NAKAYAMA, S. (1957). 'The various forms of verbal evolution in Tenrikyō Doctrine.' *Tenri Journal of Religion* 3.

55 NAKAYAMA, S. (1957). 'Women's position viewed by Tenrikyō.' *Tenri Journal of Religion* 3.

56 NAKAYAMA, S. (1958). The Missionary Spirit of the Foundress of Tenrikyō, Tenri.

57 NAKAYAMA, S. (1958). 'The Doctrine and Practice of Tenrikyō (Part 1).' *Tenri Journal of Religion* 4.

58 NAKAYAMA, S. (1959). 'The Doctrine and Practice of Tenrikyō (Part 2).' *Tenri Journal of Religion* 5.

59 NAKAYAMA, S. (1960). 'The Doctrine and Practice of Tenrikyō (Part 3).' *Tenri Journal of Religion* 6.

60 NAKAYAMA, S. (1961). 'The Anniversary of the Tenrikyō Foundress.' *Tenri Journal of Religion* 7.

61 NAKAYAMA, S. (1962). 'The Doctrine and Practice of Tenrikyō (Part 4).' *Tenri Journal of Religion* **8**.

62 NAKAYAMA, R. Y. (1979). Mind and Body. Tenri, Japan, Tenrikyō Overseas Mission Department.

63 NEWELL, W. H. and F. DOBASHI (1968). *Some Problems of Classification in Religious Sociology as shown in the History of Tenri Kyokai. The Sociology of Japanese Religion.* M. Kiyomi and W. N. Newell. Leiden, E.J. Brill: 94–100.
   This article gives a history of Tenrikyō and analyses its organization and the way in which it has changed, especially in the post-war era.

64 NISHIYAMA, T. (1981). Introduction to the Teachings of Tenrikyō. Tenri, Japan, Tenrikyō Overseas Mission Department.

65 OGURI, J. (1976). *Nihon no kindai shakai to Tenrikyō. Nihonjin no kōdō to shisō* (The Behaviour and Thought of the Japanese). Tokyo, Hyōronsha. 7.

66 OGURI, J. (1977). Tenrikyō no Tanjo to Hatten (The Birth and Development of Tenrikyō). *Nihon Shūkyōshi (A History of Japanese Religion)*. K. Kasahara. Tokyo, Yamakawa Shuppansha. II: 227–247.

67 ŌKUBO, A. (1960). '"Counselling" in Tenrikyō.' *Tenri Journal of Religion* **6**.

68 ŌKUBO, A. (1969). 'A Study of Social Welfare in Tenrikyō.' *Tenri Journal of Religion* **15**.

69 ŌKUBO, A. (1970). 'Social welfare and practicality of Hinokishin of Tenrikyō – A proposal to the International Year of the Disabled Person.' *Tenri Journal of Religion* **16**.

70 OSAKA, M. (1930). 'Tenrikyō, One of Japan's new Religions.' *Japan Christian Quarterly* **5**.

71 PUTNAM, G. (1981). 'Tenrikyō: from Japanese Folk Religion to Universal World Religion?' *Japanese Religions* **11**(4).

72 PYE, M. (1989). *Woran glauben Japans Großindustrielle? Die Religion von Oberschichten.* P. Antes and D. Pahnke, Diagonal Verlag.
   A brief survey of some of the ways Japanese industrial leaders have been influenced by a range of religious ideas and some of the overtly religious activities observable in Japanese companies. Amongst other influences, notes that of Tenrikyō on Matsushita Konosuke, founder of Matsushita Electric.

73 RAMSEYER, R. L. (1972). 'Finances in the New Religions and the Christian Church.' *Japan Christian Quarterly* **37**: 84–89.

74 REPP, M. (1995). 'The Earthquake in the Kobe-Osaka Area January 17th 1995. Its impact on religions and their response.' *Japanese Religions* **20**(2): 207–229.

75 RICCO, M. (1967). *Religione della violenza e religione del piacere nel nuovo Giappone.* Florence, Saggi.

76 SHIMAZONO, S. (1977). 'Kamigakari kara tasuke made: Tenrikyō no hassei josetsu (From divine possession to salvation: An Introduction to the origin of Tenrikyō).' *Komazawa daigaku bukkyōgakubu ronshū* **8**.

77 SHIMAZONO, S. (1979). 'The Living Kami Idea in the New Religions of Japan.' *Japanese Journal of Religious Studies* **6**: 389–412.

Discusses how the New Religions, although often classified as Buddhist or Shinto in origin have emerged from elements of folk belief. Focusing on shamanism and the idea of a 'Parent God' and the 'living kami (god)', the historical development of Tenrikyō and Konkōkyō is discussed.

78 SHIMAZONO, S. (1982). 'Tenrikyō ni Okeru Kyūsaishi Shinwa (The Heils-geschichte in Tenrikyō).' *Tetsugaku Shisō Ronsō University of Tsukuba, (Department of Philosophy)* **1**: 17–28.

79 SHIMAZONO, S. (1984). 'Shinshūkyō-kyōdan ni okeru taikendan no ichi: Myōchikai, Risshō Kōseikai, Tenrikyō (The Place of Testimonies in the New Religions: Myōchikai, Risshō Kōsei Kai and Tenrikyō).' *Tōkyō-daigaku shūkyō-gaku nenpō* **2**: 1–20.

80 SHIMAZONO, S. (1986). *The Development of Millennialistic Thought in Japan's New Religions: from Tenrikyō to Honmichi. New Religious Movements and Rapid Social Change.* J. A. Beckford. London. Beverly Hills, Sage Publications: 55–86.
This paper examines millenialistic tendencies in Tenrikyō and its offshoot, Honmichi, through a historical account of the development of these movements.

81 SHIONOYA, S. (1967). 'Tenrikyō's Future Missionary Work.' *Tenri Journal of Religion* **13**.

82 STROUPE, B. (1971). 'Healing in the History of Tenrikyō, the Religion of Divine Wisdom.' *Tenri Journal of Religion* **17**: 79–.
Outlines the history of Tenrikyō and the context within which it arose, amd examines Tenrikyō notions of disease and healing and the significance of healing in the Tenrikyō world view.

83 SUGAI, T. (1969). 'The Soteriology of New Religions.' *Japanese Religions* **6**(2): 23–46.

84 SUGIHARA, Y. and D. W. PATH (1969). *Sensei and His People: The Builders of a Japanese Commune.* Berkeley, University of California Press.

85 TAGAMI, M. (1971). 'Tenrikyō kyōso Nakayama Miki no shiseikan (Nakayama Miki: The Founder of Tenrikyō – Her View of Life and Death).' *Shintogaku* **71**: 21–37.

86 TAKAGI, H. (1954). 'Shūkyō Kyōdan no Seiritsu Katei – Tenrikyō no Baai (The Process of Formation of a Religious Organization – A Case of Tenrikyō).' *Tōyō Bunka Kenkyū-jo Kiyō* (Memoirs of the Institute for Oriental Culture, University of Tokyo) **6**: 265–338.

87 TAKAHASHI, T. (1988). 'Aperçu de la Prédication de Tenrikyō au Congo-Brazzaville.' Studies of Worldviews **1**.

88 TAKANO, Y. (1962). *Tenrikyōshi sankō nenpyō* (The Reference History of Tenrikyō). Tenri City, Yotokusha.

89 TAKANO, T. (1981). *The Missionary.* Tenri, Japan, Tenrikyō Overseas Mission Department.

90 TANAKA, K. (1982). Dust and Innen (Dust and Fate). Tenri, Tenrikyō Overseas Mission Department.

91 Tenrikyō Tenrikyō Yearbook. Tenri City, Japan, Tenrikyō Headquarters.
Yearly Handbook

92 Tenrikyō Tenrikyō Newsletter. Los Angeles, California, Tenrikyō.

93 Tenrikyō (1952). Tenrikyō gentenshu ((The Original Teachings of Tenrikyō). Tenri.

263

94 Tenrikyō (1982). The Life of Oyasama, Foundress of Tenrikyō. Tenri, Japan, Tenrikyō Church Headquarters.

95 Tenrikyō Overseas Mission Department (1978). An Introduction to Tenrikyō and its Teachings. Tenri, Japan, Tenri Jihōsha.
A collection of essays by members and a few foreign scholars.

96 Tenrikyō (1930). Tenrikyō. Tambaichi, Dōyūsha.

97 Tenrikyō (1952). Scriptures of Tenrikyō, Tenri.

98 Tenrikyō (1958). Oyasato, Guide to Tenrikyō, Tenri.

99 Tenrikyō (1960). Tenrikyō Kyōkai Honbu (A Short History of Tenrikyō), Tenrikyō.

100 Tenrikyō (1966). Tenrikyō, Its History and Teachings. Tenri, Japan, Tenrikyō Overseas Mission Department.

101 Tenrikyō (1985). The Doctrine of Tenrikyō, Tenrikyō Church Headquarters.

102 Tenrikyō Kyōkai Hombu (1951). Ofudesaki Sakuin (The Index of Ofudesaki). Tenri, Dōyūsha.

103 Tenrikyō Kyōkai Hombu (1952). Oyasama no Omokage (The Reminder of Oyasama). Tenri, Dōyūsha.

104 Tenrikyō Kyōkai Hombu (1955). Tenrikyō Yōran (The Outline of Tenrikyō). Tenri, Dōyūsha.

105 Tenrikyō Kyōkai Hombu (n.d). Tenrikyō Getenshū (Original Texts of Tenrikyō).

106 Tenrikyō Kyōkai Honbu (1949). Tenrikyō Kyoten (The Canon of Tenrikyō). Tenri, Dōyūsha.

107 Tenrikyō Kyōkai Honbu (1956). Tenrikyō kyōsoden (The Biography of the Founder of Tenrikyō). Tenri City, Tenrikyō Dōyūsha.

108 Tenrikyōgaku Dōgakkai Tenrikyōgaku Kenkyū: Tenrikyō no Gaisetsu (Journal of Tenrikyō Studies: Outline of Tenrikyō). Tenri, Tenrikyō Dōyūsha.

109 Tenrykyō Brasil Dendō Chō (1958). Tenry-kyō dendō shi (História da Tenry-kyō no Brasil), Tenrykyō sha.

110 Tenrykyō Brasil Dendō Chō (1985). Tenry-kyō Brasil dendō shi (História da Tenry-kyō no Brasil), Tenrykyō sha.

111 TOMOJI, T. (1981). The Missionary. Tenri, Tenri Overseas Mission Department.

112 UEDA, Y. (1955). The Outline of Tenrikyō Doctrine and its History, Tenri.

113 WöHR, U. (1989). *Frauen und Neue Religionen. Die Religionsgründerinnen Nakayama Miki und Deguchi Nao. (Women and New Religions. Foundresses Nakayama Miki and Deguchi Nao).* Wien, Beiträge zur Japanologie/Institut für Japanologie.
A discussion of the importance a female founder may have on the ideology and aims of a religious movement. Wöhr then goes on to give two examples: the female founders of Tenrikyō and Ōmoto, two of the oldest 'new' religions.

114 YAMADA, M. (1997). Shūkyō teki tagen shakai no kaishin ron: Hokutobu Brazil ni okeru Tenrikyō no Juyo to tenkai (Motives for Conversion in a

Religiously Plural Society: Reception and Developments of Tenrikyō in Northeast Brazil), University of Tsukuba: **159**.

This dissertation discusses the motives for conversion of Brazilians to Tenrikyō, a Japanese New Religion in what is a religiously plural society. There is also a discussion of Brazilian religiosity in the context of modernity.

115 YAMAMOTO, T. (1961). 'Tenrikyō and Medicine.' *Tenri Journal of Religion* **7**.

116 YAMASHITA, A. (1983). 'Modernization and Human Rights: The Historical Significance of the Origin and Development of Tenrikyō.' *Japanese Religions* **12**(4).

117 YAMASHITA, A. (1990). 'Tenri-ō and Henjō-Nanshi: Two Women Founders of New Religions.' *Japanese Religions* **16**(2): 1–23.

Yamashita relates the new religions boom to the women's liberation movement and feminism in Japan by examining two shamanic women, founders of two new religions: Nakayama Miki of Tenrikyō and Deguchi Nao of Ōmoto.

APPENDIX

Aum Shinrikyō: Brief History and Select Bibliography

Aum Shinrikyō, one of the new, new religions described in the introduction to this volume, stands alongside several other new religious movements from outside Japan associated with violence, death and tragedy on a large scale, and in particular the People's Temple of Jonestown Guyana (Hall, 1987), the Branch Davidian Church in Waco Texas (Lewis, 1993) and the Canadian and Swiss-based mogico-religious group the Solar Temple (Palmer, 1996).

Aum illustrates more clearly than any other religion in the contemporary Japanese context the lethal potential of mystical power. Mysticism is a difficult word to define and often refers to an inward, spiritual religion based on the experience of direct, immediate awareness of the divine. It emphasizes experience rather than theological reasoning. While these features are not being overlooked here the stress is on mysticism as a form of spiritual power that is activated by a relationship between a leader who claims supernatural powers and who regards her/himself as divinely chosen and the unswerving belief of disciples in those claims. It is a power that can be manipulated to justify the use of the most immoral and unlawful means, such as the use of sarin gas in an attack on the Tokyo underground by members of Aum Shinrikyō on 20 March 1995 demonstrated, to further what are interpreted as spiritual ends.

This brief outline of Aum looks at its teachings and practices diachronically. New religions, and Aum is no exception, tend to develop and systematize their doctrines and practices as they go along, as it were. They do not usually have from the outset a detailed map of where they are going or of how they will get there. They begin as theories, so to speak, and flesh out the meaning of the propositions which they assert to be the case in response to circumstances and demands made by members and the wider religious market. Researchers are also a factor in the formation and systematization of the teachings of new religions. Asked questions about the meaning and purpose of their beliefs and practices new movements, and, in particular, very new movements start to search for logical and coherent replies and the result is a greater systematization of doctrine. This can also arise from a desire not to appear ill-informed or lacking in those elements associated in scholarly minds and in the opinion of the law and the public generally with 'proper' religion. The development of the doctrines of many of the new religions of Japan and elsewhere bear this out.

In the case of Aum there was an important shift in emphasis from a this-worldy to an other-wordly orientation that was not obvious from the outset; it was the outcome of a process that was not always even and unilinear, and this is reflected in the changing content of the writings and activities of its founder, Shōkō Asahara. While, with hindsight, there are indications that he had begun to see himself as a divine being with a divine mission earlier, the crucial turning point in Asahara's own self understanding and in his understanding of his future role came in 1986 in the Indian Himalayas.

Shōkō Asahara was born Chizuo Matsumoto in Kyushu in 1955. Almost totally blind from birth, he was sent to a boarding school for the blind in Kumamoto prefecture, where he was reputedly a domineering personality. The future founder of Aum then went to Tokyo where he practised as an acupuncturist while waiting to enter Tokyo University and, according to Shimazono (1995: 384), it was at this point in time that he became interested in religion.

Asahara was aware that he was lacking in self-confidence and when he failed to gain entrance to Tokyo University this produced a deep sense of emptiness; it was as if he had been informed that he would not be able to fulfil the most important ambition in his life. His response was a practical solution, in that he focused his attention on making a living by setting up a business in Chinese medicine. At the same time he developed an interest in Taoism and began to study various forms of fortune-telling, but most importantly from the point of view of his future career, he became a member of Agonshū and undertook the practice of *senzagyō* in which, as Reader (1988: 253) explains, 'believers chanted Buddhist texts before an image of Juntei Kannon'. Drawing on the writings of the founder of Agonshū, Kiriyama Seiyu, Reader adds: 'Performed over a period of a thousand days, this (*senzagyō*) was believed to remove all karmic hindrances from one's family, oneself, and lastly from one's descendants' (Ibid).

When I interviewed officials of Agonshū in Kyoto in April 1997 about Asahara's participation in their movement they stressed that he was not a full member and only attended occasionally. They were also clear in their minds that he was a terrorist and had no genuine religious insights, nor were his teachings of any spiritual value. Shimazono (1995: 385) believes that the future founder of Aum did perform the one-thousand-day *senzangyō* practice, which according to Asahara himself, made him less rather than more spiritual.

Shimazono is also of the opinion (Ibid: 386) that Agonshū's belief in the necessity to eliminate karma in order to remove suffering was continued on in Aum. Asahara's thinking was also influenced while with Agonshū by the idea of returning to early Buddhism, the key notion on which Agonshū rests its claim to originality. Agonshū's founder Kiriyama criticised the corrupt state of Buddhism and emphasised the fundamental importance of the Agama sutras of early Buddhism. He also saw himself as the reformer of humanity and published a number of beliefs and practices that were later to be echoed by Asahara in his own writings. Kiriyama, for example, wrote a treatise on the Buddhist training method known as the seven subjects and thirty-seven paths, *shichika sanjūshichidōbon*, and in addition provided his own explanation of and taught the practice of Kundalini yoga, liberation from karma through the power of a guru (Ibid:387). Other writings of Kiriyama that, with hindsight, appear to have greatly influenced Asahara were: *Henshin no genri* (English: the Principles of Transformation (1971) and *Mikkyō: Chōrnōyoku no himitsu* (English: Esoteric Buddhism: The Secret of Psychic Power (1972).

To suggest that Agonshū had an influence on Asahara's thinking is not, of course, to attribute any responsibility whatsoever to that movement or its founder for the subsequent decisions and actions of Asahara and Aum Shinrikyō members on the Tokyo underground on 20 March 1995, or at any other time.

Asahara developed his own interpretations and emphases in all of these areas of belief and practice. Aum, therefore, was not in any sense a simple replica of Agonshū either in matters of belief and practice or in its orientation towards the world. Among the examples Shimazono provides of the differences between these two movements two deserve special mention as they were to become the bedrock of Aum's teachings, while they received relatively little attention, at least in the early years, in Agonshū. These were an emphasis on the Buddhist teaching of 'transcending life and death' and on that of 'absolute freedom, absolute happiness' (Ibid: 387). Moreover, initially sharing with Agonshū a positive response to society and more concerned with this-worldy benefits, Aum was later to become introversionist and hostile to the world, while, contrary to appearances, never actually renouncing this-worldy gains.

Asahara 'left' Agonshū discontented with his spiritual progress in 1984 and in February of the same year he opened a Yoga centre in the Shibuya district of Tokyo (Shimazono, 1995: 383) where he taught *kundalini* as the means to enlightenment. During 1985, in the manner of a charismatic leader, he had begun to make extraordinary claims on his own behalf including the claim to messianic status. He reported that while carrying out religious practices on a beech in Kanagawa Prefecture the Hindu deity Shiva appeared to him, appointed him the *Abiraketsu no Mikoto* or the god of light who leads the armies of the gods, and gave him a divine mission to create a perfect society called the Kingdom of Shambhala, which would be composed of all those who had attained the requisite levels of psychic power by following his teachings, methods and example. This millenarian element in Asahara's thought is traced back by Shimanzono to an esoteric Buddhist text, the *Kālacackra Tantra*, which contains the idea that the ideal king will be reborn as a messiah to conquer the infidels and establish the reign of Buddhism (Ibid: 388).

In April 1986 the group had become the *Aum Shinsen no Kai* (The Aum Association of Pure Truth) and in July of the same year it changed its name to Aum Shinrikyō, meaning when broken down into its constituent parts: the teachings (*kyo*) of the truth (*shinri*) of the creation, preservation and destruction of the present universe (*aum*). Like many self-proclaimed prophets, messiahs and millenarians Asahara was largely self taught and by this time had gathered in ideas indiscriminately from many sources, putting an interpretation on each that fitted with his own sense of himself and his purpose in life. He studied, in his own way, elements of Tibetan Buddhism, Hinduism, Taoism and Christianity, and various prophetic books, particular the prohecies of Nostradamus. From these and what he had learnt from Agonshū he constructed his teachings.

Though not a university graduate himself, Asahara was to attract a number of very successful graduates and postgraduates who were to become his devoted and obedient disciples. In an attempt to explain this paradox some observers have suggested that the emotional, moral and social life of these exceptionally talented students were neglected at the expense of their intellectual development, a neglect that resulted in their rather desperate search for a more integrated and wholesome sense of themselves. Others have detected a sense of elitism in their attitude and behaviour and have speculated that there was an inability to come to terms with being ordinary. They were driven, it is suggested, by this sense of their own superiority to go further and further beyond the normal, eventually finding in Aum the means and the outlet to experiment with ways of actually becoming higher beings. The psychological motives that led individual members to join Aum were doubtless highly complex and should become clearer with the full findings of the most notorious criminal trial in post World-War II Japanese history which is still underway and likely to last for many more years.

On his visit to the Himalayas in 1986 Asahara claimed to have received ultimate enlightenment and to have resolved his self doubts and any doubts he had previously had about his capabilities. After returning to Japan in February 1987 he was soon back in India, in Dharamsala, meeting the Dalai Lama who, he claimed, identified him as an authentic Buddha and assigned him a special mission to spread true Buddhism throughout Japan. His spiritual and mental powers now knew no limits.

This eclectic, millenarian new, new religion was registered as a religious juridical person (shūkyō hōjin) in 1989, and while Asahara was to continue to display what, to the outside observer, appears to have been little more than sheer, naked pragmatism and even Machiavellian traits, these were accompanied by a greater emphasis on the transcendental benefits to be derived from following Aum's beliefs and practices. New religions have generally undergone this 'process of spiritualization' relatively soon after they have started.

New religions at first offer tangible benefits. This has been the case in a number of movements that began as healing movements with a stress on physical cures, improved employment prospects and better interpersonal relationships, even physical immortality, only later to emphasize that the principal and much more satisfying goal is spiritual wellbeing. Asahara followed a similar path, and then moved on to offer to provide access to psychic powers for purposes of personal enlightenment. There developed a preoccupation with transcendence, with going beyond human limitations, with over-

271

coming the physical, psychological barriers to immortality, in other words with conquering death. This concern was translated into action by among other things the introduction of training to enable members to acquire the capacity to levitate, an ability Asahara claimed to possess from his time with Agonshū.

The inversion of means and ends in Aum began early in its history. Prior to 1989 Asahara had already developed his own interpretation and application of the concept of *poa* which traditionally means in Tibetan Buddhism the transference of the soul of a person to a higher realm. Although he was familiar with this meaning Asahara was also to claim,Watanabe explains, that a deliberate act of murder by a superior being was a case of poa, and, therefore, a justifiable and merciful act (1998:7). We see here the elevation of destruction and violence to the status of instruments of salvation.

Destruction and violence, a preoccupation with Armageddon, legitimated by recourse to the prophecies of Nostradamus and the *Book of Revelation*, and an emphasis on his role as saviour, as the Christ of the present age, feature in a number of Asahara's writings, particularly from 1989, and assume greater importance as his political ambitions fail. In keeping with the apocalyptic genre he wrote of a harmful power or energy that was spreading widely across the planet and predicted that a major catastrophy would occur by the year 1999. Catastrophe could, however, be avoided by 30,000 individuals accepting and practising Aum's teachings and following the example of Asahara himself. This would have the effect of providing sufficient positive energy to counteract the evil effects of the negative energy now destroying the world (Mullins, 1995).

This is the milder version of Asahara's apocalyptic message; later, he was to rule out the possibility of avoiding Armageddon. As he did so his movement became more introverted and elitist in outlook and attitude. The goal switches from saving humanity as a whole to saving a small group of specially chosen people who will survive to build a new civilization. The notion of his own followers as an elite superior to the rest formed part of his teachings on spiritual progress. Aum members who renounced the world were on a higher spiritual plane than others who were mere humans stuck in the mud of suffering. This idea of spiritual elitism reinforced the previously mentioned belief that an act of violence on the part of a true disciple of Asahara could be an act of salvation.

Despite their spiritually elevated status Aum members would need protection from the twin evils of negative energy and nuclear war that would inevitably destroy the world and so Asahara and his close advisers at the movement's headquarters in the small village of Kamikuishiki at the foot of Mt Fuji, began to address the question of constructing nuclear shelters. The original plan for a federation of Lotus villages across Japan was also looked into and abandoned in favour of a model of government and administration under the dominion of Asahara himself that replicated that of the secular state which was about to be destroyed. All the ministries, including those of health, defence, education and science and technology, had their Aum counterpart, and all were under Asahara's authority, turning Aum into a state within a state.

The effort was now on to ensure that Aum had all the basic necessities to defend itself and survive a nuclear war. This introversionism was as potentially dangerous as the teachings on *poa* and spiritual development, already referred to above. It also meant that many of the checks and balances, scientific, ethical and moral, that departments such as those of science and technology would normally be subjected to, were not in place. Ultimately Asahara's spiritual insights determined, or were used by his close associates to determine, the validity of all initiatives and innovations in this pursuit of total self-sufficiency and self-preservation.

Asahara encountered further setbacks to his ambitions in 1990 when *Shinrito*, the political branch of Aum, campaigned for twenty-five seats in the Lower House of the Japanese parliament and failed to obtain any. This failure, difficulties with the Tokyo Prefecture the previous year over recognition as a religious body, which was later granted, police raids following on difficulties with residents in other prefectures over the use of land, and difficulties with the press contributed to the emergence of a more insular and self-righteous Aum that distrusted the wider society. There was also speculation that Aum had already begun to retaliate and that in November 1989 it had kidnapped a lawyer, Tsutsumi Sakamoto, and his family, as 'punishment' for his opposition to the movement's request for legal recognition as a religious body.

Local problems such as these and the increasing tendency among members to idolize their guru combined with world events, including the collapse of Communism in the Soviet Union and Eastern Europe in the late 1980s, offering the movement the possibility of gaining access to ammunition and weapons in Russia where it had its largest following, the Gulf War of 1991, increased Asahara's sense of himself as a messianic figure. In 1991 and subsequent years the apocalyptic content of his writings became more pronounced as did the emphasis on his own salvific role. The

273

following are a sample of his writings in this messianic and apocalyptic genre in that year: 'The Truth of Humanity's Destruction', 'Proclamation as Christ Part 1' – Part 2 of this treatise followed in 1992 – and 'The Great Secret Prophecy of Nostradamus'.

Public lectures reiterated the same themes as Asahara became more precise about the date of Armageddon. He predicted that it would occur in the year 2000, that over ninety per cent of the urban population would perish and that the only means of survival was to become a 'superhuman' through spiritual training which would give resistance to atomic, biological and chemical weapons. Aum's preparations for this calamity were stepped up and included an underwater city.

Aum's introversionism and its hostility to the wider society became more marked in 1994, as did its militant disposition. While previously prepared to use violence on single individuals and their families, the sarin gas attack on the Tokyo underground on 20 March 1995 marked the worst of what is now believed to have been a number of outrages committed by Aum against members of the public from 1994. Means had become ends. Metaphorically speaking, God and the Devil had finally changed faces and places as charisma, in this final act, became utterly graceless.

Although it had global repercussions Aum was not an isolated incident, as was pointed out above in the general comments on similar tragedies involving new religions in other parts of the world. Nor did it occur independently of the rest of society. The answers to the Aum Affair do not all reside in the form and content of Shōkō Asahara's mind or in his own personal ambitions and frustrations. They cannot be found solely by investigating Aum with a view to understanding the psychology of its leader, his collaborators and the membership generally. The culture, religious, educational and political preoccupations of mainstream society also require analysis in the search for a rounded understanding of the Aum case.

REFERENCES

Hall, John H (1987) *Gone From the Promised Land: Jonestown in American Cultural History*, New Brunswick, NJ: Transaction.

Lewis, James ed., (1993) From the Ashes: Making Sense of Waco, Lanham, Maryland: Rowman and Littlefield

Mullins, Mark (1995) 'Aum Shinrikyō as An Apocalyptic Movement. A Review of Recent Japanese Responses' Paper presented to the Society for the Scientific Study of Religion (SSSR), San Francisco.

Palmer, Susan (1996) 'Purity and Danger in the Solar Temple' in *Journal of Contemporary Religion*, Vol.11, No 3, October pp. 303–319.

Reader, Ian (1988) 'The Rise of a Japanese 'New New Religion: Themes in the Development of Agonshū' in Japanese Journal of Religious Studies, 15/4, pp. 235–261

Shimazono, Susumu (1995) 'In the Wake of Aum. The Formation and Transformation of a Universe of Belief' in Japanese Journal of Religious Studies, 22, 3–4, pp 381–415.

Watanabe, Manabu (forthcoming) Religion and Violence in Japan Today. The Case of Aum Shinrikyō's Idea of Buddhist Salvation, in the *Journal of Terrorism and Political Violence.*

SELECT BIBLIOGRAPHY ON AUM SHINRIKYŌ

The following entries consist of writings by the leader of Aum Shinrikyō, Sōkō Asaharu, who is standing trial in Tokyo at the time of writing (June, 1998) charged, with among other things, the sarin gas attack on the Tokyo underground on 20 March 1995 after which twelve people were left dead and over five thousand injured. Recently on 26 May 1998 – one of his closest collaborators, Mr Ikuo Hayashi, was sentenced to life in prison for his part in the above-mentioned sarin gas attack on the Tokyo underground. Dr Hayashi, a graduate of Keiō medical school, had studied at Mt Sinai hospital in America, before joining the cardiopulmonory medicine unit, of which he later became the head, at a government hospital not far from Tokyo. The trial continues and may continue for many more years to come.

Other references cover the responses, mainly by academics, to the Aum Shinrikyō affair, and more generally the question of new religions, apocalypticism and violence.

BIBLIOGRAPHY

ASAHARA, SHOKO (1986) *Chōnōryoku: Himitsu no Kaihatsu Hō* (A Secret Method of Developing Psychic Power), Tokyo: Aum Shuppan.

—— (1986) *Seishi o koeru* (Transcending Life and Death), Tokyo: Aum Shuppan.

—— (1987) *Inishēshon* (The Supreme Initiation), Tokyo: Aum Shuppan.

—— (1988) *Mahāyanā Sūtora* (Mahayana Sutra), Tokyo: Aum Shuppan.

—— (1989) *Metsubō no hi* (The Day of Destruction), Tokyo: Aum Shuppan.

—— (1991) *Metsubō Kara Kokū: Zoku metsubō no hi* (From Destruction to Emptiness. A Sequel of the Day of Destruction), Tokyo: Aum Shuppan.

—— (1991) *Jinrui metsubō no shinjitsu*, Tokyo: Aum Shuppan.

—— (1991) *Nosutoradamusu himitsu no daiyogen*, (The Secret Prophecy of Nostradamus), Tokyo: Aum Shuppan.

—— (1991) *Kirisutu sengen* (Proclamation of Christ Part 1), Tokyo: Aum Shuppan.

—— (1992) *Kirisutu sengen* (Proclamation of Christ Part 2), Tokyo: Aum Shuppan

—— (1992) *Declaring Myself the Christ: Disclosing The True Meaning of Jesus Christ's Gospel*, Fujinomiya: Aum Shuppan.

EGAWA, SHOKO, (1995) *Aum Shinrikyō-tsuiseki 2200 nichi* (The 2200-day Pursuit of Aum Shinrikyō), Tokyo: Bungei Shunju.

HARDACRE, HELEN, (1995) *Aum Shinrikyō and the Japanese Media: The Pied Piper Meets the Lamb of God,,* New York: Columbia University, Institute Reports of the East Asian Institute.

INOUE, NABUTAKA, (1990) *Shinshūkyō jiten* (Dictionary of New Religions), Tokyo: Bungei Shinju

—— (1991), *New Religions. Contemporary Papers in Japanese Religions* (2), Tokyo: Institute for Japanese Culture and Classics, Kokugakuin University.

—— (May 1995) 'Gendai shakai no 'byo' to 'shinshūkyō' toshite no Aum Shinri kyō' (The Illness of Modern Society and Aum Shinri kyo as A New Religion), in *Shukan Asahi*, pp 35–38.

—— (et al), (1996), *Aum Shinrikyō towa Nanika?* (What is Aum Shinrikyō, ?), Tokyo: Asahi Shinbunsha.

KISALA, R (1995) 'Aum Alone in Japan: Religious Responses to the 'Aum Affair", in *Nanzan Bulletin*, 19, pp 6–34.

—— (1998), '1999 and Beyond: The Use of Nostradamus' Prophecies by Japanese Religions' in *Japanese Religions,*, Vol. 23 (1&2) pp. 143–157.

READER, IAN 1996, *A Poisonous Cocktail: Aum Shinrikyō's Path to Violence* Copenhagen: Nordic Institute of Asian Studies.

SHIMAZONO, SUSUMU (1993) 'New Religious Movements', in *Religion and Society in Modern Japan*, (eds) M. Mullins, S. Shimazono, and P. Swanson, Berkeley: Asian Humanities Press, pp. 221–230

—— (1995) *Oumu shinrikyō no kiseki* (The Tracks of Aum Shinrikyō), Tokyo: Iwanami Shoten (Trans. by R. Kisala, 'In the Wake of Aum: The Formation and Transformation of a Universe of Belief' in *Japanese Journal of Religious Studies*, 22/3–4, 1995 pp 381–415.

—— (1997) *Gendai Shūkyō no kanosei: Aum Shinrikyō to bōryouku* (Possibilities in contemporary religion: Aum Shinrikyō and Violence), Tokyo: Iwanami Shoten.

TAKEUCHI, SEIICHI (1995), *Aum 200 nichi senso* (Aum's 2000-day war), Tokyo: KK Besuto sera-zu.

WATANABE, MANATOBU (1998), 'Religion and Violence in Japan Today. The Case of Aum Shinrikyō's Idea of Buddhist Salvation', in the *Journal of Terrorism and Political Violence* (forthcoming).

YAMAMORI, TETSUO, (1995) 'Aum Shinrikyō Sounds the Deathnell of Japanese Religion' in *Japan Echo* Autumn, pp 48–53.

YOUNG, RICHARD FOX (1995), 'Lethal Achievements: Fragments of a Response to the Aum Shinrikyō Affair', in *Japanese Religions*, Vol.20, No. 2 July, pp. 230–45.

www.ingramcontent.com/pod-product-compliance
Ingram Content Group UK Ltd.
Pitfield, Milton Keynes, MK11 3LW, UK
UKHW020358010325
455677UK00021B/516